LE MANS
'THE BENTLEY & ALFA YEARS'
1923-1939

Compiled by
R.M. Clarke
with an introduction and annual race summaries
by
Anders Clausager

ISBN 9781855204652

BROOKLANDS BOOKS LTD.
P.O. BOX 146, COBHAM,
SURREY, KT11 1LG. UK
sales@brooklands-books.com

D0905683

www.brooklands-books.com

Contents

Contents - continued

Cover Illustrations

Front: Sir Henry Birkin overtaking Caracciola's Mercedes in the 1930 race. From a painting by T.V. Ballance

Back Top: The Bloch/Rossignol winning $3^{1}/2$ Litre Lorraine-Dietrich in the pits during the 1926 race. From an Autocar painting by Gordon Crosby

Back Bottom: The winning Alfa Romeo driven by Sir Henry Birkin overtaking Samuelsons MG Midget in the 1931 race. From a sketch in Light Car.

Acknowledgements

When we started our Le Mans series two years ago it was our intention to take Anders Clausager's book 'Le Mans', first published in 1983, but now sadly out of print, and expand it with contemporary reports from the worlds leading motoring journals.

Anders book covered the first 50 races and we decided to do the same but breaking the period down into seven volumes. For commercial reasons we started with the immediate post war years and proceeded up to the fiftieth race which was held in 1982. We have now with this book added the final piece to the jig-saw, by covering the colourful vintage years of Le Mans, from 1923 to 1939.

We apologise in advance for the quality of the reproduction of some of the pages. It must be remembered that we have to photograph the actual magazine pages for these books, which are now in the main 65 to 90 years old, and which were even then only printed on 'newsprint' quality paper.

Our thanks go to the publishers of *Autocar, Light Car, Motor, Motor Sport* and *Speed* for again allowing us to bring back these historic reports in this way. We are also indebted to Anders Ditlev Clausager for permission to include the excellent introduction from his book plus the annual summaries, which add depth and continuity to the series as a whole.

R.M. Clarke

Le Mans - The Vintage Years

The nice thing about the Le Mans 24-hour race is that it is such a traditional event. Anyone who had witnessed the first race in 1923 and then had been transported magically forward in time to the present would probably feel quite at home, once the initial shock of seeing such outlandish cars had worn off. Basically, the circuit is the same as in 1923 though with many improvements and somewhat shortened; and the format of the race is equally unchanged. The starting time of 4 pm on a Saturday afternoon has occasionally been moved one or two hours forward but has always returned to where it was in 1923. All but three of the races to date have taken place in June; these were the first race which took place in May, the 1956 race in July and the 1968 race in September. Of the famous traditional motor races Le Mans has survived for longer than most in the same format and on the same circuit. Only the Indianapolis 500-mile race and the Monte Carlo Rally which both started in 1911 have remained as unchanged for longer, while the French Grand Prix, the Targa Florio and the Tourist Trophy which all go back to 1906 have all been changed drastically at least once if not several times.

We owe the birth of the 24-hour race to the ideas, initiative and foresight of three men. Georges Durand, secretary of the Automobile Club de l'Ouest, wanted to organise a unique and outstanding race at Le Mans and had the idea of promoting a race to demonstrate the reliability of ordinary touring cars. He took his ideas to Paris and discussed them with Charles Faroux, editor of *La Vie Automobile* during the Paris motor show in October 1922. Faroux thought of Emile Coquille, the French agent for the Rudge-Whitworth detachable wire wheel, who had once suggested a night race to encourage improvements in lighting and electrical systems. Faroux initially suggested an eight-hour race - to be run half during daytime and half during the hours of darkness but he and Durand soon decided to make it a 24-hour race. Coquille promised to put up a trophy - the Rudge-Whitworth Cup - and made a donation of 100,000 Francs.

Durand went back to Le Mans and set about obtaining all the necessary permissions to close the roads of the circuit to the public during the race, and also undertook the organisation of the race and all the attendant facilities - not the least of the problems involved would be to arrange artificial lighting over part of the circuit. Charles Faroux set about drafting a suitable set of regulations. It was decided that Coquille's Rudge-Whitworth Cup should not go to an outright winner of the race - instead the 1923 race should be considered as the first qualifying round for a Triennial Cup which would only finally be awarded after the 1925 race. Of the three originators Faroux functioned as clerk of the course until 1956 when he was over 80, while both Durand and Coquille had died during the second World War.

The first regulations intended to make sure that the cars taking part were standard touring models. Initially it was required that exact duplicates of the cars in the race should be present at the circuit, but this was soon discontinued in favour of a solemn declaration signed by the entrant to the effect that at least 30 similar cars had been manufactured. The cars had to conform with the manufacturer's catalogue specification and had to run fully equipped with wings, running-boards and hoods in addition to lamps, horn, mirror etc. 1,100 cc cars got away with just two seats but larger cars had to have four seats, and in addition to the driver 60 kg of ballast had to be carried for every passenger seat.

During the race itself cars had to cover a minimum distance depending on their capacity - originally ranging from 570 miles for 1,100 cc models and going up to 990 miles for six-litre cars - and there were systematical eliminations every six hours of those cars which dropped behind their required averages by a certain percentage. All tools and spares to be used during the race had to be carried on the car - initially this included even jacks, pumps and cleaning materials and only the driver was permitted to work on the car during the race. All re-fuelling had to take place at the pits, using fuel supplied by the A.C.O.

These regulations were soon amended and for 1924 it became a requirement that oil, water and fuel could only be replenished after the first 20 laps, and then at 20-lap intervals. During the years 1924 to 1927 it was stipulated that hoods had to be raised during part of the race but it is interesting that the A.C.O. has right from the start been completely neutral on the question of open versus closed cars, and closed cars appeared at Le Mans very early on; ever since the popularity of either type has changed almost as fashion dictated. Before 1939, some of the bodywork requirements were relaxed a little, for instance rear seats became optional on all cars and doors were no longer required on open cars. The co-driver, and later a mechanic, were permitted to work on the car during the race. Above all the minimum distances required were steadily increased over the years and by 1939 had virtually doubled.

The original Triennial Cup was only awarded once, over 1923-4-5 races, and in 1924 a Biennial Cup still known as Rudge-Whitworth Trophy - was instituted complementing and then replacing the Triennial award. The Biennial Cup continued for many years after the war. It was awarded on the basis of an Index of Performance which took a car's actual race distance compared to the set minimum distance into account. From 1928 an annual winner was recognised, the Annual Distance Cup simply going to the car which had covered the greatest distance in the race, but for reasons of convenience and continuity it has long since been the custom to refer to 'winners' - meaning those cars which covered the greatest distances of the 1923-27 races. An annual winner of the Index of Performance was also recognised but often the same car won the Index and the Biennial Cup - 1930 was the first year in which this did not happen.

The 10.726-mile circuit which had been marked out in 1919 was only used for the first six 24-hour races. The Pontlieue hairpin was a narrow street lined with houses, and it had become a favourite vantage point for spectators; it was soon realised that this was a dangerous spot so for the 1929 race, the A.C.O. built a road - the Rue du Circuit - which cut across the Pontlieue hairpin approximately a quarter of a mile from the apex. The Rue du Circuit was not more than a few hundred yards long and began and ended with two sharp right-hand bends. The length of the circuit was shortened to 10.153 miles by this amputation, but in this form the circuit only lasted for three years before the A.C.O. decided to perform major surgery. For 1932 a new road connecting the two sides of the circuit was built on land acquired by the A.C.O. well clear of the built-up area of Le Mans.

Soon after the starting line a fast right-hand curve swept on to the new section - named Tertre Rouge, or 'Red Hillock' - which was about a mile long, taking in the Esses and rejoining the original circuit via the sharp right-hand Tertre Rouge corner. The circuit was reduced to 8.383 miles in length and in this form lasted until 1955. Two pedestrian bridges, which have since assumed the shape of Dunlop tyres, spanned the circuit in the Tertre Rouge section where on both sides of the track the fairground-like 'Village' began to grow up.

For the first race in 1923, the facilities were on the primitive side, with tents acting as pits and only a

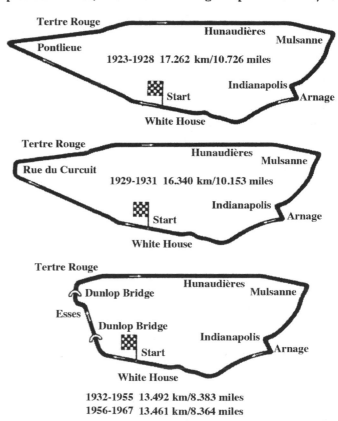

1923-1928 17.262 km/10.726 miles

1929-1931 16.340 km/10.153 miles

1932-1955 13.492 km/8.383 miles
1956-1967 13.461 km/8.364 miles

small grandstand. Then in 1925, the pits had to be moved from their original position midway between White House and Pontlieue, across the circuit to a point near Les Hunaudieres - the A.C.O. was having trouble with the original land-owner but soon managed to purchase the site so for 1926 the pits and the grandstand were back in their original place, where they still are. A permanent wooden structure was built and in 1934 a second storey was added; this was also the year in which the first high-pressure fuel systems were installed. The amenities gradually improved, with grandstands, a club house, press-box, time-keepers' boxes etc.

All beginnings are difficult and the first 24-hour race at Le Mans was no exception. For a start, the dates chosen 26 and 27 May - turned out to be too early in the season and the weather was terrible - a hailstorm, heavy rain and high winds combining to make life unpleasant for the drivers. The pits were in tents and the road surface none too good. A total of 33 cars were brought to the start at 4 pm on the Saturday afternoon; the starting time unaltered to this day.

Two entries from Voisin did not materialise but of the 33 starters only three were not French - these were a team of two Belgian Excelsiors with ohc 5.3 litre six-cylinder engines, the biggest cars and therefore given numbers 1 and 2; and a single three-litre Bentley, entered by the maker's London agent John

The pits before the 1923 race.

Duff who was partnered by Bentley's works driver Clement. Among the other entries were La Lorraine and Chenard et Walcker in the two to three-litre class, while at the other end of the scale were five cars in the 1,100 cc class - two air-cooled S.A.R.A.s, two Salmsons and an Amilcar. There were two Bugattis and a Delage; while car number 19, entered as a Montier-Special, was largely Ford Model T; its entrant-driver Charles Montier was Ford's French agent.

Three of the cars had closed bodywork and as yet there were no regulations governing the use of hoods

during the race; but most other rules were intended to make sure that the entries were true touring cars. Cars had to be fully equipped with hood, wings, running-boards and electrical equipment apart from 1,100 cc cars which had only to be two seaters, all entries had to have four seats and ballast had to be carried in lieu of passengers. Repairs could only be carried out by the driver; and while fuel consumption was unrestricted, refuelling could only be carried out at the pits.

At first the idea of a 24-hour race had been greeted with derision in some quarters - for instance by W. O. Bentley himself; nevertheless he agreed to act as Duff's pit manager and soon realised that Le Mans was exactly the kind of race that would demonstrate the capabilities of his cars. That year's event was, while undoubtedly spectacular, perhaps the least dramatic Le Mans race ever. Very soon after the start, the two Chenard et Walckers went into the lead, followed by a two-litre Bignan; they were to retain this order throughout the race and eventually finished 1-2-3. The pre-race predictions that no car would stand the pounding for the twenty-four hours were soon shamed, in fact the first retirement (a S.A.R.A.) was caused when the car crashed after the lighting system failed in early evening, and there were only two other cars which had to retire.

Much excitement was provided by the Bentley; this was an early three-litre without front wheel brakes, and the two-wheel brakes were wholly inadequate. An additional problem was created by a headlamp which was inoperative after being hit by a flying stone; another stone holed the petrol tank and the car was delayed for two and a half hours while repairs were made. At the end, Duff and Clement shared a fifth place with one of the Excelsiors; Clement had meanwhile set up a lap record (for sports cars) of 66.69 mph. The race was won by Lagache and Leonard in a Chenard et Walcker covering 1,372.94 miles at an average speed of 57.21 mph; although as yet the A.C.O. did not recognise an outright winner of the individual race, instead all finishing cars had qualified for the Triennial Cup.

1,372·5 MILES IN 24 HOURS AT LE MANS

The Wonderful Utility of Four-wheel Braking Demonstrated in Rudge-Whitworth Cup Contest. Chenard-Walcker Cars Secure First and Second Places. The Bentley Dead-heats for Fourth Place and Breaks Lap Record. By W. F. Bradley.

They're off! The thirty-three competitors were lined up in two rows in front of the grand stand and despatched in a massed start. The three cars in the front row are, numbers 1 and 2, six-cylinder Excelsiors, and number 5, a Lorraine-Dietrich.

A DISTANCE of 1,372.5 miles was covered in twenty-four hours by a 3-litre Chenard-Walcker, driven alternately by Lagache and Leonard, in the first race for the Rudge-Whitworth Cup held on a road course at Le Mans, last Saturday and Sunday. The performance constitutes a world's record for a twenty-four hour road race, with an average speed of more than 57 miles an hour, and is remarkable testimony to the reliability of the car and the endurance of the men who handled it under most unfavourable weather conditions.

A Franco–British Duel.

Immediately behind the leader a second and similar car, driven by Bachmann and Glazmann, finished with a distance of 1,317 miles. A 2-litre Bignan, with positive valve closing gear, came in third with a distance of 1,284 miles, and fourth position was tied for by another Bignan and a 3-litre Bentley, privately entered by Capt. J. F. Duff, with a distance of 1,198.5 miles.

The outstanding feature of this race, which really forms an elimination for other twenty-four hour races which will determine the ultimate winner of the Rudge-Whitworth Cup, was the duel between the Chenard-Walcker team and the Bentley, the only English car in the race. This latter secured the track record, but was robbed of a better position by the petrol tank being punctured by a flying stone, and two and a half hours

being lost in effecting a repair. The English car went through the race without any mechanical work being done on it other than that to the petrol tank, and was driven the entire distance without a change of tyres, Rapson straight sides being used. The Chenard-Walckers had as the leading articles of their equipment Scintilla magneto, Jam plugs, Solex carburetter, Hartford shock absorbers, and Michelin tyres.

Next year and the following year there will be another twenty-four hour race, and in 1926 all those qualified in the preliminaries will take part in the final to determine the holder of the Rudge-Whitworth Cup.

Good Work by Smaller Cars.

While a Chenard-Walcker of 3,000 c.c. proved the fastest irrespective of class distinctions, with an average speed of 57.1 miles an hour, the fastest average speed with a 2-litre engine was 53.5 miles an hour set up by the four-seater Bignan; in the 1,500 c.c. class the four-seater Bugatti averaged 46.3 miles an hour. The fastest 1,100 c.c. two-seater was the Salmson driven by Desvaux and Casse, with an average of 43.7 miles an hour. Even the slowest car, the 1,100 c.c. Sara, which was out for fuel emonomy and regularity, showed an average of 25.4 miles an hour for the two rounds of the clock.

At four o'clock on Saturday afternoon, the hour fixed for the start of the race, 33 cars lined up in two rows

The ubiquitous "Henry" put in an appearance in the race, but in a form so disguised as to be almost unrecognisable, and ran under the name of Montier-Ford. The car finished fourteenth with a total of 1,039 miles.

in front of the grand stand ready for the 24-hour struggle. Of those on the list of starters, only two Voisins failed to appear, no reason for their abstention being given. The start was simultaneous, and was rendered more exciting by the fact that the cars were placed in the order in which their entries had been received, small cars being mixed up with big ones in a manner which called for all the ingenuity of the drivers in jockeying for positions at the actual start and on the run down to Pontlieue hairpin turn.

Bad Weather at the Start.

The weather, which had been threatening all the afternoon, showed its worst mood as the starter's flag dropped, for at the precise moment hail began to fall, and this shower was immediately followed by heavy rain, which continued almost without interruption for nearly four hours. At this stage the race was much more severe for the drivers than for the machines, for rain and road conditions held speed down somewhat, whereas the men

were blinded with mud and water, and unable, for the most part, to wear goggles, suffered severely from sore eyes. Although the condition of the drivers of the fast cars was not enviable, they really suffered less than the men on the slower machines, for every time one of these was passed, its driver found himself in a veritable sea of mud. Windscreens were more of a nuisance than a protection, and in the case of the little 1,100 c.c. Saras were such a handicap that the drivers voluntarily broke them. For such a contest the best combination was a very low driving seat, a high scuttle, and the lowest possible glass screen.

Direct Comparison of Types.

The race for the Rudge-Whitworth Cup being open to all classes of standard cars with four-seater bodies (an exception was made for the 1,100 c.c. models), there were most interesting opportunities for a comparison of types and equipment. A couple of Rolland-Pilains came to the start with saloon bodies built under Weymann licence of wood and fabric leather. The Lorraine-Dietrich, Rolland-Pilain, Brasier, 12 h.p. Delage, and the Berliet cars had the closest approach to what the tourist considers a comfortable touring body. The rules allowed the hood to be left off, and the majority took advantage of this, while the driver of the little Corre La Licorne, on the other hand, put his hood up, and kept it up all the time.

Among the fast sporting type cars, the most promising were the three 3-litre Chenard-Walckers, Capt. J. F. Duff's 3-litre Bentley, and the pair of 2-litre Bignans. The biggest cars in the race were the two six-cylinder sporting type Excelsiors, fitted with a new overhead valve engine. They had nothing exceptional, however, in the matter of equipment, and with their roomy and comfortable bodies, were handicapped compared with some of the others.

Front Wheel Brakes Essential.

Duff's Bentley was really the most favoured in the matter of low build and racing equipment. Mudguards were down to the minimum width, the windscreen was low, the entire car was fairly well streamlined and super-

The course has an acute corner at Pontlieue. J. F. Duff is seen bringing his Bentley close in to the corner.

(Top) F. C. Clement (Bentley) effecting adjustments at the pits.

(Centre) Lagache (Chenard-Walcker), the winner, at Pontlieue.

(Bottom) de Courcelles (Lorraine-Dietrich) and Moton (Vinot) filling up. Observe empty lamp bracket and lamps damaged by flying stones.

At speed in front of the stands. The leading car is the Irat, which finished fifteenth with a total of 995 miles. The system of overhead lights for illuminating the ground in front of the stands at night is indicated in this view.

fluous weight had been got rid of. With his car fitted with Rapson straight-side tyres, Duff decided that there was nothing to be gained by carrying a spare wheel, and consequently went away without one. All the others, having beaded edge tyres, carried a single spare. Duff, however, had a most serious disadvantage in the absence of front wheel brakes, this handicap being most marked on a triangular course not much more than ten miles round, with a hairpin, two right-angle turns, and several twisty bits.

The favourites were the three Chenard-Walckers, fitted with a 3-litre overhead-valve sporting-type engine, having a most wonderful four-wheel braking system of the Perrot type with the Hallot servo-mechanism, handled by clever and experienced drivers, and backed up by perfect pit organisation.

Successful Positive Valve Operation.

Of the two Bignans, both of 2,000 c.c., the one with the positive valve closing mechanism was particularly fast for its size. Compared with its companion, having spring-operated valves, it had a gain of 800 revolutions a minute and about 10 h.p., its maximum engine speed being 4,500. With its comparatively low final gear ratio it touched 4,200 revolutions on the down stretches. Another sporting type worthy of note was the Montier-Ford, which had very much more of the Montier than the Ford construction about it, for the Frenchman who had produced it appeared to have left nothing bearing the U.S.A. mark except the cylinders and front axle.

He would have been a clever man who could have indicated what constituted the basis of the Rudge-Whitworth Cup. A minimum distance had to be covered in the two rounds of the clock, this distance being in proportion to the size of the engine and rising from 503 miles for the 1,100 c.c. Amilcar to 968 miles for the big Excelsiors. All those covering this distance would qualify for the following year's race. Such a basis, however, left the race without a winner, and was as unsatisfactory for the drivers as for the public. The first half hour indicated, however, that the great majority of the competitors had no intention of handicapping themselves by any

considerations of a minimum distance, and that for a number of them it was going to be a race throughout.

Lagache, driving No. 9 Chenard-Walcker, proved himself the fastest, followed by No. 10 Chenard-Walcker, with Duff's Bentley and De Tornaco's Bignan very close behind. The first thirty minutes showed that in the matter of speed the only cars to be considered were the Chenard-Walckers, the Bentley, the Bignans, and one of the Excelsiors. The others were either less speedy types or were being driven with a view more to regularity than covering the greatest distance.

Changing over Drivers.

One, two, three hours passed without any change in the unfavourable climatic conditions, without a car stopping at the pits, and without any mechanical incident. Soon after 7 o'clock the drivers began to come in for relief, the regulations stipulating that while there should be two men per car, only one man should be allowed to work upon it at a time. Generally, the man coming off duty filled up with petrol and oil, carried out such adjustments as were necessary, and then turned the machine to his team-mate, who only had to jump into the seat and drive away.

Duff, working to programme, remained at the wheel four full hours before turning his car over to Clement. It was then 8 o'clock, darkness had fallen, lights had been turned on everywhere, and, the rain having ceased, there was a complete transformation of scene. While the Clerk of the Weather had done his best to upset the programme, he was powerless to damp the enthusiasm of the public and the competitors. At the American bar a jazz band performed without interruption, a wireless loud-speaker reproduced a concert from the Eiffel Tower, a few couples danced, an open-air cinema depicted sporting scenes, and towards 11 o'clock a fireworks display began.

" L'Hotel Hartford."

One of the most curious scenes at the covered pits was the "Hartford Hotel." The makers of the well-known shock absorber, having no motor supplies to give out, had fitted up their replenishment station as a restaurant and hotel. As the tired, wet, and muddy drivers came off their cars they were hauled into the hotel, regaled with hot onion soup, found plates of roast chicken in front of them, and were called upon to assist in emptying innumerable bottles of champagne.

Darkness proved that the electric lighting systems were less reliable than the various mechanical features of the car, for after a couple of hours' running one-third of the cars had lost time by reason of the failure of their electric or acetylene sets, or both. Just before darkness a stone went right through one of the Bentley headlights. The Chenard-Walcker team sportingly offered to give another lamp, but the change would have taken too much time, and the car continued with one headlight working normally and the other operating intermittently.

Trouble with Car Lighting.

The most seriously affected were the two Saras, both of which had their electric systems short-circuited and could not make their acetylene sets operate. One of the drivers ran off the road and had to abandon. During the night one of the Excelsiors went right off the road and buried itself in the sand to such a depth that the engine could not be started up, and two hours were lost in digging the car out. A Vinot-Deguingand broke a valve during the night, but was able to repair and continue with a comparatively brief loss of time.

One of the Bugattis punctured its petrol tank during the night, but, refusing to admit defeat, the driver walked three miles to the pits, carried a couple of cans of petrol back to the stranded car, and on getting to the replenishment station changed his tank and continued. All this work had to be done single-handed.

Duff and Gros were the actors in another exciting night incident. Just as the Bentley was closing up on the Bignan, the latter burst a rear tyre, and the driver of the car applied his very efficient four-wheel brakes hard on. Duff, seeing nothing more than a wall of blue smoke ahead of him, ran into the grass, and as the smoke cleared away discovered that the dumb iron of his car was practically touching the Bignan's tail. Both got away without the least injury.

Sunday morning, which broke fine, found the Chenard-Walcker driven by Lagache-Leonard in the lead with the

An impression of the illumination of the replenishment pits in the hours of darkness is given by this view of one of the Lorraine-Dietrichs being filled up.

advantage of a couple of laps over the Bentley handled by Duff and Clement, the English car having been delayed by reason of its lighting system. Two other Chenard-Walckers were close on the wheels of the Bentley, and the De Tornaco-Gros-driven Bignan was a close runner-up. The 4 a.m. stop for supplies gave first two positions to the Chenard-Walckers, for the French team was infinitely better trained than that at the English stand, and although the driver only could work on the car, very much could be done in the way supplies were prepared and handed to him.

Bentley Breaks Lap Record.

While the Frenchmen had the first two positions, with a lead which at one time got nearly as high as four laps, or practically forty miles, they considered the Bentley to be dangerously near, and consequently gave orders to their men to shake him off. Lagache and Leonard set

The victorious Chenard-Walcker team. The car on the left (number 9) finished first; the other two Chenard-Walckers annexed second and seventh places.

the pace and averaged several laps at more than sixty-four miles an hour. At 9 a.m. (summer time had been applied during the night) Duff took over from Clement, filled his oil and petrol tanks, and immediately set out to catch the two Frenchmen. That Sunday morning three-cornered fight between No. 8 Bentley and Nos. 9 and 10 Chenard-Walckers was one of the finest features of a really interesting race. Duff soon got into his swing and set up a lap record at an average of 64.7 miles an hour. On the following lap he bettered this time by one second.

Sandwiched between the two Chenards, Duff found that he was overtaking the leader too rapidly on the approach to the right-angle bend at Mulsanne, and, not having front wheel brakes, was in danger of being bumped by the second Chenard on the turn itself. He was obliged, therefore, to run straight ahead down the escape road and let the second Chenard-Walcker get by him. Immediately afterwards he went in chase again, passed No. 10 in front of the grand stands, and overtook No. 9 on the fast straightaway leg. Several times during the morning Duff established lap records, and excitement was getting up to a high pitch when, about a quarter to twelve, a telephone message came in to the effect that the Bentley was stranded with an empty petrol tank three miles from the pits. Robbed of what looked like a most exciting struggle, real regret was manifested among competitors and the public alike.

Hard Work and Hard Luck.

The Jury decided that a bicycle could be made use of and that Clement could go out to the stranded car after Duff had reached the pits. Requisitioning a bicycle temporarily abandoned by its owner, Clement slung a couple of bidons of petrol over his shoulders, and as soon as Duff came in from his long trot, set out towards the car abandoned on the short cross-road of the course. On reaching the pits, with the bicycle in the back of the car, a hasty repair was carried out with corks and soap. Finally, after two hours and a half had been lost, the Bentley went away again with Clement at the wheel. It seemed doubtful whether the temporary repair would hold, and as the puncture was immediately above the exhaust pipe there was a certain danger from fire.

Evidently the work was well done, for the first lap constituted a record, the second was slightly faster, and finally the English car got the fastest lap of the day, with sixty-seven miles an hour for one round of the course. While this fast driving would do nothing to bring the Bentley in the lead, for a handicap of 2½ hours could not be wiped out in three hours' running, it helped to improve the position of the machine and finally to allow it to tie for fourth place with the De Marne-Martin team on a 2-litre Bignan.

Unfortunate Termination.

The twenty-four hours having elapsed, the cars were flagged in and stopped at the pits for the final parade. The last car to arrive, a Chenard-Walcker, came up the grand stand stretch at something like sixty miles an hour and suddenly found itself confronted with Gros, one of the Bignan drivers, who was crossing the track afoot. The man at the wheel displayed wonderful skill and incidentally gave a remarkable exhibition of the value and efficiency of a modern braking system; but he was unable to avoid striking Gros, who received serious injuries.

FINAL ORDER OF CARS, THE DRIVERS, MILEAGE AND AVERAGE SPEEDS

		Miles.	Average in m.p.h.
1.	Chenard-Walcker 3-litre (Lagache and Leonard)	1372.5	57.1
2.	Chenard-Walcker 3-litre (Bachmann and Dauvergne)	1327	55.3
3.	Bignan 2-litre (de Tornaco and Gros)	1284	53.5
4.	Bentley 3-litre (Duff and Clement)	1198.5	49.9
4.	Bignan 2-litre (de Marne and Martin)	1198.5	49.9
6.	Excelsior (Dils and Caerels)	1188	49.5
7.	Chenard-Walcker 3-litre (Bachmann and Glazmann)	1177	49.0
8.	Lorraine-Dietrich (de Courcelles and Rossignol)	1157.6	48.2
9.	Excelsior (Lecureuil and Flaud)	1134.5	47.3
10.	Bugatti 1½-litre (de Pourtales and de la Rochefoucauld)	1113	46.3
11.	Brasier (Migeot and Verpault)	1059.5	44.1
12.	Delage (Belben and Torchy)	1049.8	43.7
13.	Salmson 1,100 c.c. (Desvaux and Casse)	1049.8	43.7
14.	Montier-Ford (Montier and Ouriou)	1039	43.3
15.	Irat (Cappé and Douarimon)	995	41.4
16.	Salmson 1,100 c.c. (Benoist and Bueno)	995	41.4
17.	Rolland-Pilain (de Morguanatz and Delande)	984.5	41.0
18.	Amilcar 1,100 c.c. (Boutmy and Marcadanti)	952	39.7
19.	Lorraine-Dietrich (Bloch and Stalter)	941.5	39.2
20.	Berliet (Prost and Redon)	941.5	39.2
21.	Rolland-Pilain (Sire and Guignard)	899	37.5
22.	Bugatti 1½-litre (Marie and Pichard)	845	35.2
23.	Rolland-Pilain (Pouzet and Pichon)	845	35.2
24.	Rolland-Pilain (Robin and Marinier)	845	35.2
25.	Vinot-Deguingand (Molon Brothers)	823.9	34.3
26.	Brasier (Maillon and Jouguet)	813	33.9
27.	Corre la Licorne (Collomb and Lestieux)	791.7	33.0
28.	Irat (Milhaud and Malleveau)	781	32.5
29.	Sara (Erb and Battagliola)	610	25.4

JOTTINGS ON THE COURSE AT LE MANS.

Among the English spectators were Mr. Vernon Pugh and Miss Pugh, who motored down on an Alvis car, and Mr. T. P. Searight, who had the misfortune to sprain his ankle when walking at the back of the pits in the darkness.

* * *

The French soldier who unknowingly lent his bicycle to Clement heaved an immense sigh of relief when he saw the Bentley pull in with his old-time "véloë" in the tonneau.

* * *

Fifty chickens, 150 gallons of hot soup, 450 bottles of champagne, and unknown quantities of red and white wine were given away at the "Hartford Hotel" established in the pits. Boyce motometers were stated to be useful for taking the temperature of drivers after the meal.

* * *

Lagache, who won the first round of the Rudge-Whitworth Cup, is a body builder, and Bachmann, who came in second, is his partner. They built the bodies fitted to the Chenard-Walckers in the race.

* * *

With the exception of the Bentley, all the fast cars had front wheel brakes, with which they gave marvellous exhibitions of their ability to stop quickly without skidding.

* * *

Although the equipment generally was very complete, not a single car had a mechanical windscreen wiper.

* * *

Duff and Clement drove in the rain without headgear and without goggles. The French spectators were certain they would catch cold.

The first Bentley performance at Le Mans was to finish fourth in 1923.

1924

For 1924 the event was, put back three weeks, to 14 and 15 June, as the organisers hoped for improved weather; their expectations were fulfiled, indeed the heat was described as tropical. The number of entries had increased to 40 but the only non-French car was the Bentley of Duff and Clement; this year equipped with four-wheel brakes and proper stone guards to protect lamps and fuel tank. The entry of a three-litre Sunbeam was scratched; the other main contenders were as in 1923, the La Lorraine, the Chenard et Walcker, the Bignan and one of the newcomers, the 3.2 litre Aries.

Clement's and Duff's winning Bentley before the start of the race.

Apart from the 1924 race being the second round in the Triennial Cup, a new Biennial award was also instituted the Rudge-Whitworth Cup which remained a feature of the Le Mans until 1960.

The regulations now stipulated that after the first five laps, hoods had to be erected and remain up for 20 laps; and a minimum of 20 laps had to be covered before fuel, water and oil could be replenished.

This was a much more gruelling race than the previous year; 19 cars had retired after 12 hours, and at the finish, only 15 cars were in the running of which one did not classify as it failed to cover the minimum distance required. At the end of the first lap, an Alba and a Corre la Licorne had already retired. The opening stages of the race were dominated by the four-litre straight-eight Chenard et Walcker, the Bignans and the La Lorraines. Lagache in the Chenard pushed the lap record up to 69.076 mph before the car caught fire and burned out, while the pace proved too much also for most of the other big French cars both the three-litre Bignans, the Aries and the three litre Chenard were all out by midnight. This left the team of three La Lorraines, all with ohv 3.4 litre six-cylinder engines, as the main competitors for the Bentley, while some of the smaller cars, the two-litre Chenards and Bignans moved up the score board.

At half time Duff in the Bentley was lying second to the Lorraine of Stalter and Bloch; and during Sunday morning Duff eventually overtook the French car which ultimately retired at 1 pm leaving the Englishman in a secure lead, followed by the two remaining Lorraines. Despite losing much time towards the end of the race due to a lengthy pit stop for a precautionary change of both rear wheels, Duff and Clement were the winners; although they had covered 1,380 miles, their qualifying distance was 1,290 miles due to a misunderstanding as Duff had not realised that the long pit stop had pulled his average for the final five laps down below the statutory minimum. The lead over the Lorraine in miles, and Duff's distance less average speed was 53.783 mph.

Bentley Wins 24-hour Race at Le Mans.

Duff and Clement Victorious Over 40 Other Competitors.

LE MANS, *Saturday.*

THE sky is very blue—blue as it is seldom seen in our England. The broad road between the flag-bedecked grand-stand crowded with eager spectators and the pits, stripped for action, is empty save for the 41 cars standing in two long lines. The first 30 or so are still, waiting, curiously forlorn, for the drivers who, on the word " Partez," will set them throbbing with life at the touch of an electric button, and unloose all the vast forces latent in their wonderfully wrought engines. At the end of the two long queues exhausts still snore and rumble spasmodically as the last cars are manœuvred into position.

The silence grows more intense. The voices of a few spectators sound curiously clear in the hush. It is three minutes to four, and the afternoon sun is blazing down on the gravel road, 10 7 miles of it, which runs across the heather and pine-grown plain outside Le Mans. The minutes are thudded, one by one, by a distant maroon. Three—two—one . . . . *Partez!*

41 Cars Start Together.

With a thrilling roar and the clash of Bendix pinions 41 self-starters come into use, and 40 engines spring into life. All, that is, with the exception of poor Montier's wonderfully speeded-up Ford, which splutters and bangs and will not start until half a dozen depressions of the starter button, when he rushes gamely off in the rear of the procession.

The haze of dust and oil smoke raised by the starters has scarcely blown away when all eyes turn right. A speck in the distance grows and grows against a pale background of dust, becomes de Marne's Bignan, flies past with a roar, and is lost to sight. A few seconds later Lagache, the winner of last year's race, thunders past at a terrific pace. Then Ledure, on the new three-litre six-cylinder model Bignan, which he has not even had time to try on the course.

The passing of Duff, on the three-litre Bentley, is eagerly awaited by the few

British onlookers. Soon he comes past the stands, holding the road like a leech, raising his arm as a signal that all goes well.

With Klaxon blaring a shrill warning, Louis Chenard, on the car bearing his name, dashes past the two Omegas as they go under the bridge. Follow a succession of speeding cars, and Paul and Wallon's Corre-la Licorne, misfiring badly, draws up at the pits with a broken valve; a second or two later Hatton's Alba stops just behind with a horrible clatter coming from his valve gear also.

At this stage de Marne's speed is given for the first lap—104 k.p.h. He follows up with a lap at 114 k.p.h., and in a burst of applause tops his performance with a record lap in 9 mins. 24 secs., equal to 116 kilometres (72.5 miles) an hour.

Wonderful Hood Work.

When one of the most interesting episodes of the race—the raising of hoods and screens and driving two laps with them erected—begins, Duff gives a wonderful display of lightning hood raising.

Before he is in, however, Lagache rushes by, only to be flagged to stop for the hood test when he has nearly passed the stands. With front-wheel brakes hard on, he draws up " all standing," reverses rapidly to his pit a hundred yards back, leaps out, and begins the long fumbling with telescopic tubes which characterized fitting up the detachable hoods on the ultra-sporting bodies.

Duff, on the other hand, pulls his hood over, secures in like lightning to the screen pillars and roars off in a babel of warm-hearted applause, having taken

GETTING READY FOR THE START. THE CARS OUTSIDE THEIR PITS.

CLEMENT SCREWS DOWN THE OIL TANK FILLER CAP AFTER RELIEVING DUFF ON THE VICTORIOUS BENTLEY.

F. DUFF, AT LE MANS, PUTTING UP THE HOOD ON HIS FOUR-SEATER BENTLEY IN RECORD TIME, 41 SECS.

the record for hood raising in only 41 seconds. On his next lap he is driving at 60 miles an hour or more with one hand holding the hood in place, and of the French drivers that follow many are doing likewise. The Bignans have very neat collapsable windscreens that drop flush with the scuttle top, in front of the instrument board.

Lagache, continuing his whirlwind rush, is first in to take down his hood, but when Duff comes in he flings it down so rapidly that the spectators burst into delighted applause. In an incredibly short time he has strapped it securely and sped away.

"Fire!"

The fastest cars are doing their eighth or ninth lap when Bachmann's blue Chenard-Walcker comes to a stop at the

the next two cars were Lorraines, a Georges Irat was fourth, and the British Bentley, driven by Capt. J. Duff, was fifth.

Dusk.

Slowly the daylight ebbed away, and out of a darkening sky shone a solitary golden star. One by one the Magondeaux dissolved acetylene headlamps lit up, casting their beams along the gravel road. The stands emptied; the open-air restaurant, erected near by, became crowded to overflowing. A jazz band tinkled, and a quartet of red-coated huntsmen played prettily on French horns.

Of a sudden all eyes searched the horizon over beyond the scoring board. A pillar of black smoke, drifting slowly with the wind, betrayed the fact that a car was on fire, on the Pontlieue-Mulsanne road. This was the redoubtable Chenard-Walcker handled by Leonard, who succeeded Lagache, burning furi-

THE SIMULTANEOUS START OF THE 41 DRIVERS IN THE GRAND PRIX D'ENDURANCE 24 HOURS RACE.

MR. F. C. CLEMENT (LEFT) AND CAPT. J. F. DUFF (RIGHT) WITH THE BENTLEY, VICTORIOUS IN THE LE MANS 24 HOURS RACE. MR. W. O. BENTLEY IS STANDING BETWEEN THEM.

beginning of the long line of pits. There is a sudden scream of "*au feu!. . . les Pyrènes!*" and a wicked coil of grey-blue smoke rises from the driving compartment. Figures rush hither and thither squirting the extinguishers, and the red flames which threatened to engulf the car are conquered after a fight. A moment for the smoking cushions to cool, and the intrepid driver is off again. The race goes on. An Aries (Gabriel's) and Collomb's La Licorne are reported stopped by the gargantuan loud-speaker. There is a little ironical laughter, for Collomb has had endless trouble. Two hours have already passed, yet Brouin still struggles with his valve gear. His team-mate Paul pushes his La Licorne wearily off the course.

A Moment of Suspense.

There was a moment of breathless suspense while René Marie's Bignan, after racing side by side with Douarinou's Georges Irat, skidded across the road just in front of him in terrifying fashion, sending a pillar of dust whirling skywards. He recovered quickly and the two cars sped on, each jockeying for position. About this time Ledure's six-cylinder Bignan came to a stop with a complete and mysterious loss of power, and he retired.

At the end of the first three hours Lagache (Chenard-Walcker) led the field;

ously, and therefore out of the race. Thus the Lorraine-Dietrich, driven in turn by Bloch and Stalter, dropped into first place, with Duff, on the Bentley, a close second.

Only 24 Cars Left.

At the end of six hours there were only 24 cars left out of the 43 that started off so bravely at 4 o'clock on Saturday, and among the four that had in that time covered 33 laps, or 569.646 kiloms., was Duff's Bentley, now being piloted by Clement.

Now, in complete darkness, the scene by the pits was curious indeed. Everywhere was brilliantly lit up, the illuminated scoring board standing sharp and distinct among the brilliantly lighted advertisements above the pits. Now and then, with a whirr and a roar, the racing touring cars would dash past, headlamps blazing, with sometimes a giant searchlight beside the driver playing also upon the road.

What might have been a sore trial for the Bentley occurred when the official timekeepers credited Duff with only 19 laps when he had covered 20. At length, after a long and bitter wrangle, it turned out that the timekeeper had made a mistake.

At the Bentley Pit.

The 11.30 p.m. change of Bentley drivers was typical of the period of

darkness. For minutes before Clement was due in Duff was standing ready in the road. At length the Bentley slowed and came in, lamps were switched off, and replenishments hastily effected. Then in leapt Duff, long and spare, in brown "plus fours" and a blue berêt basque, and depressed the starter. Nothing doing. Hastily, but very cool, he sprang out, freed the sticking pinion, leapt back. There were shouts of "Lights! Lights!" from the pit, the lamps were switched on, the starter button depressed, and the engine burst into a roar. Duff let in his clutch, cheered by many a sporting Frenchman

HOW THE PITS WERE ILLUMINATED AT NIGHT AT LE MANS DURING THE GRAND PRIX D'ENDURANCE. TAKEN AT MIDNIGHT.

Lorraine at the rate of 18 secs. a lap. When Bloch stopped at the pits Clement was only 21 secs. behind him, then took first place, dropping back to second place after stopping at the pits to be relieved by Duff. The two rear Hartford shock absorbers, of Duralumin, both broke, owing to the fact that steel ones should have been used in such a race as this.

With the sky glowing lavender and yellow in a cloudless dawn, the spirits of the onlookers rose even higher than they kept all night. And ever the cars thundered by, the wonderful little air-cooled Saras, the Bignans, the Lorraine-Dietriches, Chenard-Walckers, the Amilcar, the Bentley and Rolland-Pilains lapping steadily hour after hour.

At about 9 a.m. the two leading cars Bloch (Lorraine-Dietrich) and Duff (Bentley)—are separated by 3 mins. 16 secs. In the next lap Duff gains 10 secs., and in the following lap

led on the Bentley with 1,864 kiloms., Bloch and Marie, on the Lorraine-Dietrich and Bignan respectively, being second and third, with 1,847 kiloms. and 1,760 kiloms.

At the end of 20 hours also the only complete teams were the three Lorraine-Dietriches of 3,500 c.c., two Brasiers of 2,100 c.c., and two Saras of 1,100 c.c.

Excitement High.

Well over an hour before the finish of the race excitement was at fever pitch. The Bentley supporters anxiously timed Duff's every lap as he edged nearer and nearer the lead; there was so strong an element of chance that to follow the race was almost to die of excitement.

At last the cars were flagged on their last lap, each driver applauded as he went by Great bouquets were got ready, and when at last Capt. John Duff purred up, anxiously looking for news, he was welcomed as the victor

LAGACHE, WHOSE CAR WAS LATER DESTROYED BY FIRE, ERECTING HIS AWKWARD HOOD ON THE EIGHT-CYLINDER CHENARD-WALCKER.

(and woman too), for he is wonderfully popular, went a few yards and . . . stopped. There were anguished yells of "Pressure!" and, realizing the omission, the driver pumped frantically, just caught the hesitating engine, and roared off at full speed into the blackness.

De Marne, who had been doing so well on the Bignan, lost the drain plug of his radiator, and retired, while the Majola stopped near Pontlieue. One of the imposing-looking Omega Six cars stopped with a broken valve.

Once again there were anguished moments when Duff came in with an obstruction in his gear-change gate, but at last, after a considerable amount of levering and hammering, managed to extract it—an insulated staple from the electrical wiring.

At the end of the 10th hour the two Lorraine-Dietriches driven by De Courcelles and Bloch were first and second, with the Bentley a close third.

Bentley in Second Place.

Three hours later the Bentley lay second, and was overhauling the fastest

the Lorraine bursts a tyre, rapidly changes a wheel, and dashes off again. Duff then takes the lead, which he increases steadily by 10 secs. per lap for three laps, until he leads by 1 min. 52 secs.

British Car Gets the Lead.

At the end of 18 hours' continuous running Duff (Bentley), who had just increased his lead to 2 mins., was first, with 97 laps, Bloch (Lorraine-Dietrich) second, 96 laps, Marie (Bignan) third, 93 laps.

During lunch time, to the dismay of the French, Bloch retired with serious valve trouble at his 111th lap (1,916 kiloms.). This was after being hard put to it to keep up with Clement, who took over from Duff at about 10.40 a.m. On the 107th lap, the Bentley led by 3 mins. 28 secs., and immediately afterwards he overtook Bloch for the second time, being then over a lap ahead.

When, about 2½ hours before the finish, the Bentley came in to change the rear wheels (not because it was necessary, but to avoid taking any chances), owing to bad explanations from the officials, Duff took longer than he need over the tyre change, and set off at last perspiring from the struggle with a seized wheel locking ring, with a good deal of time to make up. The last hour or so was an agony of anxiety.

In the meanwhile it is noteworthy that, at the end of 20 hours, J. F. Duff

with flowers and felicitations, having covered 129 laps (1,290.44 miles) in the 24 hours of gruelling racing, averaging 53.76 m.p.h.

A Great British Victory.

Thus a very great British victory. The only car entered from this side of the Channel, with J. F. Duff and F. C. Clement as drivers, and a perfectly standard one at that, it takes the laurels from 43 French competitors, most with an international reputation. It is of note that Rapson cord tyres were used throughout the race, and not a single involuntary stop was caused by them.

The car was entered privately by Capt. Duff, who, it will be recalled, is of Duff and Adlington, 10, Upper St. Martin's Lane, London, W.C. 2, who are the sole Bentley representatives for the Long Acre area. Prices' special racing oil was used, as were Hartford shock absorbers. and Rapson tyres, and M.L. magneto.

RESULTS.
Distances covered in 24 hours by first six.

1.—Bentley (Duff and Clement), 1,290.44 miles.
2.—Lorraine (Stoffel and Brisson), 1,280.49 miles.
3.—Lorraine (Courcelles and Rossignol), 1,276.77 miles.
4.—Chenard-Walcker (Bisard and Chavée), 1,191.65 miles.
5.—Chenard-Walcker (Manso and Dauvergne), 1,164.93 miles.
6.—Rolland-Pilain (Delalande and Guignard), 1,144 miles.

Bentley at Le Mans 1924

Clement's and Duff's car before the Start.

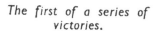

A fine action shot of sunshine and shade and the winning Bentley.

The first of a series of victories.

1925

The race on 20 and 21 June 1925 brought several innovations, chief among which was the first Le Mans start which was to be a feature of the race until 1969. The cars were lined up at an angle on one side of the road, the drivers stood opposite and when the flag fell the driver had to run across, put up the hood and start the car. 1925 was also the one year when the pits and grandstand were moved from their traditional position at Les Raineries across the circuit to the hippodrome at Hunaudieres, due to difficulties with a land owner.

Of a total of 68 entries, 49 were brought to the start; but only 16 were to classify, and five cars which were running at the finish failed to cover the minimum distance. Perhaps because of Bentley's win the previous year, there was more international interest in the race; British entries included a team of two three-litre Bentleys, Duff and Clement now supplemented by a works entered car driven by Kensington Moir and Dr Benjafield. Two of the sophisticated and fast three-litre Sunbeams with twin ohc six-cylinder engines were driven by Segrave/Duller and Chassagne/'Sammy' Davis, and while an entry from AC was scratched, an Austin Seven driven by Gordon England and Sir Francis Samuelson was, with its 747 cc engine, much the smallest car in the race. From Italy there were four Diattos - two with three-litre engines, and two two-litres, together with three O.M.s with their remarkably powerful side valve engines; and perhaps the most portentous newcomer was a lone American Chrysler 70, though ignominiously, this first American entry at Le Mans failed to qualify on distance. Among the French contingent most of the interest attached to the Chenard et Walckers - two of the big eights were entered together with two 1,100 cc models, the latter with the fully enclosed streamlined 'tank' bodywork which became a hallmark of this make - and also the team of three La Lorraines. The largest car was a 4.5 litre Sizaire-Berwick; not the British mock Austin species but the old-fashioned French model which had a side

valve four-cylinder engine with fixed 'T' cylinder head complete with valve caps. There were also two three-litre Aries in the large car class. Among the smaller cars, a famous name made its first appearance: two 1.5 litre Talbots, of the French variety, though both retired.

Initially, a fierce duel was fought out between the Bentleys and the Sunbeams from which neither team emerged victorious. Having driven flat out with the hood up, Moir ran out of fuel before the officially permitted re-fuelling stop. The other Bentley and both Sunbeams suffered from various mechanical mishaps, and the Segrave/Duller Sunbeam retired before midnight with clutch trouble. Duff and Clement in the other Bentley were put out of the race when the float chamber of one SU carburettor broke off and there was an under-bonnet fire.

Of the big French cars, the La Lorraines again proved to have the stamina necessary; one of the cars crashed while lying in third place but the other two finished first and third, sandwiching the only surviving British entry, the Chassagne/Davis Sunbeam, which completed the course with a fractured chassis. But perhaps the most impressive performance was of two of the two-litre O.M.s which finished in a shared fourth place. The 1,100 cc Chenard et Walcker 'tanks' took the honours in the Rudge-Whitworth Cup, one winning the Triennial award (which was not repeated) and the other taking the first Biennial Cup. Before retiring, Lagache in the eight-cylinder Chenard et Walcker had improved his lap record from the previous year to 70.206 mph, while the average speed of the winning La Lorraine was 57.838 mph for a total distance of 1,388.127 miles.

On a serious note, Le Mans claimed its first two deaths this year; Andre Guilbert was killed in a Ravel when practising on Saturday morning prior to the race, and Marius Mestivier lost control of his Amilcar which went off on the Mulsanne straight; he was killed instantly.

The Rudge-Whitworth Cup Race.

Chenard-Walcker Wins Coveted Trophy in Great 24-hour Road Race— High Speeds by Bentleys and Sunbeams.

(Above) P i s a r t (Chenard-Walcker) overtaking Saint-Paul (Lorraine) who eventually turned over. (Right) H Kensington Moir (Bentley) at speed.

THE great 24-hour road race for the Rudge-Whitworth Cup, which finished at Le Mans on Sunday afternoon, proved once again to be the finest test which it is possible to conceive of the reliability of the standard model. Out of 49 starters there remained at the end of the 24 hours only 19. The hot weather and the appalling surface of the road between the Mulsanne and Pontlieue corners aggravated the already severe nature of the race, which was attended by at least double or treble the number of spectators which it attracted last year.

The British contingent was strong, and our representatives were all cars with international reputations. But Fate, after decreeing that the Bentley should win last year, was against us this time, although one of the new 3-litre Sunbeams covered the second greatest mileage (2161.6 kilometres or 1,342 miles) in the two turns of the clock.

Thus the much-coveted Tri-annual cup goes to France, the actual winners being Sénéchal and Loqueneux on a 1,095 c.c. beetle-backed Chenard-Walcker

of futuristic design but astounding performance. A similar car, handled by Manso and Glaszmann, wins the first Bi-annual cup. The first race for the second Bi-annual cup was won by De Courcelles and Rossignol on a big Lorraine-Dietrich, with the new 3-litre Sunbeam, ably piloted by Jean Chassagne and S. C. H. Davis, a good second.

The Bentleys were first favourites. Even the French were convinced, at the

start, that Duff and Clement would pull off the Tri-annual cup. Yet sheer bad luck, in the shape of a broken-off float chamber causing a sudden petrol leakage which resulted in a small fire, put the car out of the running. The other Bentley, to all appearances the fastest car in the whole race, ran out of petrol only half a lap before it was due at the pits for replenishment, owing to the unforeseen increase in fuel consumption resulting from running over 200 miles with the hood up—one of the tests. As no fuel could be taken in except at the pits, the driver, H. Kensington Moir, had to retire.

Segrave and Duller's Sunbeam, which was very fast, was withdrawn owing to the clutch seizing and also slipping. E. C. Gordon-England's little Austin had its radiator holed by a great stone flung from the hind wheels of a larger car, and the A.C. was found, only a moment or two before the start, to have its main radiator fixing plate fractured, so had to be scratched.

Quite one of the most striking features of the race was the regular running of the two Italian teams (O.M. and Diatto) and the silent, effortless demonstration of the Chrysler, which ran the whole race at an excellent average without a single stop for repairs or adjustments.

One accident—alas, fatal—is to be deplored. Mestivier, a young driver-mechanic, turned turtle, owing, it is said, to one of the front brakes locking hard on on his Amilcar, and had his skull crushed. The car was completely wrecked.

It is noteworthy that out of 55 entrants there were only six non-starters. The neat little six-cylinder A.C. which V. A. Bruce and J. A. Joyce were to have driven was found at the last moment to have one of the radiator holding-down plates fractured. There were only a few minutes to go before the start and there was no time to make even the most temporary repair, so an English car of which a good performance was expected was forced to retire, as it were, at the starting line. One of the big three-litre Revals met with a head-on collision on the circuit early on the Saturday morning; the

George Duller takes over from Segrave at the Sunbeam pit.

20

Segovia (Sara) and De Courcelles (Lorraine) shortly after the start

driver had both legs crushed, and his condition is very serious. The other non-starters were a Chrysler and the three Omega-Six cars.

For sheer enthusiasm there was no comparison between the Rudge-Whitworth Cup race of this year and that of 1924. At least three times the number of spectators were present at the start. The weather was sweltering. Shirtsleeves, tinted spectacles and even pith helmets were much in evidence.

An Exciting Start.

As the loud-speaker gave out the final warnings the competitors' cars were parked diagonally down the right-hand side of the road with hoods folded and strapped down and with doors shut. The drivers stood tense and expectant on the other side of the course. Slowly the minutes ticked by until, with the dropping of a great flag and a stentorian "Partez!" from gargantuan loud-speakers the drivers raced for their cars, erected their hoods with all possible speed, leaped in, depressed the starter button, and roared off. This, at least, is what they were supposed to do. It remained for Capt. J. F. Duff, on the low, lithe Bentley speed model to show 48 other drivers how it was done. With incredible rapidity he had fitted hood and side curtains, and in a burst of warm-hearted applause from delighted spectators his engine roared up healthily as he shot away, the first driver to start. For this display he won a special prize. De Froncony, on the Sizaire-Berwick was next away, with H. Kensington Moir on the other Bentley and Minöa on an O.M. close behind. Followed another O.M., then Segrave.

With his clean, rapid getaway and a clear road before him it was expected that Duff would be an easy "first man round." Nearly ten minutes elapsed, then a speck on the distant road grew bigger second by second, was suddenly recognized as Segrave's Sunbeam, and flashed screaming up the road. Segrave was first round in his best Grand Prix style.

Kensington Moir, on a very fast Bentley, had no intention of playing second fiddle to the famous Sunbeam driver, and roared past close on Segrave's tail,

while only a little way behind was Duff on the other Bentley. Saint-Paul's Lorraine-Dietrich came, and then Lagache's great flat-bodied straight-eight Chenard-Walcker.

A thrill was provided at the end of the first lap when Pisart's Chenard-Walcker passed Minöa's O.M. under the footbridge spanning the circuit. Immediately afterwards Staltey's Lorraine-Dietrich overtook Gordon England's Baby Austin at the same point. Thereafter Segrave held the lead for many laps. His second round of the circuit occupied 9 mins. 48 secs., equal to an average speed of 105 k.p.h., or about 65 m.p.h.

Beyond an occasional stop at the pits for information by one or two drivers, there was little of interest.

On the fourth lap Moir was just behind him, and at the same time Pisart came into the pits with clouds of blue smoke pouring through the louvres of the bonnet, and climbed wearily out. After a brief conversation Elgy, the reserve driver, took his place, as he was more capable of dealing with a mechanical breakdown on the straight-eight Chenard-Walcker. The trouble, however, was only remedied temporarily after some 40 minutes' strenuous work.

Moir's Bentley, which quite evidently had an enormous reserve of power, judging by the way it accelerated, was only 18 secs. behind the leading Sunbeam at the end of five laps. Duff was some distance behind, while Chassagne, following him closely, came roaring down the "straight," overtaking, one by one, a long line of cars. The Sizaire-Berwick, handled by De Francony, came in to the pits for the second time.

A little less than ten minutes afterwards Segrave, with Kensington Moir hot on his heels, shoots past the stands screeching imperious warnings on his powerful electric horn. One sees the Frenchman swerve sharply to his right as he sees in his driving mirror the reflection of the British champion's thrusting V-nosed bonnet.

The race goes on. The thrilling roar of motors driven "flat out" vibrates in the air, comes pulsing through the pines from Mulsanne and Pontlieue. The hoods seem to be standing up to it well, and for the most part do not belly in the wind.

The Bignan, driven alternately by Martin and Matthys, comes in with a flat tyre. The wheel is changed in an incredibly short time, and the car shoots forwards once more. Scarcely has he disappeared when a blare of sirens is

Saint-Paul (Lorraine) followed by Springue (Bignan) at the Mulsanne Corner

Pisart on one of the new straight-eight Chenard-Walcker cars, followed by Duff (Bentley) approaching the stands.

heard down towards Pontlieue. Sénéchal, on one of the new beetle-backed Chenard-Walckers, is on the extreme left of the road running neck and neck with an Italian. Segrave is sounding his Klaxon fiercely, trying to get through, while Moir on the Bentley is thundering up behind ready to shoot through the gap the instant there is room.

On the ninth lap Chassagne, who is driving one of the Sunbeams, comes in to the pits with his throttle controls sticking. He seizes a great squirt and pumps petrol over the two carburetters and their operating mechanism. Then quickly and accurately he squirts oil here and there until the carburetters work freely, and off he goes with a cautious backward glance to see if any other competitor is hurtling up behind him.

Meanwhile, the Bentley, No. 10, is going faster and faster, and at the end of two hours Kensington Moir has wrested the lead from Segrave, who, half a length behind, and with his near-side wheels in the dust, is struggling to forge ahead again.

This lead Moir increases, but fate

steps in and he loses the cap of his oil level overflow pipe, so Segrave gets back into the first place while a new cap is being improvised, from a Vichy bottle cork, at the pits.

At the end of 20 laps cars were allowed to come in to the pits for supplies, when they were also permitted to fold their hoods. Leonard, driving an eight-cylinder Chenard-Walcker, was first in, and cheered with a round of applause as he shot away again with his car in normal racing trim.

The total time taken by the first Sunbeam in to fold the hood, replenish, and change drivers was about 5 minutes. Segrave carried out all the necessary work before handing over to Duller, in marked contrast to Chassagne, who got straight out and left the fresh driver, Davis, to do what was required before driving off. Duller had considerable difficulty in engaging first gear owing to the clutch sticking, while a loose ignition switch wire caused him to leave the pits with a succession of terrific reports.

As the shadows lengthened with the setting sun much anxiety was felt in the Bentley pit owing to the failure to arrive of both their cars. Clement and Benjafield, the relief drivers, had

been waiting for some time all ready to take over, when word came that both Bentleys were stuck on the course—one at Pontlieue and the other on the far leg of the circuit.

Meanwhile the high-powered electric lamps, supplied with current from a vast temporary power station, were being switched on, and in a luminous, deep-blue sky the stars began to shine one by one. The road past the stands was like a brilliantly lit bazaar, with each pit as a little shop, bright with coloured cans and half-watt lamps.

Through the dark pine forest Duff came running, obtained a necessary spare for the petrol feed, which had given trouble on his Bentley, and dashed off again through the gloom. Half an hour later he reappeared with the car, and after the necessary replenishment he set off pluckily to make up the five laps which he had lost. Thus the Sunbeam-Bentley duel continued à deux, for Duller had by this time retired owing to clutch trouble, and Moir, having run out of petrol a long way from the pits, could not continue without breaking the regulations, which ordain that petrol tanks may only be filled at the pits.

Shortly after Mestivier met his death, as is mentioned earlier in this account, one of the Lorraine-Dietrichs spun round three times and overturned, with one front spring torn right away from its shackles. The driver escaped, miraculously, with a bad shaking.

Up the Mulsanne road was the Bentley private timing installation, where silent Britishers lay in the grass by the roadside, with stop-watches, slide rules and notebooks gleaming in the light of electric torches. Every passage of Duff was carefully timed, the driver each time signalling with two sharp roars of the exhaust as he opened the throttle wide.

At 4 a.m. it was already daylight, and the enthusiasm of the crowd was such that fully half of them still thronged paddock and stands. The half-time score showed that the two Lorraine-Dietrichs were leading with 65 and 63 laps, the Sunbeam next with 62 laps, and Duff and Clement's Bentley 6th, with 58 laps.

At 6 a.m. 30 cars were still running,

Boland (La L.corne) being caught up by Kensington Moir (Bentley) near the point where Mestivier was killed

the Sunbeam now having crept up to second place, only two laps behind De Ceurcelle's Lorraine. The Bentley, however, was out of it owing to the float chamber breaking off one carburetter, and causing a small but destructive fire under the bonnet.

Thus the day went on, every hour bringing more and more spectators. At 1 p.m. only 25 cars remained out of the original 49, and at 4 p.m., when, with the usual bonquets, music and wild applause, the winners, were announced, there remained only 19.

RESULTS.

First Tri-annual Cup.
Sénéchal-Locqueneux, 1,095 c.c. Chenard-Walcker.

First Bi-annual Cup.
Glaszmann-Manso, 1,095 c.c. Chenard-Walcker.

First Race of Second Bi-annual Cup.

		km.	m.
1.	De Courcelles-Rossignol (Lorraine)	2,233	982
2.	Chassagne-Davis (Sunbeam)	2,161	6
3.	Stalter-Brisson (Lorraine)	2,149	486
4.	T. Danieli-M. Danieli (O.M.)	2,080	44
4.	Foresti-Vassiaux (O.M.)	2,080	44
5.	Wagner-Flohot (Ariès)	2,055	613
6.	Stoffel-Desvaux (Chrysler)	2,032	413

Senechal, winner of the Tri-annual Cup, on his strange Chenard-Walcker at Mulsanne

The Le Mans 24-hour Race.

The R.A.C. Representative's Interesting Report on the Event.

COL. O'GORMAN, who attended the recent 24-hour Endurance Trial at Le Mans on behalf of the R.A.C., has compiled a report on the event, which is of unusual interest. In the first place, Col. O'Gorman is of opinion that nothing less than a 24-hour race is capable of trying out the modern car, and the gruelling the cars received at Le Mans is sufficiently severe to incite the go-ahead manufacturer to enter, since it gives him a chance of proving the superiority of his productions. The change of driver every three hours permits of the utmost being extracted from the cars right through the 24 hours without any danger arising from human fatigue, whilst the almost automatic handicap gives the small and the big car a chance of running against one another, and yet gets over the humiliation with which a big car is often faced in being beaten by a little one when both have the same task to perform.

Briefly, the trial consists of an attempt by every competitor to run as far as possible in 24 hours under touring conditions. For each engine capacity there is a quota of miles that must be run in the time, and the series of quotas are plotted as a curve, on the basis of engine capacities. Above this curve a family of curves is plotted, roughly parallel to the basic curve of quotas. It is the object of each competitor, by making a large mileage in the 24 hours, to reach up to as high a member of this family of curves as possible, and so win the contest.

Col. O'Gorman did not find any substantial grounds for complaint regarding the organization, but the bodies on the British cars were far superior to the others.

Although only three British cars actually ran (against 43 of other nations), they secured a very good position; and, moreover, the engine of the British car—which finished only 50 kiloms. short of the fastest car at the conclusion of the 24 hours—was of considerably smaller dimensions.

Col. O'Gorman, in concluding his report, justifiably points out the advantages to be derived from the R.A.C. running a similar event in England. "To perform well, a car maker for the race must produce a foolproof scheme of lubrication, of petrol filtering, a minimum of petrol and oil consumption, his springs must stand up to severe shocks with a good useful load (the cars have to carry the weight of the passengers), he must study wind resistance to the utmost, he cannot use poor steel or steel alloys, he cannot win with a car frame that distorts, or a radiator that springs leaks. His brakes must be superb. The acceleration must be excellent and, therefore, the carburetter must adjust itself to all engine speeds, and the maker must cut down all wasted weight without weakening anything anywhere. Fatigue of drivers will diminish his chances enormously if his seating and the car springing is not easy. Most makers competing found it necessary to use four-wheel brakes. Devices for saving wind resistance are studied to the utmost to enable the little engine to do the big job. Why should the advantage of these studies be brought to France from all over the world and not to England?"

1926

After one year's absence the race headquarters were back at Raineries in 1926, the un-cooperative land owner having in the meantime decided to sell the area to the A.C.O. at a reasonable price. Chenard et Walcker were conspicuous by their absence this year (and indeed, would only once more return to the Sarthe circuit) so French hopes centred - again - on the La Lorraines, together with the three litre Aries and for the first time Peugeot, making one of their rare appearances at Le Mans with a team of two 3.8 litre sleeve valve cars.

O.M. was back in force but there was no other Italian entry; similarly the three Bentleys were the only British cars. A rather surprising entry came from Toledo, Ohio; the Willys-Overland company (which at the time was among America's leading mass-producers) entered a Willys-Knight with a sleeve valve engine, and two of their Overland Sixes (of which one crashed in practice).

There was still no overall winner officially but the second Biennial Cup was coupled with an Index of Performance, based on actual distance travelled by a car in relation to the required minimum distance set for its class. The Triennial Cup was abandoned. The hoods still had to be raised at the start which gave an immediate but slight advantage to the single closed car in the race, a French Jousset. There were several French entries in the 1,100 cc category - including S.A.R.A., Salmson and Aries - but nothing smaller; while the Willys-Knight was the biggest-engined car at 3.9 litres.

New pits and grandstands had been erected; also a restaurant, bars, much-increased car parks which would accommodate 3,000 vehicles, and a large scoreboard on which spectators could follow the changing positions throughout the race. The press-box was at the top of the new grandstand.

The promised battle between La Lorraine, Peugeot, Aries and Bentley duly unfolded. The dark horse, the American Willys-Knight, was, despite its advantage on engine size, never a serious threat and soon retired; its smaller stable-mate, the Overland, proved to possess more stamina in the long run and was lying sixth when it retired with less than an hour to go. The 1926 race was an unmitigated disaster for two of the favourite teams; of the Peugeots, the Wagner/Dauvergne car suffered from long drawn out electrical troubles and finally had to retire when the electrical starter refused to work after a pit stop - hand cranking was interestingly enough disallowed. Their Boillot/Rigal team mates were disqualified while lying second at half time - the windscreen had broken earlier and the jury-rigged remains had now given way. The disqualification was unpopular with the crowd of spectators and the luckless officials had to make themselves scarce until the hubbub had died down.

The Bentley team fared even worse. 'W. O.' attributed his failure to lack of preparation as Bentleys were preoccupied record-breaking at Montlhery; but there was no real reason all of the three green cars should fail and indeed they did so for different reasons. First to go, at about half-distance, was the Duller/Clement car which suffered a broken valve, and by mid-morning the Gallop/ Thistlethwayte car was out of the race with a broken rocker arm. This was particularly disappointing as this was one of the new short-chassis super sports three-litre models and it had been lying as high as second. Final hopes were pinned on the Davis/ Benjafield car which had moved up to third but was wearing out its brakes rapidly; it had covered 1,480 miles and had less than half an hour to go when Sammy Davis slid into a sandbank at Mulsanne. The Aries had both retired earlier in the race, and the result was therefore a remarkable 1-2-3 for La Lorraine; all three setting average speeds over 100 kilometres per hour, the first time this barrier was broken. Winners were Bloch/ Roissignol at 66.083 mph, total distance 1,585.99 miles. In fourth and fifth places followed two O.M.s, and Minoia and Foresti in the leading O.M. were also the winners of the Biennial Cup and the Index. Fastest lap speed was pushed up to 71.112mph by Courcelles in the second La Lorraine.

The GRAND PRIX d'ENDURANCE.

The drivers lined up in front of their cars awaiting the starting signal.

A Most Exciting 24-Hour Road Race Won by the Lorraine-Dietrich. Great Struggle Between the Winners, the O.M., and the Bentley Cars.

THE FIRST SIX CARS AND DISTANCES COVERED IN THE THIRD BIENNIAL RACE.

Car.	Drivers.	Distance.
1. Lorraine—Dietrich (3,447 c.c.)	Bloch and Rossignol	1,585·99 miles
2. Lorraine—Dietrich (3,447 c.c.)	De Courcelles and Mongin	1,574·2 ,,
3. Lorraine—Dietrich (3,447 c.c.)	Stalter and Brisson	1,493·4 ,,
4. O.M. (1,990 c.c.)	Minoia and Foresti	1,446·4 ,,
5. O.M. (1,990 c.c.)	M. Danieli and T. Danieli	1,405·92 ,,
6. Bentley (2,998 c.c.)	Davis and Benjafield	1,284·6 ,,

AFTER one of the keenest and best competitions ever seen in France, the Lorraine-Dietrich team captured first three places in the 24-hour race for the Rudge-Whitworth Cup, at Le Mans, last Saturday and Sunday.

The fastest car, driven by Bloch and Rossignol, covered a distance of 1,585.99 miles in the two rounds of the clock, thus maintaining an average of 66.08 m.p.h., which is a world's record on the road, and the two other Lorraine-Dietrichs, finishing second and third, each averaged well over 60 m.p.h.

Three and a Half v. Two Litres.

There were two races in one : the qualifying test for the third biennial, all the competitors in which set themselves the task of covering the greatest possible distance in twenty-four hours, and the final for the second biennial, for which only eleven were qualified. As the cars were of widely differing capacities, the final award was based on comparative performance, according to a table drawn up by the technical committee. After a very keen struggle with the two 1,990 c.c. O.M.'s, which were admirably handled, Lorraine Dietrich captured the

Second Biennial cup with No. 5 car driven by De Courcelles and Mongin, its distance being 1,574.2 miles compared with 1,446.4 covered by the smaller O.M.

Hard Fortune for British Cars.

Fortune did not favour the British cars and drivers. The three Bentleys made an excellent impression both before and during the race. It was recognised in France that the team was really worthy of the British industry, and while the natives naturally hoped for a French victory, it was freely admitted that the home cars would have a difficult task in defeating the invaders. The Bentleys lived up to their reputation. The first car dropped out after more than twelve hours' running, during a portion of which time it had been leading and had never been lower than fourth place. The second car, privately owned, but entered by the firm in order to comply with the rules, ran eighteen hours, during which time it was always in the leading group, before a fractured rocker arm caused it to be withdrawn. The third car, driven by S. C. H. Davis and Dr. Benjafield, met its fate during the last half-hour of the race while it was struggling to capture second place from one of the

the circuit, and yet both were withdrawn for other than mechanical reasons. Boillot's car lost its windscreen, and the one driven by Wagner was found to be without

Lorraine-Dietrichs. With the brakes needing adjustment after 23½ hours' driving on a difficult circuit, Davis took a right-angle turn at too high a speed for safety. Single-handed he could not dig the car out of the sandbank, and although he drove it away afterwards he was not among those who participated in the parade of honour before the representatives of the French Government.

Unusual Causes of Mishap.

Another team which met with ill-luck was that of the Peugeot Company. Running with a sleeve-valve engine, the two Peugeots had been most carefully prepared, they had experienced drivers in Wagner and Boillot, they showed at the beginning that they were the fastest on

liquid in its accumulators half an hour before daybreak. The headlights were functioning correctly, but the amount of current was insufficient to start the engine, and the handle was barred.

Out of forty-one starters only sixteen were present at the end, and of these two failed to cover the minimum distance necessary to qualify for next year's final for the third cup. On the other hand, the Bentley had more than covered the distance necessary to qualify, but by reason of its unfortunate twenty-fourth-hour accident it could not reach the finishing line.

This year the roads at Le Mans were in excellent condition, and did not suffer at all by reason of the race. This, in a large measure, was responsible for the high proportion of failures. A well-surfaced fast road can be more destructive of mechanism than a poor one, which

by its very nature limits speed. There had been much discussion before the race as to the possibility of maintaining an average of 100 kilometres (62 miles) for the entire twenty-four hours. This was largely exceeded, for the winner averaged sixty-six miles, and the first three cars exceeded sixty-two miles an hour. The first five averaged more than a mile a minute for two rounds of the clock, with a normal touring body carrying weight equivalent to the full number of passengers, deprived of all outside assistance, forbidden to take any supplies other than those carried aboard, and having to run more than two hundred miles with the hood raised. The value of such a contest to the motor industry in general cannot be too highly emphasised.

The management of the race was excellent throughout. Everything possible had been done by the Automobile Club de l'Ouest to facilitate the task of the competitors and to render the race interesting to the public. While the weather was not ideal, it did not interfere with the success of the race nor prevent a record crowd visiting Le Mans and remaining on the permanent circuit for the entire twenty-four hours.

Independently of the car race there was a test of three different but economical methods of road construction. A run round the circuit on Sunday evening showed that the road was in perfect condition, hardly a loose stone being visible anywhere. The Automobile Club de l'Ouest is trying to prove that these three economical systems of road maintenance could be applied advantageously all over France. The result was conclusive.

Forty-one cars placed diagonally on the right-hand side of the road, with their tails towards the replenishment pits, a white line down the middle of the highway and

27

Thellusson (O.M.) about to overtake Paris (Aries) on the S bend. He was later disqualified for a breach of the rules.

beyond this, with their backs to the spectators, the forty-one multi-coloured drivers, each with a crash helmet on his head. The starter counted off the seconds backwards, dropped his yellow flag, and immediately there was a wild rush towards the standing cars.

The rules required that the hoods should be erected and engines started after the starting signal had been given, with the result that spectators were enabled to witness a wonderful display of agility on the part of the drivers and to note—the matter is of some importance to the average motorist—that every engine responded on the first touch of the button.

Getting Away.

Foresti was the most nimble, but he was not the first to get away, for down the line was a Jousset saloon, driven by Molon, which pulled out just a second ahead of Foresti's bright red O.M., followed closely by one of the Rolland-Pilains, then by Clement and Davis respectively on Nos. 8 and 7 Bentleys. The movement was so rapid, however, that it was difficult for one pair of eyes to follow them. Balestrero's O.M. was closely behind the pair of Bentleys, the others being a Rolland-Pilain, the third of the O.M.'s, another Rolland-Pilain, and then Thistlethwayte's light green Bentley, with Boillot's dark blue Peugeot side by side with it.

But before they had covered a hundred yards many of these positions had been completely changed. The Lorraine-Dietrich men were quite leisurely, but in comparison the drivers of the two big light blue Aries, Flohot and Laly seemed absolutely lazy. They erected their hoods, fastened the straps, and buttoned the side curtains as if they were about to start for a pleasure run in showery weather, the while their team-mates, Chassagne and Duray, stood by impatiently.

The first car to appear down the winding ribbon of black highway was the low-built No. 2 sleeve-valve Peugeot, driven by André Boillot. It had a lead of about three hundred yards on Clement and Davis, very close together, on the two Bentleys, who were followed at an interval of about one hundred yards by Thistlethwayte on the third Bentley, with Bloch (Lorraine-Dietrich) hard on his heels, and Louis Wagner (Peugeot) in sixth place. Rost (Georges Irat), Stalter (Lorraine-Dietrich), Minoia (O.M.), Derny (Georges Irat), and De Courcelles (Lorraine-Dietrich) went by in a compact group which was changed when the cars got round the Pontlieue hairpin on to the fast national highway.

Half an hour was sufficient to show that the fastest cars were the Peugeots, the Lorraine-Dietrichs, and the Bentleys. André Boillot set the pace, with Bloch (Lorraine-Dietrich) very close behind, but the impression created was that the Peugeot could shake off its rival if it desired. Clement (Bentley) was third, followed by Thistlethwayte and Davis, with Wagner (Peugeot) sixth and Stalter (Lorraine-Dietrich) seventh.

Settling Down.

For three hours there was no change so far as the first two were concerned. Boillot led, with Bloch's Lorraine-Dietrich in striking distance; Clement held the third place for the first five rounds, then lost it to Stalter's Lorraine-Dietrich for three rounds, regained it on the ninth and held it until the twentieth, a distance of 214 miles. Davis (Bentley) got fourth place on the third round, but on the fifth he dropped behind both Thistlethwayte and Stalter (Lorraine-Dietrich); later he regained fourth place, only to lose it again to one of the Lorraine-Dietrichs, and to drop to seventh place after twenty rounds of the circuit.

The scene was full of life and excitement. Speeding up on the second lap, which he covered in 9m. 30s., Boillot succeeded in shaking off Bloch's Lorraine-Dietrich, but this car kept ahead of all three Bentleys. The Englishmen were driving hard. Thistlethwayte succeeded in passing Clement in the run past the grand stands, but

Kling (Ravel), Nezelof (Rolland-Pilain) and Duval (S.A.R.A.) between Arnage and La Maison Neuve.

did not hold his advantage for long, and after seven laps had dropped behind his two companions. Interest was centred on Bentley, Lorraine-Dietrich, and Peugeot, for all three teams were making a wonderful display of speed and regularity.

The first to make a stop was the Jousset saloon, and while it was at its station No. 19 O.M. pulled in just sufficiently long for its driver to say a few words to the pit attendants and came back a lap later to make a tyre change.

At the start the slowest car was No. 10, Aries, but after it had been on the road half an hour its driver, Laly, seemed to realise that he had speed and power available, for he speeded up to the record of 69 m.p.h. for one round, compared with 63.5 m.p.h., the previous record by the Lorraine-Dietrich, and shortly afterwards covered a lap at nearly 70½ m.p.h. This fast driving brought the Aries up from the tail-enders to eighth, in close company with the group of leaders.

Out, In and Out of the Race!

Officially, the first car to drop out of the race was No. 1, Willys-Knight, but soon after it was announced out of the competiton it appeared, running quite normally, only to be withdrawn permanently a few rounds later. For some reason not easy to explain, it was found impossible to get an adequate supply of petrol to the carburetters, and an hour's labour by the roadside bringing no result, the driver, Gros, declared himself defeated.

Under the rules, stops for petrol, oil, and water could be made only at intervals of twenty rounds (about 205 miles), and although there were many involuntary calls at the replenishment stations, where work was done without supplies being taken, the first official stop was that of Bloch, driving No. 6, Lorraine-Dietrich, then occupying second place behind Boillot's Peugeot. As the car came to a stop, two officials jumped out from the replenishment boxes and broke the seals on the three filler caps for oil, petrol, and water, while the driver dropped his hood and filled up, previous to handing over to his companion.

While the Lorraine-Dietrich was in, Clement's No. 8 Bentley, then holding third place, came to a stop for supplies, while Wagner went by at the same time, thus making the two Peugeots first of the field. The Lorraine-Dietrich was first away, the car starting off just as Davis came in to be relieved.

Having big capacity tanks, Boillot's Peugeot was not brought in for supplies and the lowering of the hood until twenty-two rounds had been covered, while Wagner stopped a little later after covering twenty-one rounds. Compared with racing car practice, the work at the pits seemed slow. Davis was very active; Boillot lost no time; Wagner was wonderfully agile, but the fastest at this work was Foresti on the O.M. He put the petrol pipe into his tank and let it fill automatically, the supply being by gravity from the pit, and let the tank fill to overflowing while he attended to the oil and the lowering and fastening down of the hood. The pit work by Foresti, and his companion Minoia, was really very smart.

Risks of Fire.

There was some element of danger in the way they filled the tank, for at least a gallon of petrol was spilled on the road each time, but the attendants stood by with fire extinguishers, and as soon as the car had moved off they turned a jet of their liquid on to the fuel left on the road.

By reason of these stops for replenishments, there were numerous changes, for a few rounds, in the positions of the first twelve, only the leader, Boillot on a Peugeot, being unaffected. Just before they made their stops the positions of the fastest cars were as follow :—

1. Boillot (Peugeot).	7. Davis (Bentley).
2. Bloch (Lorraine-Dietrich).	8. Thistlethwayte (Bentley).
3. Clement (Bentley).	9. Flohot (Aries).
4. Wagner (Peugeot).	10. Clauss (Bignan).
5. De Courcelles (Lorraine-Dietrich).	11. Stalter (Lorraine-Dietrich).
6. Laly (Aries).	12. Foresti (O.M.).

Two rounds later, when all had been filled up, drivers had been changed, and hoods had been lowered, Peugeot was still first, Lorraine-Dietrich second and third, Duller had run the Bentley up into fourth position, ahead of Wagner's Peugeot, while the others had held their places. The promise of an average of one hundred kilometres an hour (62 miles) was more than fulfilled. During the first three hours Boillot averaged 65.8 miles an hour, and during four hours the same car, which had then been taken over by Rigal, covered a distance of 259 miles, giving an average of 64.77 m.p.h.

The Grand Prix d'Endurance.

The harsh-toned, flat-tailed Aries had come up fast. With the hood raised Laly gained on the entire field and wiped out much of the time he had lost at the start. When Chassagne took the car over he was faster still, and for a time it looked as if the Aries could seriously threaten the Peugeots, the Bentleys, and the Lorraine-Dietrichs.

British Car Meets with Trouble.

While the pace was fast, all the competitors had kept within their limits. Duller evidently decided to put a little more vim into a game which was far from being dull, for taking over No. 8, Bentley, which Clement had maintained in third place for more than two hundred miles, he found himself in seventh place by reason of his

The first few hours revealed the severity of the contest, for while the road surface was magnificent, the pace was high, thus proving destructive to the machinery and the undoing of drivers lacking the necessary skill or caution on the bends and the turns. Two of the 2-litre Georges Irats disappeared early with mechanical trouble. Two of the Corre la Licornes required a lot of attention before they were definitely withdrawn, while early in the night the third car of the team pulled up with its left rear mudguard trailing on the ground, the front guard lying on the bonnet, and the left front wheel at an abnormal angle. It was claimed that the car had been driven into the ditch when squeezed by a competitor. Road accidents had been the undoing of one of the Th.

Bussienne (E.H.P.) leading two rivals round the sharp turn at Arnage.

supplies, then jumped up fourth a lap later, was lying third at the end of the twenty-fourth lap; ten minutes later he was second, immediately behind Rigal on the Peugeot; breaking the lap record, he went into first place after twenty-six laps, but, not satisfied with this, he drove still faster, missed the Arnage right-angle turn, and buried himself so deep in the soft earth that he had to appeal to a farmer for pick and shovel to extricate his car.

This incident cost the Bentley a couple of laps and a jammed third-speed gear. The relief of the team management at the reappearance of the car was short-lived, for Duller was bare-headed, and the rules required a crash helmet the whole of the time. It was naturally imagined that Duller had lost his head-gear while digging his car out of the sand, and as a consequence another was prepared for him, and signals were given him to stop. But Duller had so warmed up to his work that he ignored all signals and rushed by bare-headed for three or four laps, until finally several members of the team, gesticulating by the road-side and an official waving a big yellow flag, brought the impetuous driver to a standstill, when it was discovered that he had the helmet on the seat by his side.

Schneiders, a small Aries, two of the Salmsons, and an E.H.P., and occasioned their retirement.

Animated Night Scene.

Night brought a complete change of aspect, and the grand-stands, which had been well filled during daylight hours, became even more crowded and animated after the electric lights had been switched on. Opposite the grand-stands the long line of replenishment stations were hives of activity of various kinds. Where the competitors' interests were at stake, stop watches, slide rules and charts were in evidence, petrol, benzole, and oil drums were being handled, and drivers equipped themselves for their four-hour spell at the wheel.

Having nothing to sell or supply, the Hartford Hotel competed with the Rudge-Whitworth Bar and the Weymann Cabaret in distributing champagne from inexhaustible cellars, chicken and *pâté de foie gras* from spacious ice-boxes, and in slicing Prague hams and Bologna sausages on American machines. Tastefully decorated, brilliantly illuminated with electric table lamps served by white-jacketed barmen, these temporary *cafés* were comparable with the best in Paris. They differed, however, in having no charges and no tips.

Outside, the interest among the spectators was no less. Between 11 and 12 o'clock the immense open-air garage was packed with cars, and more were making their way towards the circuit than were proceeding in the direction of Le Mans, thus proving the deep-rooted interest of the French public in motoring competitions.

For at least ten days before the start of the race the weather had been inclement in France, not a single day passing without heavy rain falling. Saturday, the 12th, although threatening, was fine, and while a few showers fell, they were not sufficient to interfere with the comfort of the spectators or seriously handicap the drivers. The night of the 12th-13th was fine, with good visibility, but it was destined to be critical for many of the competitors.

Through the Night.

After losing time to replace his crash helmet, Duller again attempted to regain the lead, and was gaining on his French rivals when the breakage of a valve stem completely put an end to his endeavours. The big Aries, driven by Flohot and Duray, was saved from total destruction by the quick action of its driver. In accelerating out of a turn there was a blow back into the carburetter. With wonderful presence of mind Arthur Duray shut off the petrol supply, seized the fire extinguisher, leaped out of the car, and extinguished the fire with no more serious damage than the burning of the ignition wires.

Early in the morning Chassagne took over the 3-litre Aries from his companion Laly, and after filling up attempted to start on the electric button. The high-compression engine swung over a few degrees without firing, and repeated efforts failing to produce a result, the cruel truth had to be faced that while the generator was working the batteries were failing to store up current.

Fate hit hard at the two Peugeot cars during the wee small hours. Before midnight one of the windscreen supports had broken on Boillot's car, allowing the Triplex glass to fall out. Rigal, who was then at the wheel, kept going in the hope of finding some means of repairing, but with the morning hours the official order came either to replace the screen without outside assistance or abandon the race. No windscreen parts being carried aboard, the car had to be run into the " cemetery " while in first-class mechanical condition.

Thrilling Incidents.

Within the same hour fate was equally cruel to the second Peugeot. When Wagner took the car over from Dauvergne he found that a fuse had gone and the batteries were dry. The fuse was replaced, the lighting set functioned normally, but there was not enough current to swing the engine. The pits being on a slight gradient, Wagner put reverse into engagement, pushed the car, and as soon as the engine responded jumped aboard—to be arrested an instant later by the official diction that any other method of starting than by the use of the electric motor was contrary to the regulations.

There were thrilling incidents during the night driving, and certainly every competitor could tell of adventures which would appear miraculous to the ordinary tourist. Doubtless the most exciting was that which befell Dauvergne soon after he relieved Wagner at the wheel of the sleeve-valve Peugeot. One of the fastest cars on the circuit, the Peugeot claimed the right to pass No. 28, a 1,500 c.c. E.H.P. According to Dauvergne, the driver of the E.H.P. refused to give way, and just

as the Peugeot was about to pass swung completely into the middle of the road, causing the bigger car to run into the left-hand ditch at 70 m.p.h. By wonderful good luck Dauvergne succeeded in pulling out, but shot across the road in front of the E.H.P. and came to a complete stop in the right-hand ditch. Immediately behind was De Courcelles on No. 5, Lorraine-Dietrich, who, realising the critical situation, applied his brakes hard, swung broadside on, and came to a standstill facing the wrong way. Most extraordinarily, no material damage was done, but as the driver of this particular car had been guilty of several breaches of driving rules Dauvergne and De Courcelles lodged an official protest against him.

Positions at Half-time.

At midnight, after eight hours' running, thirty-two cars out of the forty-one starters were still running, the lead being held by No. 6, Lorraine-Dietrich, driven by Bloch and Rossignol, their distance being 514.84 miles, giving an average of 64.85 m.p.h. Last year the distance covered at this time was 471.6 miles. The two Peugeots, one of the Lorraine-Dietrichs, the Davis-Benjafield and the Thistlethwayte-Gallop Bentleys were each a lap behind the leader.

Having started at 4 p.m., half-time came at four in the morning, when thirty-two cars were still running, the positions of the leaders being as follow :—

	Laps.	Miles.
1. Lorraine-Dietrich (Bloch and Rossignol)	73	783.6
2. Lorraine-Dietrich (De Courcelles and Mongin)	72	772.2
2. Peugeot (Boillot and Rigal)	72	772.2
3. Peugeot (Wagner and Dauvergne)	70	750.8
3. Bentley Thistlethwayte and Gallop)	70	750.8
4. Lorraine-Dietrich (Stalter and Brisson)	69	740.0
5. Bentley (Davis and Benjafield)	68	729.0
5. Bentley (Clement and Duller)	68	729.0
6. O.M. (Foresti and Minoia)	66	708.0
7. O.M. (Danieli Brothers)	65	697.0
8. Bignan (Clauss and Gauthier)	64	686.0
8. Aries (Laly and Chassagne)	64	686.0
9. Overland (Duprez and Dumont)	61	654.0
10. O.M. (Balestrero and Thellusson)	59	633.0
10. Rolland-Pilain (Chalamel and Stremler)	59	633.0
11. Th. Schneider (Poirier and Fontaine)	58	622.0
11. Th. Schneider (Tabourin and Lefrancq)	58	622.0

By 8 o'clock on Sunday morning the number of competitors had been reduced to twenty-three, and while surprises were always possible one could safely forecast Lorraine-Dietrich as the winner, for car No. 6, driven by Bloch and Rossignol, had a lead of two laps, or more than twenty-one miles, over the companion car driven by De Courcelles and Mongin, and was three laps ahead of the first Bentley, driven by Thistlethwayte and Gallop. The second Bentley, driven by Davis and Benjafield, was running equally with the Stalter-Brisson-driven Lorraine-Dietrich, six laps behind the leader. Then came the two O.M. side-valve 2-litre models, driven respectively by Foresti-Minoia and the Danieli Brothers.

Single British Car Remaining

Washed and refreshed Clive Gallop took over the wheel of the Bentley about 8.30 o'clock for Sunday morning exercise around the Le Mans circuit. Half an hour later he reappeared running on three cylinders by reason of a broken rocker arm, thus reducing the British representation to a single car, driven by Davis and Benjafield. The remaining Bentley was then five laps behind the leader and three laps behind the second car.

When Benjafield took over he set out in chase of his French rivals with such good result that for half a dozen laps he gained from fifteen to twenty seconds per lap. But the Lorraine-Dietrich men were watchful, for order was given to Mongin, on No. 5 car, to go out in chase, the result being that he set up the lap record **at an** average of 71.1 m.p.h. Davis took the wheel of the Bentley for the final run, his instructions being to get one place from the Lorraine-Dietrichs, which were then holding first, second, and fourth places.

When he set out Davis realised that his brakes had lost their effectiveness, but it was the last hour, Mongin was just ahead, although behind in actual distance covered, and to stop would mean the loss of valuable seconds. Down the fast straight-away from the Pont-lieue fork to the Mulsanne right-angle turn, the Bentley waged a battle royal with the Lorraine-Dietrich. Davis realised that unless he caught the Frenchman before the bend he would have to wait until the grand stand stretch, it being impossible to pass at speed, with cars of practically equal ability, on the cross-leg through the pine woods.

distinct violation of the rules and a rather surprising action on the part of an experienced driver, the O.M. was ordered to be withdrawn.

While, during the race, attention had naturally been focussed on the biggest and fastest cars, some of the small machines were putting up excellent performances. The two air-cooled, four-cylinder S.A.R.A.'s, of 1,099 c.c., covered respectively 1,168 and 1,118 miles in the twenty-four hours, while the little Aries, of practically the same size, driven by the veteran Gabriel and a new-comer, covered a distance of 1,093 miles.

The Tyres Stand the Test.

Tyre service was excellent. Out of the 164 tyres which started in the race, only three had to be changed. The winning Lorraine-Dietrichs went through the race

Bourriat (E.H.P.) and Stremler (Rolland-Pilain) neck and neck on the tricky section between Arnage and the grand stands.

Davis drew alongside, moved ahead inch by inch, and entered the bend first to realise that he had no brakes. It was then too late to run ahead down the escape road : either the bend had to be taken or the car had to run off the road. The task proved impossible, for the Bentley plunged into the sandbank on the outside of the turn, burying itself so completely that the driver alone could not hope to dig it out. Mongin very sportingly stopped to ask if he could render assistance, but the offer had to be declined. Although he failed to finish, Davis was credited with the minimum mileage necessary to qualify for next year's race. This action of the club was much appreciated by the British contingent.

An Italian Contretemps.

This withdrawal left the Lorraine-Dietrich team in full possession of the field so far as maximum distance was concerned, but it did not relieve them of competition for the final of the second biennial cup, where the 2-litre O.M.'s were proving most redoubtable competitors.

During the last hour of the race Balestrero, driving No. 19 O.M. in conjunction with the Englishman Thellusson, was called in and asked to explain why he had stopped at Hunaudieres to take tools. This being a

with their original sets of straight-side Dunlops. The road surface was good and remained in excellent condition right up to the end of the race, but, on the other hand, the pace was much higher than ever before. It would appear, therefore, that the advance made of late in the manufacture of tyres is very real.

Equipment of winning Lorraine-Dietrich cars included Dunlop tyres, Hartford shock absorbers, and Zenith carburetters, while Castrol oil was used.

FINAL PLACINGS IN THE THIRD AND SECOND BIENNIAL RACES.

		Miles.
1. Lorraine-Dietrich, 3,447 c.c. (Bloch and Rossignol)		1585.99
2. Lorraine-Dietrich, 3,447 c.c. (De Courcelles and Mongin)		1574.2
3. Lorraine-Dietrich, 3,447 c.c. (Stalter and Brisson)		1493.4
4. O.M., 1,990 c.c. (Minoia and Foresti)		1446.4
5. O.M., 1,990 c.c. (M. Danieli and T. Danieli)		1405.92
6. Bentley, 2,998 c.c. (Davis and Benjafield)		1284.6
7. Th. Schneider, 1,954 c.c. (Tabourin and Lefrancq)		1265.5
8. Rolland-Pilain, 1,998 c.c. (Chalamel and Stremler)		1250.9
9. E.H.P., 1,203 c.c. (Bussiene and Decostier)		1194.5
10. Salmson, 1,094 c.c. (Casse and Rousseau)		1189.4
11. Corre-la-Licorne, 1,481 c.c. (Ericalde and Galoisy)		1173.5
12. S.A.R.A., 1,099 c.c. (Lecureul and Marandet)		1167.8
13. S.A.R.A., 1,099 c.c. (Duval and Armand)		1117.7
14. Aries, 1,098 c.c. (Gabriel and Paris)		1092.9

FINAL RESULTS SECOND BIENNIAL.

		Miles.
1. Lorraine-Dietrich, 3,447 c.c. (De Courcelles and Mongin)		1574.2
2. O.M., 1,990 c.c. (Minoia and Foresti)		1446.4
3. O.M., 1,990 c.c. (M. Danieli and T. Danieli)		1405.92
4. Lorraine-Dietrich, 3,447 c.c. (Stalter and Brisson)		1493.4
5. S.A.R.A., 1,099 c.c. (Lecureul and Marandet)		1167.8

The following cars did not qualify: Overland, Rolland-Pilain, Jousset, Ravel.

1927

Was this the classic 24 hour race? It may certainly have done more than any other single Le Mans to bring the event to the notice of the British public, containing as it did all those ingredients that would have been necessary for a Boy's Own Paper' version of the great race: near disaster, followed by heroic effort resulting in a British victory.

The beginnings were inauspicious; a mere 22 cars came to the start on 18 June, and most peoples' money would have been on the team of three Bentleys, two three-litre cars and one of 4¹/₂ litres. All the big French cars had disappeared with the exception of a single Aries three-litre. Otherwise there was a gaggle of French cars in the smaller capacity classes up to two-litres; notably the air-cooled S.A.R.A.s, the beautifully made twin ohc Salmsons in the 1,100 cc class, and one of Gregoire's front-wheel drive Tractas co-driven by the designer himself.

Frank Clement and Callingham drove the 4¹/₂ litre Bentley which went into the lead right from the flag. Hoods had been raised at the start but despite this handicap Clement broke the lap record on the second lap of the race. This was the last year that regulations demanded that hoods be raised for the first three hours of the race. The two three-litre Bentleys followed, driven by Baron d'Erlanger/Duller and Sammy Davis/J. D. Benjafield; the latter car was 'Old Number 7' which had crashed so close to the finish of the 1926 race. The Bentleys led the Aries driven by Chassagne/Laly, and this in turn was followed by the three Salmsons. The Aries sported somewhat ungainly bodywork, the front half was of traditional aspect but the long slab-sided tail was reminiscent of the 'tank' bodies already seen on the Chenard et Walcker.

Then at 9.30 in the evening, just as the summer night was closing in, all calculations were upset. A two-litre Th.Schneider (driven by Tabourin/Poirier) skidded at White House corner, less than a mile before the pits and came to a halt blocking the road. Callingham was just behind in the 4¹/₂ litre Bentley; taking to the ditch, he managed to avoid the French car but his car rolled over behind the stationary Th.Schneider. The melee was soon joined by a second Th.Schneider and Duller's 3-litre Bentley; then an 1,100 cc Aries added itself to this monumental pile-up, and finally came Sammy Davis in the third Bentley. Apparently he had some notion that the road ahead was not clear so he approached White House rather more slowly than he would otherwise have done; he was able to brake, bringing the heavy Bentley into a skid so that it hit the assembled wreckage sideways on.

The most remarkable thing about the White House disaster was that nobody was actually killed. Of the six cars involved, five were totally wrecked, but Davis was able to extricate his Bentley and drive it back to the pits for closer examination. The frame was bent, and so was the front axle; the offside front wing and running-board were in tatters, and the headlamp was smashed. But it was a runner; Davis frantically set about rectifying some of the worst damage as best he could - the rules stipulated that only the driver could effect repairs, and he was only allowed the use of tools carried on the car. After half an hour, the Bentley rejoined the race; and when co-driver Benjafield later took over, he reported a slight tendency to pull to the right when braking, otherwise the massive solidity of the Bentley appeared to have withstood the effects of the crash remarkably well.

By now the big Aries was leading the race, and throughout the rainy night the chase went on. During Sunday morning the French car's lead was eroded from four laps to one, as it had a lengthy pit stop with starter trouble. But with Chassagne at the wheel, the Aries was still faster than Benjafield in the Bentley; then in the final stages of the race it was apparent that the French car was in trouble. It stopped at the circuit with an hour and a half to go, and the Bentley took the lead. It was the only big car left in the race, and was followed home by a pair of 1,100 cc Salmsons; only seven cars finished, last home was the Tracta. It makes an interesting speculation that if Davis had not got the Bentley going again outright victory could have gone to one of the Salmsons which would have been the smallest-engined car ever to succeed at Le Mans. As it was, Casse and Rousseau won the Index of Performance and in addition to their third place overall.

The average speed of the Davis/Benjafield car had been 61.354 mph for a total distance of 1,472.52 miles; well below the figures achieved by any of the first three Lorraines in the previous year, but it should be remembered that the car was stopped for a long time after the crash, and its average speed was probably rather lower afterwards. Frank Clement, in the 4¹/₂ litre Bentley, set a new lap record of 73.4 mph before being put out of the race.

This then was the start of Bentley's fame if not fortunes; but as W. O. Bentley himself said, '. . . from this time we had no need to worry about publicity' If the Le Mans victories did not help towards putting the Bentley company on a sound commercial footing at least they created the legend of the green cars at Le Mans, and heritage that lives on in the name of the current Bentley 'Mulsanne' model; even if no Bentley has raced at Sarthe since 1951. As a fitting finale to the 1927 victory, the winning car was the star guest at a party given by The Autocar in the honour of the Bentley team at the Savoy Hotel soon after the race, when 'Old Number 7' still bore its honourable battle scars.

Next Saturday's 24-hour Race.

All About the Great Event for the Rudge-Whitworth Cup.
"The Motor" Report by Aeroplane.

ALTHOUGH the great 24-hour race for the Rudge-Whitworth Cup only finishes at Le Mans in Western France at 4 p.m. on Sunday, June 19th, a complete and fully illustrated report of the event will appear in *The Motor* first thing on the morning of Tuesday, June 21st. Starting for London in a De Havilland Moth light aeroplane directly the race has finished, *The Motor* representative will write his report in the air and it will be printed soon after midnight. The report will be fully illustrated with photographs and sketches by Bryan de Grineau, whose work is so well known to readers of *The Motor*.

British Participants.

The 24-hour race at Le Mans has always aroused considerable interest on this side of the Channel owing to the fact that ever since its inception Bentley cars have taken part. This year the famous British make will be represented by two of the well-known 3-litre cars and a new 4½-litre four-cylinder model with which the makers are just going into production. The race this year is likely to be of special interest, because there will be a number of dark horses in the shape of cars of makes which are either making their debut in racing or have not raced for some time.

In actual fact, two races are run concurrently. One is the final of the third bi-annual Rudge-Whitworth Cup race, and is only open to those cars which covered the minimum distance required by the regulations in last year's race. Thus there are only seven cars taking part, these being one Rolland-Pilain, two S.A.R.A., one E.H.P., one Salmson, one Ariès and one Th. Schneider. In the fourth bi-annual cup race, which is the first heat, as it were, of the race, the final of which will be run in 1928, has attracted 28 entries, representative of British, French, Italian and Austrian factories.

Cup for Best Performance.

The Rudge-Whitworth Cup is awarded to the winner on formula; that is to say, a chart has previously been got out showing a curve indicating the minimum distance to be covered in the 24 hours by cars in various categories. The car which exceeds by the greatest amount the minimum mileage imposed is declared the winner of the race. We publish on this page a table showing the minimum mileages and average speeds which have to be accomplished by each class of car. In general, therefore, the method of finding the winner of the Rudge-Whitworth Cup is similar to that

employed recently on the occasion of the Essex Motor Club's six-hour race; that is to say, a small car has just as good a chance of winning as the largest in the race.

The actual Grand Prix d'Endurance is not an award, but is the distinction of having covered the greatest distance in the 24 hours. The record so far stands at 1,586 miles, and was put up last year by Bloch and Rossignol, driving a six-cylinder Lorraine-Dietrich. It is equivalent to the distance across the Atlantic from St. John's, Newfoundland, to the Irish coast.

MINIMUM SPEEDS.

Engine capacity.		Distance. Miles.		Speed. m.p.h.
500 c.c	...	621.37	...	25.89
750 c.c.	...	839.5	...	34.97
1,100 c.c.	...	1,005	...	41.87
1,500 c.c.	...	1,139.5	...	47.47
2,000 c.c.	...	1,260	...	50.25
2,500 c.c.	...	1,337	...	65.70
3,000 c.c.	...	1,383	...	57.62
4,000 c.c.	...	1,404	...	58.50
5,000 c.c.	...	1,420	...	69.16
6,000 c.c.	...	1,430	...	59.58

The Le Mans course measures 10.7 miles around and forms a triangle, of which two sides are practically straight main roads, while the third is a somewhat tortuous section through a forest. That it is a fast circuit, notwithstanding its difficulty, is proved by the fact that Bloch and Rossignol averaged no less than 66.08 m.p.h. for the 24 hours last year. In 1924 the race was won by a Bentley car at an average of 53.75 m.p.h., the drivers then being Duff and Clement.

Lessons of Racing.

Much is learned in road racing. Finding that delays were caused last year by the accidental crossing of the threads of the radiator caps and fuel tank caps when they were hastily screwed down, the Bentley concern have this year fitted lids of the clip-on type, which can be opened or closed with extreme rapidity. Other modifications include the simultaneous adjustment of all four-wheel brakes by the driver without the need for stopping the car, as the ordinary method of adjustment proved to take too long in a race, where every second counts. A new type of carburetter is being used this year, and by fitting smaller wheels and tyres the cars are being brought lower and thus made more stable at corners. The Bentley cars will be garaged at the Hotel Moderne at Le Mans.

20 Laps with the Hood Erected.

The starting time of the race is 4 p.m. on Saturday, June 18th, and it finishes at 4 p.m. on Sunday, June 19th. The first 20 laps, i.e., 214 miles, have to be covered with the hoods erected. A standard, com-

mercially obtainable fuel supplied by the organizers must be used throughout, and only the self-starter may be used for starting the engines, whether at the commencement of the race or after any stop while the race is in progress. No replenishments may be effected until the first 20 laps have been completed.

The drivers of the Bentley team include F. C Clement, who is well known in this country for his many fine performances at the wheel of Bentley cars; Clive Gallop, who won the Boulogne Light Car Grand Prix; S. C. H. Davis, who put up the best performance in the Essex Club's six-hour race recently, and J. D. Benjafield, well known at Brooklands.

An Efficient Body.

The Automobile Club de l'Ouest, who so painstakingly organize this fine event every year, are to be congratulated on the attention which they have paid to detail. The grandstand and Press boxes are permanent structures of steel and concrete and equipped with every modern convenience. All the pits are in full view of the grandstand, while spectators are kept constantly informed as to the progress of the race by means of loud speakers. Open-air restaurants are installed, and there are as a rule special side shows and attractions to amuse spectators during the hours of darkness.

LIST OF ENTRIES.
THIRD BI-ANNUAL RUDGE-WHITWORTH CUP RACE.

1. Rolland-Pilain L
2. S.A.R.A. I.
3. S.A.R.A. II.
4. E.H.P. L
5. Salmson I.
6. Ariès III.
7. Th. Schneider I.

FOURTH BI-ANNUAL CUP RACE.

1. Steyr.
2. Rolland-Pilain I.
3. Rolland-Pilain II.
4. Rolland-Pilain III.
5. S.A.R.A. I.
6. S.A.R.A. II.
7. E.H.P. I.
8. E.H.P. II.
9. Salmson II.
10. Salmson III.
11. Tracta L
12. Fasto I.
13. Fasto II.
14. Fasto III.
15. S.A.R.A. L
16. S.C.A.P. I.
17. S.C.A.P. II.
18. Ariès L
19. Ariès II.
20. Ariès III.
21. G.M. I.
22. G.M. II.
23. Bentley I.
24. Bentley II.
25. Bentley III.
26. Tracta II.
27. Th. Schneider I.
28. Th. Schneider II.

The Le Mans 24-hour Race.

Special Report by Aeroplane.

Competitors running to their cars to erect their hoods at the start of the race. The Bentley team is in the foreground.

British Cars in Amazing Crash. Bentley Covers Longest Distance in 24 Hours. France Wins the Rudge-Whitworth Cup.

*T*HE 24-hour race for the Rudge-Whitworth Cup took place at Le Mans in the Department of the Sarthe, France. It began at 4 p.m. on Saturday, June 18th, and finished at 4 p.m. on Sunday, June 19th. The cars, which were of touring type, were required to average certain performances according to their engine capacity, the vehicle having covered the greatest excess mileage being acclaimed the winner. The distance round the course was 10.7 miles. The first 20 circuits had to be made with the hoods erected, and only the electric starter was allowed to be used for starting the engines. Within 30 minutes of the finish of the race "THE MOTOR" representative was in the air writing his report as the aeroplane sped toward England.

"WELL, you poor old devil, how are you?"

A man in khaki overalls came in to a tin-roofed pit at Le Mans last Saturday night, crash helmet in hand, as the exhaust note of No. 3 Bentley faded in the direction of Pontlieue. He was S. C. H. Davis, who had just changed places with Dr. Benjafield after escaping unscathed from one of the most amazing accidents in the whole history of motor racing. He was speaking to George Duller, another Bentley driver.

Even the "Paris-Madrid"—the race which is a classic so far as the number of crashes is concerned—never produced such an amazing sequence of events as last Saturday's and Sunday's 24-hour race at Le Mans. In the space of a few seconds, through no fault of their own, the complete team of three Bentley cars ran into each other, two being so badly damaged that they were unable to continue, while two more French cars brought up the total to six, including the car which was said to be the cause of it all.

Dusk had fallen. Through the pine forest it was dark enough for headlamps to be necessary. Callingham, in the big 4½-litre Bentley which had twice beaten the lap record for the circuit, was thundering down from

Arnage to the grand-stands when, as he rounded a sharp curve known to the team as White House Corner, he suddenly saw a dark-blue car broadside on across the road. It was Tabourin, the driver of a Th. Schneider, who had skidded into the wall as another competitor passed him and had bounced back right into the path of approaching vehicles. Callingham, taking the curve at over 70 m.p.h., made a desperate attempt to skid round the Schneider, but went into the ditch on the right-hand side of the road. The impact was so terrific that he was

THE RESULTS AT A GLANCE.

First three to qualify in the 4th (1927-1928) Rudge-Whitworth Cup Race.
1st, BENTLEY, 1,472.6 miles in 24 hrs. equals 61.36 m.p.h.
2nd, SALMSON, 1,254.8 miles in 24 hrs. equals 52.28 m.p.h.
3rd, SALMSON, 1,244.1 miles in 24 hrs. equals 51.80 m.p.h.
Winner of 3rd (1926-1927) Rudge-Whitworth Cup: SALMSON, De Victor-Hasley, 1,254.79 miles equals 52.28 m.p.h.
Winner of St. Didier Cup: SALMSON, De Victor-Hasley, 1,254.67 miles equals 52.27 m.p.h.

thrown clean out into the middle of the road, but, struggling to his feet, he staggered up the road with one idea only in his head—to warn the other drivers of their danger.

Hardly had he got clear of his car when there came another terrific crash. George Duller, roaring along in his wake in No. 2 Bentley, took the corner at speed. Seeing the Schneider, he tried the same dodge as Callingham, but was unaware that the latter's Bentley (No. 1) was already in the ditch. At the last moment, expert hurdle-race jockey that he is, he saw the obstacle and jumped clear over the steering wheel. His car crashed into the 4½-litre model with such force that it threw it bodily into the road again and fell on it.

Then came Davis's nightmare. He was approaching at some 82 m.p.h. when he suddenly sensed that something was wrong. As he came to the "White House" bend he saw the surface of the road strewn with stones and dirt and, being a very fine driver, acted immediately and "stood on everything." Well it was that he did so. Suddenly he beheld, in the darkness, an amazing, terrifying sight. On his left a large car lay blocking almost the entire road. Rising like some weird monster from the ditch, Callingham's Bentley lay half on its side with Duller's car piled up on its tail. Somewhere in the mêlée there seemed to be another car.

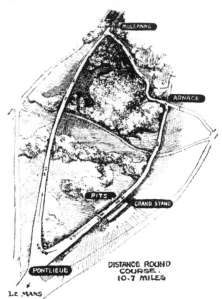

A sketch map of the course.

It looked as if the whole road was blocked, but, had the light been better, Davis might have been able to see that there was a way through. As it was, he did the only possible thing in the circumstances: he braked heavily, swinging the car round in a broad skid in the attempt to confine the inevitable damage to the tail. He could not quite manage it, and the front of his car caught one wheel of the larger Bentley, Duller's car toppling over on to him.

In the meanwhile Duller, bleeding at the mouth and badly winded, when he picked himself up out of the field into which he had been thrown, first thought he was badly hurt, but discovered that he could run. So off he went into the darkness to warn oncoming competitors, all unknowingly on the wrong side of the hedge. Consequently, Davis never saw the warning.

Then ensued what was surely the grimmest game of hide-and-seek that has ever been played in a motor race.

Leaping from his battered car, Davis ran through the hedge to look for Duller. After a little time he espied his blue-overalled figure in the gloom. "George!" he shouted. "*George!*"

There was no answer.

For one awful moment Davis thought Duller was badly hurt in the face, but, coming nearer, he was relieved to find that the only reason why he had not answered was that he was quite deaf from the persistent roar of his exhaust.

"Are you hurt, George?"

"No, but this one's *very* dead," replied George cryptically. Davis is quite positive that Duller spoke thus, though neither could recall who or what was supposed to have expired. Anyhow, seeing the ghastly mess of piled-up cars spreading across the road, the two stumbled back on to the course to see what had happened to Callingham.

The last-named, returning to the scene, had the weird experience of watching Davis and Duller hunting in the wreckage for his body!

When he joined his team-mates Davis made a dash to his car, somehow bent the off-side wing into a rough semblance of its previous shape and tore off once again. He was obsessed with the idea that, above all things, he must keep to his predetermined average speed. So, with the one remaining headlamp pointing like a finger through the inky blackness, he roared towards the pits over roads now shining black and treacherous as the result of a fall of rain.

It was a dramatic moment when Davis came up to the Bentley pit, his car battered and twisted, with several loose spokes in one wheel. "Six cars all piled up at "White House"! he explained. "A most unholy mess!"

Swiftly he changed a wheel, saw that his wing and lamps were in order and dashed off again for six laps on wet and slippery roads. Then he came in, as it was Benjafield's turn to drive, and the bacteriologist-cum-race-driver took over the car.

It requires a great deal of nerve and pluck to take over a car that one knows has been in a crash, has a bent front axle and twisted dumb-irons, and then to drive it at 90 to 100 m.p.h. on a wet road. Yet Dr. Benjafield leapt into the driving seat and went off smiling, obviously enjoying every moment of the race.

Tabourin, the driver of the Th. Schneider involved in the accident, broke his arm just above the wrist, and three ribs, but none of the five other drivers suffered any harm.

This multiple collision is without parallel in the annals of motor racing, and there is no doubt that, given reasonable luck, all three Bentleys would have held to the end and covered the greatest distance in the 24 hours.

* * *

The moments before the start held a poignancy that never fails to stir those whose pleasure it is to follow the noble

Duller on No. 2 Bentley rams Callingham on No. 1 Bentley, who had ditched himself in avoiding Tabourin (No. 12 Th. Schneider), who was blocking the road after a collision; while Davis (No. 3 Bentley) runs into the wreckage. The last-named, however, extricated himself and continued.

game of road-racing. In the hush before the dropping of the starter's flag memories crowd upon one—sad and happy memories—memories of great risks run and great victories won. And over all is the ardent desire to see the event won by a British car.

The start was not unlike that of the Essex Motor Club's six-hour race. Parked diagonally on one side of the road opposite the huge permanent grand-stands were the cars, with silent engines. On the other side stood the drivers, tense and alert. Then a great yellow flag dropped, and each man made a bolt for his car, erected his hood single-handed, depressed the starter button and dashed off towards the Pont-lieue hair-pin.

With a sharp, hard bark the engine of the big new 4½-litre Bentley sprang to life, and Clement, amid enthusiastic applause, got away first. There were cheers and much laughter. "Un anglais, comme toujours!" exclaimed the crowd. Barely a fifth of a second later Benjafield, too, let in his clutch and sped off close on Clement's heels.

It seemed that the Baron d'Erlanger, driving Bentley No. 2, was going to be

Marandet (S.A.R.A. II) leading Chantrel (Th. Schneider II) and Guibert (Scap II) on the Arnage corner. (Below) The front-wheel driven Tracta, piloted by Gregoire, in at the pits for replenishment. It was the only car of this make to start out of two entered.

(Right) Guibert (Scap II) replenishes his radiator at the pits.

next, but, possibly a little flurried at the start of his first race, the driver fumbled and let the three Fasto cars get away before he was properly off. The low, little front-wheel-drive Tracta was off next, followed by two S.C.A.P. and the crowd of Th. Schneider, Ariès, Salmson and E.H.P. cars. Only 2½ mins. elapsed between the dropping of the starter's flag and the time the last man got away, although it seemed an age.

One heard the drone of engines over across the pines, where, with open throttle, the cars raced from Pontlieue to the Mulsanne corner, then, cutting in and out, round the Arnage bends before a speck in the distance grew swiftly into the form of the first car round.

It was No. 1, the 4½-litre Bentley, holding the road perfectly and being driven beautifully by F. C. Clement, having covered the 10.7 miles in 9 mins. 35 secs. from a standing start. Some

distance behind came Benjafield in Bentley No. 2, and d'Erlanger came next in the third British car. Brosselin (Fasto) and Laly (Ariès) followed.

On his second lap Clement proceeded to beat the existing lap record for the circuit at 71.9 m.p.h., to the great joy of the numerous British spectators.

Laly, on the big Ariès, was the only serious competitor of the Bentleys as regards covering the maximum distance in the 24 hours, but, on the formula or handicap basis by which the Rudge-Whitworth Cup is awarded, the three Salmsons were dangerous rivals. Indeed, one of these, driven by de Victor, was next behind the Bentleys on the second lap, until Laly put on speed and took his place. By the fourth lap the Salmsons arranged themselves in numerical order behind the big Ariès and the three Bentleys, and held this position hour after hour.

At the end of the first hour the order was Clement, Benjafield, d'Erlanger (Bentleys), Laly (Ariès), de Victor, de Marmier, Casse (Salmsons), Bros-

After a terrific duel No. 3 Bentley takes the lead near the end from No. 4 Ariès.

selin (Fasto) and Chantrel (Th. Schneider). On the eighth lap Clement (4,379 c.c. Bentley) had lapped Laly (2,957 c.c. Ariès) and was about 300 yds. ahead of him.

Barring visits to the pits by a number of cars, no incidents occurred until 6.50 p.m., when a white-clad driver came running, breathless and panting, to the pits, leaving his car on the grass at the roadside some 500 yards away. As the result of a leaking radiator he had run out of water, but as the rules for the race forbade any replenishment with water until after the 20th lap the driver, Decostier (E.H.P.), had to retire.

Clement Beats Record.

At the end of two hours Clement had completed 13 laps, his last lap being at an average speed of 73.01 m.p.h., thus again beating the record for the course, while he covered 140.86 miles in two hours, beating last year's record by nearly nine minutes. Shortly afterwards Gregoire, the driver of the Tracta, who was injured in a motor smash on the morning of the race and very pluckily drove despite a bruised face and bandaged head, came in to be relieved.

As always, the Bentley pit work was beautiful to watch. At 7.2 p.m. Clement came in to replenish fuel, oil and water supplies and fold his hood. The latter was stowed away and properly clipped down in 35 secs. only, while the total stop, during which 27 gallons of petrol were taken in, lasted only 3 mins. 23 secs.—a really wonderful achievement when it is borne in mind that the whole of these operations had to be performed single-handed by a driver who had just come in from three hours at the wheel. Clement brought forth cries of joy from the spectators by the deft way he handled the 4½-gallon cans of commercial fuel.

It was at 7.15 p.m. that the other two

Bentleys came in together for replenishments and changes of drivers. Benjafield did all necessary work methodically, and Davis was away within 3 mins. 17 secs. Baron d'Erlanger, on the other hand, took 4 mins 43¾ secs. before George Duller could get away in his car.

The little Ariès were both having a fair amount of trouble—the complete removal and fitting of a camshaft being one of the tasks undertaken. The larger machine was going well and out

to hold its own with the Bentleys.

The three Fasto cars were almost English in their bodywork, which showed none of the regulation cheating tendencies which generally characterize the French vehicles in a race of this kind, while the air-cooled S.A.R.A. cars were well turned out. Particular interest centred upon the new 1,500 c.c. six-cylinder model. But of all noisy exhaust systems surely there is nothing on this earth that can compete with those ear-splitting S.A.R.A.s !

Callingham in first place and travelling at a terrific speed after taking over from Clement at their first stop, overhauls competitors at Mulsanne corner still with their hoods up.

38

On Sunday night rain fell heavily, this view from "The Motor" pit showing the little front-drive Tracta replenishing fuel and No. 4 Aries, driven by Chassagne, passing.

In marked contrast to the crews of the Bentleys, the drivers of the big Aries took nearly six minutes to fold their hoods, fill up and change drivers, but the Britishers found Jean Chassagne, an old friend of England, a very worthy opponent, in spite of the terrible mishap which overtook him some time ago on the Avus track near Berlin. Still, even he was only saved by the cries of the populace from dashing off with his three headlamps still encased in their waterproof covers.

At a little before 10 p.m. the extraordinary accident happened which we already have described, the net result of which was to put Bentleys 1 and 2 out of the race. So after six hours we find

that Davis, who is driving Benjafield's car, has completed 35 laps, the next car running being Chassagne's big Aries at 34. The next in the general classification is Casse, in a 1,100 c.c. Salmson, at 31 laps, and de Victor's Salmson and Brosselin's Fasto.

With the coming of darkness the circuit permanent de la Sarthe woke up. A beautifully laid dance floor in the huge open-air restaurant was not greatly patronized, but dense throngs filled the grand-stands and the various bars. The place was a veritable blaze of light.

While Benjafield and the Aries were on the same lap after seven hours, the former, who was driving magnificently

despite the handicap of a smashed headlamp and bent axle, managed to gain a lap by the eighth hour.

A Quick Repair.

It was exactly midnight when Dr. Benjafield trickled up to his pit exclaiming, "My side lamp's coming adrift." The lamp in question was on the damaged wing, so no wonder! With insulating tape and string he bound the lamp in place, but it was no good, and finally he had to lash a pocket lamp to the windscreen. Fortunately this functioned perfectly throughout the night.

As he worked Benjafield asked for information about the race. "Where's old Stick-in-the-mud—the Aries?" he asked on one occasion.

It was a foul night. Cars swished by, exhausts roaring, more like motor boats than automobiles, great columns of spray shooting from each wheel. Commissaires sportifs wandered about in dripping oilskins reflecting the light from a thousand electric lamps. The big Aries made ominous noises, suggestive of a slack big-end, but which may have been in the timing gear or clutch. During that long, wet night there was a group of cars almost continually at the pits, watched by an ever-enthusiastic crowd. . .

*　　*　　*

So the night wore on until, with a swift change of the wind, the curtain of low grey clouds rolled away, revealing a crystal-clear dawn of palest yellow—a lovely, pure morning, which cheered drooping spirits and revived weary bodies.

After a night-long battle the Bentley, sounding just as nice as when it started in the race, came in at 9.30 on Sunday morning for replenishments and a change of drivers, wherein "Sammy" Davis, before going on, insisted on making fast with string the rear wing on the crashed side. Then off he went

After the crash Davis (No. 3 Bentley) resumed the race at undiminished speed.

The Salmsons, like the Bentleys, kept close to each other throughout. Casse is here seen leading the team on a straight stretch through the woods.

once again, determined, if it was humanly possible, to keep the Ariès at bay.

Some three hours later, in which the Bentley crowd had almost (but not quite) resigned themselves to a second place, if they were lucky, Chassagne brought in the Ariès to change places with Laly and, after replenishing, it was found that the starting motor would not work owing to the sticking of the Bendix pinion.

At this stage the Ariès was four laps ahead of the Bentley, which was only gaining on it gradually, so here, at last, was a chance for the British car. Davis took it. Each time round he leant over for a good look at Laly toiling under the eyes of a sympathetic crowd.

Anxious Moments.

Speculation was rife in the Bentley camp. Would he put it right? He did, and finally got away in the same lap as the Bentley and only about four minutes ahead. The British pit were fairly confident of being able to overtake Laly before the end of the 24 hours.

Then Chassagne was put in the car, and he forthwith made things hum. There was then every likelihood of a really exciting finish, but on its 129th lap the Ariès never came round.

So the Bentley covered the biggest distance this year in the 24 hours, in spite of being terribly handicapped for no less than 18 hours. A " beau geste sportif," as the French would say, showed the sheer good-heartedness of Dr. Benjafield. Within a quarter of an hour of the end of the race he pulled up at the pits and called to Davis to take over. So Sammy Davis, who was the most unfortunate of mortals in the self-same race last year, at last tastes the fruits of victory.

And the other cars? Well, there were not so very many left at the end of those 24 hours. Still, two of the three Salmsons, despite their tiny 1,094 c.c. engines, were not far behind the Bentley. At about 9.30 p.m. on

the Saturday it was announced that the Salmson driven by Goutte and de Marmier had been disqualified owing to the starter having ceased to function. After seven hours another to retire was the Th. Schneider, driven by Chantrel and Schultz.

The little six-cylinder air-cooled S.A.R.A. continued to run and also qualified. It was driven by Mottet and Maret. The six-cylinder E.H.P. had C.I.M.E. side-valve engines and was running steadily and well. There was still a Fasto running well, while the two small Ariès had been disqualified as long ago as the sixth hour for failing to maintain the ordained average speed.

CHIEF DISTANCES COVERED IN 24 HOURS.

1. Bentley (2,989 c.c.), Benjafield-Davis, 1,472.64 miles = 61.36 m.p.h.
2. Salmson (1,094 c.c.), De Victor-Hasley, 1,254.79 miles = 52.28 m.p.h.
3. Salmson (1,094 c.c.), Casse-Rousseau, 1,244.12 miles = 51.8 m.p.h.
4. S.C.A.P. (1,493 c.c.), Desvaux-Vallon, 1,190.24 miles = 49.59 m.p.h.
5. E.H.P. (1,094 c.c.), Bouriat-Bussienne, 1,164.76 miles = 48.53 m.p.h.
6. S.A.R.A. (1,498 c.c.), Mottet-Marret, 1,146.38 miles = 47.76 m.p.h.

No less than nine cars in the race had Dewandre vacuum brakes, while every starter used Hartford shock absorbers. The Salmsons, for the first time in racing, were using Silentbloc bushes in their universal joints.

By effecting the fastest lap in the race F. C. Clement, driving the 4½-litre Bentley, won a prize of 1,000 francs offered by the Boulogne section of the Automobile Club du Nord de la France and one of a similar amount offered by the Morris-Léon Bollée concern of Le Mans.

The Bentley team. Left to right: F. C. Clement, L. Callingham, Baron d'Erlanger, G. Duller, S. C. H. Davis, and Dr. J. D. Benjafield.

A Gordon Crosby impression of the scene at White House Corner when five cars crashed in the Le Mans 24-hour race of 1927.

Twenty Years After

Memories of an Exciting Moment in the 1927 Le Mans Race

Dr. J. D. Benjafield with some of the model aircraft he makes today.

QUITE a while ago, when we were very young, Dumas's *Twenty Years After* thrilled. Yet there was the odd feeling of what would it be like when we, too, counted twenty years from some valued adventurous incident. On June 18 it was twenty years from that famous crash following which a much-battered Bentley won at Le Mans. To-day, looking back at that incident, it seems to both "Benjy" (Dr. J. D. Benjafield) and myself as fresh as when it happened; and not even the modifications that the long-bearded old gent with the hour-glass timepiece has power to introduce have made the memory one whit less satisfactory.

It all remains so clear. The moment when, as the twilight deepened to dusk, old Number Seven came fast round White House turn, and there in front, uncertain in the head light's beam, was the tangled mass that was our other team cars, plus some French, all across the road. There was no time to be frightened in the ensuing seconds, only to do automatically all that one's training had taught; to slew the car violently so that the ensuing slide would bring it up all standing, sideways instead of endwise, with a noise that suggested masses of steelwork falling downstairs. Clearly, too, comes back that odd moment when, on impact, I put up a futile arm to guard myself.

Came then the sickening feeling that we, the Bentley team, were in the soup, the knowledge of what "W. O." in the pit would have to say and the absolute determination to go on somehow. Then there was our determination at all costs to prevent "W. O." seeing what the real damage was when the car got to the pit. The unpleasant surmises as to the state of the steering, especially the drop arm

ball joint, are still vivid, as also is our subsequent run with the brakes timed one, four, two, three—and bits dropping off in all directions. Never has partner driven more stoutly, any time, any place, than Benjy in that subsequent hectic run when anything might have happened.

Crystal clear also remain our feelings when "W. O." ordered increased speed, having noted odd noises from our principal rival; increased speed, mark you, when we were all of a tremble practically every metre of the darned course. And the subsequent magnificent feeling when we saw poor Chassagne's car stationary at the roadside and knew that "W. O.'s" hunch was dead right. Mark you, even when we caught "petit Jean" Chassagne he switched off and went down to the side at once to let Number Seven pass. Drivers, especially petit Jean, were like that then.

Finally, the extraordinary feeling when Benjy deliberately pulled in to let me have those last few laps to victory—note again the act—and the hair-raising subsequent run when it seemed that we should be off the road any moment and our names mud when a win was in sight. But in one corner of a cupboard there is still an old piece of faded yellow bunting, the flag that signalled the end of the last lap, the victory of old Number Seven.

And Number Seven? Well, somebody bought her, fitted a closed body, and painted the whole yellow! And she, very properly, went off into a lamp post and crashed beyond repair. "Chass" is dead—may his soul find rest; Benjy—a little larger in the bore—does great things with model aircraft, and I have a chassis that gets skinnier and more wrinkled every day, more bushy about the prawn-like eyebrows — but then, a memory persists.

S. C. H. D.

S. C. H. Davis covers many miles of road today on a less exciting form of transport.

41

The two 3-litres in line-astern.

Battered but unbeaten No. 3 (old No. 7) relaxes after victory.

The first appearance of the 4½ litre was in this year.

1928

Undoubtedly all the publicity generated by Bentley's dramatic win in the previous year had helped to increase British interest in Le Mans and apart from three 4¹/₂ litre Bentleys, there were teams of two-litre Lagondas and 1¹/₂ litre cars from Aston Martin and Alvis; the last-mentioned entries were two of Alvis' front-wheel drive cars. Aston Martin also had two cars, neither of which finished, so it was an inauspicious start for what, over the years, became the most consistently entered British marque - 25 races to 1964, two private entries since and Aston Martin engined cars in 1967 and 1982.

1928 was also the year in which the American challenge had to be taken seriously. The biggest-engined car was a 4.9 litre straight eight Stutz, and this was backed up by four Model 72 Chryslers with 4.1 litre engines. Two two-litre Italas were the sole representatives of Italy - this marque's only appearance at Le Mans. The only French contender for victory was the Aries which had challenged Bentley in 1927; otherwise the French entries were all in the classes below two litres, including, among others, two Salmsons and three Tractas. The total field numbered 33 cars.

For the first time, an annual distance award was officially recognised in addition to the Biennial Cup and the Index of Performance. First car to lead was the Brisson/Bloch Stutz, and the lap record was broken in rapid succession by Woolf Barnato in a Bentley, then the Stutz, then Clement in another Bentley, all in the first hour of the race. The big Aries had the dubious distinction of being the first car to retire, after only two laps. From then on the battle became Anglo-American; Bentley v. Stutz and Chrysler. Birkin in the third Bentley driving on a punctured tyre (he carried no jack) suffered a collapsed wheel and his car went off the road; his co-driver Chassagne struggled for three hours before being able to rejoin the race. During most of the night the Stutz led followed by the Barnato/Rubin Bentley, one of the Chryslers and the Clement/Benjafield Bentley; but the latter had to retire with a cracked chassis frame, caused by metal fatigue induced by vibration, and this in turn pulled the radiator hose away.

Bentley's three-car team was therefore effectively reduced to one, and as the cars were all similar the Bentley team fully expected the Barnato/Rubin car to succumb to the same problems as the Benjafield/Clement car. Meanwhile, one of the Lagondas had got stuck in the sandbank at Mulsanne corner; it was rammed by the second Lagonda driven by the Baron d'Erlanger who was, however, able to continue and finished the race in eleventh place. One of the Chryslers dropped down the field and finally retired; another had only lasted ten laps but the two surviving cars kept well up with the race leaders.

Meanwhile Birkin and Chassagne were working their way up through a depleted field of smaller cars; in his efforts Birkin ultimately set a new lap record of 79.29 mph and finished fifth. The Bentley-Stutz duel for the lead was intensified when, on Sunday afternoon, the Stutz lost its two lower gears; but it was apparent that Barnato too was in trouble. He had passed the American car while it was being re-fuelled, but now had to slow down and from the Bentley pits it could be seen that the 4¹/₂ litre was beginning to distort its shape - the sign of a cracked chassis. As his radiator began to leak water Barnato lowered his speed, nursing the car through the last few laps to win at a margin of less than eight miles from the Stutz. The winning car's average speed was 69.108 mph and the total distance 1,658.6 miles, handsomely beating the 1926 record. Two Chryslers followed in third and fourth places and the first of the Alvises was a very creditable sixth, its team mate ninth. All three Tractas also finished, and for the second year in succession, Casse and Rousseau (who finished tenth overall) took the Index and the Biennial Cup with their 1,100 cc Salmson.

If lacking the spectacular drama of the 1927 race, 1928's race provided more excitement as the outcome was in doubt right up to the end; although there is no doubt that the excitement and the worry were more pronounced in the Bentley pit than on the grandstand. Bentley's third victory, and the second in succession, did nothing to harm the already excellent reputation of the make; but the 4¹/₂ litre's hitherto undiscovered tendency to fracture its chassis under strain was a warning to the company.

WILL BRITAIN WIN AT LE MANS?

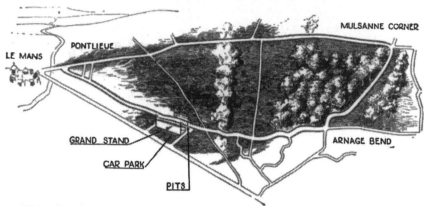

Plan of the Sarthe circuit, 10.7 miles round, over which the race will be run next Saturday and Sunday, starting and finishing at 4 p.m. on the days mentioned.

A FRONT-WHEEL-DRIVE RACE. LAST MINUTE NEWS OF NEXT SATURDAY'S RACE FOR THE RUDGE-WHITWORTH CUP.

DESPITE its distance from the British Isles, the Grand Prix d'Endurance for the Rudge-Whitworth cups held annually by l'Automobile Club de l'Ouest at Le Mans continues to attract more and more interest on the part of British motorists.

This year there is a strong international flavour about the race, for Great Britain is represented by no fewer than eight cars. There are five American vehicles, three Italians and a veritable army of French racers—in all 50 entries comprising 44 different cars have been received, and it is confidently expected that there will be very few non-starters among them.

An important feature of the race is that no fewer than five front-wheel-drive cars—two Alvis and three Tracta—are taking part. The

Tracta ran with considerable success in last year's race and was equipped with a 1,100 c.c. engine. The Alvis car is of the 1,500 c.c. type.

The Bentley team comprises such experienced drivers as F. C. Clement, Woolf Barnato, Dr. J. D. Benjafield and H. R. S. Birkin, the two other drivers, one of which is J. Chassagne, both being of French nationality. At the time of going to press, Bloch, who drove with M. Weymann in the Hispano-Stutz duel at Indianapolis recently, is mentioned as likely to be the sixth Bentley driver. The three Bentleys are all 4½-litre models and are excellently prepared with the thoroughness which characterizes this marque when it goes racing. They are, moreover, distinctly faster than the 4½-litre which ran at Le Mans last year.

Promising Lagonda Cars.

The Lagonda cars have given very good accounts of themselves in practising and are well-finished attractive-looking cars closely resembling the standard speed model. The drivers include the Baron d'Erlanger

Minimum Distances which have to be Covered in the 24 Hours.		
500 c.c.	746 miles	= 31.1 m.p.h.
750 c.c.	900 miles	= 37.5 m.p.h.
1,100 c.c.	1,053 miles	= 44 m.p.h.
1,500 c.c.	1,188 miles	= 49.6 m.p.h.
2,000 c.c.	1,303 miles	= 54.4 m.p.h.
3,000 c.c.	1,370 miles	= 57.3 m.p.h.
4,000 c.c.	1,427 miles	= 59.5 m.p.h.
5,000 c.c.	1,450 miles	= 60.5 m.p.h.
6,000 c.c.	1,463 miles	= 61.1 m.p.h.

(Left) Rear view of one of the Le Mans Bentleys, showing the special wings and method of carrying the spare wheel. (Right, reading from left to right) Birkin, Clement, Barnato, and Benjafield. The figure in the cap is Chassagne.

44

and Captain R. C. Gallop, who both drove Bentleys in last year's 24-hour race; W. D. Hawkes, a well-known driver who took part in the 1922 Tourist Trophy race in the Isle of Man driving a Bentley, and who has also driven at Indianapolis; W. L. Handley, the famous racing motorcyclist; F. H. P. Samuelson, who has raced with Ratier and Austin Seven cars, and F. King, the sales manager of the Lagonda concern. The spare drivers are Major Hayes and S. Hammond.

Front-drive Alvis Racers.

The Alvis team consists of two of the new four-cylinder front-wheel-drive sports models, the drivers being Major C. M. Harvey, who has driven Alvis cars consistently and with marked success at Brooklands, Boulogne and elsewhere, while he has also driven on the Le Mans circuit some years ago. The others are S. C. H. Davis, who is taking part in the race for the fourth consecutive year; W. Urquhart Dykes, who has raced at Brooklands and Boulogne; and H. W. Purdy, the well-known Brooklands exponent of Bugatti and Thomas Special racers.

The Aston-Martin Team.

Then there is the Aston-Martin concern, which will be represented by two cars. These are super-sports models similar to the examples shown at the last Olympia Exhibition but with different wings and the body lengthened to comply with the regulations for the race. Like the Alvis, these cars are of under 1,500 c.c. and have four-cylinder engines. The drivers will

be A. C. Bertelli, who thus returns to racing after a lapse of many years; G. E. T. Eyston, the famous Bugatti road and track racer; Cyril Paul, who drove an Austro-Daimler at Boulogne last year and did exceedingly well in hill-climbs when these were permitted; and J. Bezant, at one time a mechanic in the Bentley racing team and a successful rider in the Amateur Motorcycle Tourist Trophy Race.

Finally comes D. M. K. Marendaz, driving a car bearing his name which is also in the 1,500 c.c. class.

The Lagonda and Aston-Martin teams crossed over to France last Friday, the Bentley and Alvis on Saturday and Marendaz on Sunday

last, and all are at the time of publication hard at work practising on the course.

The race will be run over the Sarthe permanent circuit on the outskirts of Le Mans and about 140 miles south-west of Paris. The course is in excellent condition and is on the whole of a flat nature, although there are a few gentle rises and descents. There are several long straight sections, one or two tricky bends in densely wooded country, and, while it is a fast course, the Sarthe circuit is one which tests the skill of drivers and the endurance of cars to the utmost. The distance round the course is 10.7 miles and the aim of every competitor is to cover as many laps as possible in the 24 hours between 4 p.m. Saturday and 4 p.m. Sunday.

The American Contingent.

This year five American cars consisting of four Chryslers and a Stutz will be taking part, while the Italian contingent consists of an

Alfa-Romeo and two Italas. The French entries include Ariès, Tracta, Sara, E.H.P., S.C.A.P. and Salmson cars, one of which will be driven by George Newman and J. Halsey, who drove in the Six-Hours' Race at Brooklands. Other entries include Lombard, B.N.C., Alphi and d'Yrsan.

A feature of the Le Mans race is that three Rudge-Whitworth cups are competed for at the same time. The winner of the 6th Grand Prix

One of the points which makes the Grand Prix d'Endurance so interesting is that competing cars must conform with the description published in the ordinary maker's catalogue issued before January 1st, 1928. Minor alterations such as variations in the compression ratio, timing, diameter and lift of the valves, gear ratios and the weight, shape and material of the connect-

must have four comfortable seats. The coachwork must be of the bona-fide touring type and must include windscreen, wings, side lamps, headlamps, hoods, warning devices, starter, driving mirror and an efficient silencer.

Latest News from the Course.
[FROM OUR OWN CORRESPONDENT.]
Le Mans, *Saturday.*

We have made a close examination of the course and found it in perfect condition for its entire length. The arrangements for competitors and spectators,

of 24 hours is the car that has covered the greatest distance during the race. The annual Rudge-Whitworth cup awarded for this performance becomes the definite property of the winner. The 4th bi-annual cup will be won by one of the six cars which qualified in the eliminating race for this event last year, these consisting of a Tracta and Sara, E.H.P., Salmson, Bentley and S.C.A.P. Finally, there is the preliminary, if it may be so described, for the 5th bi-annual cup in which all cars entered in the race take part; those that in the 24 hours have covered the minimum distance imposed by the regulations will be qualified to run in the final next year.

A front-wheel drive Alvis similar to those which will run at Le Mans. Above are three of the drivers : H. W. Purdy (left), S. C. H. Davis (centre) and C. M. Harvey (right).

ing rods and pistons, are allowed. Cars must be equipped with comfortable touring bodies, those of 1,100 c.c. or less having two-seater coachwork, while three seats are required of cars up to and including 1,500 c.c. Above this capacity cars

always excellent at Le Mans, are better than ever this year. The pits are much improved in construction, arrangements for access are improved, and the public restaurant has been enlarged in view of the enormous crowd expected.

Shell petrol will be used exclusively by every competitor, and will be supplied in sealed cans of just over two gallons each by the organizers of the race, l'Automobile Club de l'Ouest. The cans are small drums 8 ins. in diameter and 12 ins. high, with a 4-in. pouring orifice. Some smart and amusing " fill-ups " are likely to be witnessed.

1928 RUDGE-WHITWORTH CUP RACE ENTRIES.

Fourth Rudge-Whitworth Cup Race (Final).

1. Tracta (1,100 c.c.), *F.* Grégoire.
2. S.A.R.A. (1,806 c.c.), *F.* Chanterelle and Maret.
3. E.H.P. (1,100 c.c.), *F.* Bouriat and Bussienne.
4. Salmson (1,100 c.c.), *F.* Casse and Rousseau.
5. Bentley (4,398 c.c.), *G.B.* Clement and Chassagne.
6. S.C.A.P. (1,100 c.c.), *F.* Lemesle and Godard.

Fifth Rudge-Whitworth Cup Race (Eliminating).

7. B.N.C. (1,100 c.c.), *F.* Michel Doré.
8. Tracta (1,100 c.c.), *F.* Grégoire.
9. Tracta (1,100 c.c.), *F.* ——
10. Tracta (1,100 c.c.), *F.* ——
11. Alvis (1,496 c.c.), *G.B.* S. C. H. Davis and W. U. Dykes.
12. Alvis (1,496 c.c.), *G.B.* C. M. Harvey and H. W. Purdy.
13. S.A.R.A. (1,806 c.c.), *F.* Chanterelle and Maret.

14. Aries (3,000 c.c.), *F.* Laly and Rigal.
15. Aries (3,000 c.c.), *F.* ——
16. Aries (1,100 c.c.), *F.* ——
17. Aries (1,100 c.c.), *F.* ——
18. Aston-Martin (1,500 c.c.), *G.B.* Bertelli and G. E. T. Eyston.
19. Aston-Martin (1,500 c.c.), *G.B.* Bezant and C. Paul.
20. Aston-Martin (1,500 c.c.), *G.B.* (Scratched.)
21. E.H.P. (1,100 c.c.), *F.* Bouriat and Bussienne.
22. Alphi (1,500 c.c.), *F.* De Costier and Bernard.
23. Salmson (1,100 c.c.), *F.* G. Newman and Hasley.
24. B.N.C. (1,100 c.c.), *F.* ——
25. Lombard (1,093 c.c.), *F.* Desvaux and Goutte.
26. Lombard (1,093 c.c.), *F.* ——
27. Lombard (1,093 c.c.), *F.* ——
28. Lombard (1,093 c.c.), *F.* ——
29. Lombard (1,093 c.c.), *F.* ——
30. Lombard (1,093 c.c.), *F.* ——
31. d'Yrsan (1,100 c.c.), *F.* Simas and Ego.
32. d'Yrsan (1,100 c.c.), *F.* Syran and de Soussay.
33. Bentley (4,398 c.c.), *G.B.* F. C. Clement and J. Chassagne.

34. Bentley (4,398 c.c.), *G.B.* H. R. S. Birkin and C. Bloch.
35. Bentley (4,398 c.c.), *G.B.* Woolf Barnato and J. D. Benjafield.
36. Stutz (5,000 c.c.), *U.S.* Brisson and Anderson.
37. Marendaz (1,500 c.c.), *G.B.* D. M. K. Marendaz and P. L. Densham.
38. Chrysler (4,100 c.c.), *U.S.* Chiron and Stoffel.
39. Chrysler (4,100 c.c.), *U.S.* Lepori and ——
40. Chrysler (4,100 c.c.), *U.S.* ——
41. Chrysler (4,100 c.c.), *U.S.* ——
42. Lagonda (1,954 c.c.), *G.B.* F. King and F. H. B. Samuelson.
43. Lagonda (1,954 c.c.), *G.B.* Gallop and Handley.
44. Lagonda (1,954 c.c.), *G.B.* Hawkes and d'Erlanger.
45. S.C.A.P. (1,100 c.c.), *F.* Guibert and Lefevre.
46. S.C.A.P. (1,500 c.c.), *F.* ——
47. Itala (2,000 c.c.), *I.* Dauvergne and Benoist.
48. Itala (2,000 c.c.), *I.* Sabipa and Charrier.
49. S.A.R.A. (2,000 c.c.), *F.* Mottet and Duval.
50. Alfa-Romeo (1,500 c.c.), *I.* Ivanowsky and Rachevsky.

BRITISH TRIUMPH AT LE MANS.

A Great Duel Between the Bentleys and the Stutz and Amazing Speeds the Chief Features of the 24-Hour Race for the Rudge-Whitworth Cups.

SPECIAL REPORT, PHOTOS AND SKETCHES BY AEROPLANE.

The 24-hour race for the Rudge-Whitworth Cups took place at Le Mans, in the Departement of the Sarthe, France. It began at 4 p.m. on Saturday, June 16th, and finished at 4 p.m. on Sunday, June 17th. The cars, which were of touring type, were, with slight alterations, production models, and were required to average a certain performance according to their engine capacity. The vehicle which covered the greatest excess mileage was the winner, although a cup was also given for the greatest distance covered in the 24 hours. The distance round the course was 10.7 miles. Within 30 minutes of the finish of the race "The Motor" representative was in the air writing his report, as his aeroplane, specially chartered for the purpose, sped towards England.

Two sketches by Bryan de Grineau of incidents in the 24-hour race. In the upper picture, Birkin, on No. 3 Bentley, at full speed, with a rear tyre gone, skims the sandbanks on the S-bend between Mulsanne and Arnage, hotly pursued by the Stutz. (Below) No. 5 Chrysler runs up the bank of the Arnage turn to let the Bentleys pass.

THE RACE DESCRIBED HOUR BY HOUR.

Front or Rear-wheel Drive? Four or Three Speeds? America's Challenge to Europe in 24-hour Race.

A LITTLE while ago all Europe and all America were talking of the Hispano-Stutz duel which took place recently at Indianapolis. There was talk then of a Bentley entering the lists against these two redoubtable foreign marques. The chance came last Saturday for the Bentley to meet one of these—the Stutz—and after an epic battle on the road for two rounds of the clock the Bentley proved its supremacy to the hilt.

The scene was the annual 24-hour race for the Rudge-Whitworth Cups held at Le Mans. The duel in question, therefore, was in actual fact an incident, or rather a feature, of a great race in which British, American, French and Italian cars set out to prove their value. Representatives of every country concerned put up such good performances that it is impossible to come to any decision regarding which nations turn out the best automobile.

The very serious and successful American participation provided a most interesting lesson. Subject to modifications, a good-class American car can, it seems, now be driven hard for long periods without suffering from any ill-effects. Speed can now be obtained without sacrificing flexibility, as witnessed by the fact that the Stutz and the four Chrysler cars which started

HOW THE CUPS WERE WON.

Special Rudge-Whitworth Cup for greatest mileage in 24 hours: **Bentley** (No. 4), Woolf Barnato and B. Rubin, 1,658.68 miles = 69.11 m.p.h.

Final for 1927-1928 Cup: **Salmson** (No. 35), Casse and Rousseau, 1,372.32 miles = 57.18 m.p.h. This cup is awarded for the best performance based on cylinder capacity.

Eliminating Race for 1928-1929 Cup. The following qualified:—**Chrysler** (No 7), C. Ghica and G. Ghica; **Chrysler** (No. 8), Stoffel and Rossignol; **Bentley** (No. 3), H. Birkin and Chassagne; **Alvis** (No. 27), C. M. Harvey and H. W. Purdy; **B.N.C.** (No. 32), **Doré** and Treunet; **Itala** (No. 12), R. Benoist and Dauvergne; **Alvis** (No. 28), S. C. H. Davis and W. Urquhart Dykes; **Lagonda** (No. 16), Baron d'Erlanger and D. Hawkes; **Tracta** (No. 29), M. Benoist and Balart; **Lombard** (No. 38), Desvaux and Goutte; **E.H.P.** (No. 36), Bouriat and Bussienne; **Sara** (No. 19), Duval and Mottet; **Tracta** (No. 31), Boursier and Vasena; **Tracta** (No. 42), Gregoire and Vallon.

only had three-speed gears, the ratios being sufficiently wide apart for second gear, at any rate in the case of the Chryslers, to be the lowest that would be required anywhere in the race.

Another feature of the event was the success of the front-wheel drive cars; two Alvis and three Tracta cars of this type started and the same number finished after, to all intents and purposes, no-trouble runs.

The grand-stands and the pits at Le Mans grow bigger and bigger. This year they stretched like same vast village for a good 300 yards up each side of the road. Over them fluttered the tricolour of France, the Stars and Stripes, the Union Jack, and the red, white and green of Italy. Between each group of pits were vast hoardings gay with advertisements in crude colourings. The whole circuit was, in fact, an advertiser's paradise.

A little before the start squalls of rain blew gustily across the heather-clad plain south-west of Le Mans. But above the pine trees a patch of blue sky grew swiftly, magnifying exceedingly, so that the road in front of the grand-stand was bathed in sunshine when Mr. Coquille, the director of the French branch of Rudge-Whitworth, Ltd., raised his yellow flag as a signal that the race was about to start.

With eyes fixed on the starter, the drivers stood or crouched on the opposite side of the road to where the cars waited silently for the touch of a starter button to bring their engines to life. Then the flag fell; there was a scurry of white-clad figures, the crash of engaging bendix pinions and the violent slamming of doors. Then a group of cars, notably the Stutz, Bentley and Ariès, moved away towards the

Baron d'Erlanger on the Lagonda runs into the back of Samuelson in a car of the same make, after the latter had charged the sandbank at Mulsanne.

The Bentley-Stutz duel at Pontlieue corner. (Centre) The start at 4 p.m. on Saturday was a fine spectacle. In the lower illustration W. D. Hawkes makes hurried repairs on his Lagonda after its collision with Samuelson. Note the broken lamp and bent wing.

again, this time starting their third lap, Birkin leading, with the black Stutz on their tails. But where was Laly, who looked like passing the American a lap before? Instead, there came Stoffel's Chrysler, humming smoothly, yet fast, followed by another of the same make, and the Lagonda hanging doggedly behind. Then, in a lull, came the thrilling news that Clement, on his very first lap, had beaten all existing records for the

Pontlieue corner. The most leisurely starters were Samuelson (Lagonda) and Davis (Alvis), who did not seem in the least hurried.

Long after the rest of the field had roared away into the distance one car, painted green, stood inert at the roadside. D'Erlanger, its driver, seemed unhurried. Slowly he climbed out of his Lagonda and lifted the bonnet on the carburetter side. His investigations betrayed nothing, so he raised the other side and changed his plugs, which were wet with petrol after overmuch "strangling" when starting. At length, amid cheers from British supporters, he got away.

In the meanwhile three fleet green cars loomed rapidly from the direction of the Arnage bends. Bentleys! More or less what one had expected, of course. But on their heels, very close behind, raced a long, low black car—a Stutz—its driver determined to strive for the lead. Behind came Laly's blue beetle-backed Ariés and the four Chryslers, with Samuelson's Lagonda and the two red-bonneted Italas after a short interval. In the throng that clamoured behind the Alvis and Aston-Martin entries were well placed, and a stern battle between British, French, Americans and Italians seemed promised.

Incredible! Here were the Bentleys

course on his 4½-litre Bentley, averaging 72.7 m.p.h. from a standing start!

As the remainder of the competitors filed by, Goutte, in the attractive low-built Lombard, "fell out" at the pits, stopped a moment, and dashed off again. Then, almost at the tail end of the procession, Laly came in slowly, driving the very car with which Chassagne put up such a valiant fight against the Bentley at Le Mans last year. For a time a consultation was held over the vehicle, but, at length, after it was driven silently away, it was announced as having retired with a run-out big-end bearing.

By the third lap it was obvious that the Bentley team formed a powerful coalition to keep the Stutz at bay. Birkin (Bentley) still led, but Clement's car had closed on it a little, while Barnato also had made up a certain amount of leeway. When they went faster, however, the Stutz speeded up also, and already one began to wonder for how many hours this pace could be maintained without mechanical trouble setting in. The British cars were putting up excellent performances and, indeed, the 2-litre Lagondas showed that they were the fastest vehicles in their class in the race, Samuelson and Gallop coming round regularly sand-

Prince Ghica's Chrysler pursues an E.H.P.

wiched between two pairs of Chrysler competitors. Among the smaller fry there was keen competition between the Alvis and Aston-Martin, although a special 1,500 c.c. Salmson set the pace in this class.

Birkin and Barnato beat the record for the course several times in close succession, the former by covering the 10.7 miles at an average speed of 120.666 k.p.h. (74.98 m.p.h.), and the latter at 119.276 k.p.h. (74.11 m.p.h.). Each time round, however, there was the black American car waiting, waiting its opportunity to take the lead; doing a special spurt, the driver of this car put in a lap at an average speed of 121.373 k.p.h. (75.421 m.p.h.).

A Protest.

There seemed to be some doubt as to whether the Stutz had sufficient speed to pass the Bentleys, or whether it was trying all the time to do so, yet never quite succeeding. The driver, however, evidently thought he ought to be able to get through if the Bentleys gave him more room, and, following a protest on his part, the Automobile Club warned Woolf Barnato that a repetition of such a complaint would lead to serious trouble.

On the fourth and fifth laps a struggle was going on between the Aston-Martin and Alvis teams, the drivers of the latter cars preferring to let the low-built, olive-green vehicles, which were their chief rivals, get just in front of them. By the sixth lap the Stutz had started to drop behind, but a few minutes later, when it came round again, it was slightly closer to No. 4 (Barnato's Bentley), notwithstanding a sharp shower of rain, which caused many to be alarmed for the weather conditions during the event.

One of the first cars to be definitely out of the race was the white Chrysler driven by Zehender and Ledure. During the latter's preliminary spell at the wheel the dogs for the starting handle, which are normally secured at the forward end of the crankshaft inside the vibration damper, became loose, and, unscrewing outwards, tore away the lower tank of the radiator.

The leading positions did not then change for a time, except that the Stutz seemed to be falling farther and still farther behind. On the eleventh lap it was announced, amidst excitement, that Brisson, who was driving the big Stutz, had beaten the lap record at 122.329 k.p.h. (76.01 m.p.h.), but almost immediately afterwards Barnato put in

Nearing the end: A spirited sketch by Bryan de Grineau of the Bentleys overtaking the Stutz. An hour-and-a-half before the end the Stutz lost its top gear. (Below) No. 38 (Lombard) skids round the bend where Samuelson was busy digging out his Lagonda.

a lap at 76·16 m.p.h.—best so far.

The Lagonda team, splendidly managed by Kensington Moir, was, up to this stage, a model of what a good team should be. Samuelson was signalled several times to reduce the speed of his Lagonda, but apparently did not see the signals, while d'Erlanger, who had a lap to make up, was instructed to push ahead gradually until he had acquired the position he would have occupied but for his unfortunate failure to start in the first instance.

Then occurred a curious incident, which reminded one irresistibly of the

The permanent grand stand at Le Mans showing part of the crowd.

case the gearbox was then found to have been damaged and the car was therefore withdrawn from the race.

With the higher speeds now attained in road racing the minimum number of laps which have to be covered before a car may come into the pits for replenishments are completed in a much shorter period than hitherto. Thus, it was only about three hours after the start of last Saturday's race that Bentley No. 2, with Clement at the wheel, came in for petrol and oil and to change over with Dr. Benjafield. The whole of the work was completed in 2 mins. 20 secs.—no mean accomplishment, considering the amount of petrol it was necessary to pour into the tank of such a large car, and the further handicap that the sealed cans of " Shell " petrol only held about two gallons each !

The Tragedy of a Jack.

The minutes dragged by and still Bentley No. 3 (Birkin) did not come round at his appointed time. For a long while there was no news. Then the driver of one of the other British cars looked in at the Bentley pit and announced that Birkin had punctured a tyre at Mulsanne and was trying to change a wheel.

Those in the pit, however, knew that there was no jack in the car and wondered how the driver was getting over this difficulty. Lap after lap was completed by other cars and still No. 3 did not arrive, but presently the news filtered through that it had got going again and had reached Arnage, where the driver was trying to jack up one wheel. Ultimately a white figure came running along the road across the open heath from Arnage. It was Birkin in search of a jack. Seeing his exhausted condition, Chassagne, his team mate, slung the jack over his shoulder and went rapidly up the road on foot to find the car. The wheel was changed and all was well, but the Bent-

famous Bentley triple crash of last year. Samuelson's cornering, which had been very wild, as more than one competitor had come round the Mulsanne bend only to find him skidding broadside on, was this time the cause of the trouble.

Baron d'Erlanger rounded the Mulsanne corner safely only to find Samuelson's car running backwards off the sand banks on to his vehicle and he was unable to dodge it. Consequently, although he skilfully reduced the effects of the accident to a minimum he was unable to avoid running into the back of his team mate's car. Whereas only one rear dumb-iron was damaged on Samuelson's car, both front dumb-irons, a spring leaf, a tyre and other components on d'Erlanger's car were seriously affected. Consequently, when the car came round to the pits, d'Erlanger, who was slightly grazed about the eyebrow and the bridge of the nose, changed places with Douglas Hawkes, who took the car for a slow lap to see what sort of work would

have to be done on it to make it fit for fast driving.

After a lap he found the near-side front Hartford shock absorber dangling idly a few inches from the ground. That had to be removed and, to equalize matters, the other Hartford was slacked right off. Then the springs were no longer considered adequate to take the full power of front-wheel brake application. It was all the more marvellous, therefore, to consider how later in the race average speeds of 65 m.p.h. were maintained without front brakes or front shock absorbers.

Fortunately, Gallop, who was driving the third Lagonda some 400 yards behind d'Erlanger, saw the crowd running to the corner, although he could not know the cause ; slowing down to about walking pace, therefore, he was able to get past without doing any damage.

Samuelson did not get his car out of the sand banks into which it had been pushed still farther by the impact with its team mate until he had expended two hours in frenzied digging. In any

In the glare of the lights of a following Bentley: Urquhart-Dykes, on an Alvis, leads Goutte (Salmson) and Benoist (Tracta) round the Pontlieue hairpin.

ley had to make up, in all, for a delay of no less than three hours.

One of the British drivers who followed Birkin's car for a time saw the rim gradually crack under the strain of running at 80 m.p.h. without a tyre on the road from Pontlieue to Mulsanne. Such is the strength of Rudge-Whitworth construction, however, that none of the spokes was fractured.

At 7.15 p.m. on the Saturday, during a five-minute stop, Woolf Barnato (Bentley No. 4) drew up at the pits, refilled the car as required and it was taken over by Rubin.

The Aston-Martin pit work was very smart. For instance, when No. 25 came in to the pits at 7.25 p.m. Bertelli had all replenishments effected and Eyston in the driving seat inside 2 mins. 50 secs. The Alvis stops were rather longer; they occupied 4 mins. 15 secs. for Purdy to take over from Harvey, who had already filled up with petrol and oil, although the time was somewhat reduced in the case of Urquhart-Dykes taking over from S. C. H. Davis, as only 4 mins. 2 secs. were taken.

The Lagondas (i.e., with the exception, of course, of No. 15) were doing very well, Hawkes, in spite of his damaged chassis, keeping up well over 64 m.p.h. despite the handicap of lack of front brakes and shock absorbers.

After 29 laps (i.e., about seven hours' running) the 1,500 c.c. Salmson driven by Hasley and Perrot was forced to retire.

The Stutz and Bentley duel became very much more exciting when, after competing a certain distance, re-

plenishments were necessary. Some idea of the changes in the lead during the early part of the race is shown by the fact that the Bentley, driven by Birkin and Chassagne, led up to the 20th lap, that driven by Barnato and Rubin led on laps 21 and 22, the Stutz led on lap 23, but lost its position for laps 24, 25 and 26 to Barnato. After this, however, the Stutz led for an appreciable time.

One of the low and businesslike

Capt. Woolf Barnato and his co-driver, B. Rubin, photographed after their victory on Sunday evening.

Aston-Martins was put hors de combat after 31 laps, i.e., at about 9 p.m., owing to the fracture of the rear-axle casing. It is said, however, that another car compelled the Aston-Martin to go right into the gutter, where one of the rear wheels struck a very deep gulley.

As the afternoon wore on, giving place to a beautiful starlit night, the grand stands and pits became illuminated with thousands of electric lights, giving a most attractive effect. The dense crowds showed no signs of diminishing and thronged round the space in the large open-air restaurant, where a dancing floor had been laid down. There was an air of festivity about the whole thing and, but for the thunderous exhausts of powerful cars rushing by every two or three minutes, one almost had the impression that one was visiting a country fair.

Just after midnight d'Erlanger, driving very stout-heartedly despite his crash, came into the pits. "Can't see a darned thing!" exclaimed d'Erlanger, and then discovered that the near-side headlamp bulb had burnt out. It turned out that apart from the filament having gone in one bulb the lamp brackets were loose, allowing the projectors to tilt rearwards and upwards. The calm Kensington Moir, speaking in a quiet, distinct voice that would soothe the most troubled or excited enthusiast, gave exact instructions as to the position of the spares, etc., that d'Erlanger might require.

While on the subject of Lagondas, it is worth while pointing out that the venture of running these three cars in their first race was an entirely sporting idea to which the 16 leading British Lagonda agents subscribed. The cars were prepared with meticulous care, and but for the unfortunate mishap right at the beginning all of them might have finished the course. The Lagondas were very fast, it being possible to get up to a speed of 95 m.p.h. in the neighbourhood of the bend between Pontlieue and Mulsanne.

The sporting character of the Bentley-Stutz duel was appreciated by spectators of every nationality, and when the British and American cars chanced to be in at the pits together and the Stutz got away first, Rubin, who had just taken over from Barnato, was sent off in a burst of cheering and the wishes of nearly everyone present that he should catch the Stutz in the near future. All eyes, therefore, turned to the southernmost end of the road, past the grand stands, a few minutes later in order to see what difference existed between the positions of the two cars. Another cheer went up when a lap later Rubin came thundering past on his great Bentley only 30 yards behind the low, black Stutz, but a lap later most hearts were gladdened by the healthy note of his exhaust before his time, and he came round 100 yards ahead of the American, to be increased ere long to a quarter of a mile.

In the cool of a lovely dawn C. M. Harvey brought his Alvis in for a quick and methodical fill up. A feature of the changes in drivers of this car was that Purdy, with Tarzan-like agility, would take a flying leap from the counter of the pit straight into the driving seat and seemed to alight exactly in place with his foot on the starter button. Harvey, at all times very calm, gave precise instructions as to the manner in which the car had been running in the last four hours, with warnings to his successor to beware of the treacherous mist which was now drifting in the hollows.

The small hours of the morning saw Bentley No. 2, driven by Clement and Benjafield, put hors de combat. With

Harvey on the Alvis taking the
Pontlieue hair-pin.

a loud knocking of the engine, it was driven slowly past the pits to the dead-car park, where it was left what time the announcers described the trouble as being due to a broken water-pump joint.

As the sun rose the spirits of drivers and pit attendants rose also, and, despite the fact that by that time owing to the failure of a cylinder-head gasket to hold out on one of the Lagondas, only one car of this marque was left in the running, the Lagonda equipe was full of high spirits and joking cheerfully about their prospects in the race.

As noon on Sunday approached the Stutz-Bentley duel became more fierce than ever, Barnato (Bentley) gaining 15 seconds on one lap and 50 seconds on the next, finally passing the Stutz when the latter stopped at the pits. Purdy came into the pits, having lost his spare wheel en route, but he obtained permission to continue round the course to look for it. He succeeded in finding it on the next lap, however, and fitted it with straps.

At 2.30 in the afternoon, with only 1½ hours to run, the climax of the great Anglo-American duel which had stirred so many hearts was reached when the Stutz came in slowly to the pits with no top gear left. Thus it was no longer a serious competitor to the

Bentley, although by its magnificently regular and trouble-free running up to this point the Stutz had covered a mileage far in excess of what was required in order that it might qualify for next year's final.

At last 4 o'clock drew near, crowds pressed against the barriers so far as one could see, not only in the pits and public enclosures, but far down the roads on either side. Until the very last moment it was touch and go whether Clement would jockey his Bentley through the last few minutes sufficiently well to enable it to qualify for the final, and this, amidst wild excitement, he at last succeeded in doing.

When considering the results which we give hereafter every credit should be given to the fine performance put up by the 1,100 c.c. Salmson, which won the Fourth Bi-annual Cup, as this car never faltered in its running from beginning to end of the 24 hours.

Those qualified for next year's finals (competing for the Fifth Bi-annual Rudge-Whitworth Cup):—

1. **BENTLEY** (No. 4), Barnato and Rubin, 1,658.68 miles in 24 hours=69.11 m.p.h.
2. **STUTZ** (No. 1), Brisson and Bloch, 1,594.26 miles in 24 hours=66.42 m.p.h.
3. **CHRYSLER** (No. 8), Stoffel and Rossignol, 1,549.52 miles in 24 hours=64.56 m.p.h.
4. **CHRYSLER** (No 7), C. Ghica and G. Ghica, 1,498.93 miles in 24 hours=62.45 m.p.h.
5. **BENTLEY** (No. 3), Birkin and Chassagne, 1,451.18 miles in 24 hours=60.46 m.p.h.
6. **ALVIS** (No. 27), Harvey and Purdy, 1,420.75 miles in 24 hours=59.19 m.p.h.
7. **B.N.C.** (No. 32), Dore and Treunet, 1,410.61 miles in 24 hours=58.77 m.p.h.
8. **ITALA** (No. 12), R. Benoist and Dauvergne, 1,403.22 miles in 24 hours=58.46 m.p.h.
9. **ALVIS** (No. 28), Davis and Dykes, 1,396.91 miles in 24 hours=58.20 m.p.h.
10. **LAGONDA** (No. 16), Baron d'Erlanger and Hawkes, 1,353.56 miles in 24 hours=56.39 m.p.h.
11. **TRACTA** (No. 29), M. Benoist and Balart, 1,280.33 miles in 24 hours—53.34 m.p.h.
12. **LOMBARD** (No. 38), Devaux and Goutte, 1,253.17 miles in 24 hours=52.21 m.p.h.
13. **E.H.P.** (No. 36), Bouriat and Bussienne, 1,240.31 miles in 24 hours=51.67 m.p.h.
14. **S.A.R.A.** (No. 19), Duval and Mottet, 1,227.04 miles in 24 hours=51.12 m.p.h.
15. **TRACTA** (No. 31), Boucier and Vasena, 1,183.76 miles in 24 hours=49.32 m.p.h.
16. **TRACTA** (No. 42), Gregoire and Vallon, 1,162.18 miles in 24 hours=48.88 m.p.h.

Nearing the end : A S.C.A.P., followed by Stoffel's Chrysler, at Pontlieue
in the 22nd hour.

High-speed Motor Racing.

Some Further Details of the 24-hour Race at Le Mans, Reported Last Week.

FRONT-WHEEL drive has come to stay. The Alvis and Tracta teams in the recent 24-hour Race at Le Mans for the Rudge-Whitworth Cup were the only teams to finish complete. All the cars in these two teams, moreover, had absolutely no-trouble runs for the entire 24 hours.

* * *

The Americans really seem to have learned how to make cars stand up to prolonged high-speed work. The Chryslers were equipped with auxiliary oil tanks connected to the sump by a number of pipes with taps controlled by the driver. The Stutz also was modified in various respects. Nevertheless, both makes of car were very little different from the standard models as sold to the public.

* * *

The great surprise of the race was the amazing performance of the 1,099 c.c. B.N.C. driven by Doré and Treunet, which finished seventh in the general classification of an average speed of 58.77 m.p.h., thus beating several other cars of bigger cylinder capacity.

* * *

A feature of the race this year was that the Bentley which put up the best performance and beat the record for 24 hours on the road, was one of the cars that ran at Le Mans last year.

* * *

Accessories are always important in a race of this nature, and it is interesting to note that the Bentley which won the sixth Rudge-Whitworth Cup (the Grand Prix of Endurance) was equipped with Smith lighting, K.L.G. plugs, Young's accumulators, Tecalemit greasing, Castrol oil, Shell petrol, Hartford shock absorbers, Dunlop tyres and Rudge-Whitworth wheels.

* * *

The finest performance in the whole race was the last lap put up by H. R. S. Birkin, driving Bentley No. 3. In a desperate but successful attempt to make the car qualify for the final next year, Birkin averaged 79.126 m.p.h. for his last lap. When it is considered that there were still about 15 cars on

An outstanding performance by an 1,100 c.c. car: The unsupercharged Salmson which won the Fourth Rudge-Whitworth Cup at Le Mans is the only car to have won the premier event for two years in succession. The illustration shows a quick "fill-up" in the course of the race. The drivers were MM. Casse and Rousseau.

the course and that there is a sharp hairpin and many right-angle bends in the circuit, some idea may be formed of the excellence of this performance.

* * *

Although one of the Salmsons was stated in the official programme to have an engine of 1,426 c.c., it should be realized that the car had in actual fact a 1,095 c.c. engine equipped with a supercharger. The regulations for the race handicapped supercharged cars by making them cover the same distance as unsupercharged cars of 30 per cent. greater cylinder capacity.

* * *

Shell petrol was the only fuel allowed in the race, and was supplied in special two-gallon cans by the organizers of the event.

* * *

It should be realized that, provided a car qualifies to run in the final next year there is no point in it being driven at a higher speed than is necessary. A little restraint during the race one year may enable a car to win in the final in the subsequent year.

* * *

The Motor aeroplane piloted by Capt. T. Neville Stack, A.F.C., covered the 320 miles between Le Mans and Croydon in 310 minutes. The machine was a D.H.9, supplied by Messrs. A.D.C. Aircraft, Ltd. This enabled us to publish in *The Motor*, on sale everywhere last Tuesday, a seven-page report, illustrated from sketches as well as photographs, of an event finishing on Sunday at 4.30 p.m. 300 miles away.

* * *

Birkin's Bentley, which put up the record last lap in the 24-hour Race at Le Mans, one of the front-wheel drive Alvis cars which competed, and possibly also one of the Lagondas will be on exhibition at Henlys, Ltd., Devonshire House, Piccadilly, London, W., all this week.

An All-British Cigarette.

CIGARETTE smokers have the opportunity of changing their brand and to give a trial to a cigarette made entirely of Rhodesian tobacco. Such has been introduced by Messrs. Lambert and Butler under the name of "Rhodians." They are sold at the popular price of 6d. for 10, and are of extra large size.

Fuel replenishment was speeded up by means of huge funnels—but not without waste. The Stutz refilling.

1929

The entry of 25 cars was composed largely as in previous years - French cars in the minority, and of these the biggest were 1.8 litre S.A.R.A.s. The Bentley team consisting of five cars were the favourites; there were four 4½ litre cars of which three had run in the previous year's race their chassis now suitably strengthened - but Woolf Barnato and Sir Henry 'Tim' Birkin were entrusted one of the new Speed Six models: Bentley's first six-cylinder car, a 6½ litre developed to challenge the Rolls-Royce Phantom but in short chassis sports form a formidable weapon in their Le Mans armoury. Ranged against the Bentleys were the American cars: a straight eight 5.3 litre Du Pont, three Stutzes, now of the twin ohc DV.32 model with four valves to each of the eight cylinders, and two Chryslers. A potential British challenge might come from a lone 4½ litre Invicta, and there were also single entries from Lagonda, Alvis and Lea-Francis. There were no Italian cars entered, and in the absence of Salmson, the most important French entry was that of four Tractas. A 749 cc d'Yrsan provided an almost comic contrast to the enormous Bentley Speed Six.

The circuit was shortened fractionally as the Pontlieue hairpin virtually in Le Mans itself - was cut off by a new road, the Rue du Circuit, in the interest of safety; the distance was now 10.153 instead of the original 10.726 miles. This arrangement was, however, of a makeshift nature and only lasted three years before the much more radically altered Tertre Rouge stretch was opened.

As expected, the Bentleys took the lead from the start, only two the Stutzes keeping up with them. Lord Howe, who was driving a 4½ litre Bentley together with Bernard Rubin had trouble first with plugs, then with the magneto, and was obliged to retire at the end of the afternoon; but nothing could impede the progress of the other Bentleys. At 8 pm the Bentleys, and one of the Stutzes driven by the British record breaker

Captain George Eyston, had lapped the rest of the field.

And so the race went on. Little short of a multiple disaster, as in 1927, or wholesale mechanical breakdown, could have destroyed the Bentleys' lead which was gradually extended. Their opponents did not fare so well. One of the Stutz drivers was badly burned when petrol was spilled on the red-hot exhaust pipe during a pit stop; his co-driver bravely continued in the face of a possible 18 hour solo drive but was eventually put out of the running with a leaking petrol tank. A similar fate overtook Eyston's Stutz, leaving only the Bouriat/Philippe car in the race. The Du Pont had retired early when the ballast it carried fell through the floor and damaged the prop shaft! And the Invicta ran a big end early on Sunday morning.

In the end, it was a rather predictable Bentley walk-over; with Bentleys in the first four places, the most magnificent victory so far at Le Mans, and not equalled before 1957. It was also the most impressive demonstration of the qualities of the Bentley, speed coupled with stamina and reliability. The green cars were followed home by the surviving Stutz in fifth place, and two Chryslers were sixth and seventh after an undramatic race. Only three more cars finished; the Lea-Francis, and two of the Tractas. The winning Bentley was the Speed Six; Birkin set the lap record for the new circuit at 82.984 mph, and he and Barnato also won the Biennial Cup and the Index of Performance - the biggest-engined car ever to win this Index which has tended to favour cars of smaller capacity, but a good measure of the margin of performance enjoyed by the big Bentley. For the first time all three major awards therefore went to the same car, a feat only repeated twice in Le Mans history. The winner's average speed was 73.627 mph and the distance covered was 1,767.07 miles.

TO-MORROW'S GREAT RACE

Concerning the Conditions, the Competing Machines, and the 10.1 - Mile Le Mans Course.

By S. C. H. DAVIS.

IN France to-day, at the little town of Le Mans, the cars competing in the Grand Prix d'Endurance and for the Rudge-Whitworth Cup are slowly passing through the inspection stage under the care of the officials of the Automobile Club de l'Ouest, and a mile or so outside the town finishing touches are being put to the big grandstand, the advertisement-decorated pits, and to the course itself.

There is no race quite like this one, for it entails twenty-four hours' driving, and racing during the night by the light of the cars' headlamps. It is a really gruelling test almost to destruction of some of the best sports cars there are, and because it is so long the problem of how to blend speed with reliability is exceedingly difficult to solve beforehand.

The race needs a certain amount of explanation, but not so much as it did in years gone by, for the Essex Six-Hour and the Junior Car Club Double-Twelve events were purposely run under rules of the same kind so that English competitors should become accustomed to the conditions and spectators obtain a more correct perspective. But the Le Mans race differs in one important particular: it is really two races combined.

One of these races, the Grand Prix d'Endurance, is a straightaway affair not in the least complicated; the winner is the car which averages the highest speed, and therefore covers the longest distance—quite obviously a race for a big car. But the second race, running at the same time, for the Rudge-Whitworth Cup, is exactly the same as the Junior Car Club Double-Twelve; all the cars are placed on a basis of equality by a handicap curve setting minimum distances to be covered, and the winner is that car which shows the best figure of merit, exactly as Ramponi's Alfa-Romeo did in the British race.

Stern Endurance Test.

To this second race, however, is attached another condition. A car to be eligible for it has first to compete in the Grand Prix d'Endurance—to run, that is, for twenty-four hours maintaining all the while a minimum average—and, that done, it is allowed to compete for the Rudge-Whitworth Cup the following year. Winners of the Rudge-Whitworth Cup, therefore, have raced for two successive years and for forty-eight hours, not for a mere twenty-four hours in actual fact.

To make both tests more difficult the cars have to cover 210 miles with sealed tanks; no fuel, no water, and no oil may be put in after the car has started until 210 miles have been completed. Then the seals are broken and the cars can be refilled by the driver working single-handed, after which another 210 miles have to be completed before the next refill.

Further, the only spares which can be used are those that are carried on the car from the start, and the only tools allowed also have to be carried, the necessary work being accomplished not by driver and mechanic, but by the driver alone.

There is one more handicap. The cars throughout the race carry, in effect, four persons, one the driver, the other three represented by ballast, and all the cars this year carry four-seater bodies. Concerning this there was a big outcry by the entrants of the smaller machines, who deemed it unfair that they should have to take the same weight and the same body as the largest cars in the race, a fact which has limited entries this year.

Each car is handled by two drivers, who take turns throughout the race, and each car is allotted six wheels, five to be on the machine, one in the pit, so that a wheel with a punctured tyre can be exchanged for the one in the pit as and when necessary.

This year there is to be a terrific battle between the five Bentleys, three Stutz and the Chryslers for the Grand Prix d'Endurance. What may be termed the storm section of the Bentley team consists of two of the new supercharged cars of $4\frac{1}{2}$ litres.

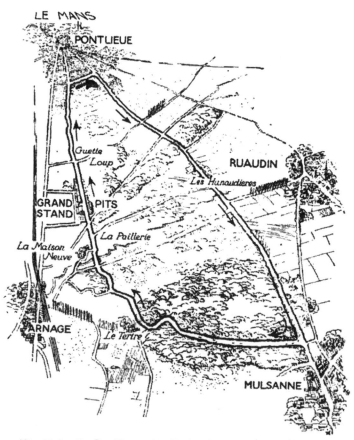

The 10.1-mile Le Mans circuit, showing the altered Pontlieue turn, which is being used for the first time.

tactically under Birkin, and the big six-cylinder which ran in the Double-Twelve, from the engine of which still more power has been obtained. Quite what the supercharged cars will do nobody knows. They are very fast, and they have been tested very thoroughly, but one never knows what a car in its first race will do.

The six-cylinder is even faster and should win. It is running for the Rudge Cup as well as for the Grand Prix d'Endurance, and the only possible point is that it is a very deceptive machine and liable to have one off the road before its real speed is realised, which, after all, is up to the drivers. The remaining two cars are ordinary $4\frac{1}{2}$ litres, one of which is running for the Rudge Cup. They are so well known and so well proved that they ought to do creditably in the present struggle.

The Stutz team is composed of Brisson's private car, a machine entered by Warwick Wright, and

Three of the extremely business-like-looking Bentleys.

The Le Mans Lea-Francis to be driven by Newsome and Peacock.

another entered by the Paris agent, all three running as a team under Brisson. The cars are short-chassis straight-eight Bear-Cat Stutz, and one, or perhaps two, may have Roots superchargers driven from the crankshaft front end. These cars are bigger than all the Bentleys except the six-cylinder. They are much faster than they were last year, have four speeds, and were ready in plenty of time.

British Straight Eights.

The Chryslers put up an extraordinarily good show last year, and probably will be better still this year. Two of them are running for the Rudge-Whitworth Cup, and they ought to be formidable opponents.

The remaining cars for the Rudge-Whitworth Cup—cars, that is, which qualified last year—are the Lagonda, a little B.N.C., one of the three Stutz, three front-drive Tractas, an air-cooled S.A.R.A., and the two new straight-eight, supercharged, front-wheel-drive Alvis. These machines are decidedly faster than they were

last year and much lighter. They have the transverse rear suspension, a considerably modified gear box and clutch, and a very neat little overhead camshaft straight-eight engine with a Roots blower at one side. They ought to have a very good chance for the Cup if anything happens to the six-cylinder Bentley and they are able to stay the course, because this type of engine has not previously been engaged in the Le Mans race, though it ran for nearly the full twenty-four hours in the Junior Car Club event.

The single Lagonda is very much of the type which ran last year, but

considerably lower and with all the advantages of experience in the Double-Twelve-Hour behind it.

In the Grand Prix d'Endurance only there are an American Oakland, two more B.N.C., an extra Tracta, two d'Yrsan, another S.A.R.A., two Du Pont, a single Lea-Francis, and a single Invicta, all of them running for a good position relative to their engine size in the Grand Prix d'Endurance, and all of them qualifying to run for the Rudge-Whitworth Cup next year.

As to drivers, Chiron is with Brisson, and both should give a fine account of themselves. Chassagne is with the Bentley team once more, and there are five drivers in the English teams who have been on the winning car one year or another. Clement, Benjafield, Davis, Barnato and Rubin, provided, of course, that the last-mentioned has sufficiently recovered from an injury to his leg to be able to drive this year.

Pontlieue Modified.

Unfortunately, the Automobile Club de l'Ouest have been forced to make some modifications to the circuit by cutting out the old hairpin corner at Pontlieue and taking the cars round a new corner made just short of the village. This has been done for the convenience of the inhabitants, but the alteration to the distance of one circuit, which now is 10.1 miles, upsets all the drivers' calculations and makes comparison

The Le Mans Stutz fitted with buffers to protect the supercharger

with previous times quite impossible. The circuit itself is triangular, with one nearly straight, very fast leg from the new hairpin, then the right angle at Mulsanne and an easy run through the forest ending in a bad S turn which has been called Arnage, after which the road is a series of slight and not too easy bends back towards the grandstand, and a little way before the latter comes the historical and nasty bend at La Maison Neuve, or, as we call it, White House, where the Bentleys' crash occurred two years ago.

The grandstand and pits are brightly illuminated at night, and among the pits are little cafés, while *The Autocar* is running, as before, a special tea " room " in the pits which also serves breakfast, and is a sort of club for the English drivers. The spectators generally, who stick it all through the night, have their own restaurants, dances, and other entertainments.

Last year's Grand Prix d'Endurance was won by the 4½-litre Bentley driven by Barnato and Rubin, which averaged 69.1 m.p.h., and this car, by the way, is running again this year. It was actually the first 4½-litre of this *marque* to compete in any race. The Rudge Cup was won by Casse and Rousseau on a Salmson at an average of 57.17 m.p.h., this being the Salmson's second win and the Bentley's third. Below is a list of the cars entered for the event, those eligible and nominated for the Rudge-Whitworth Cup being shown separately.

Early Practice Spins.

On Monday and Tuesday of this week the Bentley, Alvis and Lagonda cars were out for some unofficial practice, but no especially good times were

TO-MORROW'S GREAT RACE (*continued*).

put up. The weather then was all that could be desired, and the circuit itself was found to be in good condition.

The altered turn at Pontlieue,

One of the most consistent performances in the Le Mans race has been that of the Salmson, which won the Rudge-Whitworth Cup last year and in 1927. Casse, who drove on both occasions with Rousseau, is seen on the run down to Pontlieue.

which is being used in its present form this year for the first time, provided a certain amount of difficulty, the surface here being loose. To drivers who know a circuit very thoroughly, as many do the Le Mans course, it always takes some little time to become accustomed to a violent change in a famous corner such as Pontlieue.

On Wednesday morning the six-cylinder Bentley did a lap at 78 m.p.h., one of the " four and a halfs " covered a round at 73 m.p.h., and an Alvis at 67 m.p.h. Neither of the supercharged Bentleys had then arrived.

The usual amount of work on the cars was giving teams all they wanted in the way of worry and excitement, the Lagonda team lowering the gear ratios and the Lea-Francis fitting stronger springs.

The Bentley camp was making efforts to enter the " Double-Twelve " 4½-litre No. 5—driven recently for twenty-four hours at Montlhéry by Mrs. Bruce—but with men drivers.

Official practice with the properly closed road took place only yesterday (Thursday) and to-day (Friday).

LIST OF CARS ENTERED IN THE RACE.

GRAND PRIX d'ENDURANCE.				RUDGE-WHITWORTH CUP.	
Tracta.	B.N.C.	Du Pont.	Invicta.	Tracta.	S.A.R.A.
Tracta.	Stutz.	Du Pont.	Bentley.	Tracta.	Bentley.
Tracta.	Stutz.	d'Yrsan.	Bentley.	Tracta.	Bentley.
Tracta.	Stutz.	d'Yrsan.	Bentley.	B.N.C.	Chrysler.
B.N.C.	Oakland.	S.A.R.A.	Bentley.	Stutz.	Chrysler.
B.N.C.	Alvis.	S.A.R.A.	Bentley.	Alvis.	Lagonda.
	Alvis.	Lea-Francis.		Alvis.	

NOTES, NEWS AND NOTIONS

EARL RUSSELL AT TRANSPORT MINISTRY.

TO motorists the appointment of Earl Russell as Parliamentary Secretary to the Ministry of Transport is interesting.

Lord Russell should be an admirable man for the post if long experience of cars and road matters counts for anything. He became a member of the R.A.C.—then the Automobile Club of Great Britain and Ireland—in 1899, and was a prominent figure in the development of the new locomotion in the early days, taking part in many of the trials promoted by the A.C.G.B.I.

More recently Lord Russell has been active in making suggestions to the Minister of Transport regarding desirable modifications in regulations and orders. It was, for example, he who secured, shortly after the Roads Act was passed in 1920, a concession enabling a car owner when disposing of a vehicle to retain the old registration number—in Lord Russell's case A1—for use on a new car, the fee charged for this small favour being £5!

Presumably Lord Russell, as Parliamentary Secretary, will now have an opportunity of putting into practice some at least of the theories he has so stoutly and consistently championed.

HISTORICAL.

NOT only users of Morris cars, but all those interested in the development of the British automobile industry should make a point of writing to Morris Motors (1926), Ltd., Cowley, Oxford, for a copy of an extremely interesting booklet, " At Cowley," which has just been produced. The whole history of the beginning and rise of the great Morris undertaking is given, together with a good deal of interesting information regarding the methods of production in vogue at the Cowley and other Morris plants. The illustrations in this booklet are particularly good.

BRITISH VICTORY at LE MANS.

BENTLEY CARS SWEEP THE BOARD.

Fine Effort by Lea-Francis and Chryslers. Only One Stutz Finishes. Two Front-drive Tractas are Only French Cars to Finish.

The start of the race. Bentley No. 1, the ultimate winner, is first away followed by the white Du Pont.

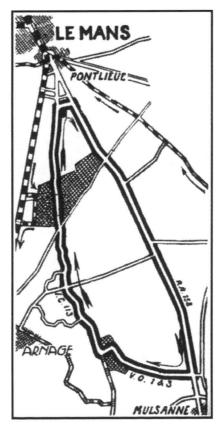

The 24-hour race for the Rudge-Whitworth Cups took place on Saturday, June 15th, and Sunday, June 16th, at Le Mans, in the Departement of the Sarthe, France. A modified course was used this year, cutting out the famous Pontlieue hair-pin bend. The cars, which were of touring type, were, with slight alterations, production models and were required to average certain performances according to the size of their engines. The vehicle which covered the greatest mileage above that required by the rules was the winner, although a cup was also given for the greatest distance covered in the 24 hours. As usual, the report of this race was written in the air as "The Motor" representative hurried back 350 miles to England immediately after the event.

TOURING pleasantly over an amazingly green countryside, with our Moth flying very low to keep out of the wet, misty clouds that drift barely 400 feet up, we seem to be creating something of a sensation. A mare and her foal have just galloped madly away from our threatening shadow. A yokel has gazed at us spell-bound. He is probably more thrilled at the sight of an aeroplane over the Mairie gables than we have been at any moment during the Le Mans race this last week-end.

For it was not a thrilling race. Yet it was, in its way, very wonderful. Three nations—France, America and Great Britain—were striving to win a classic road race in which they won the right to run in a similar race last

year. The French could not hope, with the small cars they had entered, to cover anything like the maximum distance in the 24 hours. But they did hope to win under the rules of the race, which took engine size into consideration. It was a foregone conclusion that one of the big cars would succeed in doing so; but not until the race had been going on for a few hours could one safely foretell that a British Bentley would triumph.

Indeed, the much-vaunted Black Hawk Stutz cars proved less of a menace to the British team than did the two white Chryslers. The latter, through silent, speedy running, were never very far behind and finished immediately after the only Stutz that stood the ordeal.

Beautiful workmanship, magnificent driving and, above all, the most minute preparation enabled the Bentley team to pull off the double victory. For this year, not content with covering the biggest distance in the 24 hours, a Bentley also won the final of the race on a cylinder-capacity handicap basis. Moreover, on the score of distance, three other Bentleys were respectively second, third and fourth, and they finished together, crossing the finishing line like a squadron of battleships in "line-ahead."

Another British achievement that calls for the highest praise is that of the lone Lea-Francis, privately owned and driven by a couple of amateur enthusiasts. Without any works backing,

Taking the new corner at Pontlieue. Boursier's Tracta is leading, followed by Clement's Bentley and Lejeune's B.N.C.

this 1,500 c.c. car ran steadily right through those gruelling 24 hours at an average speed of 57.7 m.p.h. and qualified, with points to spare, for next year's final.

Of the other representatives of Britain —the Alvis, Lagonda and Invicta—it can be said that they went down with colours flying, having, in their respective classes, averaged extremely creditable speeds until trouble overtook them.

Where were the big French cars, the products of La Belle France which once held the proud distinction of leading the world in automobile construction? We asked this question of Charles Faroux, the greatest authority on motoring in France, and he cried "C'est une honte! It is a disgrace! I am ashamed for my own country! Perhaps next year . . . ." Yet the French wonder why the Americans are establishing themselves on the French market, selling their cars well despite the formidable price-handicap of a 67 per cent. import duty!

The French entry was limited to small firms trying to make a name for themselves. The most interesting were, perhaps, the front-wheel-drive Tracta cars, two of which were, incidentally, the only French vehicles to finish. Then there were the air-cooled S.A.R.A. entries, interesting not only technically but because they are the prototype of the new Scotsman car and because three out of the four drivers were British. The B.N.C. cars were component-built with good proprietary makes of engines, the same applying to the single d'Yrsan.

* * *

While the foregoing was in process of writing the sun came out. Fulford, the pilot, has just handed over a stick of chewing gum to try to keep me awake. The country looks singularly lovely. . . But this is no time for gossip. On with the race !

* * *

Right up to the moment of the start no man could have foretold what sort of weather would be experienced. A lowering sky, a gusty south-westerly breeze and a certain dampness in the air suggested rain. The last announcement was made on the loud-speakers and the deathly hush which always precedes the start of a big road race was broken for a moment by a rattle of drums and blare of trumpets as the Champion plug band, in white coats and jockey caps, strutted past the front of the grandstand. Then silence fell once more on the crowd that surged against the barriers, and   it began to drizzle.

The drivers, lined up on the far side of the road from their cars, turned up the collars of their overalls or raincoats and crouched ready to sprint away as the starter dropped his flag. Then the flag fell, there was a rush for the cars and the whirring of starter pinions. Who would be first away?

From the line of cars parked diagonally across the road shot a low, black and white sports model—the Lagonda ! But

The solitary Lea-Francis, driven by Newsome and Peacock, just after passing Pontlieue.

At the Arnage bend. Miranda's Du Pont leading from Stoffel's Chrysler and Brisson's Stutz.

hardly had it reached the crown of the road when, with a deep rumble from its exhaust, the big Six Bentley, Birkin driving, leapt into the fray and, ere the bridge spanning the road was reached, led the procession.

Twenty-five cars started, and among the leaders past the end of the enclosures were Clement's and Benjafield's two Bentleys, the two Chryslers, the S.A.R.A. driven by Hutchinson, and the Invicta. Immediately behind were the Alvis and the Lea-Francis. Almost the last to get away was the eight-piston, four-cylinder, two-stroke Tracta, with clouds of blue smoke pouring from every nook and cranny of chassis and body.

One car remained behind—a d'Yrsan—which Trilland (replacing Siran, who was ill) pushed miserably into the middle of the road. Long after the rumble of exhausts had died away in the direction of Pontlieue the wretched man tottered up the almost imperceptible incline past the pits, pushing his refractory cyclecar, until at last the engine spluttered and burst into life. He started off, seven precious minutes lost.

While the crowd, aware of the Big Bentley's great speed, craned their necks in the direction of Arnage, news came through from the first of the two new corners (the course was

modified a little this year) that the Big Bentley and three of the "4½-litres" were leading at Le Tertre Rouge. Behind were two Black Hawk Stutz, a Chrysler and the big white Du Pont.

The announcer was still speaking when there came a gasp of awe from the spectators. Away in the direction of Arnage appeared a dark speck; as it roared round the two slight bends within view of the grand-stand it rapidly took form. It was Birkin's six-cylinder Bentley. Amid huge excitement it tore past the pits, having completed a standing-start lap in 7 mins. 57 secs.—about 76 m.p.h.!

Clement, Glen Kidston and Benjafield were next, with Bouriat and Eyston, on Stutz cars 5 and 6, behind, Lord Howe, the two Chryslers and the Du Pont next. Benoist's Stutz stopped at the pits after only one lap, but was soon off again, what time the Lagonda swept by, with Cyril Paul (Alvis) trying to overtake Doré's B.N.C. on his heels. Behind another B.N.C. came the Invicta and Newsome's Lea-Francis.

There seemed hardly breathing space before Birkin came roaring round once more—this time in 7 mins. 44¾ secs.—with four Bentleys following this time, for Lord Howe had passed the two Stutz. There was an enormous gap—three-quarters of a mile, perhaps—before any of the smaller cars came into view. The difference in speed was so obvious that there seemed to be two quite separate races going on—one for the large cars and another for the "little fellows."

On the next lap the difference was even greater. The Lagonda came along all by itself, midway between two gangs of cars. The leader of the second

The straight-eight front-wheel-drive Alvis at Pontlieue.

LE MANS.—Contd.

pack, however, was the Alvis, and this was fast spanning the distance separating it from the car in front. By the fourth lap the Alvis had overtaken the Lagonda and was on the heels of the great white Du Pont.

After three-quarters of an hour's running Lord Howe stopped at the pits. His Bentley engine was misfiring. Soon he had to take drastic steps to cure it. First the sparking plugs were changed and then, as there was no improvement, a new magneto was fitted. The onlookers, anxious for the big car to get going again, seemed quite impatient at Lord Howe's steady and deliberate working on the car. Eventually, when the task was done, Rubin took over the car—apparently with a view to forming an opinion as to what was the matter.

The result was evidently not very satisfactory, as Rubin brought the car back and Lord Howe again worked on it—for just about an hour. This time the magneto was replaced and eventually the car got going again. The respite was only temporary, however, for somewhere about 6.30 on the Friday evening, when he was some six minutes overdue at the pits, Lord Howe was reported as having stopped by the ninth kilometre post, not far short of the Mulsanne corner. Long afterwards the news trickled through that the cross-shaft driving the two magnetos had broken—a hitherto unheard-of source of trouble which may possibly have been due to the too hasty fitting of the new magneto.

There had been other calls at the pits in the meanwhile—one of the S.A.R.A.s, Benjafield's Bentley, the Invicta and No. 5 Stutz had been in—the last mentioned several times—but the first retirement was that of the d'Yrsan, which was pushed back down the slope beyond the pits and parked in the pit enclosure.

H. R. S. Birkin, driving the big "Speed Six" Bentley, was doing wonderfully well. After a number of extremely fast laps he proceeded to beat the record for the circuit by lapping in 7 mins. 37 secs., which is equal to 79.78 m.p.h. The previous record of some 79 m.p.h. was made by Birkin last year in the course of his historic last lap in the 4½-litre Bentley.

Barnato and Birkin's victorious six-cylinder Bentley taking the corner at Mulsanne.

Barnato's and Kidston's Bentley passing the stands.

From the lofty Press stand—probably the finest of its kind in Europe—the distant scene was extraordinarily calm. A gentle breeze idly fanned the Union Jacks, Tricolours and Stars and Stripes with which the grand-stand enclosure was decorated. The soft greens and blues of the feathery-looking pines and the blue, tree-covered hills in the far distance were very restful if the eyes had for long gazed at the advertisements in crude primary colours, more vivid than ever this year, which gave such a gay aspect to long rows of pits. Over to the left, where a great arch representing a section of a Dunlop tyre spanned the path, one could see a never-ending stream of people scurrying like ants to and from the other "leg" of the course, 900 metres distant.

After two hours, four Bentleys still led, with one of the Stutz, driven by G. E. T. Eyston, on their heels. With the high averages maintained by the Bentleys, it was not surprising that they were in to the pits for replenishments, which were only permitted every 20 laps, in a much shorter time than in previous years. Birkin came in, filled up very quickly and very efficiently and handed over the car to his team-mate, Woolf Barnato. When he had taken off his "crash hat" and goggles and the queer fingerless gloves he uses for

These drivers beat all records for the race.

again beat his own record, his speed working out at 81.12 m.p.h. With such valiant deeds being done it was an extraordinary but a true thing that by quarter to nine on Saturday evening it was almost impossible to believe that a race was in progress. It was a beautiful, calm evening, with a soft, south-westerly wind; from a suitable position one could look up and down the course for a considerable distance without seeing a car. The bulk of the spectators, too, were eating in the large, open-air restaurant adjacent to the grand-stands, which left the paddock in a singularly deserted condition.

The Du Pont, which had been notably unsteady on corners for several laps, was withdrawn at the 20th lap with a bent propeller shaft. The reason for the failure of the shaft was curious. The ballast shifted, broke through the floorboards and fell on the shaft, with the dire results which we have mentioned.

After it had covered only 28 laps the Lagonda, which, driven by Rose Richards, had been doing so well, came into the pits because the floorboards had been on fire. For a considerable time it was thought that one of the exhaust-pipe joints had gone and that it was simply a question of fitting a new joint for matters to be put right. Eventually, however, the fire was traced to an escape through the cylinder-head gasket. This actually sounded the death-knell of the Lagonda so far as this race was concerned, because if a new gasket were fitted all the water would have to be run out of the radiator and cooling system.

Now, in the Le Mans race fuel, water and oil may only be taken in every 20 laps. As the Lagonda had done 28 laps at the time, it therefore meant that if the gasket were replaced the car would have to cover another 12 laps before any water could be put in the engine. It was not practical, and the drivers had regretfully to signify their retirement and the car was pushed off the course. This Lagonda, it will be

driving he was absolutely radiant. The car, he declared, was wonderful, and so far he had only "toured" the circuit. It had never been necessary to hurry at all. It went more than fast enough for the purposes of the race without the accelerator pedal ever being fully depressed.

Just as Barnato let in his clutch to go roaring up the slope towards Pont-lieue, Clement dashed up to the pits in Bentley No. 8; his filling up with petrol was wonderful to behold. It was a great jangle of empty tins, which were thrown bodily into the interior of the pit and oil and water supplies were taken in at the same time. Then Chassagne, a veteran now, but still a splendid driver, stepped from the pit counter into the driving seat and re-started, the total stop having occupied 3 mins. 27 secs.

No. 9, driven by Kidston and Dunfee, was also quick, four tins at a time being emptied into the giant, galvanized-iron funnels. In his haste Kidston slammed down the lid of the petrol filler and there was a chorus of shouts of "Open it," and after one or two attempts he got it satisfactorily closed. So full was the tank after this replenishment that the driver had to scoop excess fuel out of the tank with his hands, throwing it all over the road. Dunfee took over from him immediately afterwards, so that the total stopping time of this car at the pits was only 2 mins. 8 secs.

In the hours which followed Birkin

Bouriat's Stutz taking the Mulsanne corner.

Barnato's Bentley, Watney's Stutz and Hutchinson's S.A.R.A. passing the pits.

remembered, was privately entered for the race by a syndicate of enthusiasts and was being run independently of the manufacturers. So successful did the car prove in practice that it was prepared in ample time for the event. Hearing that a certain amount of mechanical trouble had been experienced with the Lea-Francis car, however, two of the Lagonda mechanics came round to the Lea-Francis headquarters and voluntarily offered to work for seven hours on the car, although they had already been working all day themselves. This shows the true sporting spirit that prevails in a race of this nature.

An Amusing Incident.

The Lea-Francis, by the way, was going round very well and the driver had to be called in in order to be told to switch on his lights. There was a certain amount of laughter when it was realized that the driver was still apparently unaware that opaque covers were fitted over all his lamps. He had until then been blaming the lamps for not giving enough light !

The big, supercharged Stutz, driven by Brisson and Chiron, was not running any too well, and there was a pronounced spitting from the carburetter. A few minutes later this car came into the pits and during replenishments some petrol was accidentally spilt on the white-hot exhaust pipe. The result was an immediate and alarming outbreak of fire which, fortunately, was got under with commendable promptitude. Practically every Pyrene in the pits for their entire length was called into requisition and soon there were no flames visible and only a black plume of smoke, looking very evil in the glare of the electric lights, showed that anything was wrong.

Poor Brisson got considerably burnt ; so much so that he had to be taken away on an ambulance and was unable to drive for the remainder of the race. Chiron was, therefore, left in the position to drive himself for 24 hours, but as his car subsequently had to be withdrawn from the race owing to pronounced and apparently incurable clutch slip, fate shortened the drive for both of them.

When we visited the Stutz pit, which was still a centre of excited conversation, we saw Colonel Warwick Wright dashing about to see what could be done and uttering hopes that the car

would be able to restart. Eventually the car got going again at 10.15 p.m. with Chiron at the wheel. In his haste, however, he had overlooked the fact that his tail light, if it existed at all, was not visible, and a few laps later he was called in and told to make a proper job of his lamp.

At the sixth hour the six-cylinder Bentley was leading with 44 laps, Kidston and Dunfee's car having completed the same number of circuits. The other two Bentleys, driven by Clement and Chassagne and Benjafield and d'Erlanger, had both 43 laps to their credit, while the foremost Stutz,

The Du Pont (in the foreground), Watney's Stutz, and Benjafield's Bentley taking the new Pontlieue corner.

The winning Bentley passing de Vere's Chrysler. At the pits is Lord Howe's Bentley.

driven by Bouriat and Philippe, occupied fifth place in the general classification with 42 laps; another Stutz and the two Chryslers had all, by this time, covered 41 laps.

As late as 11.30 p.m. the enormous crowds showed no signs of going home, and opposite the Bentley pits a strong contingent of Britishers seated in the grand-stand called out at intervals, not unmusically, "B-e-n-t-l-e-y," Bentley! and they sang loudly, also, to keep themselves awake.

Slowly darkness crept in and one by one the cars were called in to their pits to remove lamp covers, while the pits and all the buildings in the grand-stand enclosure were lit up in the most attractive fashion. It is probably this unique feature of the Le Mans 24-hour race which makes it always attract such a large crowd of people. The sight of an exceedingly long row of pits lit up like so many shop windows is one which will not easily be forgotten. At 10.15 p.m. the S.A.R.A. driven by Motett and Douglas Hawkes retired.

The night hours were calm and rather devoid of incident from midnight until nearly 3 a.m. The four Bentleys still led, with No. 6 Stutz a bad fifth, nearly four laps behind the last Bentley. No 1 Bentley continued its astonishing career, frequently breaking its own lap records, whilst second, third and fourth positions alternated between Nos. 9, 8 and 10. Shortly before 3 o'clock, however, the Stutz began to increase speed and on No. 9 Bentley coming in to the pits it climbed into fourth place. At ten minutes to three d'Erlanger, on No. 10, at that time running second, was reported in trouble with his lights at Arnage corner. He came in shortly after 3 o'clock and handed over to Benjafield. The lamps appeared to be all right; but a water leak had developed. This proved to be at the pump joint and Benjy put matters right with quiet encouragement from Kensington Moir. The leak stopped, Benjafield got into the car, but the starter refused to work. "Look at the leads; take the lid off the battery boxes." Nothing doing! "Kick the batteries." This had the desired result, and the car got away again. Much time had been lost, however, and the Stutz was close on his heels, followed by No. 14 Chrysler. Shortly afterwards the Stutz came in for a change over and the Chrysler took fifth position. At half time (4 a.m.) the four Bentleys were still leading, but Chrysler and Stutz were only a few minutes behind Benjafield.

The curious two-stroke Tracta which had been making frequent pit stops retired shortly before the end of the 12th hour with a broken petrol pipe. By 5 a.m. No. 14 Chrysler managed to pass No. 10 Bentley and get into fourth position. Amongst the rest of the field the Invicta and Lea-Francis were doing best at this time, followed by a Tracta, a B.N.C., and a S.A.R.A. The Invicta retired at 5.30 a.m. Ran out of oil and then ran out a big-end. Stoffel and Benoist had evidently been holding back

Barnato and Birkin after their fine victory.

The all-British finish at the end of 24 hours—three of four Bentleys about to cross the line.

their Chrysler, for the car steadily increased speed from 5 o'clock onwards, until by the 14th hour the car had been worked into third place. No. 8 Bentley came into the pits a little before six, and this gave the Chrysler its chance. The ballast had shifted and fouled a brake-control rod. The latter, unfortunately, broke off short in the joint and the repair proved difficult, delaying the car for over an hour. Clement worked at the job like a galley slave, and finally drove off amidst cheers. By this time the Chrysler had reached third place, it was running less than two laps behind Kidston and Dunfee's Bentley No. 9.

At 7.30, No. 19 S.A.R.A. (the only remaining one) stopped about a kilometre from the tribunes and the driver walked in.

No. 6 Stutz retired in 15th hour. Only 12 cars now left in the race. The Chrysler held its position well, and the two Stutz cars now ran into fifth and sixth places after Benjafield and d'Erlanger's Bentley, No. 5 Chrysler being very close indeed. At the 16th hour the Chrysler was barely a lap behind the second Bentley.

When the crowd began to trickle back to the tribunes on Sunday morning they found only 10 cars still running. Of these five were British, three American and two French. As usually occurs at Le Mans, those which were still running fairly easily on the Sunday morning were still capable of a good performance at 4 o'clock in the afternoon, when the 24 hours had expired.

Of those that fell by the wayside the Invicta deserves mention, because it had been putting up a valiant show notwithstanding the fact that trouble with the oiling system had resulted in a big-end bearing being run. The repairs that were needed were only completed at 11 o'clock on the day on which the race started. The car was very fast and behaved well until the oil pressure failed once more in such

a way that the occupants of the car knew that the end had truly come.

Knowing that their engine was likely to burst any minute, the driver continued to press on the accelerator and actually succeeded in covering three laps, or over 30 miles, at a very high speed before, with a somewhat distressing noise, one or more big-ends went again. The two drivers, Davies and Feinnes, who had done so well up to this time, then returned to the town in a taxi and gave up racing, at any rate so far as that race was concerned!

The Alvis Retires.

Another car that retired in the night was the 1,500 c.c. supercharged straight-eight Alvis. This had been putting up a very good show, lapping consistently at between 68 m.p.h. and 70 m.p.h. Unfortunately, however, the cylinder block cracked and the water poured out. It was impossible to do anything and the car was parked in the pit enclosure. The performance of this car was exceptionally fine in view of the fact that it had to carry ballast equivalent to the weight of four persons, including the driver, while four-seater bodies were also compulsory. Incidentally, in our opinion, the eight-cylinder Alvis looked better with a four-seater than with a two-seater body.

In the early morning, when George Eyston had only one lap to go before coming into the pits to fill up, he ran out of petrol and found the cause to be a split petrol tank. With the supercharged Stutz out of the race with clutch trouble, only one car of this make, that driven by Bouriat and Philippe, remained. This put up a very good show considering the cumulative effect of the many small stops which occurred throughout the race. The Tracta, with the curious engine which we have already mentioned, retired at 3.55 a.m., the reason being given as a broken petrol pipe.

For the rest of the race there was really nothing of very great importance and certainly nothing of a thrilling nature. Some of the Bentleys came in at intervals for minor adjustments and replenishments, while the Chrysler handled by Stoffel and Benoist developed some sort of transmission trouble, so that all four wheels had to be jacked off the ground for examination. After losing a considerable amount of time, however, the car was able to continue and finished at a satisfactory speed.

A feature which makes the Lea-Francis performance all the more meritorious is that, owing to the breakage of one shock absorber and a shock-absorber bracket, the car had to be driven the last four hours of the race without any form of spring dampers. The car, by the way, is a 1929 T.T. chassis, similar to those prepared for the Double-twelve Hours' Race.

There were extraordinarily few tyre changes in the race, and all the cars that finished were running on Dunlops. The big Bentley changed its first and only tyre after 12½ hours' running as a precautionary measure; a flint cut a tyre on the Lea-Francis, without, however, penetrating as far as the tube, and two back wheels were changed on Kidston and Dunfee's Bentley. Otherwise all the cars that finished ran for 24 hours on the same tyres as those with which they started.

When the result of the race already seemed certain, and some journalists were engaged in sending out wires giving the results, it was suddenly announced that the Tracta driven by Gregoire and Valon had run into the ditch near White House corner. The driver, however, was unhurt. By a herculean effort he managed to extricate his car and, amid loud cheers, finished the course on time.

Fifteen minutes before the end of the race the Bentleys went by in slow and solemn procession amidst a buzz of

LE MANS.—Contd.

animated conversation from the enclosure. Every man, woman and child who could get on to a pit counter did so and all eyes were fixed on the bend in the road towards Arnage. Then from the green of the distant trees four shapes became detached. They were the victorious Bentleys coming into the finish unhurried, dignified, superb, disposed in line ahead like a squadron of battleships. This slightly theatrical finale created an enormous impression, and those that thought of this striking little procession deserve every praise.

There was not time to wait for more. As the cars were being arranged in front of the grand-stand, with their occupants almost hidden beneath gigantic bouquets of beautiful flowers, we sped to the aerodrome on one of the latest straight-eight Ballot cars which had been put at our disposal by its manufacturers. A few minutes later and we were in the air speeding towards England.

THE SEVENTH GRAND PRIX OF ENDURANCE.

	Car.	Drivers.	Miles.
1.	Bentley	Barnato and Birkin	1,765
2.	Bentley	Kidston and Dunfee	1,692
3.	Bentley	Benjafield and d'Erlanger	1,620
4.	Bentley	Clement and Chassagne	1,593
5.	Stutz	Bouriat and Philippe	1,565
6.	Chrysler*	Stoffel and Benoist	1,550
7.	Chrysler*	De Vere and Mongin	1,513
8.	Lea-Francis	Peacock and Newsome	1,375
9.	Tracta	Balart and Debengny	1,303
10.	Tracta	Grégoire and Valon	1,236

* Did not run in eliminating race for Sixth Rudge-Whitworth Cup.

FIFTH BI-ANNUAL RUDGE-WHITWORTH CUP (FINAL).

(Cars which ran in this had to qualify last year.)

	Car.	Drivers.	Miles
1.	Bentley	Barnato and Birkin	...1,765
2.	Bentley	Benjafield and d'Erlanger	1,620
3.	Chrysler	Stoffel and Benoist	1,550
4.	Chrysler	De Vere and Mongin	1,513
5.	Tracta	Balart and Debengny	1,303
6.	Tracta	Grégoire and Valon	1,256

Hartford shock absorbers and Dunlop tyres were fitted to every car that finished. The six-cylinder Bentley used Champion plugs, but the 4½-litre models used K.L.G. plugs. The Bentleys used Super Shell oil, Lucas lamps, Young batteries, and Rudge Whitworth wheels. Shell petrol was the official fuel for all cars.

Bentley at Le Mans - 1929

No. 1 leads the way from the Start.

Chassagne cornering in No. 8.

Barnato bringing the winning car round Mulsanne.

LE MANS: A FINE BRITISH VICTORY.

How Bentleys Swept the Board at the Famous French Classic —Excellent Performance by a Solitary Lea-Francis — The Alvis Again Pursued by Bad Luck.

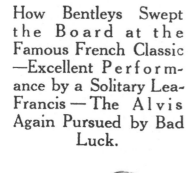

FOR the first time for some years a car of over 1,500 c.c. has won the famous Rudge-Whitworth Cup Race at Le Mans. As this award is made on a handicap basis in which the cylinder capacity is taken into account it frequently happens that the small cars do relatively better than the larger vehicles. This year, however, all cars having engines of 1,000 c.c. or more had to carry four-seater bodies and ballast equivalent to three passengers; consequently they were severely handicapped, for not only were their power-weight ratios adversely affected, but wind resistance was noticeably increased. The results show that out of 25 starters only three light cars finished the 24 hours' strenuous racing. The fastest of these was the 1929 T.T.-type Lea-Francis, driven by Peacock and Newsome.

The only French cars to finish had engines of under 1,000 c.c. in order that they need carry only two-seater bodies. These were a couple of front-wheel-drive Tractas, driven respectively by Balart and Debeugny and Gregoire and Valon. The only other British car having an engine of under 1,500 c.c. was the straight-eight supercharged Alvis, driven by Cyril Paul and W. Urquhart Dykes. This put up an amazingly good show, frequently lapping just short of 70 m.p.h., right up to the moment when during the night a mechanical breakage caused the cracking of the cylinder block.

Considerable ingenuity was shown by the French; the four Tractas, for example, all had engines of different cylinder capacity, three of them had more or less orthodox power units of 993 c.c., 985 c.c. and 984 c.c. respectively, but that driven by Bourcier and Thibeaudeau had a 999 c.c. engine of weird and wonderful construction. It was the

(Above) Showing the Bentleys finishing the race in line-ahead formation, and inset (left) Woolf Barnato and Birkin, the victors. (Oval) The Lea-Francis on the Mulsanne turn. (Inset) Peacock and Newsome, who drove the "Leaf" alternately.

production of a mechanic living on the outskirts of Paris who spends his Sunday mornings demonstrating his latest engines to an awe-stricken crowd of French motorcyclists.

Hitherto he has confined his activities to producing some fairly efficient but noisy motorcycle units. The engine which he produced for the 24-hour-race Tracta was not only wonderful to behold but amazingly efficient considering the enormous bulk of the car which it had to propel. The bonnet stretched the entire width of the car, and under it was what appeared at first sight to be two water-cooled Morgan engines stuck together. In actual fact, the unit was a four-cylinder with two banks of cylinders at 90 degrees. In each cylinder were two pistons, acting like those in the famous Gobron-Brillé engine of pre-war days, and, in addition to all this, the engine worked on the two-stroke

principle and had an enormous Cozette supercharger fitted between the cylinder blocks. The sound of the exhaust was like the splitting of calico and dense volumes of blue smoke poured from every joint of body and chassis.

The B.N.C. and D'Yrsan were component-built vehicles, the latter being a four-wheeled edition of the well-known three-wheeled cyclecar.

The race was run on the Sarthe circuit on the outskirts of Le Mans over a road course measuring 10.1 miles round. This year the famous Pontlieue hair-pin had been eliminated by the substitution of two easier bends, which had the effect of shortening the circuit slightly. There are sundry slopes in the course, none of which, however, could properly be described as hills, and there are quite a number of bends in addition to about five real corners.

The race was started at 4 o'clock in the afternoon of Saturday, June 15th. The competitors had to line up on one side of the road, and at the fall of the starter's flag dash across, set their engines in motion by means of the starter and get away thereafter as quickly as possible.

Somewhat unsettled weather during the day crystallized in a miserable drizzle just as the race commenced. The first car to pull out of the line outside the pits was the British Lagonda, driven by T. E. Rose-Richards, but hardly had he reached the crown of the road when with an impressive roar the great six-cylinder Bentley, driven by H. R. S. Birkin, dashed off up the road leading the whole procession.

In the struggle for position on the first lap the Alvis and Lea-Francis were well to the fore with two Tractas and one of the B.N.C. cars behind. The only car that would not start immediately was the D'Yrsan, driven, in Siran's absence through illness, by Trilland. The wretched driver pushed it miserably into the middle of the road, and so unlikely to start did the engine sound that there was some fear that the large cars would be round before he could get out of the way. Still pushing his car, the unhappy man tottered up the almost imperceptible rise past the pits until, having presumably cleared the cylinders by pushing the car in gear, he got off.

Needless to say, Birkin's big Bentley was first past the pits, having averaged about 76 miles per hour from a standing start. There was a very long gap between a group of large cars and the smaller vehicles, and the first light car to appear was Cyril Paul's Alvis going extremely well. Next came Lejeune's B.N.C., separated by the Invicta from Newsome's Lea-Francis and the rest of the field.

On the fourth lap the Alvis caught and passed the Lagonda and so led the under-1,500 c.c. cars by a considerable distance. Bourcier's two-stroke Tracta came round lap after lap heralded by a great blue smoke screen which obliterated the view for a distance of fifteen yards or so above it and on each side.

For some time the race went on, the first retirement being that of the D'Yrsan, which completed only nine laps. After running for about 2½ hours and being in the same lap as the fastest cars, Paul's Alvis began to drop back and finally had to be withdrawn from the race owing to a cracked cylinder block. The other Alvis, which was to have been driven by S. C. H. Davis and Cushman, had been unable to start owing to the crankshaft having got out of line subsequently on the failure of a big-end bearing.

During the fourth hour the B.N.C. driven by Doré and Treunet retired, the reason given being valve trouble, and at about the same time the big Du Pont—an American entry—retired because the ballast fell through the floor and bent the propeller shaft; soon after Earl Howe's Bentley stopped with a broken magneto drive. Another B.N.C. retired at 8.4 p.m. in the evening of the first day just a quarter of an hour before it was decided that the Alvis could not continue. At 9.50 p.m. the Lagonda retired with a leaking cylinder-head gasket, the cumulative effect of all these retirements being that the Lea-Francis, which was running extremely well, worked its way up, and after six hours' running was only nine laps (just under 100 miles) behind the leading Bentley.

For some hours nothing further occurred, darkness fell on the scene, the pits and grand-stand were brightly illuminated and the cars tore round the course with blazing headlamps.

The two-stroke Tracta retired at 3.35 a.m. and another vehicle of the same make retired at 5.55 a.m., by which time the Lea-Francis had worked its way up to ninth place.

The only remaining B.N.C., driven by Devaud and Caralp, retired at 8.30 a.m., after which the Lea-Francis ran into eighth place and the positions remained more or less unchanged until the end. It is always a feature of the Le Mans race that those who are running at about breakfast time on the second day generally manage to hang together until the finish at 4 o'clock on the Sunday afternoon. When the Bentleys had come in taking the first four places and the surviving Stutz and the two Chryslers had been duly applauded, the Lea-Francis, driven by Peacock and Newsome, swept by, going every bit as well as when it started 24 hours before. The car ran extremely well notwithstanding the fact that it had to cover the last four hours with one broken shock absorber bracket.

GRAND PRIX RESULTS.

	Car.	Drivers.	Miles.
1.	Bentley	Barnato and Birkin	1,765
2.	Bentley	Kidston and Dunfee	1,692
3.	Bentley	Benjafield and d'Erlanger	1,620
4.	Bentley	Clement and Chassagne	1,593
5.	Stutz	Bouriat and Philippe	1,565
6.	Chrysler	Stoffel and Benoist	1,550
7.	Chrysler	De Vere and Mongin	1,513
8.	Lea-Francis	Peacock and Newsome	1,375
9.	Tracta	Balart and Debengny	1,303
10.	Tracta	Grégoire and Valon	1,236

RUDGE-WHITWORTH CUP RESULTS.

	Car.	Drivers.	Miles.
1.	Bentley	Barnato and Birkin	1,765
2.	Bentley	Benjafield and d'Erlanger	1,620
3.	Chrysler	Stoffel and Benoist	1,550
4.	Chrysler	De Vere and Mongin	1,513
5.	Tracta	Balart and Debengny	1,303
6.	Tracta	Grégoire and Valon	1,256

HARD LUCK FOR ALVIS CREW.

After making a splendid impression in the early stages of the race the Alvis was put out of the running by a cracked cylinder. The photo on the left shows the car being pushed off the course after its retirement. (Inset) Cyril Paul and Urquhart Dykes, the drivers: a photo taken before the race started.

1930

The result of the 1929 race led to violent criticism of the passivity of the French motor industry in not entering Le Mans with cars which had a chance of winning on distance; but there was no sign that such criticism had been heeded for the 1930 race, indeed, if anything, the French interest was even less - of the 17 starters (the smallest-ever field) only three cars were French, two Tractas and a 1.5 litre Bugatti; the first time the Molsheim factory had been represented at Le Mans since 1923, and the first time a female crew- Mesdames Mereuse and Siko had been permitted to start in the race.

However, it is likely that the economic depression had affected manufacturers in general; the American entries were down to two Stutzes, but two important newcomers to the Sarthe circuit were Mercedes-Benz and Alfa Romeo, with one entry each. The race was still somewhat of a British, not to say Bentley, benefit: there were ten British cars entered, of which five were Bentleys. This year the Bentley entry came from two different stables, the factory team ran a trio of Speed Sixes led by Barnato and Kidston in 'Old Number One' which had won the 1929 race; they were supplemented by two supercharged 4½ litre 'Blower' Bentleys, from the team of the Hon. Dorothy Paget. Two Talbots from the British company were entered: 2.3 litre machines, their tall bonnets hiding Roesch's compact six-cylinder engines and they could easily be identified from their three closely-set headlamps. A Lea-Francis was the sole contestant in the 1½ litre class apart from a Bugatti, and finally there were two MG M-type Midgets, of the 'Double-Twelve' type which had won the team prize in the British equivalent of Le Mans, the Brooklands Double-Twelve hour race.

The race that unfolded proved to be a Mercedes-Bentley duel; the Stutzes were never really in the running, One car set itself on fire and the other broke its rear axle. Caracciola (whose co-driver was Werner) took the lead from the start in the Mercedes, but was passed on the fourth lap by Birkin in one of the blown Bentleys. In doing so Birkin shed a tyre tread and although he continued at first, the tyre ultimately burst forcing him to stop to change it. The other Bentleys continued the chase, after the first pit stop the Barnato/Kidston Speed Six was less than two minutes behind the Mercedes, and the two cars passed and re-passed each other several times as the evening wore on. Then, in the middle of the night, the Mercedes failed to restart after a pit stop; it seems the dynamo had stopped charging and the battery was flat, and of course Le Mans regulations forbade pushstarting as well as the use of a starting handle.

This left the Bentleys firmly in control of the race, if anything the two teams could indulge in some private sport but as it turned out, the 'Blower' Bentleys lived up to their reputation for mechanical unreliability and both had retired by midday Sunday. Lower down the scale, the Alfa Romeo driven by Lord Howe and Callingham challenged the pair of Talbots but was unable to pass either of them. Both the MG Midgets had retired, and in the end only nine cars finished, led home by the Barnato/Kidston Bentley which also took the Biennial Cup, its average speed was 75.876 mph and distance 1,821.02 miles. The Clement/Watney Bentley followed, then came the two Talbots and the Alfa Romeo; the Lea-Francis beat the Bugatti in the 1½ litre class, and the two Tractas rounded off the list, despite Gregoire in one of the Tractas getting stuck in the ditch on the last lap, getting free only just in time with a little unofficial help from the spectators standing by. The Index of Performance went to Talbot, and Birkin - before retiring pushed up the lap record to a remarkable 89.696 mph.

After this, their fifth victory, the Bentley works team retired from racing; indeed, the original Bentley company lasted only just another year, as the receiver was appointed in July 1931 and eventually control passed to Rolls-Royce. For three years a single Bentley was entered privately at Le Mans but without any success, and although a Rolls-Royce type Bentley put up an impressive performance in 1949 and 1950, it was not really competitive. The Bentley days were over on that June Sunday in 1930, but what a splendid final chapter in their saga.

Clement refuelling No. 2 with the five-gallon churns while a " plombeur " waits to put the seal on the radiator which has just been replenished.

1st and 2nd cross the Line. Kidston driving No. 4 and Clement No. 2.

The LE MANS 24-HOUR RACE

A Terrific Bentley-Mercedes Duel. Barnato and Kidston (Bentley) Cover the Greatest Distance. Talbots Win the Eliminating Race. Birkin (Bentley) Breaks all Records

(REPORT BY AEROPLANE)

Hindmarsh (Talbot) stops at the pits to make adjustments to his headlamps, meanwhile the others flash by in the glare of the lights.

LE MANS is fading rapidly into the blue distance astern. Below us is a patchwork pattern of tiny fields bounded by rows of spiky poplars, of orchards and rich red furrows. Roads wind like yellow ribbons across the sunny countryside. The noise is terrific, for it is too hot to wear a flying helmet, but our Gipsy Moth really does seem to be getting on with the job.

*   *   *

It has been a very wonderful weekend. The most exciting, the most thrilling race that has ever been run on the famous Sarthe circuit was held on Saturday and Sunday last, June 21st and 22nd, when some of the finest cars in the world were pitted against each other for the honour of winning the two Rudge-Whitworth cups—one for the highest speed, the other for excellence of performance on handicap.

This year the race took on an entirely fresh character. So far Bentleys have had it all their own way for a number of years. The result was that few foreign makes could be persuaded to race against them, and a sort of inferiority complex germinated in the minds of the French, although the race was held in their country.

" Why enter," they would ask, " when Bentleys are sure to win? They are unbeatable on the Sarthe circuit ! "

So when Rudolf Caracciola, a young and famous German driver, threw down the gauntlet by entering his white Mercédès his sporting challenge was taken up at once by the British. Six green Bentleys were entered : two teams of the finest water against a lone but formidable entry !

Elaborate Team Tactics.

Such is the reputation of the famous German marque for speed and stamina that elaborate team tactics were adopted by the two Bentley groups— the respective captains of the Bentley Motors, Ltd., team and the Hon. Dorothy Paget's racing stable. The only way to " crack up " the Mercédès, it was considered, was to make its drivers use the supercharger as much as possible, so Birkin and Chassagne, in a 4½-litre supercharged Bentley, and Barnato and Glen Kidston, in a Speed Six, took turns, all the first afternoon and evening, in luring the German on to unwise speeds. That the pace was positively killing was proved later, for in due course the Mercédès and both of the two supercharged Bentleys were obliged to retire.

Tyres played an unusual part in this race. One has got so used to expecting extraordinary mileages, even from tyres on racing cars, and in speed contests, that, in a modern road race over decently surfaced highways, one practically rules out the possibility of bursting a tyre or flinging off a tread.

Yet again and again last Saturday both types of Bentley engaged had tyre trouble whenever they started to travel really fast, so that they lost almost as much as they gained. It seemed as

Earl Howe (Alfa-Romeo) leading Lewis (Talbot) round the Pontlieue corner.

though it cost them a tyre each time they passed the Mercédès!

The extraordinary thing about it was, however, that the Mercédès had no trouble at all with tyres. Yet both marques were running on the same make of tyre!

The very real struggle going on all the time between the British and German cars kept the crowds out on the course, in vast numbers, until late at night. But when at length the Mercédès withdrew the interest evaporated very largely, so that Sunday morning seemed to bring fewer visitors to the course.

When Fate Intervened.

It seemed as if nothing more would happen, and that the Bentleys must inevitably form a procession unto the very end. But fate intervened, and at the 20th hour the two supercharged Bentleys both gave trouble and their drivers retired, and the new Talbots swung into second and third place.

It had been obvious, even the night before the race, that we were going to see the greatest race Le Mans has ever known. On the Friday night the heat had been terrific. We had turned in early to keep fresh for the event, yet all night through, at intervals of half an hour or so, we would wake up, sweltering, and listen to the endless horn-blowing, the interminable chatter and clinking of glasses from the cafés in the Place below.

Dawn came, then clear sunlight flooded the square. Sleep was out of the question. There were a thousand-and-one things to be done before the race. . . .

It was going to be a wonderful race. There was an electric quality in the air, for all the blazing heat of the morning. We knew quite definitely that we could not, would not, leave the pits during the night. So out we went, loading the staff Vauxhall with suitcases and coats and cameras and sketching materials, ready, when the job was done, to race to our waiting aeroplane and go roaring back to England. . . .

Mme. Mareuse and Mme. Siko, who successfully completed the course with their Bugatti.

The hours dragged by. An endless stream of vehicles brought thousands upon thousands of spectators to the great permanent grand-stands and the beflagged enclosures. A faint breeze blew down the course. Outside the gaily decorated pits stood 18 cars—only 18, but among them some of the finest and fastest the world has ever seen: Bentley, Mercédès, Stutz, Alfa-Romeo.

. . .

The sun blazed torridly down out of a sky flecked with small cumulus clouds. The drivers, wearing nothing at all under their overalls, stood, very tense, on the *tribunes* side of the road. M. Coquille, the donor of the Rudge-Whitworth cups, stood with a great yellow flag poised in mid air. Then, in the hush that always comes on these occasions, the flag dropped, there was a scamper of feet, and the drivers raced across to their waiting cars.

Caracciola First Away.

Who would be first away? Caracciola took a flying leap into the driving seat of his low, white Mercédès. Kidston, Davis and Clement slammed the doors and pressed the starter-buttons and the engines of their big Speed Six Bentleys burst into life. Almost together they were off, but the German car was just in front. "Tim" Birkin, who was really expected to set the pace for the race, got away between a brace of black American Stutz cars which were themselves trying to get clear of the throng. The off-side wheels of Birkin's 4½-litre supercharged Bentley churned the dust in the gutter as he tried to scrape by.

Clive Dunfee (No. 3 Bentley) charges and burrows deep into the sandbank at Pontlieue. The Lea-Francis is seen passing close to the palings, followed by another Bentley.

But he had to wait until the file had strung out a bit before he got where he wanted to be—close behind the Mercédès and the Bentley "Sixes," which had got a few yards start of him.

It was a magnificent sight to see the cars, their exhausts thundering, stringing out on the up-grade before the descent to Pontlieue.

Then came, in swift succession, messages from round the course. At Pontlieue, where there are two right-angle bends close together, Caracciola led, with Glen Kidston, S. C. H. Davis and F. C. Clement, in the three Big Bentleys, on his heels. At les Hunaudieres, by the famous Hippodrome Café, Davis had got into second place. At Mulsanne the order was the same, but on the S-bends Birkin, in the smaller Bentley, nipped into third place.

The Mercedes Leads.

In a riot of enthusiasm the leaders tore past the pits. One heard the shrill, sing-song wail of the Mercédès supercharger as the white car appeared, at incredible speed, from among the trees in the direction of Arnage. Some distance behind, but well within striking distance, two Bentleys roared side by side. On the last right-hand curve before the pits Birkin swung out, passed Kidston, and went shrieking after the fastest car in the race.

Then began a battle royal that thrilled to the backbone every man,

woman and child that clustered, close-packed, against the railings round the 10.2-mile circuit. Cost what it might, Birkin was going to make the Mercédès travel. He was going to force it to use the supercharger—which is engaged by means of a clutch—all the time, in the hope that the sorely-stressed mechanism would ultimately fail.

So down went his foot on the accelerator and he crept up and up, nearer and nearer to the German "ace." Caracciola averaged 87 m.p.h. for his second lap. Birkin immediately capped with a lap at 87.13 m.p.h.

The speeds were fantastic! On the wide, straight road before the Mulsanne corner the Bentley was right on

Glen Kidston and Woolf Barnato after their fine drive.

The fierce duel between Caracciola's Mercedes and Birkin's Bentley at the commencement of the race. Birkin, after passing the German car, bursts a tyre at the S-bend at Arnage. The tread had previously come off at Mulsanne, breaking the wing.

the white car's tail. Then down went Birkin's foot, and he shot past his adversary at 126 m.p.h.! What a car, and *what* a driver!

It was a tremendously dramatic moment when the 4½-litre four-cylinder British Bentley thundered past the pits only a few yards ahead of the gigantic German six-cylinder Mercédès. He had accomplished this lap, his fourth, at the incredible average speed of 89.66 m.p.h., thus beating handsomely even the lap record of the Sarthe circuit, set up recently by an out-and-out Bugatti racing car.

On the 5th lap Birkin still led, having covered 50 miles in only 35 minutes. But when he next tore past the immense grand-stand there were shouts of dismay from the crowd. His off-side rear tyre was in ribbons, pieces of rubber flying in all directions, the cord foundation whirling like a flail. Did he know it? How could he be told of his peril when he was already past, when he was shrieking down to the wicked Pontlieue corners at 120 m.p.h.?

Birkin v. Caracciola.

It was a sickening time of anxious waiting. It seemed an age before the mechanics in the Bentley pit slowly pushed a spare wheel and tyre to the very edge of the pit counter. Kensington Moir, the pit manager of Miss Paget's 4½-litre team, stood on the platform, a burly black-shirted figure, a great orange flag clutched in his hands. Caracciola came by first a lap later, and after what seemed an age, Birkin's car crawled in, a lame warrior, pitifully slowly. The driver sprang out and quickly set to and changed the wheel. He was off again in no time, but had lost a lap to the Mercédès car. He drove like the wind, using all the skill, all the experience at his command. The German driver, however, had "let up" a little. Now that he was no longer so closely threatened he could afford to spare his engine by using the supercharger less frequently.

But Birkin was after him. Soon afterwards, in a burst of cheering, he came round only 10¾ secs. behind, while

H. S. Eaton and Brian Lewis who were first in the eliminating race.

on the next lap he led the German by 5⅜ secs. They came together, these two astonishingly fast cars, with a little green M.G. Midget between them. On this exciting lap Birkin had been driving at 120 m.p.h., when there was a sudden crack like the bursting of a shell. Out of the corner of his eye he say half his off-side rear wing hurtling through the air, smashed off by a flying tyre tread. He kept on, however, passed the Mercédès in another amazing display of dash and skill, but the tyre could not last for long with the tread thrown completely off. At Arnage the tyre gave way, the Bentley turned completely round, and once again the Mercédès took the lead. When Birkin drew up at the pits on this occasion, however, Chassagne, his co-driver, took over the car. He started 3 mins. 40 secs. behind the German, made up 11 secs. on the next lap, but dropped back a little on the one after.

And so this individual "dog fight" between Bentley No. 9 and the Mercédès continued, but the tyres did not seem able to stand the speed and the hot weather. In the early hours of the race Birkin had to change four tyres, and the Mercédès none at all, so the drivers of the British car deserve every praise for their magnificent performance.

A Battle of the Giants.

While this battle of giants was progressing, however, an exciting incident occurred at Arnage. Philippe, driving a Stutz, took the S-bends apparently too fast, failed to make the last turn, and crashed at great speed into the bank For a moment the big black car was hidden under a cloud of earth, dust and small stones. Then its driver managed to reverse on to the road, tearing down branches and shrubs so that the car looked as if it had been decorated for a floral fête. He got off again in a matter of a few seconds, and then came round to the pits to examine the car for possible failures. A brief glance satisfied him that nothing was apparently amiss, but, alas! a broken axle later put the car out of the race.

The thrilling duel between the Mercedes driven by Caracciola and Werner and No. 4 Bentley piloted by Barnato and Kidston.

The two M.G. Midgets were acquitting themselves right manfully. For lap after lap, they came round, close together, always ahead of the bigger-engined front-drive Tractas. The two Talbots, too, were doing extraordinarily well, lapping steadily at about 72 m.p.h., and looking as if they might continue to do so for the whole of the 24 hours. The Lea-Francis was also going round very fast.

Both the Tractas, neat little front-drive two-seaters, with engines of 988 c.c. and 986 c.c. respectively, had a bit of bother with sparking plugs. They had been changing them only a minute or two before the start, and at about 5.40 p.m. on the Saturday they were both in at the pits, leaving again with engines spluttering—evidently not much improved.

The greatest joke was the 2-litre B.N.C. When the starter had dropped his flag and all the other cars had disappeared, it was seen stationary at its pit with a lot of very excited gentlemen trying to fill the petrol tank. When they had finished they tried to start the car, but without avail, so the driver retired before he had covered so much as a yard!

Owing to the bother they were having with tyres, Birkin and Chassagne, in Bentley No. 9, gradually dropped back, allowing Davis, on the Speed Six Bentley No. 3, to take second place. This position was occupied at about 6.30 p.m. by Davis when, having completed 20 laps he came in for replenishments and a change of drivers. His face was bleeding slightly, and the pair of Meyrovitch-Acetex goggles that hung round his neck were in a sad state.

A Narrow Shave.

When he was following the Mercédès at about 112 m.p.h. a stone thrown up by the back wheel of the latter car was flung straight into his right eye. Fortunately the goggles, although badly smashed, did not splinter, but several small fragments of glass did, in fact, get into his eye.

Bentley No. 3 was taken over from Davis by Clive Dunfee; he had a short but sweet career. Less than two

One of the successful Talbots, driven by Hindmarsh and Rose Richards, coming out of the bend at Pontlieue.

They are seen at the Arnage bend.

miles down the road he tried to round the Pontlieue corner much too fast, and crashed into a huge sandbank. The car was irrevocably ditched. The driver dug like a navvy for nearly two hours, the perspiration soaking his garments, without any apparent result. Then, wearily, he threw up the sponge and came back to the pits.

Presently a little, lonely figure detached itself from the confused background of the pits, and set off, at a steady purposeful jog-trot, up the hill towards Pontlieue. It was "Sammy" Davis off to see if *he* could dig out the car. We watched him disappear over the crest in the failing light, and it was nearly two hours before he returned, exhausted, having dug tons of sand away with a headlamp glass, which was just about as hopeless as trying to drain the North Sea with a teaspoon. Incidentally, he discovered that the front axle was irreparably bent and two wheels buckled. So that was that; and he returned to face cheerfully what we know to have been a bitter disappointment.

Wheel Changing.

At about the same time as Clive Dunfee buried his car, mole-fashion, in the sand, Glen Kidston dashed up to the pits. Rapidly the replenishments were effected and, when the last "plombeur" had jumped out of the way and Woolf Barnato was letting in the clutch, there was a howl of alarm from the public enclosure. The tread was entirely missing from the off-side rear tyre!

So out hopped Barnato, pushed a jack under the axle, hammered off the locking ring, and changed wheels. It was only then that Kidston remembered when he threw the tread. The car was so steady, he said, that he increased speed again and was driving well above the 100 m.p.h. mark without feeling that anything was amiss!

No sooner was Barnato away than Clement arrived. In 95 secs. the car was off again, having been refilled with petrol, oil and water, but not before there had been a veritable hue and cry for Dick Watney, who had got lost at

a highly inconvenient moment. And even then there was more excitement, while the general public gesticulated and pointed at the surplus oil drip tray which had been left by mistake beneath the sump. Clement told us that driving in the appalling heat was very hard work indeed, and the tar had melted on some of the bends, making braking rather a tricky business.

For a long time the Lea-Francis had been putting up a wonderful show. With a full four-seater body it had averaged 68.7 m.p.h. for the first two hours. Unfortunately, soon after 6 p.m., it came to rest at the roadside only about a quarter-mile from the pits. Twenty-seven precious minutes were wasted there, curing some elusive plug trouble, but eventually the car was got going again and proved as fast as ever.

The M.G. Midgets were going amazingly well. Sometimes averaging over 60 m.p.h. per lap, they were cornering faster than almost any of the other cars except the Mercédès. The French people were astounded at the performance of these little English cars, always a long way ahead of the larger-engined Tractas, holding the road splendidly, safe and fast.

Barnato Overhauls the Mercedes.

With Birkin falling back, Barnato pushed ahead on the Big Six Bentley, gaining steadily, until he was on the tail of the Mercédès. Then, at 8.26 p.m., amid tremendous cheers from British supporters, he came roaring past the pits some 50 yards ahead of the German car. On the next lap, however, by a very stout piece of work, Werner, who was driving, was again in front, with Barnato 100 yards astern and Clement, whose car was actually three laps behind him, sandwiched in between. A few minutes later, however, Werner came by again, his supercharger whining furiously, with Barnato only 6 secs. behind him!

What a race! And all the time those low, black Stutz were going round, unobtrusively, almost silently—a force to be reckoned with, maybe, later in the

Brisson and Rigal's Stutz followed by Neale and Hicks's M.G. Midget at the Arnage bend.

The hounding of the Mercedes. Caracciola is seen leading No. 4 Bentley, driven by Barnato, who is waiting to pass at the Hippodrome. On the left is Samuelson's M.G. Midget.

race, when speed must exact its toll and the slower but possibly more reliable cars creep up, and are still running, unharmed, when the sun rises on the second day's racing.

Amid all this fast, thrilling driving, a blue two-seater Bugatti—an apparently very ordinary sports car, driven in turn by two Frenchwomen, Mme. Mareuse and Mme. Siko—ran round and round with wonderful regularity. Everybody laughed at them; said they wouldn't last a lap. Yet lap after lap they came round, trouble free, safe. . . .

Then, at 9.47 on Saturday evening, the Mercédès appeared through the misty woods, the sun glinting redly on its narrow strip of windscreen. Right on its heels, ready to dart by the moment the opportunity arose, drove Barnato, magnificently holding his own.

For a moment there was peace. The flags on the grand-stand hung limp as rags in the windless air. Then a hard, thunderous exhaust came from Arnage way, and the Bentley roared across the open heath 7¼ secs. ahead of the German car. The Mercédès driver seemed to have the blower in action all the time now; his foot hard down, he tried not to lose more ground to the English "dreadnought" . . .

Almost unnoticed, because of the stirring Anglo-German duel in progress, Samuelson's M.G. Midget came into the pits for a little while, only to get off again very quickly.

Lord Howe, driving his blue Alfa-Romeo, came round lap after lap with Hugh Eaton on a Talbot, although actually the English car was two laps ahead. On handicap, as a matter of fact, the two cars were running almost equally, for the Italian engine, being supercharged, brought it almost on an equality with the larger but unsupercharged Talbot power unit.

At 9.1 p.m. there came an ominous announcement. No. 5, the Stutz which at that moment was being driven by Rigal, had burst into flames along the straight between the Hippodrome and Mulsanne. Looking over the trees in the direction mentioned we saw coils of black smoke rising into the tranquil evening sky, spreading out fanwise, as it grew in height. The ill-fated car

Peacock and Newsome's Lea-Francis at Arnage.

The American hope, a Stutz driven by Brisson and Rigal catches fire and is rendered hors de combat after putting up an excellent show. The car was practically destroyed.

continued to burn for the best part of an hour, and relays of fire-extinguishers were even sent round, several miles, in the official cars. In the end only a gaunt skeleton of twisted metal remained, but while the blaze was at its height many drivers actually found it extremely dazzling to drive past.

Only a minute after the announcement of the Stutz fire there was much animation in the Bentley camp.

Earl Howe (Alfa-Romeo) and Lewis (Talbot) at Mulsanne.

First, although No. 4 (Barnato and Kidston) Bentley still led, the Mercédès was only 2¾ secs. behind it. At the same moment Clement dashed up in a supercharged 4½-litre job and demanded a new tyre. Hardly had the new spare wheel been fitted when Chassagne also came into the pits, with the tread completely gone from the off-side rear tyre. As the car got away again, with Birkin at the wheel, from the pits there was a

great bang, a vivid red flash of flame from the exhaust and a dense puff of black smoke; enough to startle the onlookers, in all conscience, but signifying little except that the driver had not sufficient air pressure in the petrol tank.

Not long after this Barnato tore up to the pits. As he stopped there came a musical howl from behind and Werner swung out and shot past.

Barnato was not losing a second and Glen Kidston helped to the best of his ability. It was a lightning-like fill up, although petrol surged over the tonneau cover, so that it had to be scooped out with the bare hands before it was safe to start the car.

Soon afterwards it was No. 1, the giant Mercédès, which led, but only 2 mins. 38 secs. behind him came No. 4 Bentley.

At 9.10 p.m. on the Saturday Kindell, one of the drivers of an M.G. Midget, had to retire, and it was ultimately found that the cause was traceable to foreign bodies which found their way into the engine lubricating system.

An incident occurred when Brisson tried to protest against the fact that the Bentley wings were damaged as the result of the impact from the tyre treads flying off. We gathered eventually that the true reason for the withdrawal of Bentley No. 7 was due to the fuel causing overheating. After an enormous number of experiments it was finally

At Pontlieue—the Bugatti driven by Mme. Mareuse and Mme. Siko followed by the victorious Bentley and Lewis and Eaton's Talbot.

decided to use pure benzole, which necessitated raising the compression.

It was impossible, however, to effect the necessary alteration to all three cars, so that only Nos. 8 and 9 were able to start. Just after this the Mercédès No. 1 was due in at the pits and

Frau Caracciola, to make sure that there were no mistakes, herself saw to the arrangement of everything required.

It is extremely difficult to be awakened from a deep lumber to be put straight away on to driving a fast and powerful car. We happened to be

in the Talbot pit just when Brian Lewis had to be called in order to take over Hugh Eaton's car. He was fully alert immediately, however, and rapidly asked those questions which experience told him to be the most necessary.

At Mulsanne—Davis and Dunfee's Bentley leading from Barnato and Kidston's Bentley cond Earl Howe and Callingham's Alfa-Romeo.

The finish—the two leading Bentleys crossing the line.

"Tim" Rose Richards was the next to go, and exclaimed laughingly, "I never felt less like driving a car in my life."

"Oh! you'll soon get into it," was the cheery reply.

"That's just the trouble," laughed Rose Richards.

Eaton wandered across to talk to us. He had passed the Mercédès, he said, before the pits. It was going very slowly. Its lights, however, were switched fully on and gave a remarkably brilliant light. Eaton's surprise can be imagined, therefore, when only two or three laps later he heard that the reason why the Mercédès had retired from the contest was because the battery was completely run down.

We saw Werner standing before his pit, while a knot of officials gathered round, trying to find the real cause of the trouble, for the car could not be started away from the pits, either on the starter or even by pushing, which would in any case have entailed disqualification. According to Mr. Neubauer, the head of the racing department, this sudden discharging of the battery was due to a short circuit in the dynamo, which effectively drained the accumulator without putting in any more current.

An amusing incident occurred when Merton Neale, driving an M.G. Midget, slid right into the fence at Pontlieue, owing to the fact that the local inhabitants had scattered sand there to prevent skidding. The result was that he only skidded worse than ever, and was quite unable to straighten out the car before rounding the bend. When striking the wooden fence, Merton Neale reversed, taking it with him. So incensed was he, however, by this time that he seized the pieces of broken fence and threw them at the troops who were guarding the course!

Conditions in the afternoon altered. Rain descended in torrents, and the cars came shooting by in sheets of spray. Fortunately for them, however, the shower did not last long.

Ultimately, amid scenes of considerable enthusiasm, the Grand Prix of Endurance came to an end. There are in all nine competitors who are qualified to take part in the final for this event during the coming year.

Here the lone Bugatti is seen being passed by Newsome (Lea-Francis), Callingham (Alfa-Romeo) and Eaton (Talbot) at Arnage Corner.

THE EIGHTH GRAND PRIX D'ENDURANCE.

	Cars.	Drivers.	Kiloms.
1	Bentley	Barnato and Kidston	2930
2	Bentley	Clement and Watney	2832
3	Talbot	Lewis and Eaton	2651
4	Talbot	Hindmarsh and Rose Richards	2625
5	Alfa-Romeo	Howe and Callingham	2607
6	Lea-Francis	Peacock and Newsome	2291
7	Bugatti	Mareuse and Siko	2164
8	Tracta	Gregoire and Vallon	2105
9	Tracta	Bourcier and Debeugny	2013

Barnato and Kidston averaged 122.11 k.p.h., which is a record for the race.

THE SIXTH BIENNIAL RUDGE-WHITWORTH CUP. (FINAL.)

1	Bentley	Barnato and Kidston
2	Bentley	Clement and Watney
3	Tracta	Gregoire and Vallon
4	Lea-Francis	Peacock and Newsome

THE SEVENTH BIENNIAL CUP.

			Fig. of Merit.
1	Talbot	Lewis and Eaton	1.176
2	Bentley	Barnato and Kidston	1.172
3	Talbot	Hindmarsh and Richards	1.164
4	Alfa-Romeo	Howe and Callingham	1.156
5	Bentley	Clement and Watney	1.133
6	Tracta	Gregoire and Vallon	1.054
7	Lea-Francis	Peacock and Newsome	1.041
8	Bugatti	Mareuse and Siko	1.016
9	Tracta	Bourcier and Debeugny	1.009

SIDELIGHTS ON LE MANS

Why Only Five Bentleys Started—Why Not Brassards?—Talbot Dependability—The Mercedes Retirement—M.G. Misfortunes

The two surviving Bentleys, which respectively averaged 75.8 m.p.h. and 73.3 m.p.h. for 24 hours, finishing together at Le Mans.

LE MANS this year provided more thrills than it has ever done in the past. Indeed, I am not sure that it was not the most exciting race of any kind to be held for at least five years.

The journalist's bugbear, lack of space, together with the need for getting to press with the report of the Le Mans race as fast as was humanly possible, prevented me from crowding in the stories of many incidents which went to make the race the wonderful event that it was.

* * *

Some may wonder why No. 7, the supercharged 4½-litre Bentley, which was to have been driven by Harcourt Wood and Jack Dunfee, did not start. The official story was that the car was being saved for the Belgian 24-hour race at Spa, which starts on Saturday next, July 5th.

There is no doubt that all three supercharged Bentleys would have taken part in the race had they been ready in time. The real trouble was that the fuel used, together with the intensely hot weather, caused a certain amount of overheating. The Bentleys were not the only cars to be affected in this way and much last-minute work of a more or less severe nature had to be carried out on several other competitors' cars.

After unsuccessful experiments with a mixture of petrol and benzole, it was decided that pure benzole would have to be used. The results were still not altogether satisfactory, so at the last moment the compression on the other two supercharged Bentleys was raised. This meant all-night work for the loyal band of mechanics, and it was utterly

impossible to complete the work on No. 7 in time, so that it was finally decided to keep this car for the great Belgian event.

* * *

In marked contrast to the tyre trouble experienced by the Bentleys, the Talbot cars ran right through the race on one set of tyres. Even after 1,646 miles at an average of 68.6 m.p.h. all four Dunlops on the Talbots looked as new as they were at the start. The Mercédès, also using Dunlops, had no tyre trouble, so why the Bentley cars should have had so much trouble is a mystery that is at present engaging the attention of the Dunlop technical staff.

Wonderful Reliability.

The bonnet was never lifted, throughout the race, on No. 4, the winning Bentley—a wonderful testimony to the engine's reliability.

* * *

The Automobile Club de l'Ouest, as usual, deserve the fullest possible marks for the organization of the race. Everything was carefully thought out, scrupulously effected. The Press arrangements, too, were masterly. But why, oh, why! should there be this mania for paper badges and tickets? In the old days of coloured brassards the police and marshals could see at a glance to what privileges one was entitled. But now it is a question of ticket-punching every time one passes through a gate or over a foot-bridge, even though one passed over twice a minute! Let us have brassards, messieurs, in future!

* * *

Everyone will sympathise with Carac-

ciola and Werner for having been put out of the race because of exhausted batteries. At the same time, it should be realized that there may have been other reasons for the car's failure. It is known that the brakes were rapidly losing in efficiency, for whereas at the beginning of the race the Mercédès drivers could leave braking until much later than the big Bentleys, as the hours went by the Germans had to apply their brakes when much farther from the corners than the British car drivers.

Moreover, Hugh Eaton, driving a Talbot, actually passed the Mercédès on one part of the course. The German car was travelling very slowly, but its lights were unmistakably excellent. The Mercédès had also caused anxiety owing to the flickering of the oil-gauge needle. It is worth noting that when the Mercédès engine could no longer be set in motion by its starter, an attempt was made to start the car by pushing both forwards and backwards without success. As the car was too heavy to push off the course, it was abandoned outside the Mercédès pit.

* * *

The wonderful success of the Talbots in finishing first and third in the eliminating race for the seventh biennial cup delighted everybody. That these two cars, with engines of only 2,276 c.c. and comfortable four-seater bodies, could run with such faultless reliability for the whole of the 24 hours excited everybody's admiration. Where they get their speed from is a mystery which only Mr. Roesch, the talented designer of the cars, can solve.

Although at first it appeared as though the real excitement of the race had evaporated when the Mercédès retired, a considerable amount of excitement was still reserved for those in the know. After running second on handicap for a long time, the Talbot driven by Brian Lewis and Hugh Eaton actually got into first place on handicap. With only an hour to go before the end of the race, a whole lap was lost owing to the advertising transfers off the petrol tins having got mixed with the petrol and coagulated in the filter, so that there was a petrol shortage on full throttle. This allowed No. 4 Bentley, driven by Woolf Barnato and Glen Kidston, to resume the lead on handicap, but by really stout driving the Talbot was once more brought to the lead with a figure of merit only .004 higher than that of the Bentley. The Talbots, by the way, were privately entered and run by that very sporting concern Fox and Nicholl, Ltd., Tolworth Service Station, Kingston By-pass, Surrey, and not by their manufacturers.

*   *   *

Much hilarity was caused by the enterprise of a local photographer in Le Mans, who took snapshots with a kind of reckless abandon, attributing to his portraits quite incorrect names. Thus, a singularly bad photograph of Mrs. Lionel Martin was purported to represent Miss Paget, while an equally bad picture of Saunders Davies, one of the M.G. Midget team, was labelled as "le constructeur Bentley."

Everybody was sorry when the gallant M.G. Midgets were put out of the race, after one had run for about five hours and the other for twelve hours.

The two M.G. Midgets which ran so well at Le Mans rounding the Pontlieue corners.

Both stoppages were due to lubrication troubles, and in the case of the car driven by Samuelson and Kindell a piece of insulating tape was found blocking the oil filter. Foul play was suspected when Rex Mundy, the K.L.G. representative, recalled that he had himself taped four high-tension leads, and pointed out that the piece of tape in the filter had quite evidently been removed from one of the high-tension leads.

Although one has every sympathy with the crews of the two Midgets, one cannot help feeling that they would have been wise if they had confined their use of the cars purely to the practice periods. They were, practically speaking, the only cars competing in the race which were driven about the town on ordinary hack jobs and which were left unattended for quite considerable periods. Had the cars been locked up and guarded when not being used they could have come to no harm.

*   *   *

We have received a letter from M. E. H. Brisson, referring to a passage in *The Motor* report of the Le Mans race, in which it was stated that he tried to protest against the Bentleys because their wings were damaged and no longer complied with the regulations.

M. Brisson states that neither he nor any member of the Stutz équipe or pit staff tried to make any protest against any make of car either before, during, or after the race. GRAND VITESSE.

FLYING BACK WITH THE REPORT

An Excellent Journey from Le Mans by Gipsy Moth

THIS year, for the third time. *The Motor* report of the great Le Mans 24-hour race was brought back from the scene of the contest in a De Havilland Moth aeroplane. Altogether, we have used aeroplanes on six occasions for getting back in a hurry from Le Mans to London, but some of the machines have been of much greater power.

The machine used this year was a Gipsy Moth, supplied by Messrs. Brian Lewis and C. D. Barnard, Ltd., the aircraft specialists, of 30, Conduit Street, London, W.1. It had already seen considerable service, as it was formerly the property of Mr. H. S. Eaton. It was a coincidence that Mr. Brian Lewis and Mr. H. S. Eaton were co-drivers in the victorious Talbot which won the 7th Rudge-Whitworth cup eliminating race.

The machine was flown over on the morning of the race by Mr. Bamber, who parked it with various other aircraft under the lea of the barrack buildings on one side of the great sandy expanse used for a parade ground. This year a body of bright young men wearing coloured armlets and waving flags efficiently marshalled the crowds and saw to the safe departure of the machines. They were members of the Aero Club du Mans. Incidentally, they saw to the filling up of our petrol tank some hours prior to our departure.

Immediately after the race we drove as fast as we could to the parade ground, Mr. Bamber started up the engine and soon after 5 p.m. on the Sunday afternoon we were circling over Le Mans, gaining height. It was interesting to see the streams of traffic blocking every road leading from the circuit to Le Mans. Soon we were away over open country, cruising with the engine throttled down at an air speed of about 75 m.p.h. Owing to a strong following wind, however, we were actually making more than 100 m.p.h. Approaching Rouen, we flew some miles to the right as there were wild jagged clouds betokening a storm low over the old French city.

For some time we flew in company with one of the Imperial Airways Handley Page machines, so close that we could see the faces of the occupants of the air liner. Presently we saw another machine ahead and when we landed at St. Inglevert to clear Customs at about 7.40 p.m. we found two big air liners and a small monoplane already on the ground. The pilot, who had a splitting headache, here rushed off on a bicycle to try and get some aspirin. He nearly came to an untimely end, however, as, when halfway down an extremely steep hill he discovered the cycle had no brakes! By being very clever with his foot on the front tyre, however, he managed to avert disaster and returned in time to resume the flight.

The remainder of the journey across the Channel and over Kent was without incident, but was actually the most interesting section of the whole flight, as the country was more familiar to us. Finally we landed at Heston Aerodrome at about 9 p.m.. having had a thoroughly enjoyable trip.

As on previous occasions, we found the Gipsy Moth a thoroughly comfortable, fast and dependable machine.

PROVED ON ROAD & TRACK

BRITISH DOUBLE-TWELVE HOUR RACE

LE MANS

Behind every Bentley is a series of racing triumphs without precedent in the annals of motoring. No other car has been so thoroughly proved in international events on road and track. The extensive and valuable experience gained in these strenuous tests is utilised to the full in the production of all Bentley models, resulting in an ever-increasing degree of reliability and safety.

AUTOMOBILE CLUB DE L'OUEST DE LA FRANCE

THE EIGHTH GRAND PRIX D'ENDURANCE
24-HOURS INTERNATIONAL ROAD RACE
LE MANS JUNE 21st & 22nd, 1930

1ST 6½ LITRE BENTLEY
at 76·31 m.p.h., covering 2,930 Kilometres.
(RECORD FOR THE COURSE).

2ND 6½ LITRE BENTLEY
at 73·08 m.p.h., covering 2,830 Kilometres.
Also Winners of the Rudge-Whitworth Cup.

Won for the fifth time—four times consecutively—by BENTLEY
(Subject to official confirmation)

BENTLEY

BENTLEY MOTORS LIMITED
POLLEN HOUSE, CORK STREET, LONDON, W.1   'Phone: REGENT 6911.   'Grams: "BENMOTLIM, PHONE, LONDON."
NORTHERN SALES DEPOT: 3, SANDYFORD ROAD, NEWCASTLE-ON-TYNE.   WORLD EXPORTERS: ROOTES, LTD., PICCADILLY, W.1

The thunder of the 1930 Bentleys as the Speed Six cars driven by Davis and Dunfee (3) and Barnato and Kidston sweep into Mulsanne corner followed by Earl Howe and Callingham's Alfa Romeo.

BENTLEYS at LE MANS

by Grande Vitesse

IT is probably true to say that no other single race has put British sports cars into world headlines so often or with greater prestige than the classic Twenty Four Hours Grand Prix of Endurance organized by the Automobile Club de l'Ouest on their famous diamond-shaped circuit outside Le Mans, in the Department of the Sarthe.

This competition, as long as eight Grands Prix of modern times, with twice the number of cars competing than we normally see on a Formula I starting grid, captured and retained public interest in every motoring country from its inception as a daring innovation in 1923. Not even the tradition of the Tourist Trophy nor the high drama of the Mille Miglia, nor battles on the long curves of Spa or the wild ride through the Eifel mountains at Nürburgring have dimmed the peculiar lustre which surrounds the words "Le Mans."

To many enthusiasts of the present day who, it suddenly dawns on me, never saw Brooklands or Donington, Le Mans 24 Hours means "Jaguar"—victor in 1951, 1953 and the three years running—'55, '56 and '57, three times at record speed and twice at well over 100 m.p.h. But to those whose interest in motor racing goes back even a generation, the race will always be irrevocably linked with the magic name "Bentley"—the first British marque to explode into startled headlines as a leading sports model in a world accustomed to Bugatti, Darracq, Delage, Lorraine, Mercedes, Alfa Romeo, Fiat and the rest of that great fraternity.

In the years when W. O. Bentley's creations were in active production, they won the race five times—and four years in a row. The day when the name passed into the keeping of Rolls-Royce Ltd., many were the enthusiasts who mourned the inevitable evolutions of commerce within the industry.

In the early years the circuit was very different from the one raced on these days. It was two miles longer—about 10¾ miles round—rough and stoney in places, alarmingly narrow by modern standards, and went down from the pits to Pontlieue hairpin among the houses on the outskirts of the city, thus extending the Mulsanne Straight which is the main road to Tours by about a mile, with an uphill start after Pontlieue. The far end of the Straight, the right-angle turn just short of Mulsanne village, was then surrounded by pinewoods which were razed during the war for the making of a concentration camp. Farther

along towards Arnage Corner—the Old Esses—the road was cobbled—hence the name "Indianapolis Corner" which has stuck ever since.

A few years later the course was changed again, cutting out Pontlieue hairpin by means of a lane which ran past garden fences and allotments to join the Mulsanne Straight. Later still, the club purchased land and constructed the curling road which leads through the New Esses to the straight at Tertre Rouge, thus shortening the circuit still·more to its present 8.4 miles. And of course, the even more recent modifications have entirely changed the general appearance of the area surrounding the pits and grandstands. Perhaps the greatest change that the pre-war drivers would notice apart from the fine width and surface is the easing of the approach to the famous White House corner, about a mile and a half from the pits, a bend which is now taken by many drivers at well over 100 m.p.h. but which, in the old days, could not be attempted at much above 90 m.p.h.

A glance at the record reveals at once the indelible stamp the majestic green Bentleys left on the race: 1923—Lagache and Leonard (2.9 Chenard-Walcker), 57.07 m.p.h. 1924—Duff and Clement (3.0 Bentley), 53.78 m.p.h. 1925—De Courcelles and Rossignol (3.5 Lorraine), 57.72 m.p.h. 1926—Bloch and Rossignol (3.5 Lorraine), 65.98 m.p.h. Then:

1927—Dr. Benjafield and Sammy Davis (3.0 Bentley), 61.35 m.p.h., with a car crumpled and hardly steerable after smashing into the pile of cars during the night at White House. 1928—Woolf Barnato and Bernard Rubin (4.5 Bentley), 69.1 m.p.h. 1929—Barnato and Sir Henry Birkin (6.5 Bentley), 73.6 m.p.h. leading three more

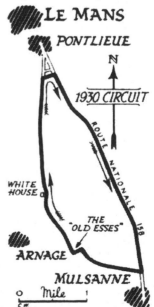

LE MANS
PONTLIEUE
N
1930 CIRCUIT
ROUTE NATIONALE 158
WHITE HOUSE
THE "OLD ESSES"
ARNAGE
MULSANNE
0   Mile   1

Hare and hounds—but not as planned by Bentley. Caracciola streaks away from his starting position at the head of the line-up while the Bentleys roar in pursuit of the white German car.

BENTLEYS
at LE MANS

Bentleys home in line ahead. 1930—Barnato for the third time, and Glen Kidston (6.5 Bentley), 75.9 m.p.h. And after that the firm raced no more.

A point of interest, by the way, is that in the old days the race was on handicap-formula which, then as now, stipulated a given number of laps to be covered according to the size of the engine. The main award, the Rudge-Whitworth Cup, went to the car which exceeded its set distance by the greatest margin. There were class prizes as well, and a somewhat secondary prize for the drivers who covered the greatest distance of all. These days the limelight centres on the speed irrespective of category rather than on the handicap race, although equal prizes are given for each. Nor is the Rudge Cup still in competition. As a matter of fact it reposes in the offices of the British Racing Drivers Club in London.

Moreover, all the cars had to be catalogued models open to sale in the normal way, with very few modifications permitted, but there was no limitation on the size of car that could be entered. As in the very early days of French motor racing, all spares and tools had to be carried on the cars all the time, except for supplementary spare wheels which could be held in the pits.

The Le Mans car of between the two wars presented a picture beloved to this day by true enthusiasts. High off the ground, close-up mudguards, great radiators and huge head-lamps, all protected by wire-mesh grilles against the constantly flying stones when one car overtook another, four-seater bodies with hoods and tonneau covers over the unoccupied seats, and in most cases great twin horns on the front dumb-irons to clear the way through slower traffic. And of all of them, probably the most imposing was the massive Big Six Bentley, stately and gleaming in its British green with an unostentatious Union Jack on the side.

I quote Tim Birkin: "There can be no praise allowed this firm without recalling the man whose name it bears—W. O. Bentley (or, to give him the title by which he is best known, "W.O."). He is the finest team manager I have ever driven under; he controls his cars as if they were toy trains and he was manoeuvring them with levers in the pits. He moves them forward or pulls them back at will, by a special arrangement of signals, and Heaven help the driver who disobeys him. For "W.O.", in ordinary conversation quiet and oysterlike, has as sharp an edge to his tongue as a piqued prima donna. He is quite impassive; if a team of 20 of his glorious cars either came in the first 20 places or crashed in the first 20 minutes he would be equally

unruffled; and yet he has a generous nature and gives more help to the drivers who want it than any other man in the sport. On those who ask sincerely for his aid, he bestows it without resting, and in return his word is law, his frown almost a social barrier to its recipients, and his smile something to live on for days." A great tribute from the greatest British driver of his time.

In my mind if there was one more outstanding Bentley triumph than another, it was the 24 Hours of 1930. In that year the Hon. Dorothy Paget, a wealthy lady well known on the Turf, purchased Birkin's two 4½-litre blown Le Mans Bentleys in order to keep them in racing, his famous single-seater Brook-lands car, and added another to the string. Then it became known that Rudolf Caracciola, the Mercedes champion who in his career won more races than any other driver, was entering a car for the race to break up the monotonous succession of Bentley victories if he could.

Practice week started off badly for the Paget-Birkin Bentleys. One car had big-end trouble, another flung its flywheel into the hedge, and the mechanics had no leisure. Even the imperturb-

The duelling pair, Mercedes with co-driver Werner at the wheel in this picture, and the Barnato-Kidston Bentley rush together into Arnage.

Down the narrow, fenced road into Pontlieue the victorious Bentley and the handicap-winning Talbot driven by Brian Lewis and H. S. Eaton prepare to overtake the Bugatti driven by Mmes. Mareuse and Siko.

able "W.O." betrayed faint signs of lack of serenity. The headlamps pointed awry, the engines were running hot on the stipulated fuel mixture. Before practice finished, therefore, Birkin and "W.O." hatched a plot to run their cars as a single united team against the Mercedes.

The German car, which they knew would be superbly handled, was faster outright and, with its screaming blower that came in when the driver put his foot down to full throttle, faster on acceleration. It was therefore a part of the plot to raise the compressions of two blown 4½-litre cars and run on the only permitted alternative fuel, pure benzole. This, it was calculated, would produce even more speed than the 7½-litre eight-cylinder Mercedes, but, as they well knew, was going to stress the engines to the limit of reliability.

The obvious Mercedes strategy was to hound the Bentleys until the last few laps and then, using all its power and with supercharger fully in use, to slash past and win. The counter-measure was to send a Bentley out in front from the start, fully extended, to lure the Mercedes driver to lap just that little bit faster than he liked, and if one Bentley blew up, to signal another to take its place until sooner or later, either they ran out of Bentleys or the Mercedes ran out of breath. A more exciting proposition can hardly be imagined.

Birkin, chosen as the man to make the running, thought so in a big way, although he was apprehensive about his tyres in the

blazing heat of that June day. The works Bentley drivers had been warned to let Birkin past, for the Mercedes was at the head of the starting line, Birkin at the far end. As there were only seventeen actual starters, in contrast with the present-day field of 60-odd, the problems of overtaking were appreciably reduced, and with the usual fall-out of some 50% of starters, the last few laps should find a car only every few miles.

Kidston (6½-litre Bentley to be shared with Woolf Barnato himself) was chasing the Mercedes down Mulsanne Straight before Birkin could get within striking distance, but Kidston waved him on after Arnage, and as he came roaring up past the pits, he could see Caracciola's dust cloud ahead. As he flashed past the row of pits which look so like a street of shops, Birkin glimpsed signal boards shown to the German, and, as the Mercedes rushed on at undiminished speed, he deduced they were not signals to slow down ; in which case, he thought, their plot might work. . . .

Birkin made his great effort on the Mulsanne straight on the third lap, averaging 88 m.p.h. Grimly he closed on the dust cloud through which he could now see the white Mercedes thundering along, its supercharger emitting that famous high-pitched wailing which meant Caracciola was on full bore. Then, as Birkin pulled over to pass, there was a bang, a rear tread stripped, mangling its mudguard, but he pressed on. Caracciola, oblivious of the challenge, was somewhat in the middle of the road. Birkin passed with two wheels on the grass at 125 m.p.h. and both drivers changed down, slammed on the brakes for the Mulsanne corner, juddering and snaking.

Caracciola afterwards said he hadn't the slightest idea anyone was within sight of him until he suddenly saw Birkin go rocketting past in a shower of dust and stones with a bald strip on the rear wheel, and was considerably shaken thereby.

Birkin lost the complete tread but raced on, although the chaps in the pits were dancing up and down and spectators were screaming and pointing. On the next lap, however, coming out of Arnage, the Bentley swayed madly and slid sideways. The tyre had collapsed, and as the Mercedes tore past again, Birkin trundled to the pits. Sammy Davis was signalled forward, over-took Glen Kidston and went after the Mercedes, lying second in the race for the next 130 miles, Birkin back in seventh position, and still having treads flying off. But Caracciola could not slow down without losing his lead, a Bentley on his tail hour after hour.

The sun set, twilight turned to night and still the battle went on. Caracciola was relieved by Werner, Birkin by "Chass" Chassagne, that wily old hand, Davis by Clive Dunfee and Bentley's chairman, "Babe" Barnato took over from Kidston and held second place with the Big Six. The Mercedes change of driver and refuelling stop was slow and with Werner on board, the car was not going at Caracciola's pace; Barnato was

closing in. Birkin sat in the pits fidgeting; Dunfee was overdue. Dunfee was down at Pontlieue frantically trying to dig the Bentley out of a sandbank—as so often happens, on his first lap after taking over, he had misjudged his corner. Dunfee panted back to the pits in despair, but Sammy Davis went off at once to spend the next hour digging with a headlamp glass until he uncovered the front axle and found it hopelessly bent.

The order now was Mercedes-Bentley-Bentley-Bentley-Stutz-Stutz-Bentley. Then one of the American Stutz caught fire and blazed at the roadside, leaving little room for the passing cars.

Soon after dark Barnato passed the Mercedes. Then Caracciola took over again and regained the lead. About 9.30 Barnato passed him again. Two hours later Caracciola went by yet again for half an hour. Barnato repassed. Caracciola held him for a few laps and then overtook. Two laps later the Bentley slammed by again and came to the pits for the routine stop. Almost at the same moment the Mercedes came in to its pit close by, and it was observed that the German car needed a great deal of oil. The gauge was flickering. Birkin restarted first but, as he accelerated from the pit area, the Mercedes shrieked past. An hour later its headlights were dimming and blinking, and as the Bentley swept into the lead once more, Caracciola was at the pits. The batteries were flat, and what was worse than the dead headlights, the starter would not turn the engine. The dynamo had packed up. After dominating the race for ten hours, the Mercedes was out. And whether the five Bentleys had indeed harried it to its fate is still hotly debated.

The Bentleys at once took command of the race in one-two-three order and eased their speed.

The Bentley-Mercedes duel naturally was the principal focus of interest, but behind them great racing was going on. The entries included Brisson and Parke with two 5.3 Stutz (American), four Spanish Nacional Pescara (one of which I remember at Shelsley Walsh driven by Juan Zanelli, now Lord Essendon) with a 2.3 Talbot and Tim Rose-Richards and Johnny Hindmarsh with another (British cars designed by Georges Roesch), two Alvis which were scratched, a 2-litre B.N.C., a 2-litre Scotsman-S.A.R.A., Lord Howe and Leslie Callingham (1,752 Alfa Romeo), Sammy Newsome and Kim Peacock (1500 Lea Francis), Jack Hicks and Murton-Neale (850 M.G. Midget), F. H. B. Samuelson (now Sir Francis) on another, and Madame Mareuse and Madame Siko with a 1500 Bugatti, who took the grins off everybody's face by their steady driving. Two 980 c.c. front-drive Tractas replaced the Alvis entries, but could get nowhere near the M.G.s, which averaged 60 m.p.h., until one went into the fence at Pontlieue (and out again) because over-zealous spectators had sprinkled sand on melting

Large American and small British contenders leave Arnage corner: Brisson and Rigal's 5.3-litre Stutz and the Neale-Hicks 850 c.c. M.G. Midget.

tar. One M.G. retired after five hours, the other after twelve, both with lubrication trouble. In one oil filter they found insulating tape which gave rise to the rumour that there was sabotage (the cars were driven around the town and parked during the days before the race).

The Talbots made a deep impression, lapping at around 72 m.p.h. and second on Index of Performance handicap to Barnato's Speed Six. A few hours from the end the Eaton-Lewis Talbot took the handicap lead, lost it at 3 p.m. with fuel blockage, and regained it in the last few laps by the bare margin of 0.004 marks. The Talbots were private entries.

BENTLEYS DOWN THE YEARS

1924: 3-litre car driven by John Duff and F. C. Clement, won the race, at 53.8 m.p.h. Lone entry.
1925: Two 3-litre models entered. One ran out of fuel before the permitted minimum distance had been reached, the other caught fire (float chamber broke).
1926: Three 3-litre models. One remained fast in a ditch when second in the race with 20 minutes to go, the others had minor mechanical trouble and retired.
1927: Two 3-litre cars, one 4½-litre. The latter and a 3-litre were involved in the White House multiple pile-up. The survivor won the race (Benjafield and Davis) at 61.3 m.p.h.
1928: Three 4½-litre cars. Barnato and Rubin won at 69.1 m.p.h. Another retired, the third lost much time with a flat tyre and finished within qualifying time by dint of very fast laps.
1929: Barnato and Birkin (Speed Six) won at 73.6 m.p.h., 4½-litre cars second, third and fourth in general category, first and second in the Rudge Cup (handicap).
1930: 1st (6½-litre Speed Six) at 75.8 m.p.h. (Barnato and Kidston): 2nd, 6½-litre at 73.9 m.p.h. One-two for the Biennial Cup.

LE MANS 1930

RESULTS

8th Grand Prix of Endurance (Distance)

1	Barnato—Kidston (6.6 Bentley) 75.9 m.p.h. (record)	1,819.5 miles
2	Clement—Watney (6.6 Bentley)	1,818.7 miles
3	Eaton—Lewis (2.3 Talbot)	1,646.3 miles
4	Hindmarsh—Rose Richards (2.3 Talbot)	1,630 miles
5	Lord Howe—Callingham (1.7 Alfa Romeo)	1,618.9 miles
6	Peacock—Newsome (1.5 Lea Francis)	1,422.7 miles
7	Mmes Mareuse—Siko (1.5 Bugatti)	1,343.8 miles
8	Grégoire—Vallon (998 Tracta)	1,305.6 miles
9	Boucier—Debeugny (996 Tracta)	1,248.5 miles

7th Biennial Cup 1930-31 (Handicap)

1	Eaton—Lewis (Talbot)	1.176 fig. merit
2	Barnato—Kidston (Bentley)	1.172
3	Hindmarsh—Richards (Talbot)	1.164
4	Lord Howe—Callingham (Alfa Romeo)	1.156

6th Biennial Cup 1929-30

1 Barnato—Kidston (Bentley).
2 Clement—Watney (Bentley).
3 Gregoire—Vallon (Tracta).

As "old number one" Bentley, carrying the number 4, crosses the line to win Clement and Watney's Speed Six draws alongside to make it a team finish.

1931

There was a marked contrast between the line-up of cars for the 1931 race and those that had gone before. There were fewer works teams, and more private entries and even if there were remembrances of the past in the form of single entries of Bentley, La Lorraine and Stutz, more importance attached to the presence of works teams from Bugatti (three 4.9 litre Type 50s, managed by Jean Bugatti) and Alfa Romeo (three 8C-2300s, a brand new model that had made its first appearance in the Mille Miglia two months previously; although only two came to the start). Most important among the bigger cars was an SSK-type Mercedes similar to the one that had been entered in 1930; it was the only German car, while two Chryslers represented America. Apart from the privately entered Bentley, British hopes centred on two three-litre Talbots, and among the smaller cars were three 1½ litre Aston Martins and a brace of supercharged C-type MG Midgets. A perhaps unlikely entry was a lone 2.6 litre Arrol-Aster complete with sleeve valves, the only time a Scottish-built car has contested the race, but its performance hardly compared with that of the Ecurie Ecosse cars 25 years later. But it was encouraging that a total of 26 cars started, and for the French more encouraging still that the Bugatti works team held out the prospect of victory.

With such hopes riding on the three black Bugattis, it is difficult to understand the reason for the events that followed. If, as has been claimed, the Bugatti's tyres had already proved unreliable, and further misadventures had occurred in practice with treads being lost at high speed, it is surprising that the tyres were not changed altogether - one wonders whether national pride played a role, as the Bugattis rode on Michelin and to change to a non-French make of tyre would undoubtedly entail a loss of face. In any case, as Dumont has argued, the road holding and the stability of the Type 50 were hardly sufficient for its top speed of 112 mph. But whatever the real reasons, ostensibly it was the tyre problem which caused Bugatti's difficulties at Le Mans: first the Chiron/Varzi car threw a tread; then, at 6.30 pm, the tread of the left rear tyre wound itself round the brake drum of the car being driven by Maurice Rost. He went off the road, hitting several spectators of whom one was killed and several injured. Rost was thrown clear and badly injured; he never raced again. The car was a complete wreck. Chiron's car lost another tread, and Jean Bugatti decided to withdraw the remaining two team cars. This was not Bugatti's year: two privately entered cars retired and the women's team, Mesdames Mereuse and Siko, were disqualified for re-fuelling too early.

This left the race between the Alfa Romeos, the Mercedes-Benz and the Talbots. One of the Alfa Romeos crashed, and one of the Talbots retired with a cracked chassis. But the remaining Alfa Romeo, driven by Lord Howe and Sir Henry Birkin, was the first car home, at an average of 78.13 mph and a total distance of 1,875.1 miles - a fraction over the 3,000 km barrier which was broken for the first time in the history of Le Mans. Howe and Birkin took the 'triple crown' by also winning the Index, and the Biennial Cup. They were followed by the big Mercedes-Benz driven by Iwanowski and Stoffel; Iwanowski put up the fastest lap but failed to break Birkin's 1930 record. The surviving Talbot was third, and this was amazingly enough followed by the ancient La Lorraine. Only two more cars finished, an Aston Martin and a 1.1 litre Caban; this was the smallest number of cars ever to have finished at Le Mans. One of the MGs finished but was not classified; it had broken a piston but managed to keep going, but took more than the permitted 30 minutes to complete the final lap.

The first victory for Italy, and for Alfa Romeo, brought congratulations from Mussolini; yet both drivers were British and experienced veterans from the Bentley team; indeed, it was Sir Henry Birkin's second win.

BRITISH DRIVERS' WIN AT LE MANS

Earl Howe and Sir Henry Birkin Break all Records and Average 78.13 m.p.h. with an Alfa-Romeo and Win the Grand Prix d'Endurance and Rudge-Whitworth Cup. Mercedes-Benz Second, Talbot Third, Lorraine Fourth, and Aston-Martin Fifth. A Wonderful Race Marred Only by a Fatal Accident. Bugatti Official Team Withdrawn. Full Report by Aeroplane

Sir Henry Birkin with the winning supercharged Alfa-Romeo at Pontlieue. With his co-driver Earl Howe he averaged 78.13 m.p.h.

LORD HOWE and Sir Henry Birkin showed what British drivers could do when they won the Grand Prix d'Endurance and Rudge-Whitworth Cup at Le Mans last Sunday, June 14th. Driving in turn an Italian straight-eight 2½-litre Alfa-Romeo, they not only made the fastest time of the day but won the trophy for the best performance on handicap.

It was a wonderful race. For the first few laps it was a close fight between a giant Mercedes-Benz car, the new big Bugattis, and the almost equally new straight-eight Alfa-Romeos, with the London-built Talbots very close rivals. Then a fatal accident, coupled with serious tyre trouble, caused the withdrawal of the official Bugatti team. The Alfa-Romeos and the Talbots then set about the Mercedes, which, for various reasons, mostly the "throwing" of its tyre treads, lost speed progressively and only regained it towards the end after fitting a tyre of British make.

The number of non-finishers was very great, which testifies to the severity of the event. The early promise of a big proportion of the nine British cars finishing intact was, unfortunately, not realized, for a Talbot, a Bentley, an M.G. Midget, an Aston-Martin, and an Arrol-Aster had to retire in the closing stages. All the American cars failed to cover even 20 laps, while six French cars and one Italian were withdrawn for one reason or another.

Many of those that fell by the wayside put up a game fight. All through

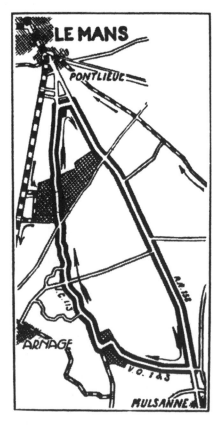

Sketch map of the circuit.

the race one could almost afford to ignore the handicap characteristic of the event and consider it as a "scratch" speed contest pure and simple.

The unsupercharged 3-litre Talbots, for instance, for a long time ran second and third behind the supercharged Alfa-Romeo, and in front of a car of the same type and a huge supercharged Mercedes-Benz. But unexpected fatigue of the metal used, the consequences of the gruelling Double-Twelve Hour Race held recently at Brooklands, put the leading Talbot out of the race, just as it eliminated one Aston-Martin and lost the other two a vast amount of time.

On formula, the little M.G. Midget, which astonished everybody, took third place, but at the conclusion of the event it was announced that it had been disqualified owing to taking two minutes too long on the final lap. This was extremely hard luck, for it was due to a misunderstanding, as Samuelson thought he had two minutes to spare.

The race took place for the most part over dry roads, although during the night a violent storm burst over the course. The event was held on the Sarthe Circuit, just outside the town of Le Mans in western France. It commenced at 4 p.m. on Saturday, June 13th, and continued until 4 p.m. on Sunday, June 14th.

All records were broken for the distance covered in 24 hours on the road by Lord Howe's Alfa-Romeo, which gave a magnificent demonstration of sustained speed over a distance of some 3,017 kiloms. (1,875 miles) in the hands of its very capable drivers. They averaged 78.13 m.p.h. The previous best performance in the race was that of Capt. Woolf Barnato and the late Lieut.-Commander Glen Kidston, who last year, with a 6½-litre Bentley, covered 1,820.7 miles at an average speed of 75.87 m.p.h.

The second car to finish was the big Mercedes, driven in turn by Stoffel and

Earl Howe and Col. Lindsay Lloyd step out to congratulate F. H. B. Samuelson (M.G. Midget) at the finish. The car, unfortunately was disqualified.

Ivanovsky, at an average speed of 75.21 m.p.h., while T. E. Rose-Richards and R. O. Saunders-Davies, on one of the new "105" model Talbots, finished third at an average speed of 73.46 m.p.h.

* * *

The Le Mans race may be viewed by the ordinary person in two ways: either as the Grand Prix d'Endurance, in which everybody is assumed to be going as fast as he (or she) can manage; or as the Coupe Bienniale Rudge-Whitworth, which is a handicap based on the speeds of which cars of varying cylinder capacity are expected to be capable, just like the handicaps in the R.A.C. Tourist Trophy race, the Irish Grand Prix, or the "Double-Twelve." Each car is expected to cover a certain mileage in the 24 hours and anyone who can make a car cover a proportionately bigger excess mileage than those of his competitors becomes the winner.

At Le Mans everybody gets a "biggest distance" complex, including the officials, so one hears little of the handicap side of the business. Only the competitors themselves, and other highly scientific people, who work it out for themselves, are aware of what is happening on handicap. It is only towards the end of the race that this aspect of it is pointed out to the spectators.

The Rudge-Whitworth Cup is called a Biennial award because, in order to win it, one has to do well for two successive years. The first race is an "eliminating" contest, of which the survivors take part in the final the following year.

On this occasion there were only four entries for the "final," these being Lord

Howe's Alfa-Romeo, the two Talbots put in by Fox and Nicholl, and Mme. Mareuse's Bugatti.

* * *

For this race, which promised to be the most exciting, as well as the most interesting, ever run on the Sarthe circuit, some of the fastest sports cars in Europe had been got ready. Yet never, in all the races that we have witnessed, have we seen more frantic last-minute work nor heard such wild and conflicting rumours.

Before the race, we had said: "Alfa-Romeo will win." But as we listened to the endless arguing of high officials of the famous Milan concern and saw one car after another being stripped down, on the eve of the race, in the old-world courtyard of the Hotel Moderne, we began to have our doubts.

It seemed as though their pride would not allow the Italians to learn. If any modification were suggested to them, they coldly replied: "It is *quite* all right! We have won the 1,000-mile race." So it was when the question of fitting of smooth-treaded tyres to the front wheels was raised, and so, also, when it was suggested that pure benzole should be used instead of the "70-30" mixture that was giving trouble during practising.

"We have won the 'Mille Miglia.' We have nothing to learn!" was their invariable reply.

Only two nights before the race the suggestion of running on pure benzole was finally adopted. This meant raising the compression ratio and involved changing the pistons. Giovanini, the head of the Alfa-Romeo racing department, rushed off to Paris to make arrangements in Sir Henry Birkin's "Speed-Six" Bentley saloon. At five o'clock next morning The Motor aeroplane was requisitioned to dash to Paris to collect the pistons. Eventually, at about 4.30 p.m., the necessary parts arrived, and soon after midnight the engines were reassembled and the necessary running-in of the new pistons commenced. During this progress one of the Alfa-Romeos "blew up," while another, entered by Lord Howe, was only ready for the race by 5.30 a.m. on the day of the event.

The new supercharged 4,900 c.c.

The "105" Talbot, which driven by T. E. Rose-Richards and R. O. Saunders-Davies put up such a good fight, taking the Pontlieue corner.

Bugattis arrived at the last moment for scrutineering, looking beautifully prepared and embodying many new and interesting features. They were fitted with an entirely new Michelin tyre, having a very heavy tread which had only been tried once before—in the recent Targa-Florio, a different type of race, and in very wet weather. How it would stand up to the 24-hour gruelling remained to be seen.

The cars had black fabric four-seater

bodies of somewhat square-cut lines, with no attempt at streamlining. In order to avoid the need for raising the bonnet the oil-filling orifice, as well as a second spout for the supercharger oil supply, projected through the bonnet. Both filler caps to the large tank at the back of the body could be opened by light thumb pressure and closed equally easily. A novel system of cable bracing was used to support the wings, one cable passing over the radiator and the other over the back of the bodywork, while the brakes, of new design, could be entirely changed in a few minutes.

The most extraordinary rumours that the Bugattis were not going to start were being circulated in Paris for several days before the race. Even when the cars reached Le Mans, after being driven all night from Molsheim, there were stories that they would be withdrawn at the last moment. But, to everybody's relief, they arrived, looking most impressive at the start.

Only Three Non-starters

As the cars were lined up opposite the pits, therefore, there were found to be only three non-starters—a straight-eight Alfa-Romeo which was to have been driven by Campari and Marinoni, and two small Ariès cars.

* * *

The scene at the start was pretty enough. The sun shone brilliantly down on the hot, sticky, tarred road. Flags of all nations fluttered in a stiff breeze; the lurid blues, reds and yellows of the advertisements above the pits made a vivid splash of colour against the green of bracken and pinewood, and the soft blue of the distant hills.

An eager crowd pressed against the barricades, filled the grandstand, and wandered slowly to and fro in the enclosures. Women in brightly-hued, sleeveless summer frocks (and one or two in silk blouses and plus-fours!) jostled their more soberly-garbed menfolk to get a better view. Everywhere there was animation and chatter.

An exciting moment at the Arnage bend when Birkin (Alfa-Romeo) and Stoffel (Mercedes-Benz) arrived at the corner simultaneously and go round practically side by side.

Stoffel calls at the pits to change a wheel on his Mercedes-Benz.

Then, shortly before four o'clock in the afternoon, Capt. Woolf Barnato, last year's winner, drove round the course with Sir Henry Birkin in a magnificent eight-litre Bentley tourer, in order to declare the circuit free for the race.

* * *

The onlookers, a little awed, lowered their voices as the timekeeper called out the last few seconds before the start. The drivers stood, alert and watchful, on the far side of the road from their cars. Then the yellow flag dropped, the drivers tore across the road, sprang into their seats, pressed the starter buttons, and roared up the slope towards Pontlieue.

Sommer (4,650 c.c. Chrysler) enjoyed a brief moment of glory, as he was first away of the 27 cars that started. But ere the sharp, right-angled turn in Pontlieue was reached the huge 6,313 c.c. Chrysler and two of the 4,900 c.c. Bugattis were in front.

We heard a muffled roar from across the forest as the whole pack thundered along the straight past the Café de l'Hippodrome and towards the Mulsanne corner. Here the leaders turned right and plunged down the tricky, winding stretch between the pines, finishing by slowing to 30 m.p.h. or so for the wicked S-bend at Arnage.

Chiron was in the lead now, driving the great black Bugatti with all his skill. Close behind was Divo, on another Bugatti, with Stoffel's gigantic white Mercedes-Benz screaming fiercely on his tail.

At the end of the first lap the Mercedes was in second place, with only Chiron ahead of it. Then came Divo, and, not far behind, Sir Henry Birkin's low, red Alfa-Romeo. Behind was the third "official" Bugatti, followed by a privately owned 2,300 c.c. supercharged car of the same make.

A Battle Royal

It was obvious, then, that the expected battle royal between the Mercedes, Bugatti and Alfa-Romeo drivers was developing. By the second lap, driving like a fury, Birkin had passed

Birkin had to skim the palisade in order avoid a collision.

and tightened his shock-absorbers to the accompaniment of much shouting by the Italian pit staff. This let Divo into third place and Marinoni into fourth place, with Rost fifth and the two Talbots sixth and seventh. Bevan's 4½-litre Bentley was in at the pits with plug trouble and, as Couper helped in work on the car, he had to take the car round for a minimum of one lap.

Suddenly the crowd gasped. The position of the leaders had changed in the twinkling of an eye. Stoffel brought the Mercedes into the pits with the off-side rear tyre flapping on the rim. In the two minutes which he took to change the wheel, Marinoni had taken the lead, with Divo and Rost, in the Bugattis, on his heels. Chiron came in to the pits and also changed a wheel, with the result that Birkin became fourth and the Talbots fifth and sixth.

But Stoffel was picking up speed so fast—he was lapping at 135 k.p.h. (83.8 m.p.h.)—that by the end of 13 laps he was back in fifth place, behind Marinoni, Divo's and Rost's Bugattis and Nimme's 2,300 c.c. car. He could afford to "ease up" a little then, and we noticed that he was using his "blower" less. De Costier's big Chrysler was at the pits with plug trouble and Couper brought in the Bentley for Bevan to take over.

The Talbots Lead on Handicap

After about two hours' racing it was announced that Lewis and Rose-Richards, on the Talbots, were respectively running first and second in the final for the 1930-1931 Rudge-Whitworth Cup, which was disputed on a handicap basis like many of our British races.

Chiron was making desperate efforts to regain the lead, and passed Birkin, just before the pits, in a thrilling skid down in the dusty gutter. Roaring down the opposite side of the course, one of the heavy treads of his rear tyres was flung off and he lost all the advantage that he had gained as he swerved

Divo and was running third behind the much larger French and German cars. while on the third lap the Alfa-Romeo was only a quarter of a mile behind Divo's Bugatti.

In the meanwhile the Talbots, driven by Brian Lewis and "Tim" Rose-Richards, were coming up well. Within the first 30 miles they had both overtaken the huge Chrysler, which had an engine more than double the size of their power units, while the big supercharged Stutz came banging its way slowly into the pits. The three Aston-Martins came by, making an excellent impression by their steady running. while Samuelson, in the little M.G. Midget, buzzed merrily along, having covered a lap at just under 60 m.p.h. average speed.

Chiron Runs Off the Course

Next time round, however, Stoffel's big white Mercedes was in front, for Chiron, unable to slow sufficiently for the right-hand turn at Mulsanne, overshot the corner and had to reverse back

on to the course. Seizing his opportunity, the driver of the German car squeezed past and soon afterwards increased his lead to such an extent that he led by more than a mile, with Chiron and Birkin, close together, more or less tieing for second place.

Next came the other two big Bugattis of Divo and Rost, with the 2,300 c.c. model of Nimme and Ano behind. Then followed Marinoni's Alfa-Romeo and the two Talbots, with the Chryslers some distance behind them. An interesting duel was taking place between various members of the Aston-Martin team and Balard's old 3½-litre Lorraine, who were constantly passing and repassing one another.

The "Two-three" Bugatti, however, was losing speed; the Mercedes was averaging over 80 m.p.h. and the two Alfa-Romeos were close on the heels of Chiron's Bugatti. The leaders were averaging 127 k.p.h. (78.9 m.p.h.), except for the Mercedes driver, whose speed was 135 k.p.h. (83.8 m.p.h.).

After nine laps Birkin came in to the pits slowly, changed a sparking plug

Trevor and Balard's Lorraine in at
the pits for replenishments.

Rost's Bugatti on a perfectly straight stretch of the course flung a tyre tread when doing nearly 130 m.p.h. It became entangled in the brake gear, locked the wheel and caused the tyre to burst. The car headed off at a tangent, leapt a ditch, tore its way through yards of fencing and straight into the spectators. The Bugatti then spun round and came to rest. Unfortunately one spectator was killed and four injured, whilst Rost although escaping with his life, was badly injured.

Picked out by the headlights of the following Mercedes-Benz driven by Ivanovsky, T. E. Rose-Richards (Talbot), with only one headlight in action, and Earl Howe (Alfa-Romeo) skid around the bend at Mulsanne during a terrific thunderstorm.

Ivanovsky and Stoffel's Mercedes-Benz and the Stutz driven by Brisson and Cattaneo rounding the Mulsanne bend.

wildly before regaining control of the vehicle. This dropped him back behind the Talbots, who were at that stage seventh and eighth, and at about this time the first retirement was announced —Sommer's Chrysler which had a hole in the radiator. Only four laps later De Costier, the driver of the other Chrysler, had also to retire.

Then occurred a tragedy that was to plunge homes into mourning and, eventually, to cause the withdrawal of the rest of the official Bugatti team.

Marinoni fled by on his twentieth lap, Then came Divo. So far, so good. But instead of Rost's Bugatti the white Mercedes screamed up the road, Nimme's and Birkin's cars in pursuit.

A little blue car slowed down by the Talbot pit. The driver shouted something and pointed back over his shoulder. Must mean something bad, a racer slowing down like that to give the news. Other drivers, too, slowed and made unintelligible signs. An ambulance started off down the road. An accident . . .

A Tragedy

But who was involved? Rost, obviously, for he was missing. But the Talbots? We felt sick with fear as we hurriedly checked our time sheets to see if they were overdue. Before we had time to do so both purred smoothly past the grandstand at 95 m.p.h., running as regularly as clocks. Thank goodness they were all right . . .

It was a long time before the truth came out. It appears that Rost, "flat out" on a perfectly straight stretch of the course, flung a tyre tread, which promptly became entangled in the brake gear, locking the wheel. Unprotected by the rubber, the tyre overheated owing to the friction and promptly burst.

The driver could do nothing to save himself. He felt the car lurch and hurtle off the road at a tangent. It must have been doing something like 130 m.p.h. as it leapt the ditch and tore its way through yards of chestnut fencing and straight into the closely packed spectators. It spun round in the middle of them, facing whence it had come and came eventually to rest; the casualties were one dead and four injured, besides the driver, who had a torn scalp and a pain in the chest that suggested a smashed rib.

Positions at End of Third Hour.

Drivers and Car.	Laps.	Time. h. m. s.		
1. Divo-Bouriat, Bugatti ...	23	2	56	26
2. Marinoni - Zehender, Alfa-Romeo	23	2	57	16
3. Ivanovsky - Stoffel, Mercedes-Benz	23	2	59	32
4. Chiron-Varzi, Bugatti ...	22	2	53	3
5. Lewis-Hindmarsh, Talbot...	22	2	54	7
6. Rose-Richards - Saunders-Davies, Talbot	22	2	54	11

The other Bugatti drivers put on speed. Chiron immediately put in a lap in 7 mins. 14 secs., at the record speed of 135.7 k.p.h. (84.32 m.p.h.). Both Alfa-Romeos came into the pits. Zehender took over the leading car after a 3½-minute pit stop, while Lord Howe took over his own car, after a stop of 8 mins. 45 secs., from Sir Henry Birkin. Stoffel stopped, too, and Ivanovsky, the relief driver, took over the big Mercedes. This let the Talbots into fifth and sixth places, and a dangerous rival was removed when the privately owned 2,300 c.c. supercharged Bugatti of Nimme and Ano broke a universal joint.

In the meanwhile Divo was in at the pits and handed his car over to Bouriat, who got away very quickly.

Charier (Lombard) nearly skids broadside when taking the corner at Arnage.

Two of the Bugattis, Divo leading, at Mulsanne.   Behind is Rost, who crashed shortly after.

A moment later, however, Chiron arrived with yet another tyre tread missing. The mechanics pushed a massive jack under the axle, but the driver waved them away. There was a hurried consultation and then Chiron, hatless, drove the car slowly up the road and into the " dead car " park. A few minutes later M. Jean Bugatti, the son of the founder of the famous Molsheim concern, stood out in the road with a large white plate bearing a red St. Andrew's cross : the " Stop " sign.

Why the Bugattis were Withdrawn

As Bouriat came in to the pits in obedience to the signal, the official decision of the Bugatti entrant was promulgated : " Owing to incidents not connected with the construction of his cars, M. Bugatti found himself obliged to withdraw his cars."

Immediately there was uproar. Cat-calls, whistles and booing rang across the enclosures. The unsporting element in the crowd shouted down the more reasonable spectators, who understood the wisdom of withdrawing the two remaining cars rather than risk another and possibly even more deplorable accident.

The race then resolved itself into a struggle between the Talbots, the Mercedes and the Alfa-Romeos. So long as the big German car kept going at speed there was the possibility that the Alfa-Romeo drivers would " scrap " it and court trouble in the process. But presently the Mercedes, which was running on Englebert tyres, began to come in

rather frequently for spares, and, in consequence, lost a great deal of time.

Not until 8 p.m., or after four hours' steady running at an average speed of 75 m.p.h., did the Talbots come in for replenishments. No. 10, driven by Brian Lewis, stopped first, and the driver complained of a sore hand, caused by the knob coming off the gear lever. Owing to carburation difficulties caused by the fuel used, also, he found that he could only use half throttle. So it was a wonderfully good show, on his part, to be running third, while his team-mate, Rose-Richards, was driving equally well and holding fourth place.

It was a pity that Hindmarsh, who took over from Lewis, should have had to come in, on the next lap, owing to the continued blowing of one fuse. This, together with the original pit stop, lost him the best part of seven minutes, equivalent to nearly a lap.

Positions at End of Sixth Hour.

Drivers and Car.	Laps.	Time. h. m. s.
1. Marinoni - Zehender, Alfa-Romeo	46	5 56 20
2. Earl Howe - Birkin, Alfa-Romeo	45	5 53 29
3. Rose-Richards - Saunders-Davies, Talbot	45	5 59 41
4. Lewis-Hindmarsh, Talbot	42	5 39 19
5. Ivanovsky - Stoffel, Mercedes-Benz	42	5 53 44
6. Bezzant and Cook, Aston-Martin	40	5 53 17

The light was fading now, but there was the promise of a fine night ahead. One by one the drivers switched on their headlamps and presently the pits, the scoring boards and grand-stands were scintillating with brilliant electric bulbs, The cars had to drive with their lights

on from 9.20 p.m. on Saturday to 4.30 a.m. on Sunday.

Just at dusk poor Couper, who was driving Bevan's Bentley, met with bad luck. As he lifted his foot to slow for the Pontlieue corner there was a rending crash and the crankshaft broke. No longer having the engine as a brake he only just managed to stop, right down by the barriers, short of rushing headlong into the town of Le Mans !

British Cars in Trouble

The three Aston-Martins, which had been lapping with great regularity at a commendable high speed, began to suffer from the most maddening trouble. They had fitted Zeiss headlamps in order to ensure a really good driving light, but these were so much heavier than the make normally fitted that the bolts securing the brackets were continually shearing. This was all the more distressing because, at the time the trouble began, two of the cars were occupying sixth and seventh places. However, the crews of each car set busily to work with straps and things to make the lamps point at the road instead of towards the tree tops.

While the Aston-Martin people worked on their cars, the Hon. A. D. Chetwynd wandered about looking very worried. His wife's M.G. Midget was more than 20 minutes overdue, and no news could be obtained as to its whereabouts.

Suddenly a little, limping figure in overalls came within the range of the pit illumination. It was Stisted, perspiring of brow but inordinately cheerful, who had abandoned his car about a mile down the road. He reported that, whatever he did to it the engine would only give "two bangs and a *whoof*." The ignition, fuel supply and so forth were all in perfect working order. Everything worked, in fact, except the engine. Long afterwards the

And so the race went on. Midnight struck. Lord Howe's Alfa-Romeo, after a short stop at the pits, set off again, the leader of the race. The other Alfa-Romeo was in a moment later for only two minutes. Rose-Richards's Talbot was running third, the Mercedes fourth, the other Talbot fifth and the Aston-Martin, driven by J. Bezzant and

enabled the driver to get free, but only after having lost a great deal of time. An 1,100 c.c. Lombard, driven by Charier and Royer, retired because of "a broken oil-pressure gauge."

For a long time, as the cars thundered through the dark pine-woods, lightning had flickered in the sky.

At about 2.30 a.m. a particularly livid flash, followed by a deafening thunderclap, announced the beginning of a short but violent storm. The crowd dissolved as if by magic and vanished under cover as the rain fell first in great drops and then with torrential intensity.

Positions at End of Ninth Hour.

Drivers and Car.	Laps.	h.	m.	s.
1. Earl Howe-Birkin, Alfa-Romeo	69	8	54	36
2. Marinoni - Zehender, Alfa-Romeo	69	8	56	12
3. Rose-Richards - Saunders-Davies, Talbot	65	8	52	48
4. Lewis-Hindmarsh, Talbot ...	65	8	56	50
5. Ivanovsky - Stoffel, Mercedes-Benz	64	8	56	30
6. Bezzant - Cook, Aston-Martin	59	8	57	43

In the midst of the downpour the three Aston-Martins came in for refuelling, which they got through with commendable dispatch. Zehender came in to raise his windscreen. This done, he set of with "Tim" Rose-Richards close behind. At "Indianapolis Corner"—the brick-paved bend at Arnage, the Italian suddenly became aware of the car on his tail. He got rattled. He twisted his head, accelerated violently, and—shot off the road.

Bad Boys

A lamp and a wing were damaged as a result and the car was never the same

At the Pontlieue hairpin—the Chrysler driven by Sommer and Delemer leading from the Arrol-Aster piloted by "W. P. Lockwood" and Bartlett.

car was pushed into the pits and, after an examination, into the "dead car park" for the trouble, a sheared key in the timing gear was too great to be cured on the spot.

The other M.G. Midget, driven in turn by Samuelson and Kindell, was putting up a magnificent performance, lapping with the most complete regularity not far below the mile-a-minute mark.

The Two Women Drivers

We happened to look in at the pit of Mme. Mareuse just as she was handing over her Bugatti to her friend and co-driver, Mme. Siko. These two sporting ladies did very well in last year's race and qualified to run in the final this year.

Mme. Mareuse, a fairly well-built woman, staggered weakly from her car and had to be helped to a chair; she complained of the cold. And where was Mme. Siko?

The latter attractive young woman was at that moment sleeping peacefully in a large saloon motorcar behind the pits, and it was some moments before she arrived. Mme. Mareuse twittered like a whole aviary of canaries. "Oh, dear! Oh dear! Why *wouldn't* the girl hurry?"

Eventually all was well, the car went off again and Mme. Mareuse was enveloped in a large fur cloak. It was a pity that, owing to some miscalculation, the car stopped two laps too soon for a replenishment and was thus debarred from competing further.

Rost's wrecked Bugatti after a crash which involved the death of a spectator and injuries to the driver and four other people.

H. W. Cook was sixth. Samuelson's M.G. Midget was ninth fastest car in the race.

Within the next hour—from midnight to 1 a.m. on Sunday—one of the Caban racers got stuck on the sand at Pontlieue. Much hard digging eventually

again. Finally, the back axle broke on the 98th lap and there was nothing more to be done. The unhappy crew, it was stated, were immediately sent home in disgrace, to report themselves to Signor Jano, the managing director of the Alfa-Romeo concern.

During the hours that followed the cars thundered around the course what time the spectators, sated with speed, danced energetically until daylight in the big tin-roofed restaurant or sought new thrills watching daredevil motor-cyclists ride round the "Wall of Death." For a whole hour Hindmarsh, on a Talbot, sat on the tail of the big Mercedes, which seemed unable to lose him. For several laps Birkin sat on the tail of one of the Talbots which, driven by Hindmarsh, covered a lap in 7 mins. 35 secs. (80 m.p.h.).

Dawn came, and with it an ink-washed sky, across which scudded ragged grey clouds. Presently the sun burst forth with tropical intensity and the dancers desisted from their antics. A new day had begun.

Positions at End of Twelfth Hour.

			Time.	
Drivers and Car.	Laps.	h.	m.	s.
1. Earl Howe-Birkin, Alfa-Romeo	92	11	56	47
2. Marinoni-Zehender, Alfa-Romeo	88	11	53	10
3. Lewis-Hindmarsh, Talbot ...	86	11	56	27
4. Rose-Richards - Saunders-Davies, Talbot	86	11	59	49
5. Ivanovsky - Stoffel, Mercedes-Benz	84	11	59	43
6. Bezzant - Cook, Aston-Martin	79	11	59	15

As the heat increased, Samuelson came in to the pits, having driven a wonderful race on his M.G. Midget. Something was bumping ominously beneath the floorboards and the propeller-shaft tunnel had to be removed in order to investigate matters. Eventually, however, the trouble was traced to the slacking-off of the rear spring bolts, which allowed the axle to get out of line. After over 50 minutes hard work the matter was rectified and Samuelson and his co-driver, Kindell, were able to proceed in their appointed turns at as high a speed as ever.

Positions at End of Fifteenth Hour.

			Time.	
Drivers and Car.	Laps.	h.	m.	s.
1. Earl Howe-Birkin, Alfa-Romeo	115	14	58	10
2. Lewis-Hindmarsh, Talbot ...	109	14	59	31
3. Rose-Richards - Saunders-Davies, Talbot	108	14	57	18
4. Ivanovsky - Stoffel, Mercedes-Benz	107	14	55	51
5. Cook-Bezzant, Aston-Martin	95	14	54	54
6. Harvey - Bertelli, Aston-Martin	94	14	28	20

At 8.20 a.m. it was announced that the Arrol-Aster driven by "Lockwood" and Bartlett had been withdrawn on the far side of the course by Les Humandières. This fine car made a most impressive sight as it swept round the course at a useful speed, and had it completed the 24 hours should have figured well up in the results.

Positions at End of Eighteenth Hour.

			Time.	
Drivers and Car.	Laps.	h.	m.	s.
1. Earl Howe-Birkin, Alfa-Romeo	138	17	54	16
2. Rose-Richards - Saunders-Davies, Talbot	131	17	56	39
3. Ivanovsky - Stoffel, Mercedes-Benz	131	17	57	16
4. Lewis-Hindmarsh, Talbot ...	129	17	31	30
5. Balard-Trebor Lorra,ne ...	111	17	52	23
6. Harvey - Bertelli Aston-Martin	110	17	45	57

Nothing of note happened for an hour or two, and then the spirits of those in the Talbot pit sank to zero, for Hindmarsh, who was running second, brought in his car with the fuel tank wobbling ominously behind. The chassis frame was cracked on the near side, just about where it is upswept to clear the back axle. Brave efforts were made with

Two Aston-Martins, driven respectively by A. C. Bertelli and C. M. Harvey and J. Bezzant and H. W. Cook close in company near Mulsanne.

straps and ropes, using tommy-bars as turniquets, and two more laps were actually covered before, fearing that the tank might fall off and cause an accident, Arthur Fox ordered its withdrawal.

Aston-Martins Have Bad Luck.

Almost simultaneously Bezzant, on an Aston-Martin, had to retire also, for the near-side front wing dropped right off and could not be replaced. Indeed, these Aston-Martins, that never faltered mechanically throughout the 24 hours, were dogged throughout by the breakage of wing, lamp and shock-absorber brackets. It seemed as though these parts, which stood the gruelling of the Double-Twelve Hour race so well, must have crystallized almost before the start of the Le Mans race.

And so the number of cars left in the race became steadily less and less. Ivanovsky, who was driving the great Mercedes as hard as he knew how, broke the lap record for the 1931 race again and again, sometimes averaging close on 140 k.p.h. (87 m.p.h.). In due course he overtook the surviving Talbot and thus moved into second place—a position he had not held for many a long hour. Incidentally, it was only after Ivanovsky had come begging and praying for Dunlops and been supplied with them by a compassionate concessionaire, that he was able to make full use of the car's speed capabilities.

Positions at End of Twenty-first Hour.

			Time.	
Drivers and Car.	Laps.	h.	m.	s.
1. Earl Howe-Birkin, Alfa-Romeo	162	20	58	38
2. Ivanovsky - Stoffel, Mercedes-Benz	155	20	58	31
3. Rose-Richards - Saunders-Davies, Talbot	152	20	56	23
4. Balard-Trebor, Aston-Martin	130	20	50	40
5. Harvey - Bertelli, Aston-Martin	124	20	55	58
6. Peacock-Newsome, Aston-Martin	119	20	51	42

There was little enough change in the closing stages of the race. Only the Aston-Martins fell back, while Samuel-

son's M.G. Midget, a little Caban (a little-known French make) and a B.N.C. more or less held the positions to which luck, plus reliability and a fair turn of speed, had led them. Among them was Ballard and Trebor's old Lorraine, which had won fourth place, by the 20th lap, through sheer, sturdy merit.

The crowds of spectators still poured into the enclosures, although it was three o'clock in the afternoon, and the race was nearly over. Anticipating the result, the officials already began to proclaim the winner. Lovely bouquets were got ready and the onlookers pressed close to the palings the better to see their heroes.

Samuelson came "tuff-tuffing by, his Midget emitting clouds of smoke. "Il ne terminera pas," muttered the gloomy prophets. But finish he did, albeit at a reduced speed, only to have the hard luck eventually to be disqualified.

There were scenes of rare enthusiasm as Sir Henry Birkin crossed the finishing line at well over 90 m.p.h., having won the 24-Hour Race at Le Mans, on the wonderful Alfa-Romeo, at a speed higher than it has ever been won before, and having, at the same time, driven one of the finest races of his career.

THE NINTH GRAND PRIX D'ENDURANCE.

	Miles.	m.p.h.
1. Earl Howe and Sir H. R. S. Birkin, Alfa-Romeo ...	1,875	78.13
2. B. Ivanovsky and Stoffel, Mercedes-Benz ...	1,805	75.21
3. O. Saunders-Davies and T. E. Rose-Richards, Talbot ...	1,763	73.46
4. Trebor and Balard, Lorraine ...	1,624	67.67
5. C. M. Harvey and A. C. Bertelli, Aston-Martin ...	1,420	59.56
6. Vernet and Vallon, Caban ...	1,260	52.53

THE RUDGE-WHITWORTH BIENNIAL CUP FINAL.

	Fig. of merit.
1. Earl Howe and Sir H. R. S. Birkin, Alfa-Romeo	1.26
2. O. Saunders-Davies and T. E. Rose-Richards, Talbot ...	1.19
3. B. Ivanovsky and Stoffel, Mercedes-Benz	1.12
4. Trebor and Balard, Lorraine ...	1.016
5. C. M. Harvey and A. C. Bertelli, Aston-Martin	1.015
6. Vernet and Vallon, Caban ...	1.002

LE MANS—AN ARTIST'S IMPRESSIONS

Although only two light cars figured in the results at Le Mans last week-end, some fine performances were put up. (Top) An impression of Newsome (Aston Martin) at Arnage. (Centre) Sir H. Birkin (Alfa-Romeo) passing Samuelson (M.G. Midget) on the straight approaching Mulsanne. (Below) One of the Cabans skids into the safety bank at Pontlieue.

Hard Luck for Light Car Drivers in
GREAT RACE AT LE MANS

ALTHOUGH eleven sports cars of under 1½-litre capacity were entered for the great 24-hour race at Le Mans, which took place on Saturday and Sunday last, June 13th and 14th, only two figured in the final results. These were an Aston-Martin driven by C. M. Harvey and A. C. Bertelli, which averaged 59.56 m.p.h., and a Caban Special of 1,097 c.c., driven by Vernet and

Only Two Under-1,500 c.c. Machines— an Aston-Martin and a Caban Special—Figure in the Results—British Drivers' Victory

(Left) The two Aston-Martins at speed. No. 24 was fifth in the Endurance Race and in the Biennial Cup Final. (Above) Samuelson and Kindell with their share of the spoils. Their M.G. Midget put up a fine show and is seen (right) at speed.

Vallon, which averaged 52.53 m.p.h.

The race was of an exceptionally gruelling nature. The road conditions were not really bad, but apparently the surface was not sufficiently hard, for bumps which had not been there at the start developed after a time; moreover, in the depth of the night a violent thunderstorm broke over the course, leaving the roads treacherous and wet.

The Aston-Martins ran with extraordinary regularity and high speed at the beginning of the race, but presently —presumably owing to the buffeting that they had received in the Double-Twelve Hour Race at Brooklands— the wings and lamp brackets began to give way and an enormous amount of time was lost in fastening up these parts. Indeed, one of the team had to be withdrawn when a wing fell off, much to the chagrin of Bertelli, who, too late, discovered that he could have run with the various detached parts in the back of the car and popped them on or tied them on with string at the very last moment.

The two M.G. Midgets created a wonderful impression among the French, who had never seen anything quite so

small move quite so fast. One was driven by the Hon. Mrs. Chetwynd and H. Stisted, while the other was handled by Captain F. H. B. Samuelson and Kindell—a mechanic employed in the racing repartment of the M.G. works at Abingdon.

Samuelson managed to complete the entire course, although trouble on the very last lap slowed him down so much that he just failed to qualify for next year's final by the narrow margin of two minutes; he could actually have gone much faster, but he imagined he had these two minutes well in hand. He was lapping the course steadily at 60 m.p.h. and had no trouble except on the morning of the second day, when the rear axle shifted somewhat in the spring clips, thus allowing the propeller shaft to get out of line and hit the tunnel provided for it in the floorboards.

Mrs. Chetwynd's Midget also ran extremely well, although a slight delay was caused by oil leaking into the distributor. Finally, however, Stisted came running up to the pits, having abandoned the car about two miles up the road with everything working properly—except the engine! The cause of

the trouble could not be discovered and at first it was reported that a key had sheared in the timing gear; later, however, it was discovered that there was nothing more serious than a seized rocker shaft, due to dirt collecting round the oil-pressure reducing pin. Unfortunately, as this was discovered too late, it was not possible to resume.

An interesting French entry was the 1,496 c.c. Bugatti driven by Mme. Mareuse and Mme. Siko. These ladies qualified in last year's event to run in the 1931 final, and put up a very good performance, although they found the race very tiring and got rather excited about things. Unfortunately, owing to some miscalculation, the car came in at the end of its eighteenth lap for refuelling when it should not have come in until 20 laps had been completed.

The only small French car to finish was a Caban of 1,097 c.c., driven by Vernet and Vallon. This had one of the new Ruby two-camshaft engines and put up a very good performance indeed, although it was naturally slower than the Aston-Martin.

Another Caban and a Lombard with engines of the same type also ran, but did not finish; nor did the 1,495 c.c. B.N.C. and another 1½-litre Bugatti.

The race was run on a circuit of slightly over 10 miles on the outskirts of Le Mans in the Department of la Sarthe. It started at 4 p.m. on Saturday last and finished at 4 p.m. on Sunday. It was marred by a fatal accident, in which one of the 5-litre Bugattis shot off the road at 130 m.p.h., killing one spectator and injuring four others, besides the driver.

The ultimate winner of the event was the 2½-litre Alfa-Romeo car, driven in turn by its owner—Earl Howe—and Sir Henry Birkin. This shows that British drivers can hold their own against the best that the Continent can produce, by putting up the amazing average speed of 78.13 m.p.h. over a distance of 1,875 miles, which, of course, includes all stops of any description.

The second car to finish was a supercharged Mercedes-Benz driven by Ivanovsky and Stoffel, which averaged 75.21 m.p.h. for 1,805 miles, while the third was a 3-litre Talbot driven by T. E. Rose-Richards and O. Saunders-Davies. This car put up the excellent average speed of 73.46 m.p.h. for 1,763 miles.

The fastest lap of the race was put up by Chiron (Bugatti) just prior to the withdrawal of the team—following the accident—at 84.32 m.p.h.

HERE AND THERE ON THE COURSE.

Rounding Mulsanne—the Caban Special which qualified and was sixth in the race.

(Above) Mrs. Chetwynd (M.G. Midget) pursuing the Lombard past the grandstands.

Another view of the straight; the other Caban following in the wake of an Aston-Martin.

(Left) Mrs. Chetwynd (M.G. Midget) leading the Lombard. (Above) The victors, Sir Henry Birkin and Lord Howe. (Right) A glimpse of the B.N.C. from above.

SPORTS JOTTINGS

WELL, after Le Mans, it can no longer be said that there is no driver in this country to stand on equal terms with the best that the Continent can produce. I refer, of course, to Sir Henry Birkin and Earl Howe. Continental drivers who, admittedly

STARTING IN THE SUNSHINE. —— Le Mans race drivers answering the maroon's call to action last Saturday. The very large number of "boaters" worn by the crowd was particularly noticeable.

are remarkable people, have the advantage that throughout the whole season there is at least one road race of importance every week-end!

Earl Howe once remarked that after a driver had put in a few laps on M. Ettore Bugatti's private course at the Molsheim factory he should be competent to tackle the Targa Florio with confidence. The noble earl has lapped on the Bugatti track—the noble earl went shockingly fast at Dublin and Le Mans. . . .

THE CRASH AT LE MANS.

Two photographs taken soon after Rost (5-litre Bugatti) left the road at 130 m.p.h. and crashed through the fencing. The driver was badly injured and one spectator was killed. The fence, it will be seen, was demolished for a considerable distance.

1932

This was the first year of the 'new' circuit; a new road had been built specially to the A.C.O.'s requirements across the circuit just after the pits and grandstand, rejoining the original circuit at Tertre Rouge. This new stretch included the 'Esses'. The new circuit cut out the Pontlieue section completely and kept well clear of the suburbs of Le Mans. The Tertre Rouge section soon became a favourite vantage point for spectators, and the centre of the gradually growing 'Village' with all its side-shows and fun fair atmosphere. The circuit was somewhat shortened and the lap distance was now 8.383 miles; in this form, the Circuit Permanente de la Sarthe survived largely unchanged until 1967.

Another small field of 26 cars, numerically dominated by seven Alfa Romeos: six 2.3 litre cars, two works entries with some assistance also given to last years winners, Howe and Birkin, and one 1,750 six-cylinder model. Ranged against these were only three big engined cars, all privately entered by French drivers: a Mercedes-Benz, a Stutz and Sir Henry Birkin's old Blower Bentley. There was a single British Talbot, and two 2.3 Bugattis - the Type 55s. Aston Martin brought three works cars and there were single entries of Alfa and MG but no other British cars. Among the smaller French cars a 1.1 litre Citroen made a unique appearance for a make renowned for endurance in long-distance record attempts, but hardly capable of the speeds required to be competitive at Le Mans. It soon retired . . .

From the start it seemed to be mainly a question of which Alfa Romeo would take the lead, individual drivers jockeying for position. But on the first lap, the French driver Trevoux overturned the old Bentley at White House, setting in motion a train of events that seemed to be almost a repetition of the 1927 drama, and would probably have been far more serious, had it happened after dark. As it was, the Bentley merely proved an irritating artificial chicane, defeating all efforts to

shift it, until just after 6 pm when Minoia in one of the works Alfas came down towards White House too fast and, trying to avoid the wreck, skidded into a field. Here it was soon joined by the Stutz and, eventually, Marinoni's Alfa Romeo also fetched up against the immovable bulk of the Bentley.

Of the remaining Alfa Romeos, the Schumann/Dreyfus car rolled at Arnage, and at 3 am Birkin's head gasket blew and with it his and Lord Howe's chances of a repeat win. The Mercedes-Benz and the Bugatti Type 55 driven by Chiron/Bouriat had both retired, so the main contestants were now The two Alfas of Sommer/Chinetti and Cortese-Guidotti (the remaining works car); the other Bugatti driven by Czaikowski and veteran driver Ernest Friderich (his only drive in the 24-hour race, but as the winner of the 1920 Voiturette was no stranger to the Sarthe circuit); and the Talbot. This would in fact have been the finishing order had it not been for the retirement of the Bugatti at noon on Sunday.

The Cortese-Guidotti Alfa was constantly plagued by parts working loose and falling off, and its mudguards gradually took on a distinct non-regulation shape; meanwhile Raymond Sommer in the leading Alfa had to drive solo, as Chinetti was taken ill after only three hours at the wheel. The Talbot in third place also had its troubles to contend with; it was running on only five cylinders and was harassed by the little 1,750 cc Alfa Romeo which eventually finished fourth. In the end the race was Raymond Sommer's; his winning average was 76.48 mph and the distance 1,835.55 miles; even if the figures were lower than 1931's record, it was a remarkable performance by this French driver whose second Le Mans this was - in the previous year he had driven a Chrysler which had retired. Sommer also won the Index. The Biennial Cup was taken by one of the finishing Aston Martins, just snatching it, away from a faltering Caban which had finished ninth and last.

THE LE MANS 24-HOUR RACE

An artist's impression of the Mulsanne Corner during the Le Mans 24-hour Grand Prix d'Endurance.

WELL, to-day should see the British competitors in the 24-hour Grand Prix d'Endurance crossing the Channel en route for Le Mans. To-morrow morning I shall be climbing into my Puss Moth and flying there in time for the first night's practice.

The race starts next Saturday, June 18th, at 4 p.m., and continues until 4 p.m. the next day. It is run over the Sarthe circuit. which, as the result of a recent shortening, now measures only 8.4 miles round and includes a new fast curve and a tricky S-bend.

Of the 31 cars entered nine are British, nine French, three German, six Italian, three American and one of unspecified nationality. Such diverse makes as Mercedes-Benz, Talbot, Bentley, Stutz, Chrysler, Bugatti, Ford, Alfa-Romeo, Salmson, Aston-Martin, Caban, Amilcar, Alta, M.G. Midget, Rally and G.A.R. are entered.

The British Entries

IT is not to be expected, however, that all these cars will appear at the start. There will, for instance, be only one Talbot, as it is too soon after the J.C.C. 1,000-mile race for a second car to be overhauled in time. It will be driven by Brian Lewis and "Tim" Rose-Richards. Capt. F. H. B. Samuelson will handle the only M.G. Midget in the race, as Mrs. Chetwynd's car will not be rebuilt in time after its recent internal collapse. The three Aston-Martins are "works" entries, the Bentley has been tuned by Birkin and Couper, Ltd., and will be driven by two Frenchmen, and a Monsieur Ludovic Ford is handling an Alta, which thus makes its début in a racing event. Lord Howe and Sir Henry Birkin will drive a straight-eight 2,337 c.c. Alfa-Romeo and will endeavour to win outright the 8th Biennial Cup, which they qualified for last year. The Talbot and one of the Aston-Martins have also qualified for the final.

The full entry list is as follows:—

LE MANS 24-HOUR RACE ENTRIES.
Final of the Eighth Biennial Cup.

		c.c.
3. Mercedes-Benz (de Tatarinoff)	...	7,100
9. Talbot (A. W. Fox)	...	2,970
11. Alfa-Romeo (Lord Howe)	...	2,337
18. Aston-Martin (Aston-Martin, Ltd.)		1,496
25. Caban (Labric)	...	1,096
31. (Undeclared, Labric)	...	undeclared

Tenth Grand Prix of Endurance and Eliminating Race for Ninth Biennial Cup.

		c.c.
1. Mercedes-Ben: (Henry Stoffel)	...	7,100
2. Mercedes-Benz or X (Prince Djordjadzé)		7,100
3. Mercedes-Benz (de Tatarinoff)	...	7,100
4. Stutz or X (E. H. Brisson)	...	5,355
5. Bugatti (Guy Bouriat)	...	4,900
6. Chrysler (R. Sommer)	...	4,900
7. Bentley (J. Trévoux)	...	4,398
8. Ford (Lebas)	...	3,282
9. Talbot (A.-W. Fox)	...	2,970
10. Talbot (R.-I. Nicholl)	...	2,970
11. Alfa-Romeo (Lord Howe)	...	2,337
10. Talbot (R.-I. Nicholl)	... ...	2,970
11. Alfa-Romeo (Lord Howe)	... ...	2,337
12. Alfa-Romeo (Soc. An. Alfa-Romeo)		2,337
13. Alfa-Romeo (Soc. An. Alfa-Romeo)		2,337
14. Alfa-Romeo (R. Sommer)	...	2,337
15. Alfa-Romeo (Heldé)	...	2,337
16. Bugatti (Comte Czaykowski)	...	2,300
17. Alfa-Romeo (Mme. Siko)	...	1,750
18. Aston-Martin (Aston-Martin, Ltd.)		1,500
19. Aston-Martin (Aston-Martin, Ltd.)		1,500
20. Aston-Martin (Aston-Martin, Ltd.)		1,500
21. Bugatti (Druck)	...	1,500
22. Bugatti (J. Sébilleau)	...	1,499
23. Rally (Jean Danne)	...	1,360
24. Salmson (J. E. Vernet)	...	1,096
25. Caban (Labric)	...	1,096
26. Amilcar (C.-A. Martin)	...	1,092
27. Alta (Ludovic Ford)	...	1,074
28. G.A.R. (A. de Choqueuse)	...	750
29. M.G. (Hon. Mrs. Chetwynd)	...	750
30. M.G. (Capt. Samuelson)	...	746
31. X (Labric)	...	undeclared

How the Race is Run

THE Le Mans race is really two races run concurrently. One is a species of handicap, in which each car has to exceed, by as big a margin as possible, the speed it is required to do by the regulations. Examples of the speeds imposed are:—750 c.c.: 64.5 k.p.h. (40.1 m.p.h.); 1,100 c.c.: 74.37 k.p.h. (46.2 m.p.h.); 1,500 c.c.: 87.08 k.p.h. (54.2 m.p.h.); 2 litres: 89.58 k.p.h. (55.8 m.p.h.); 3 litres: 101 k.p.h. (62.8 m.p.h.); 6 litres and over 108.3 k.p.h. (67.5 m.p.h.).

Last year Lord Howe and Sir Henry Birkin won the race at 78.13 m.p.h. and broke all records.

The winner of the 10th Grand Prix d'Endurance is the entrant of the car which covers the greatest distance in the 24 hours.

The Alfa-Romeo team, led by Sir Henry Birkin, get well away at the start, leaving the Bentley on the line.

LE MANS, 1932

Grand Prix d'Endurance Won by a Privately Owned Alfa-Romeo, Driven by Sommer and Chinetti, at 76.48 m.p.h. Sommer Drove for 20 Out of the 24 Hours

WHEN the Le Mans series of races started the principal and only prize was the Rudge-Whitworth Biennial Cup, given to the car which made the best performance in relation to its engine size in one 24-hour race, having previously qualified by completing the 24-hour race of the year before. Gradually, as we have pointed out from time to time, the character of the race was changed, and of late years the sensationalism of the larger cars was separately rewarded by a cup given as though each race was a Grand Prix, ignoring engine size, which inevitably would be won by a big car as things are to-day.

In 1929 and 1930 Bentleys succeeded in winning both races; in 1931 Alfa-Romeo did the same; this year a 1½-litre Aston-Martin driven by A. C. Bertelli and L. P. Driscoll was the victor, after a really fine battle with the Talbot, Lord Howe's Alfa-Romeo, a Caban, which proved to be remarkably fast, and a B.N.C., the only machines qualified to take part as a result of last year's event.

To gain the cup it is essential that the cars are controlled with some knowledge of the difficult conditions the handicap curve imposes, and at the start of this

FINAL OF THE BIENNIAL CUP, KNOWN AS THE RUDGE-WHITWORTH CUP, WON BY ASTON-MARTIN DRIVEN BY BERTELLI AND DRISCOLL

by

W. F. BRADLEY,

Continental Correspondent of " The Autocar"

year's race the intense heat was an additional handicap with which no one had reckoned, especially when the opening rounds were run at an altogether exceptional speed.

Lord Howe's Alfa-Romeo at first led, with the Talbot second and the Caban a good third, the B.N.C. being fairly early in trouble, but the fight among the leaders was too furious to last, and the Alfa-Romeo had to retire with serious trouble.

For the rest of the long and strenuous race the battle lay between the Aston-Martin, the big Talbot, and the smaller Caban, each car's every lap being jealously watched and assessed by rivals, and the thing being the more interesting because, as usual at Le Mans, none of the machines was altogether trouble-free.

The night having aided the A.M. considerably, as its pace was maintained relatively high, for hours after the dawn there was scarcely a decimal point between the three cars; especially close were the respective figures of the Caban and the Aston-Martin. Then the Talbot was much delayed, coming into action later, however, at a speed which made it dangerous to its two rivals to the end, and the gradual improvement in the Aston brought that car into the lead, only to suffer from an irritating delay caused by the breaking of some bolts of unknown French steel in the supplementary wing stays, while the Caban developed an irregular misfiring that

Almost a repetition of 1927. A second catastrophe at White House Corner. Brisson's Stutz crashes in an endeavour to avoid the wreckage of the two Alfa-Romeos and the Bentley.

necessitated several time-losing visits to its pit.

Anything more interesting to those who know the game it is impossible to imagine, and it was not until the last hour that the Aston-Martin succeeded in maintaining the highest relative speed, finally to cross the line victorious after a serious leak in the top water pipe had been dealt with, an incident that reminds one of the fact that two previous winners of the Grand Prix d'Endurance have crossed the line practically air-cooled.

Incidentally, of the remaining Aston-Martins one retired owing to a flaw in a rocker boss, the other won the 1,500 c.c. class from a Rally, two Bugattis and the Citroën, both these machines being used tactically to aid Bertelli's car.

This year, by the way, although the cup is still presented by its original donor, it is no longer called the Rudge-Whitworth Cup, owing to some change in the donor's business interests, but to all who follow this great race only the original name conveys a definite meaning.

Congratulations are due to a relatively small British firm in upholding our prestige on the Continent, and to the drivers, one the designer of the càr and the other a famous Brooklands motor cyclist.

* * *

THERE was a real tang of excitement in the air. At the start, when the drivers had been aligned on the left of the road, their cars placed opposite them, diagonally, tails to the pits, Faroux had to wave them back to their places again and again, so impatiently were they straining at their imaginary leashes. When the starter's five fingers were raised for the last five seconds, the men were uncontrollable, and with still two seconds to go some of them were half-way across the road and half a dozen had vaulted into their seats ere the big yellow flag touched the ground.

And this was the start of the great twenty-four-hour race—two rounds of the clock, during which anything and everything could happen. It was like the start of a fifty-mile sprint, to be decided on a split second. To use a colloquialism, the drivers were "crazy," or, at any rate,

a majority of them, and they carried the minority with them. There were twenty-six cars before the long line of gay, beflagged pits, and among them were seven British productions, with, in addition, the British team of Earl Howe and Sir Henry Birkin on an Italian Alfa-Romeo.

Before the start G. E. T. Eyston had been sent away on the elongated boat-type Panhard, with which he recently broke the world's hour record, and immediately after him Lord Howe and Sir Henry Birkin accomplished a *tour d'honneur* on the former's blue Alfa-Romeo, winner of last year's twenty-four-hour race. Then the secretary of the Automobile Club de l'Ouest called for one minute's silence in memory of the late André Boillot. With heads bared and bowed, drivers, assistants, officials, and thousands of spectators stood in impressive silence to the memory of the fine sportsman who had gone before.

It would be difficult to say who started first. At the head of the line was the big white Mercédès which ran last year, and it naturally had an advantage, but right on its heels were the three bright-

Three cars in line ahead approaching the fast but treacherous S bend on the new section of the course, a point where tar oozed through the road surface.

Swinging round the wide and slightly banked bend at the commencement of the new section of the course.

red Alfa-Romeos, driven respectively by Sommer, Birkin, and Minoia. When the twenty-six went into the broad, banked, right-hand bend forming the new cross-road, used for the first time this year, they were patches of red, green, blue, and white, jockeying for positions, passing to left or right, every man for himself, and the devil take the hindmost.

This new road, linking up the grand-stand stretch with the Tours highway, changed the race entirely for the grand-stand spectators and modified it for the drivers, first by reducing the distance round to 8.38 miles, and by making the pace a little faster. First up hill, then down hill with an elongated S, followed by a right-angle turn into the Tours road, the loop offered no particular difficulty for drivers, although there was much apprehension at the start regarding the tar and the tackiness of the top dressing.

Looking down the circuit to the bend hiding White House Farm, we espied a patch of red, then a second, then a third. Cortese's Alfa-Romeo was leading, followed by Minoia and Birkin, the white Merc., Marinoni on the red Alfa, and then by Dreyfus on the same make of machine, Bouriat on the 2,300 c.c. super-charged Bugatti, and Sommer on the privately owned Alfa. These eight flashed by in such close formation that one had hardly time to jot down their numbers before they were out of sight.

Surprises came quickly. The usually most reliable Talbot limped over the line and came to a stop at the end of the first round, misfiring badly. At the same time the three Aston-Martins successively pulled up, also misfiring. The Alta was in trouble from the very outset and was pushed off the circuit within the first hour. As the supercharged Bentley failed to appear, the début of the race was far from being brilliant for the British contingent. Both the Aston-Martins' and the Talbot's trouble was soon traced to unsuitable fuel which, aided by the heat, was playing havoc with plugs. Before a remedy could be applied, however, much valuable time had been lost.

Meanwhile, extraordinary scenes were happening on the circuit. The Italian drivers had lost all sense of proportion. Passing and re-passing one another on the straightaway, shaking fists at team-mates, overtaking on corners and cutting-in short, it was a war without mercy. Observing the chief engineer's ruling that revs should not exceed 5,100, Birkin found himself being left by Cortese and Minoia, and then, on the third lap, was overtaken by Marinoni.

The leading cars in close formation manœuvring for the first corner after the start. A photograph which shows the commencement of the new Pontlieue by-pass.

A point where the loose surface of the road proved difficult.

Two laps more and Marinoni was in the lead, having passed both the veteran Minoia on No. 10 and the youthful Cortese on No. 11.

But the impetuous Italian's glory was short lived, for on the sixth round he failed to appear, and rumours were circulated of a crash. Almost at the same instant the report came in that No. 12, the fourth of the leading Alfa-Romeos, driven by Dreyfus, the son of a French deputy, had run off the road. As the news concerning the Bentley was meagre and unreliable, it seemed that the centre of interest was not at the grandstands, but around the circuit. The opportunity of reaching that centre came in the form of an official Bugatti, which was about to make a tour of inspection. Jumping aboard, we were soon speeding over the new road, thickly lined with spectators, then on the Hippodrome stretch, towards Mulsanne.

Just around the first bend of the S's, No. 12 Alfa-Romeo was found in a wrecked condition, its chassis battered, but its engine still capable of running, as we proved by starting it up. In his eagerness to keep pace with the leaders, Dreyfus had gone into the right-hand turn at a rate far in excess of the safety limit. Realising his danger, he braked hard, which got him round the bend, but put the car broadside on. Dreyfus struggled hard to regain control, but the road at this place is decidedly narrow and the stretch between the two bends is short. Charging the sandy banking on the left-hand side, the car got out of control, then again charged the bank, rolling over partially. The race was over so far as No. 12 was concerned.

Determined to beat his team-mates, Marinoni got the lead on the fifth round, hard chased by Minoia and Cortese, with Birkin driving fast but playing a safer game. No. 14 roared down the Hippodrome highway with these three on its heels, swung round the Mulsanne corner, sped through the pine woods at a rapid rate, negotiated the first bend of the S's, but crabbed the second and buried itself deeply in the sand and brushwood bank. Both Cortese and Minoia, only a few yards in the rear, missed the disabled car and went on with their personal scrap.

Examination showed Marinoni that his car was not damaged in any way, but it was entirely off the road, and to get it back to the highway he had to rely on himself and the tools and implements aboard the car. Silent, ignoring the gratuitous advice offered by spectators from the safety of the adjoining fields,

pletely wrecked his car. Trevoux was picked up with a broken wrist and two dents in his "tin hat," either of which might have been fatal had they been direct on the skull. The car was a hindrance to the other drivers, but a commissionaire with a yellow flag immediately warned them of their danger, and, furthermore, it was broad daylight.

Minoia's and Cortese's Alfas were scrapping like fiends, first one and then the other getting the advantage by a few lengths. Birkin was holding himself in third place, within striking distance, puzzled at this mad display of the Italians and at the failure of the Alfa-Romeo chiefs, who were present in full force, to curb the ardour of their men. That a youngster like Cortese should indulge in dirt-track, sprint-race methods could be understood; but that a veteran like Minoia, a man of ripe experience, thoughtful, reasoning, trained to all the tricks of car racing, should

 The winning Alfa-Romeo accelerating away from the right-hand bend at Arnage.

Marinoni began to dig, to pull, to push, in almost superhuman efforts to get the car back on the road. For an hour and a quarter he toiled without remission, not a word escaping his lips, not a thought being given to anything but this one task of getting back into the race. Then his patience was rewarded, and with a healthy crackle from the exhaust he returned to the fray. It was 6 p.m., and he was the tail-ender, with a tremendous lee-way to try to make up.

Then the White House Corner became the centre of interest. On the first round Trevoux showed more speed than discretion in his handling of the big supercharged Bentley, for he utterly failed to negotiate the corner and, after spinning wildly, rolled over and com-

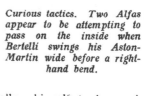 *Curious tactics. Two Alfas appear to be attempting to pass on the inside when Bertelli swings his Aston-Martin wide before a right-hand bend.*

allow himself to be carried away was beyond comprehension.

Minoia, on No. 10, approached White House Corner at the highest possible speed. But it was just a fraction too high on this narrow road, reduced in width by the presence of the Bentley and the various officials and idlers discussing the means of getting the car out of the way. Minoia realised that the situation was full of danger; he manœuvred skilfully, but when the car spun round twice in the restricted space there was no hope of regaining control, and he crashed, with moderate damage to his car and nothing more than superficial cuts to his face.

Just before entering the bend Minoia

 Marinoni endeavouring to get No. 14 Alfa-Romeo back on the course after his crash at White House Corner

Friedrich refuelling the Bugatti.

George Eyston starts his Tour d'Honneur on his record-breaking Panhard.

Cortese's Alfa during a pit stop.

White House Corner. Minoia's Alfa-Romeo, only slightly damaged, was pushed through a convenient gate into an adjoining field, but the heavy Bentley, completely wrecked, and the big Stutz, lying partially on its side, were serious obstacles. Drivers were flagged to stop, but nobody obeyed the rule. Indeed, some of them were so defiant that they hardly reduced speed, and even passed other cars on the bend. This was the case with Marinoni who, feverishly burning up kilometres in the hope of regaining some of his lost time, overtook one of the small cars just before White House, and rushed into the bend with his off-side wheels on the grass. In endeavouring to straighten out he got broadside on and brought the tail of his

had overtaken Brisson on the big Stutz. Brisson was not fighting the wild cats. His big unsupercharged Stutz was slower than the nimble Alfa-Romeos, and he was content to play a safe game which never got him better than ninth position. But when Brisson swung round the blind corner at White House he saw an Alfa-Romeo fifteen yards ahead of him, spinning like a top, and occupying the entire width of the road.

The only hope lay in brakes. Brisson applied them, and a fraction of a second later hit something and found himself floating through the air. He has distinct

Mechanics working hard on Brian Lewis' Talbot.

recollections of looking down and, as he saw the car shooting away from under him, the reassuring thought passed through his mind, "Well, at any rate, it will not crush me." With the footballer's instinct, Brisson drew his head between his shoulders as he struck the bank. Putting his hand into his pocket he found that his cigarettes were crushed beyond use. "You might give me a cig.," he remarked to a native who was standing open-mouthed by the side of the road. For reply the astonished farmer uttered one word, made famous by a French general at Waterloo.

With the wreckage of three cars on this narrow road, pandemonium reigned at

Alfa-Romeo into violent collision with the projecting portion of the Bentley.

There were thus four wrecked cars in a stretch of forty or fifty yards, on a road only just wide enough for two vehicles. A man stood in a most exposed position and waved a white flag. A gendarme blew his whistle and jumped for safety; if it was an Alfa-Romeo he gave two quick blasts and made a lightning jump. This alacrity was essential for safety, for

Throwing sand on tar brought up by the intense heat.

with the exception of Lord Howe, who drew forth the commendation of the commissaires, the drivers were most unreasonable. One Englishman, one Italian and one Frenchman were particularly objectionable in the way they rushed through this mass of wreckage at sixty miles an hour.

Marinoni's Alfa-Romeo was dragged across the road into the field occupied by Minoia's machine. The Bentley was dragged upside down into a ploughed field on the right of the road. A rope was attached to the Stutz' axle and some

Officials and police around the wrecked Bentley.

twenty-five men hauled. The rope broke and twenty-five figures sprawled on the ground until a blast on the gendarme's whistle brought them to their feet, jumping for safety. Finally, the Stutz was dragged out, its engine started, and with a steady stream coming from its oil radiator it made its way slowly towards the pits. The road was cleared. Five cars had been wrecked, while a Rally, a B.N.C., an Alta, and a Citroën had been abandoned by the roadside with mechanical defects. Yet the race was not four hours old.

If the grandstand spectators did not get the details of the sensational crashes, they witnessed plenty of activity. By the

Cortese and Minoia adopted Grand Prix methods on the sweep into the new road. Just over the brow of the hill they overtook Bertelli somewhat near the middle of the wide road. One of the Alfa-Romeos swished by on the right, and the other to the left of the English car. Birkin went by making signs: it was the signal that Minoia was off the road. This accident put Birkin into second place, just behind the tempestuous Cortese. At 6.15 No. 11, the leading car, came in for supplies, having covered the regulation twenty-four rounds. Cortese overshot the mark. There was excitement at the pits. Guidotti jumped down on the road and was called back by the pit manager, for Cortese had decided to continue. Before he got away, the two other official Alfa-Romeos came in, and Birkin turned over to Howe. Pit work was quick, being accelerated by the new system of overhead fuel supply tanks, but there was a certain lack of precision and order.

While the three Alfas were in front of their pits, No. 1 Mercédès came in

The winner of the Grand Prix d'Endurance approaching the last turn at Arnage, with the Caban in front.

second round five Alfa-Romeos were in the lead, with the white Mercédès in fifth place, followed by Bouriat on the 2,300 c.c. supercharged Bugatti, Sommer, the private owner of an Alfa, Count Czaikowski on a Bugatti, Brisson on the Stutz, and Bertelli's Aston-Martin.

Plug trouble affected the Aston-Martins, Bertelli and Newsome coming in together after four laps, while Brian Lewis, who had had to make a pit stop at the end of the initial lap, had his Talbot in again after three laps. This trouble, which was common to both the Aston-Martins and the Talbot, seriously jeopardised the chances of British success in the race. The M.G., on the other hand, ran with remarkable regularity, climbing from twenty-fifth position at the end of the first round to twelfth after twenty-four laps.

Four derelict cars on White House turn after a series of disastrous crashes.

with a seized piston, due to a failure of the lubrication system, and at the same time the announcement was received that Bouriat's Bugatti had run out of fuel. Later it was ascertained that a stone had wedged between the axle housing and the recess in the fuel tank, and had worn a hole through the latter.

All these rapid changes modified the entire aspect of the race, and when we took stock at 8 p.m., after four hours' running, it was to find Cortese and Guidotti's Alfa still in the lead, with Earl Howe a close second, and Sommer in third place, followed by Count Czaikowski's Bugatti and Newsome's and

Madame Siko coming out of the S bend on the Pontlieue by-pass.

Bertelli's Aston-Martins. Of the fifteen left in, Samuelson's M.G. was next.

In view of the quality of the official Alfa-Romeo team, not much attention had been given to Sommer, a young man driving his private Alfa-Romeo—last year's model—with the assistance of an Italian mechanic. For the benefit of those who followed the early flying movement, it is interesting that the eventual winner is the son of Roger Sommer, one of the early French flyers, who for a certain length of time was also an aeroplane manufacturer. The assistant driver, Chinetti, being worn out with his preparatory work on the car, Sommer drove for twenty out of the twenty-four hours.

Soon after 10 p.m. Cortese was held up with a broken windscreen, allowing Birkin to get in the lead and Sommer to secure second place. At 11.25 Birkin came in for water, oil, fuel, and a change of plugs. After 2 min. 13 sec. the car was taken over again by Earl Howe, who went away in the lead. At the end of the next lap, however, Howe came in sounding his horn, while Cortese was at

Two Alfa-Romeos on the first bend on the new road.

be lost. About the same time No. 22 Aston-Martin, driven by Peacock and Bezzant, broke a rocker arm. This was changed by the crew, but on the following round the rocker bracket gave way, causing the car to be withdrawn.

Howe's plug change just before midnight was indicative of trouble ahead, for between 3 and 4 a.m., while Birkin was leading and on his 109th lap, it was realised that a cylinder head gasket had blown. Thus daybreak saw the race in the hands of either Cortese and Guidotti on the official Alfa-Romeo, or Sommer on the unofficial mount. Sixty miles astern, however, was No. 16 Bugatti, driven alternately by its owner, Count Czaikowski, and the Bugatti agent, Friedrich. They had decided to play a waiting game, and now was the time to strike, for the front wings on Cor-

Driscoll with the Biennial Cup winner on Arnage.

the pits. The engine had a feeble sound, but the mechanic soon detected a shorted plug, by reason of a water leak. This stop allowed Sommer to get in front for the first time, with Cortese still third.

At midnight the three Alfas, driven by Sommer, Howe and Birkin, and Cortese and Guidotti, were in the lead, followed by No. 16 Bugatti and Newsome's and Widengren's Aston-Martin. The witching hour, however, was fatal to the M.G., driven at that time by Norman Black, which had run without an involuntary stop, until one of the tank bolts gave way, causing all the fuel to

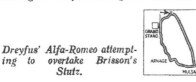

Dreyfus' Alfa-Romeo attempting to overtake Brisson's Stutz.

Madame Siko and Sabipa who were fourth with an Alfa-Romeo.

Newsome and Widengren, fifth with the Aston-Martin.

tese's machine were beginning to drop off.

Again and again either Cortese or Guidotti came in and tied up with straps and copper wire, of which the car seemed to have an unlimited supply. The battery box began to drop off, but more straps were available; the head light supports gave way, but the supply of wire was inexhaustible. Meanwhile, the Bugatti was creeping up, lap by lap, to the delight of the spectators, who saw the possibility of a French victory. They were disappointed, soon after noon, when the Bugatti came to a stop with a broken piston.

The final result of the race had been settled, for, with the exception of No. 11 Alfa-Romeo, which was in danger of shedding its wings and accessories, the really fast cars had been eliminated, and Sommer had only to maintain a steady pace to keep ahead of the nine others in the running.

These successive eliminations had brought the Talbot up to third position, thirty-six laps behind the leaders and just ahead of the six-cylinder supercharged Alfa driven by Mme. Siko and Sabipa. Newsome and Widengren were fifth on the Aston-Martin, while Bertelli and Driscoll, who led in the classification for the final of the Ninth Biennial Cup, occupied seventh position. There was some anxiety in the Aston-

(Top) Sommer and Chinetti, who won the Grand Prix d'Endurance. (Centre) Cortese and Guidotti, who were second in an Alfa-Romeo. (Bottom) Rose-Richards and Brian Lewis, who were third with the Talbot.

Martin camp, however, for Bertelli's engine had developed a water leak, and both the cars required their front wings to be tied up with rope. During the afternoon a valve spring had to be changed on the Talbot, and although this gave the six-cylinder Alfa-Romeo an opportunity of getting uncomfortably close, so much time had been lost in the early stages by reason of plug trouble that it made no real difference to the final result.

During the last four hours Sommer was able to take things easily, nevertheless, he had driven pluckily, and had suffered much by reason of the loss of his exhaust box, on the left-hand side of the car. This had dropped off, leaving a short exhaust pipe which ejected black fumes over the car and driver, and a useless tail pipe.

Although there was a little doubt, for a certain time, as to the ability of the Talbot to accomplish the minimum distance required under the rules, the end of the race was tame to the onlooker compared with the excitement of the opening hours. The mad pace of 83.8 m.p.h. maintained up to the end of the first hour, with a record lap at 89 m.p.h., dropped at the end to an average of 76.48 m.p.h.

Thus ended the battle between cars on level terms irrespective of engine size, but the other, and equally important, competition for the Biennial Cup provided quite a lot of excitement for those who had been able to follow it with private score sheets and slide rules in the pits, and the enthusiasts in the grandstand who knew how to read the excellent scoreboard. To them the Grand Prix d'Endurance was just a battle between the Alfa-Romeos and the Bugattis. The Biennial Cup was more complicated, but not beyond the understanding of the majority of the spectators. The scoreboard stated the number of laps covered and the number which had to be covered, and the dingdong struggle between the Aston-Martin, the Talbot and the Caban provided more excitement than the sight of the Alfa-Romeos dashing through between pits and grandstand.

Each of the competing cars had its petty troubles, mainly due to plugs overheating through the strange fuel they were burning, and it seemed that fate was playing a pretty game with them all, for no sooner did one of the three lead than it had to make a call at the pits. Then one of the other two would take the lead, and then their positions would be changed by a stop.

And so it went on, the Talbot going like the wind and driven magnificently by those two fine English sportsmen

Berielli and Driscoll after winning the Ninth Biennial Cup with the Aston-Martin.

Brian Lewis' Talbot taking the right-angle corner at Arnage.

who so closely resemble each other—Rose-Richards and Brian Lewis. Bertelli and Driscoll, with the Aston-Martin, knew that they had no time to waste if they were not to be beaten by either the Talbot or the Caban. The latter car ran like a clock. It was not an easy victory for the Aston-Martin.

[*The key maps with the illustrations indicate from what positions the photographs were taken.*]

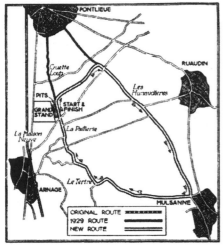

The course as it is to-day, with the new short cut after the grandstand.

RESULTS
Grand Prix d'Endurance

	Miles Covered.
1. Sommer and Chinetti, Alfa-Romeo.... (Average speed, 76.48 m.p.h.).	1,835.57
2. Cortese and Guidotti, Alfa-Romeo	1,819
3. Brian Lewis and T. Rose-Richards, Talbot	1,517
4. Mme. Siko and Sabipa, Alfa-Romeo ..	1,502.2
5. S. H. Newsome and H. Widengren, Aston-Martin	1,459.6
6. Sebilleau and Delaroche, Bugatti......	1,446
7. A. C. Bertelli and L. P. Driscoll, Aston-Martin	1,409.3
8. Martin and Bodoignet, Amilcar	1,269.5
9. Giraud Cabantous and R. Labric, Caban	1,231

Final of the Ninth Biennial Cup (1931-1932), generally known as the Rudge-Whitworth Cup.

	Figure of Merit.
1. A. C. Bertelli and L. P. Driscoll, Aston-Martin	1.137
2. Giraud Cabantous and R. Labric, Caban	1.109
3. Brian Lewis and Rose-Richards, Talbot	1.100

Causes of Withdrawal
1. Mercédès, lubrication troubles.
3. Stutz, accident.
5. Bentley, accident.
9. Alfa Romeo, cylinder head joint.
10. Alfa-Romeo, accident.
12. Alfa-Romeo, accident.
14. Alfa-Romeo, accident.
15. Bugatti, leaking fuel tank.
16. Bugatti, oil leak and seized engine.
19. Citroën, ignition troubles.
22. Aston-Martin, valve gear.
24. Bugatti, accident.
25. Rally, ignition defects.
27. B.N.C., seized piston.
28. Salmson, clutch trouble.
30. Alta, clutch trouble.
32. M.G., leaking fuel tank.

EQUIPMENT
Jaeger instruments on all cars to finish race. Champion plugs on first three cars, and also on Cup winner. Englebert tyres on winning Alfa-Romeos. Ferodo brake linings, Alfa-Romeo and Aston-Martin. Dunlop tyres, Aston-Martin and second Alfa-Romeo. Pratt's oil, Aston-Martin. S.U. carburetter, Aston-Martin. Rotax, Aston-Martin. Rudge-Whitworth wheels, Alfa-Romeo and Aston-Martin. Andre shock absorbers, Alfa-Romeo and Aston-Martin.

1933

Although surely a well-meant gesture, undertaken in all innocence by the pious burghers of Le Mans, the building of a small chapel at the track might have had somewhat cynical overtones - the French are primarily a practical race. Mass was said here on Sunday morning during the race. For those in peril on the track . . .?

A total of 29 cars were brought to the start on 17 June after a record 13 entries had been scratched. Again, there were seven Alfa Romeos; five 2.3 litre eight-cylinder models, of which two were short chassis Mille Miglia replicas, and two 1.75 sixes, of which the Rousseau/Paco car was a coupe. Among the Alfa drivers, the partnership of last year's winner Sommer with the Italian master Tazio Nuvolari (his only Le Mans appearance) attracted attention. The Frenchman Louis Chiron had been tempted away from the native Bugatti into another Alfa, together with Cortese; another change of allegiance was the British duo of Lewis and Rose-Richards who had taken the Talbot into third place in 1932 but were now to be found in an Alfa.

Among the more unusual entries was Prince Nicholas of Roumania, in a giant 6.9 litre Model J Duesenberg; Trevoux persisted with the old Bentley, and Labric-Daniel with an equally venerable La Lorraine. The last big car was a single five-litre Bugatti. Apart from the Bentley, all the British cars were small fry, comprising three Aston Martins in the 1¹/₂ litre class (in one of these Sammy Davis had his last Le Mans drive), two 1,100 cc Rileys (these were the Nine Brooklands models; one had won the 1932 TT, and it was Riley's first entry in the 24-hour race) and finally a Singer Nine, two MG Midgets and an Austin Seven. All the remaining entries were various small French cars, including a farewell appearance of that Le Mans stalwart, the air-cooled S.A.R.A.

Right from the start a most punishing pace was set up, the Alfa Romeo driven by Sommer eventually set up a new lap record of 90.96 mph, at last beating Birkin's record from 1930. The five 2.3 Alfa Romeos led, and were followed by the Bentley and the Duesenberg; but the final Le Mans appearance of a classic Bentley soon ended in the sandpit at Mulsanne, while the Roumanian prince was disqualified for re-fuelling too soon. The only car left to threaten the Alfas was the big Bugatti, driven by Mesdames Desprez and Tarante. Before 2 am the first of the 2.3 litre Alfas, that of Moll/Cloitre, retired with lighting trouble. Otherwise the lead still changed between Sommer/Nuvolari, Chinetti/Varent and Chiron/Cortese, with Lewis and Rose-Richards never far behind.

Early Sunday morning, Nuvolari stopped for 16 minutes while a leaking fuel tank was plugged, and shock absorbers were also a cause of trouble. Then Cortese had a dramatic accident, turning a somersault at the Esses, while the Bugatti had given up with mechanical trouble. Nuvolari had managed to regain the lead after some brilliant and furious driving but was still challenged by the Chinetti/Varent car; particularly as his fuel leak grew steadily worse, despite much dedicated gum-chewing by Nuvolari, Sommer and even the entire pit crew of Lewis and Rose-Richards. The last hour of the race was of a drama unparalleled in Le Mans history; Nuvolari led by two minutes at 3 pm; fifteen minutes later Varent was in the lead, but Nuvolari passed yet again. At 3.52 pm Chinetti (who had taken over from Varent and who was spurred on by a promised 60,000 francs bonus should he win) passed a stationary Nuvolari at the pits; Nuvolari got going again, and on the last lap the lead changed three times. Finally, Chinetti missed a gear change at Arnage, he went off the road and Nuvolari got by; when Chinetti resumed the chase, he found the road blocked by a smaller car and Nuvolari won by a margin of a quarter of a mile, or about ten seconds.

The winner's average was 81.4 mph and the distance 1,953.61 miles, handsomely beating the previous records set up in 1931. Sommer and Nuvolari also won the Biennial Cup. They were followed home by Chinetti (who got his 60,000 francs bonus all the same) and Varent, and in third place was the Alfa of Lewis and Rose-Richards. Fourth was the little Riley of von der Becke and Peacock and this team won the Index of Performance; they were followed by an Aston Martin, the supercharged MG J4 Midget and the other Aston Martin driven by Bertelli and Sammy Davis. The closed Alfa was eighth, and the next four places were occupied by small French cars; thirteenth and last to finish was the Singer Nine.

Thus ended a most memorable race; Nuvolari's only Le Mans drive, resulting in a dramatic victory at one of the narrowest margins ever in the history of the 24-hour race. But Alfa Romeo's 1-2-3 victory was tinged with regret; after having run into financial problems, the company had been taken over by the state-owned I.R.I. organisation which had announced the withdrawal from racing of the Alfa works team at the end of the 1933 season.

TEN SECONDS DECIDES
LE MANS 24-HOUR RACE

Alfa-Romeos First, Second and Third—Nuvolari and Sommer Win from Chinetti and Varent and Secure the Rudge-Whitworth and Biennial Cup at an Average Speed of 80.98 m.p.h.—All Records Broken—The Hon. Brian Lewis and T. E. Rose-Richards Third—Aston-Martin Second and Fourth in the Biennial Cup—Good Riley Performance

ALL records were broken by Nuvolari and Sommer with a straight-eight supercharged 2,336 c.c. Alfa-Romeo when winning the Rudge-Whitworth Cup, and covering the greatest distance in the classic Le Mans Race held on the permanent Sarthe Circuit on Saturday and Sunday last.

They covered 1,943.70 miles over the 8.37-mile course at an average speed of 80.98 m.p.h. The previous record was held by Earl Howe and Sir Henry Birkin (Alfa-Romeo), who, in 1931, covered 1,875.12 miles at an average speed of 78.13 m.p.h. It was Sommer's second successive win, for last year he partnered Chinetti, who this time also broke the course record, to finish second only 10 secs. behind the winner.

British drivers—the Hon. Brian Lewis and T. E. Rose-Richards—finished third, and five British cars survived the gruelling test, namely, two Aston-Martins, a Riley, an M.G. Midget and a Singer Nine Sports.

There were originally 41 entries, but only 29 actually started. Of these eight were running on a formula basis for the Rudge-Whitworth Cup, which entails two successive wins to secure it, and the remainder were out to cover the greatest distance in 24 hours and so earn the right to participate in

THE 29 STARTERS
Duesenberg (6,882 c.c., S.), Prince Nicolas of Roumania and Cattaneo.
Bugatti (4,965 c.c., S.), Tarante and Mme. Desprez.
Bentley (4,398 c.c., S.), Gas and Trevoux.
Lorraine (3,483 c.c.), R. Labric and Daniel.
Alfa-Romeo (2,357 c.c., S.), Chinetti and Varent.
Alfa-Romeo (2,337 c.c., S.), Moll and Cloitre.
Alfa-Romeo (2,338 c.c., S.), Sommer and Nuvolari.
Alfa-Romeo (2,338 c.c., S.), The Hon. B. E. Lewis and T. E. Rose-Richards.
Alfa-Romeo (2,338 c.c., S.), Chiron and Cortese.
S.A.R.A. (1,818 c.c.), Mottet and Maraudet.
Alfa-Romeo (1,768 c.c., S.), Mme. Siko and Sabipa.
Alfa-Romeo (1,742 c.c., S.), Rousseau and Paes.
Bugatti (1,493 c.c., S.), Czaykowski and Gaupillat.
Aston-Martin (1,496 c.c.), Bertelli and S. C. H. Davis.
Aston-Martin (1,496 c.c.), Driscoll and Penn-Hughes.
Aston-Martin (1,496 c.c.), Goodall and Mrs. Wisdom.
Rally (1,309 c.c., S.), Duruy and Danne.
Salmson (1,092 c.c.), Vernet and Vallon.
Riley (1,087 c.c.), Van der Becke and Peacock.
Riley (1,087 c.c.), Sebilleau and Delaroche.
B.N.C. (1,087 c.c.), Alin Brothers.
Amilcar (1,074 c.c.), Buquet and Clouet.
Amilcar (1,066 c.c.), de Gavardie Brothers.
Tracta (999 c.c.), Quinault and Podrault.
Amilcar (990 c.c.), Martin and Bodoignet.
Singer (972 c.c.), Barnes and Langley.
M.G. (746 c.c., S.), Hendy and Parker.
M.G. (746 c.c., S.), Ford and Baumer.
Austin (742 c.c.), Metchim and Masters.
(S. denotes supercharged.)

the Rudge-Whitworth Cup for 1934.

Organized by the go-ahead Automobile Club de l'Ouest, and starting at 4 o'clock on the Saturday afternoon, it was a race for sports cars as distinct from the ordinary Grands Prix cars run with bodies to conform to specific dimensions, and are equipped with screen, headlamps, wings, etc.

The event, to use a much-abused word, is unique in every respect. It is the greatest race of its kind in the world, one in which the atmosphere has to be experienced to be appreciated. The course, which has a splendid tarmacadam surface, lies some 4½ miles south of the town, and in glorious, wooded country. There are two long S-bends, the famous right-handed Arnage and Mulsanne bends, and the Mulsanne downhill straight, where speeds of 120 m.p.h. were attained.

Le Mans goes en fête for this festival, shops being closed during the proceedings. Hundreds of thousands of people line the circuit, and at night the lighting effects of the tribunes and pits, coupled with the dispensation of music, give a wondrous effect. The weather, with the exception of a few showers, was very good, and consequently a very big percentage camped out and saw the proceedings through.

Hon. Brian Lewis (Alfa) was in the lead from Chinetti, Sommer, Moll and Chiron. Next came Prince Nicolas of Roumania, with the big Duesenberg, and right on his tail Trévoux, with a 4½-litre supercharged Bentley once

ran orange-coloured Austin Seven, sans blower, and Hendy, with one of the two supercharged M.G. Midgets.

Sommer Soon in the Lead

By the time the competitors had reached the Arnage bend Sommer, last year's winner, with his beige and red Alfa, was in the lead, and he came round past the grandstands in front of Chiron. Then a slight gap, and Chinetti and Brian Lewis came by in close company. Another interval, and then Moll, Prince Nicolas, Tarante and Trévoux.

(Left) Nuvolari and Sommer, who won the race by the narrow margin of ten seconds.

(Right) Chinetti and Varent, who were second.

The Start

And now to the race. As in previous years, the cars were lined up against the pits with the drivers on the opposite side of the road. The loud-speaker belched forth the ever-decreasing minutes to zero hour—five, four, three, two minutes. Then Col. Lindsay Lloyd dropped the Tricolour and the drivers raced across the road to their cars.

The five supercharged 2.3-litre Alfa-Romeos drew out practically simultaneously, and as the cars that had got away quickly reached the right-hand banked bend, some 300 yards away, the

driven on the same circuit by Sir Henry Birkin. In practice overnight the car had developed clutch trouble. The aid of that famous veteran, Jean Chassagne —now a Castrol representative in France—was sought and, thanks to his assistance, the Bentley was able to start. Last to pass the grandstands on their 24-hour trek were Metchim's vete-

Count Czaykowski, with one of the new twin o.h.c. 1,500 c.c. Bugattis, followed nearly two minutes later. The leader had taken exactly 5 mins. 55 secs. for the standing lap of 13.5 kiloms., his average speed being 136.82 k.p.h. (approximately 85 m.p.h.). Bertelli brought in his Aston-Martin for a minor adjustment, but was away again in a few

Van der Becke and Peacock's Riley Nine, which secured fourth place, leads Buquet and Clouet's Amilcar round the sharp bend from the new road on to the old course.

private scrap on their own, with the advantage in favour of the British car, which, as it transpired a little later, was too fast for the American. At this stage the Aston-Martins, Rileys and M.G.s were running consistently, while Lewis

outstanding interest, although Chiron gave the spectators at the grandstands a thrill by cutting across the bows of Tarante's 4.9 Bugatti. After one hour's running Sommer was still in the lead by a big margin from Chiron. They had

Gas (Bentley) charges the sandbanks at Mulsanne corner, breaking the palisade and embedding the car deeply in the sand.

seconds, and then in came Ford, who lost several minutes in working on his M.G., while Sommer, on completion of two laps, had lapped Metchim's Austin.

Sommer's Lead Increased

In the third lap Sommer increased his lead over Chiron, but two circuits later the last-named cut down the margin considerably. After another 10 minutes'

was in third place in front of Chinetti, and nearly three parts of a minute behind Chiron.

On the eighth lap Czaykowski had to pull in, but was away in a few seconds

(Below) The Hon. Brian Lewis and T. E. Rose-Richards (Alfa), third.

each covered 10 laps, the leader's time of 57 mins. 43 secs. being 1 min. 55 secs. faster than Chiron. Third came Lewis, in 54 mins. 30 secs., with 9 secs. separating him from Chinetti. Next in order

K. S. Peacock and A. Van der Becke, (Riley Nine) who finished fourth.

running, however, Chiron fell behind again, owing to a brief call at the pits. Meanwhile Trévoux, with the old Bentley, and Prince Nicolas, with the big twin o.h.c. Duesenberg, were having a

with a cigarette between his lips. Hendy had an enforced halt near Mulsanne, and then called in and rectified matters at the pits on the same circuit.

For some time there was nothing of

were Moll, Tarante, Trévoux, Prince Nicolas, Mme. Siko, Driscoll, Rousseau's Alfa saloon, Sebilleau, Labric and Van der Becke.

Riley's Long Pit Call

At 5.40 p.m. Sebilleau was in with his Riley, a stop which eventually cost him half an hour. Meanwhile two hours had elapsed, and Sommer was only just short of lapping Lewis and Chinetti, who was now close on the Englishman's tail. The following lap Lewis was passed by Chinetti, and shortly after Lewis came into the pits, losing over a minute before the car was away, with Rose-Richards driving. At 6.15 p.m. a small sensation was caused by the non-appearance of Chiron. Eventually he came in slowly, and left after a 4-minute halt.

Sommer's Record Laps

Sommer's lead was now over two laps, whilst his fastest lap so far was 143.278 k.p.h.—a record for the circuit.

After 2½ hours Lewis had covered 24 laps, the requisite distance before fuel or water can be taken aboard, and he came in and was quickly away after re-fuelling. Moll was in simultaneously. Sommer was still going strong and increasing his advantage on every circuit, and he again beat the lap record on the 25th lap, his average speed being the wonderful figure of 143.702 k.p.h. (89.25 m.p.h.).

Many Changes of Driver

Pit stops were now becoming frequent. Tarante brought in his black Bugatti, and after five minutes it was taken over by his partner, Mme. Desprez. Sommer refuelled after 27 laps, and then Nuvolari took over. At the same time—7 p.m. —Sabipa relieved Mme. Siko, who had been driving splendidly. Gas drove into the dead car park with the Bentley. Prince Nicolas of Roumania gave over to Cattaneo, and Driscoll, after bringing in his Aston-Martin for fuel, handed his car over to Penn-Hughes. Then S. C. H. Davis made his first re-appearance in racing since his accident at Brooklands, taking over Bertelli's Aston-Martin, likewise Gaupillat relieved Czaykowski, and Mrs. Wisdom superseded Maurice Goodall. Labric's Delage also made frequent pit calls.

It transpired that the Bentley had charged the Mulsanne bunker head on.

A fine drawing by Bryan de Grineau of Mme. Siko's crash; her Alfa-Romeo struck a tree with terrific force and the wreckage burst into flames.

Making its first appearance in Continental racing, the Singer Nine, driven by Barnes and Langley, put up a very good performance.

It smashed through the wooden palisading and hit a tree, bringing down a shower of branches. Gas, who had just taken over, was on his first lap and approached the corner far too fast. He was slightly cut about the mouth, and although the car was driven back it was out of the race.

Leaders at Three Hours

At the end of three hours Sommer's car, in the hands of Nuvolari, had an advantage of 4 mins. 18 secs. over Chinetti and Varent's Alfa, the leader's time for 30 laps being 2 hrs. 52 mins. 28 secs. Next were Rose-Richards and Moll, whose respective times were 2 hrs. 54 mins. 13 secs. and 2 hrs. 58 mins. 7 secs., while Cattaneo had got the Duesenberg into fifth place, despite the fact that it did not appear to be firing regularly. Sixth was Cortese, with Chiron's car, and tenth came Driscoll and Penn-Hughes's Aston-Martin, followed by Van der Becke's Riley. Five minutes later—8.5 p.m.—Sebilleau retired with No. 31 Riley.

The driver, fortunately, was not seriously injured. The tree was snapped off and Driscoll had to drive his Aston-Martin through the branches.

The positions at the end of four hours were as follow :—

1. Nuvolari and Sommer, 40 laps, 3 hrs. 54 mins. 20 secs.
2. Chinetti and Varent, 39 laps, 3 hrs. 56 mins. 50 secs.
3. Lewis and Rose-Richards, 39 laps, 3 hrs. 59 mins. 50 secs.
4. Moll and Cloitre, 38 laps, 3 hrs. 59 mins. 25 secs.
5. Chiron and Cortese, 37 laps, 3 hrs. 57 mins. 20 secs.
6. Prince Nicolas and Cattaneo, 37 laps, 3 hrs. 59 mins. 59 secs.

The first three positions remained unaltered at the end of the fifth hour, but Moll and Cloitre lost fourth place to Chiron and Cortese owing to the fact that the Alfa, driven by the last-named pair, had a jammed starter pinion when getting away from the pits. Most of the cars were running with unfailing regularity, the British contingent of Aston-Martins, M.G.s, and the lone Riley and Singer showing up well.

At the sixth hour the first four were still in the same order, but the 4.9 Bugatti was now in the fifth position; owing to the disqualification of the Duesenberg. This announcement was greeted with considerable disapproval,

for the car had covered 50 laps. The reason was that Prince Nicolas had taken on fuel one lap too early—on the 23rd instead of the 24th lap. And yet the car had been allowed to run all this time without notification !

Then in the seventh hour the Alfa. which had been magnificently handled by Brian Lewis and Rose-Richards, jumped into second place behind Sommer and Nulovari, with Chinetti third and Chiron fourth.

High Speeds After Nightfall

Night had now fallen, and the scene had taken on a wonderful aspect, and at the same time it caused the elimination of Czaykowski (Bugatti), who went out with trouble connected with the lighting equipment. It was also announced that Sommer and Nuvolari had covered the first 500 kiloms. at a higher average speed than was put up at Montlhéry the previous week by Campari, the winner of the French Grand Prix.

By the eighth hour Sommer's advantage was down to 48 secs., and Chiron had become second in front of Chinetti. while Lewis and Rose-Richards's Alfa was in fourth place, the car having been delayed at the pits just over 4 mins. with a jammed starter pinion. In fifth place came Mme. Desprez, driving a remarkably steady race with her Bugatti. The British contingent were, however, performing very well, Aston-Martins lying seventh and eighth, with the Riley ninth, Ford's M.G. eleventh, and Mrs. Wisdom's Aston-Martin next

Positions at Midnight

The times of the leaders at midnight were :—

1. Sommer and Nuvolari, 79 laps, 7 hrs. 55 mins. 38 secs.
2. Chiron and Cortese, 77 laps, 7 hrs. 56 mins. 24 secs.
3. Chinetti and Varent, 77 laps, 7 hrs. 56 mins. 33 secs.
4. Lewis and Rose-Richards, 76 laps, 7 hrs. 56 mins. 22 secs.

The order remained unchanged for the next hour, and the only incident of note was the retirement of Moll and Cloitre's Alfa. The engine was running splendidly, but the battery lugs had broken, and it was impossible to restart from the pits without a push-start, which is barred.

Another popular British entry was Metchim and Masters's Austin Seven, seen here on the new Esses bend, followed by an Aston-Martin and Alfa-Romeo.

Nuvolari (Alfa-Romeo) on the sharp Mulsanne bend, with Hendy's M.G. Midget in the rear.

3. Chinetti and Varent, 116 laps, 11 hrs. 58 mins. 31 secs.
4. Lewis and Rose-Richards, 114 laps, 11 hrs. 55 mins. 2 secs.
5. Tarante and Mme. Desprez, 104 laps, 11 hrs. 58 mins. 7 secs.

Twenty-five minutes later, and just as dawn had broken, Nuvolari brought in the leading Alfa with the off-side front wing adrift. Sommer immediately jumped from the pit to the rescue. He and his mechanic worked feverishly, but in the middle of the job there was a cry of "essence!" which was simply pouring on to the road. Driver and mechanic dived under the car, and before the two things were rectified 16 mins. had elapsed. Further excitement ensued as the starter refused to get the engine going. Sommer, however, let the car roll back on the down grade, and, engaging reverse, the engine sprang into life.

Excitement Prevails

Meanwhile, Chiron had taken the lead. Simultaneously, Lewis came in and departed minus a headlight. More excitement. Tarante's Bugatti looked to be on fire, being enveloped in white smoke. Something was wrong with it, however, and on the next lap he made a very lengthy stop. Meanwhile, the British cars were performing very well, with Ford's M.G. the admiration of everyone.

Positions were unaltered at 2 a.m. Just after Davis, with Aston-Martin No. 24, came in with a near-side front spring gone, and despite heroic efforts by driver and mechanic a replacement cost them an hour. Sommer also came in, and, losing 3 mins. thereby, enabled Chiron to pick up considerably. At the end of the 11th hour Alfas still filled the first four places, while Sommer and Lewis were running respectively first and second in the Rudge-Whitworth Biennial Cup.

Leaders at Half-time

With the race half over the positions were :—
1. Sommer and Nuvolari, 118 laps, 11 hrs. 54 mins. 47 secs.
2. Chiron and Cortese, 116 laps, 11 hrs. 58 mins. 26 secs.

Cortese (Alfa-Romeo) got into a terrific skid on the new Esses bend, turning right round and damaging the off-side front wheel, causing his retirement.

LE MANS 24-HOUR RACE—Contd.

One hour later—the 13th—the order was Chiron, Chinetti, Sommer, Lewis and Mme. Siko, all Alfas, Tarante, Driscoll and Van der Becke. At this period Aston-Martin No. 26, driven by Mrs. Wisdom, had retired, and Metchim's Austin was still bringing up the rear with unfailing regularity, although slow. And 20 cars were still in the battle.

Chinetti Takes the Lead

There were some striking changes before the end of the 14th hour. A pit stop by Chiron cost him the lead, and for the first time Chinetti was at the head of affairs by a margin of 2 mins. 31 secs., with Sommer third and Rose-Richards next, three laps behind the three named. Mme. Siko was fifth.

Now Chiron is in Front

At 6.40 a.m. Chinetti and Chiron came into view, bonnet to tail, the last-named trying unsuccessfully to pass on the hill past the grandstands. Past White House they roared together, but between Arnage and Mulsanne Chiron went to the front, and by the end of the 143rd lap he held a lead of half a mile.

The second crash during the race occurred just before 7 o'clock on the Sunday morning. The victim was Mme. Siko, who, driving an Alfa-Romeo, had all along been well placed. Her car skidded on the first bend before reaching the famous "S" on the Mulsanne-Arnage stretch. Getting completely out of control, the Alfa-Romeo cut down two big pine trees and overturned against a third, the impact breaking the tree off half-way up. Mme. Siko was conveyed to hospital, where it was found that her injuries were more or less of a superficial nature.

At 7.15 a.m. Rose-Richards, still lying fourth, came in for fuel, changed both rear wheels, made some minor adjustments, and after 4½ minutes' delay, handed over to Lewis, while Roger Labric, who had patronized the pits quite a lot with his Lorraine, gave up the struggle with clutch trouble, and drove into the dead car park. Next Bertelli was in with his Aston-Martin, and some strong cord was requisitioned to secure the near-side front wing, which was coming adrift. Chiron also came in and handed over to Cortese. After 15 hours it was Chiron, Chinetti, Nuvolari and Lewis, with the Riley now in sixth place, followed by Penn-Hughes.

A plucky show was also being put up by Ford and Baumer, who had brought their M.G. into tenth place with 109 laps. At this stage 19 were running, including seven British cars.

Four Alfa-Romeos Lead

The positions at the 16th hour were:

1. Chiron and Cortese, 155 laps, 15 hrs. 54 mins. 22 secs.
2. Sommer and Nuvolari, 155 laps, 15 hrs. 57 mins. 57 secs.
3. Chinetti and Varent, 154 laps, 15 hrs. 54 mins. 29 secs.
4. Rose-Richards and Lewis, 151 laps, 15 hrs. 54 mins. 29 secs.
5. Van der Becke and Peacock, 127 laps, 16 hrs. 58 mins. 5 secs.

After another half an hour Nuvolari and Cortese, running abreast, came down the straight to the grandstands. and a few yards later Nuvolari passed amid cheering, and on the following circuit led by 11 secs. This was increased later to half a minute, but at 9.25 a.m. Nuvolari had to come in for fuel. He also adjusted his brakes and handed over to Sommer, all in 40 secs. Sommer quickly began to reduce the gap, and exactly at 10 a.m. he came past the grandstands waving his handkerchief to denote his rival's undoing.

Cortese had a terrific broadside on the Esses before White House. Thus, Chinetti became second and Lewis third.

Thirteen out of the 29 had now fallen by the wayside—one of the Amilcars

and the Rally with fractured radiators, Sebilleau's Riley with seized rocker gear, and the Lorraine and Austin with clutch trouble. With the retirement of Chiron and Cortese considerable interest had also gone out of the struggle, for Sommer and Nuvolari's, which had so far broken the lap record nine times, was three laps to the good from Chinetti, who was the same distance in front of Lewis. Sommer's Alfa was also leading in the Coupe Biennial with Driscoll's Aston-Martin second.

British Cars Performing Well

By the 19th hour it was Sommer, Chinetti and Lewis, and the next three places were filled by British cars, Driscoll's Aston-Martin. Van der Becke's Riley and Ford's M.G., all of which were going remarkably well. Then shortly after, the M.G. driven by Parker and Hendy, which had been pretty consistent, retired after covering 123 laps, which was insufficient to qualify for next year. The leader's time was 18 hrs. 57 mins. 47 secs. for 185 laps. One hour later the first three positions were the same, but the Riley had moved up fourth in front of the Aston-Martin, and had also displaced Sommer's car on handicap for next year's qualifying race.

Sommer was in at 12.10 p.m. for fuel, change of drivers, and for again lashing up a front wing, while the pits were showing signs of anxiety about the petrol tank. Nuvolari also came in twice with fuel running from the tank.

Three Hours to Go

With three hours to go it was anyone's race, for the tank of Nuvolari's car was now leaking badly. Rose-Richards also made a fairly lengthy pit stop, whereas Chinetti's car was running trouble-free. British cars, Van der Becke's Riley and Ford's M.G., were at this stage running first and second on handicap, with Sommer next, while the last named had covered the greatest distance, his time for 194 laps being 19 hrs. 54 mins. 15 secs.

A fine speed picture of the Hon. Brian Lewis (Alfa-Romeo) passing de Gavardie's Amilcar.

At 1.15 p.m. Nuvolari was in again, but, having been passed by Chinetti, he went on without any attempt to stop the leak. Quickly he got the lead back. All eyes centred on the Italian. Would he be able to cover the full 24 laps before he could refuel at the rate he was losing the precious essence? There was a fever of excitement as he wiped off lap after lap.

The Alfa's Pit Calls

Then out went the stop sign. He came in on the following lap. An attempt was made to minimize the leakage, and Nuvolari was off, still in the lead. Then at long last the pit signal was "1." Had he got enough to take him 13½ kiloms.? At 2.47 p.m.

Count Czaykowski (Bugatti) finds time to look round as he comes out of the Arnage corner.

Penn-Hughes (Aston-Martin) hot on the tail of Rousseau's Alfa-Romeo on leaving the new road and entering the old course.

the question was answered. Nuvolari coasted safely into the pits, took aboard the precious fuel and was away before Varent came past with Chinetti's car. The rest seemed easy, for the leading Alfa was much speedier.

At this period it was still Nuvolari, Chinetti, and Lewis, and British cars now filled the next four places—Van der Becke (Riley), Driscoll (Aston-Martin), Ford (M.G.), and Bertelli (Aston-Martin).

Nuvolari Loses the Lead

More excitement was yet to follow, for Nuvolari was far from being out of his troubles. At 3.15 p.m.—only 45 mins. to the finish—he came into the pits. Quickly he removed the seat cushions, apparently in an endeavour to get at his tools. The Varent-Chinetti Alfa-Romeo rushed by at the moment into the lead, which caused Nuvolari to alter his mind and go in pursuit. Then, 6 mins. later, both Varent and the Italian were in together. Half an hour passed. The pair came in sight abreast on the long stretch to the grandstand. Then Nuvo-

lari drew clear and Varent had to come in to refuel. The race now looked as good as over, but, like all the big events this year, the Le Mans classic had to provide a sensation.

With 8 mins. to the hour they were racing abreast again. Past the Arnage bend Varent was in front. On the fast leg by the Café l'Hippodrome Nuvolari's speed told to good effect, but his brakes were weakening, and when the Esses were reached it was Varent again. When the road opened out the Italian once more trod hard on things, and he was first home by the small margin of 10 secs. after one of the sternest struggles ever seen.

British Car Positions

Both men received a wonderful ovation, and T. E. Rose-Richards, who with the Hon. Brian Lewis had driven such a fine race, finished third.

British cars were fourth, fifth, sixth, seventh and fourteenth. The Aston-Martins ran splendidly. Ford's M.G. Midget more than surprised the spectators, and the Riley, driven so well by Van der Becke and Peacock, more than

upheld the reputation of the manufacturers and the prestige of the British light car.

Last but one came the Singer Nine sports four-seater, which it can truly be said gave a great account of itself. Likewise credit must be given to drivers of the other foreign finishers: Alfa-Romeo, Tracta, Salmson, B.N.C., S.A.R.A. and Amilcar all covered themselves with glory.

What a race, indeed! One worth going a very long way to see. Sommer was nearly overcome with excitement.

THE 11th GRAND PRIX d'ENDURANCE RESULTS

1. Sommer and Nuvolari, 3,144 kiloms. = 80.98 m.p.h.
2. Chinetti and Varent, 3,143 kiloms.
3. Hon. Brian Lewis and Rose-Richards, 3,043 kiloms.
4. Van der Becke and Peacock, 2,581 kiloms.
5. Driscoll and Penn-Hughes, 2,548 kiloms.
6. Ford and Baumer, 2,385 kiloms.
7. Bertelli and S. C. H. Davis, 2,352 kiloms.
8. Rousseau and Paes, 2,250 kiloms.
9. Quinault and Podrault, 2,176 kiloms.
10. Vernet and Vallon, 2,155 kiloms.
11. Alin Brothers, 2,047 kiloms.
12. de Gavardie Brothers, 2,005 kiloms.
13. Barnes and Langley, 1,900 kiloms.
14. Mottet and Maraudet, 2,034 kiloms. (broke down before 24 hrs. were completed).

All these covered the minimum distance required, which is calculated from the cylinder capacity. They are qualified for the final of the 10th Coupe Biennial, 1933-1934.

THE 9th BIENNIAL CUP

1. Sommer and Nuvolari (Alfa-Romeo).
2. Driscoll and Penn-Hughes (Aston-Martin).
3. Hon. Brian Lewis and Rose-Richards (Alfa-Romeo).
4. Bertelli and Davis (Aston-Martin).

London-Edinburgh Results
Correction

IN the tabulated results of the London-Edinburgh Trial, published on page 823, R. G. M. Paul, E. C. Weiss, J. M. Pybus, Junr., and M. P. Tenbosch are included in the Frazer-Nash list, whereas they all drove Hillman Minx cars, the first three gaining premier awards.

The French Grand Prix Lap Record

IN our report of the French Grand Prix, published last week, it was stated that Etancelin equalled the circuit record of 5 mins. 24 secs. on his fourteenth lap (175 kiloms.) and the speed of 136.116 k.p.h. was given; this was Etancelin's average for the 175 kiloms., the lap speed being 138.888 k.p.h., which Campari subsequently increased to 139.318 k.p.h.

1934

Although there were no further changes to the circuit, the aspect of Le Mans was changed drastically for the 1934 race as impressive new two-storey pits had been erected, and new high-speed fuel pumps had been installed courtesy of the petrol companies. The new pits would cater for a maximum of 60 cars a figure which was occasionally reached in the 1950s although since then the number of entrants has normally been limited to 55.

Perhaps because of the much improved amenities, perhaps because of Nuvolari's dramatic victory the year before, the 1934 race attracted 44 starters, of which Britain provided the biggest number, but none with the chance of an outright win as the biggest British cars were the Aston Martins, Rileys and Singers in the 1½ litre class; Britain also dominated the 1,100 cc class with MG Magnettes, a Lagonda Rapier and Riley Nines, and in the small car class there were Singer Nines, MG Midgets and a single Austin Seven. The total number of British cars was 23; but the favourites were yet again the 2.3 litre Alfa Romeos, of which four were entered privately, making up for the absence of the Milanese works team. France fielded 17 cars, including five Bugattis ranging from 1½ to five-litres; the old La Lorraine; assorted small cars, including the last appearance at Le Mans of Rally, Tracta and Salmson, although the last mentioned would make a brief reappearance in 1955-6; and two of the new front wheel drive Derbys with two-litre V-8 engines, one driven by Englishwoman Mrs Gwenda Stewart.

Raymond Sommer in one of the Alfa Romeos led from the start, closely followed by the other three cars of this make; but after less than two hour's racing, the Sommer car caught fire and had to retire, putting the British entered Alfa of Lord Howe and Rose-Richards into the lead. Sommer's early retirement was a bad omen for the Alfa camp; another British crew in an Alfa, Saunders-Davis and Clifford, had to retire during Saturday evening, and after having dropped down the field due to lighting problems, Lord Howe and Rose-Richards were finally defeated with clutch trouble.

As Sunday dawned it therefore appeared that the remaining Alfa Romeo driven by Louis Chinetti and Philippe Etancelin would have the race in the bag, if it would last; but there seems to have been a repeat of the leaking fuel tank problem which all but defeated Sommer and Nuvolari in the previous year. Of their rivals, the five litre Bugatti had already retired the previous evening; so had one of the 2.3 litre Bugattis while the other was disqualified. The three-litre Bugatti and the venerable La Lorraine still kept going but they were well down the scoreboard, behind many of the smaller cars; indeed, the leading Alfa was hunted by a pack of assorted Aston Martins, Rileys and MGs. But when the Aston Martin which was running second retired, Chinetti had a comfortable lead over the following Riley which enabled him to relax a little. He finished the race as winner but without breaking any records - the average speed of the Chinetti/Etancelin Alfa Romeo was 74.74 mph and the distance covered 1,793.85 miles, lower figures than at any time since 1929, nor was the lap record broken.

Apart from the victorious Alfa Romeo, the honours of the race went to British cars; of 23 finishers, 16 were British, and the achievement of Riley was particularly noteworthy: of six cars entered, six finished, taking second, third, fifth and sixth places, while the Riley of von der Becke/Peacock, which finished fifth, also won the Index of Performance and the Biennial Cup. One of the MG Magnettes was fourth, MG's best ever Le Mans placing, and Singers filled seventh and eighth places.

With four consecutive victories to their credit, the Alfa Romeos were obvious rivals to the Bentleys for the best overall performance at Le Mans, but the Italian cars still needed a fifth victory to equal the achievement of the British cars. This is exactly what Alfa Romeo entrants intended to do in 1935...

On ROAD and TRACK

by Grande Vitesse

Action! Philippe Etancelin swinging his G.P. Maserati round a bend in the recent Montreux Grand Prix.

LE MANS ENTRIES

GREAT BRITAIN
Up to 1,100 c.c.
M. Collier (M.G. Midget).
R. Eccles (M.G. Magnette).
Singer, Ltd. (two Singers).
L. Ford (M.G. Magnette).
Lord de Clifford (Lagonda).
G. Hendy (Singer).
Riley, Ltd. (four Rileys).
Miss D. Champney (Riley).
A. A. Rigby (M.G. Midget).
B. Metchim (Austin).

1,500 c.c.
F. S. Barnes (Singer).
Aston-Martin, Ltd. (three Aston-Martins).
A. Vincent (Aston-Martin).
J. C. Noel (Aston-Martin).
A. W. Fox (Singer).

3-litres.
Lord Howe (Alfa-Romeo).
Mrs. G. Stewart (Derby).
R. P. Gardner (Singer).
T. E. Rose-Richards (Alfa-Romeo).

FRANCE
Up to 1,100 c.c.
Soc. Anon. Tracta (two Tractas).
R. Gaillard (Rally).
J. E. Vernet (Salmson).
C. Poire (Amilcar).
C. A. Martin (Amilcar).
De Gavardie (Amilcar).

1,500 c.c.
G. Boursin (Amilcar).
B. Bodoignet (Bugatti).
J. Trevoux (Riley).

3-litres.
Mlle. Helde (Alfa-Romeo).
L. Chinetti (Alfa-Romeo).
P. Felix (Alfa-Romeo).
N. Mahe (Bugatti).
Equippe Braillard (Maserati and Bugatti).
C. Brunet (Bugatti).

Over 3-litres.
J. E. Vernet (3½-litre Lorraine).

Not Declared
R. Sommer, R. Labric, V. Bayard, the brothers Alin, Mme. Itier, L. Villeneuve and Mme Siko.

ROUMANIA
Over 3-litres.
Prince Nicholas of Roumania (5½-litre Duesenberg).

AND NOW—LE MANS!

Excellent Entry for 24-hour Endurance Race — Britain Dominates the Lists

SO here we are on the eve of Le Mans, or near enough for all intents and purposes. Of all the races held to-day, and their name is legion, Le Mans continues firm in our affections. This classic race has atmosphere, glamour, drama—call it what you will. It is a race which grips the imagination even more than the wild Grands Prix run at incredible speeds which have become the order of the day. Le Mans is unique; it stands alone, and stands alone particularly for British enthusiasts. On the Sarthe Circuit, at least, British cars have been supreme and have built up a reputation which has made a British entry something to be reckoned with, even in these days when the majestic green Bentleys no longer go thundering down to Mulsanne.

Three Races in One

At first sight the Le Mans 24-hour Endurance Race seems to be a somewhat complicated affair in which every driver appears to be competing in several races at the same time. Simplified, this is what happens. First of all there is a free-for-all 24-hour Grand Prix in which there is no handicap and in which the drivers (for there are, somewhat naturally, two per car) who cover the greatest distance in the two days are the out-and-out winners. Next there is the Rudge-Whitworth Cup. This event is run in two parts—an eliminating round and a final, held in successive years, so that to compete in the final the entrant must have had a car qualify in the eliminating round of the preceding year. Thus next week-end we have the final round of the 10th Rudge Cup and the eliminating round of the 11th (next year's) Rudge Cup.

All this means that every car which starts on Saturday will be competing in the 24-hour Endurance Grand Prix and in the eliminating round of next year's Rudge Cup. The few which qualified last year (13 are eligible) will fight out the final of the 1934 Rudge Cup between them. A manufacturer or private entrant who qualified with a car last year can run one car of any make or type this year for each car he qualified last year. Thus, Aston-Martins have two cars eligible for this year's final. I do hope all this is clear.

The Le Mans races are open only to standard A1 sports cars, blown or unblown. Except the Grand Prix d'Endurance, they compete on a handicap basis which sets a minimum distance for each category. The driver who improves most on his set distance is the winner.

The Famous "Le Mans Start"

At the start the cars are drawn up in echelon, with their backs to the line of pits. The drivers stand on the opposite side of the road. When the flag drops, there is a scurry of feet, the men dash to their machines, leap into the seat, press the starter button and roar off down the road. It is one of the finest sights in modern racing.

Great Britain has always been a formidable opponent at Le Mans. This year we are represented by an entry of no fewer than 25 cars—easily the largest number of any nation in the race. France comes next with 18 cars, then Italy with 7. There is one American and two entries which have yet to be named.

The race starts at 4 p.m. on Saturday. The cars race all that night, changing drivers as their pit chiefs direct, and finish at 4 p.m. on Sunday evening. Throughout the race all spares and tools to be used must be carried on the cars, with a few exceptions.

The permanent circuit of the Sarthe, over which this great race is annually run, is one of the finest in France. It measures 13 kiloms. (8.08 miles). There is one long straight where speeds of over 140 m.p.h. are attained, leading down from the Pontlieue end of the course to Mulsanne Corner. The opposite side of the circuit is difficult, with the dangerously fast "Esses" and famous White House and Arnage corners. The old circuit used to run through the village of Pontlieue at the north end of the course, but this is now by-passed by a new leg specially built, bringing the cars back to the beginning of the Mulsanne Straight. For some distance the road runs through dense pine forests. Thousands of French people camp out all night in the woods, lanterns hang from the trees, marquees do a roaring refreshment trade, and the strains of dance bands beat upon the night air. Certainly, Le Mans has an atmosphere of gaiety and enthusiasm unequalled anywhere else to-day.

In the list of entries given on page 830 I have grouped the names according to the nationality of the entrant. At Le Mans they have a knack of leaving the name of the car as the enigmatic " X " until almost the eve of the race, which explains the " Not Declared " section so late in the day.

All those given in this list are eligible for the Grand Prix d'Endurance and the eliminating round of the 1935 Cup. Those running this year in the Final are: two factory Aston-Martins, a works Riley, and a Tracta, and among the private entries, Sommer, Chinetti, Brian Lewis (Arthur Fox's entry), Ludovic Ford, Andre

Rousseau, Vernet, Adrien Alin, de Gavardie and F. S. Barnes.

The Riley contingent consists of four 1,089 c.c. models and two 1,455's. The former are to be driven respectively by MM. Gas and Trevoux, the Monte Carlo Rally experts, Miss Champney and Mrs. K. Petre, S. H. Newsome and E. McLure, A. Von der Becke and K. S. Peacock.' The larger cars will be handled by Jean Sebilleau and G. Belleroche, F. W. Dixon and C. Paul.

Lord de Clifford will drive a Lagonda Rapier—the first time this car has appeared in racing. The Singer entered by Arthur Fox will be driven by the Hon. Brian Lewis and is the car he drove in the Mannin Beg.

F. S. Barnes and A. H. Langley will drive a 1½-litre Singer in the final as well as the Grand Prix d'Endurance, and the other Singers are Nines, to be handled by J. D. Barnes and T. H. Wisdom, J. R. Baker and Norman Black.

The Aston-Martin team drivers will be A. C. Bertelli (designer-driver) and C. Penn-Hughes, T. S. Fothringham and J. C. Elwes, G. Morris-Goodall and R. J. Appleton.

The mantle of prophecy has never really descended on my shoulders, but Alfa-Romeo seems to have a winning sound about it. . . .

Incidents in the Mannin Races

BEFORE carrying on with the hundred and one things there are to talk about this week, I think there should be a word about the recent Mannins.

That week in the island was not unmarked by incidents—one, unfortunately, grave, but many, happily, gay. There was, for example, the occasion when the R.A.C. officials forgot to wake up for the first day's practising and were duly summoned from their couches by a sturdy sergeant of police, specially and very hurriedly detailed by the Chief Constable. There was also the gentleman who looks after the roads who, when asked if he had put down any material on a certain bump said, " Yes, a little. About eight tons."

Apart from these matters, the R.A.C. staged what approximates to a British Grand Prix over a circuit which, given a few less bumps, would be first class, and is in any case immeasurably superior to that used last year—and vastly more agreeable to the good people of Douglas. The race is no longer a " Round-the-houses " circus.

The driving of Freddie Dixon was the subject of general comment amongst drivers. There was that incident with Rose-Richards in the Mannin Moar (which was sketched by Bryan de Grineau). Rose-Richards, hearing the squeal of Dixon's brakes behind him as he was about to take the Onchan hairpin, slowed up, and thus avoided

E. G. Frankl, the Bugatti driver, who was killed in the recent Eifel meeting on the Nurburg Ring.

being charged broadside. There was a similar incident at Broadway Corner when Dixon was making up time. Whilst it may be appreciated by the public and daily Press, this spectacular kind of driving is deplored by racing motorists who see it from a more intimate angle.

P. L. Donkin's Retirement

We hear that P. L. Donkin, who drove an M.G. Magnette in the recent Mannin Beg race, objects to the use of the words " Driver Warned Off " which were used as a sub-title in our report of that event, feeling that this casts a personal reflection upon him. It was not intended in this way, as, naturally, there was no suggestion of irregularity on his part, as our description of the incident emphasized. Our information is that the M.G. had damaged an axle during the race and, having been flagged in for inspection, was withdrawn as being unsafe for further participation in the event.

The Eifel Meeting

THE wonderful circuit of the Nurburg Ring saw a tremendous race on June 3 between the new Mercedes and P-wagen Grand Prix cars and the Ferrari Alfa-Romeo. This time the 3-litre Mercedes (which is said to have an even more amazing wail than the giant 7-litre models ever had) came into its own, and with Manfred von Brauchitsch at the wheel, won the unlimited race at 76.5 m.p.h. He led throughout the race, with Hans von Stück in the rear-engined P-wagen hard on his heels and Louis Chiron (Alfa-Romeo) some distance behind. This was the finishing order, with the Mercedes 1 min. 20 secs. ahead of the P-wagen.

Lord de Clifford at the wheel of the 1,100 c.c. Lagonda Rapier which he is to drive in its first race—Le Mans—next week-end. The car has shown great promise in trials at Brooklands.

GRAND PRIX D'ENDURANCE

		m.p.h.
1.	Alfa-Romeo (Etancelin—Chinetti)	74.74
2.	Riley (Sebilleau—Delaroche)	70.07
3.	Riley (F. W. Dixon—C. Paul)	69.60

RUDGE-WHITWORTH CUP

		Figure of Merit
1.	Riley (A. Von der Becke—K. S. Peacock)	1.3697
2.	Singer (Hon. B. E. Lewis—J. Hindmarsh)	1.2549
3.	Singer (F. S. Barnes—A. Langley)	1.2389

FACTS ABOUT THE 24-HOUR RACE

The race goes on from 4.0 p.m. on Saturday afternoon through the night till 4.0 p.m. on Sunday afternoon.

* * *

As well as the prize for the longest distance, the Rudge-Whitworth Cup is open to those cars which fulfilled a minimum distance considering their engine size in the race in the previous year, thus qualifying for the next year. The award for this "race within a race" is decided on formula, whereas the Grand Prix is irrespective of engine size.

* * *

Cars are allowed to refuel only at intervals of 24 laps or more, and replenishments of fuel, oil, and water must be simultaneous.

* * *

All fuel is of a standard grade, and is issued by the organising club, the Automobile Club de l'Ouest. Benzole or oil in the fuel are allowed, however.

* * *

All tools and spares to be used must be carried on the car, except one extra spare wheel, jacks, and fuel, oil and water, which are at the pits.

* * *

One mechanic only is allowed to assist a driver in adjustments. An assistant must also be provided to fill the petrol tanks, but is not allowed to help in any other way.

* * *

Last year Nuvolari and Sommer, driving an Alfa-Romeo, covered 1,953.6 miles at an average speed of 81.5 m.p.h., thus winning the Grand Prix d'Endurance and the Rudge-Whitworth Cup.

They're off!

Alfa-Romeo Wins Grand Prix d'Endurance, Driven by Etancelin and Chinetti. British Riley Wins the Rudge-Whitworth Cup

LES *Vingt-Quatre Heures du Mans*— the great French 24-Hour Race! Only in France could such scenes of enthusiasm for a motor race be experienced. Yet British cars achieved great success in last Saturday's and Sunday's epic race, for out of the field of forty-four starters twenty-three cars finished, and sixteen of these were manufactured in this country. The winner of the Grand Prix d'Endurance—the award for the longest distance covered in the twenty-four hours—was, it is true, an Italian car, the Alfa-Romeo driven by Chinetti and Etancelin, which averaged 74.74 m.p.h., but British cars occupied the next seven places, and the Rudge-Whitworth Cup—the biennial award on formula for the best figure of merit according to engine size—was won by a Riley, drivers: Von der Becke and K. S. Peacock!

Le Mans is justly proud of the "Circuit Permanent de la Sarthe," and every year the town is *en fête* for the occasion of the race. Glorious hot weather—really, it was almost too hot—saw the entire countryside making its way out to the course on foot, on the inevitable French bicycles, or in cars with equally inevitable incessant hooting, such a characteristic of the country. From far and near they rolled in, till even the crowds of past years were exceeded, and car park after car park glistened in serried ranks.

Much of the circuit, 8.3 miles in length, lies among beautiful pine woods, and here tents and caravans were set up, while thousands came prepared to spend a night in the open. Picnic parties spread themselves out, booths sprang up like mushrooms, and lilting French airs from the innumerable loud-speakers greeted the gaily decked throng—women in summery frocks of unmistakable French taste, the men in short-sleeved pull-overs and small, round berets.

This year the pits—always permanent structures fitted with electric light—had been provided with an upper storey, reaching indeed a standard of magnificence unparalleled in motor racing. Beneath them were lined up the cars— seventeen carried the blue of France, twenty-three the English green, and four the Italian red—all arrayed pointing diagonally in the direction of travel at

TWENTY-FOUR-HOUR RACE AT LE MANS

the side of the road, and the vivid advertisements of various accessories, so characteristic of a Continental road race, lent additional colour to the scene. As four o'clock approached a stentorian voice announced "*Messieurs les gendarmes, prenez garde à la route,*" or words to that effect, and the task began of getting the chattering throng off the road. But the French have all the instincts proper to a road race, and soon all was clear.

Round the stands and along each side of the new road after the start there are avenues or paths marked in picturesque style after famous names connected with the race. One saw thousands of eager spectators pressing to the railings around such signs as the Esplanade Dunlop, the Avenue Bentley, and the Esplanade Guy Bouriat, after the late French driver.

* * *

The drivers took up their stations on the opposite side of the road to the cars, and all eyes were fixed on the starter, with the French tricolour raised. As he let it fall they dashed across, leapt into their *voitures*, and one after the other got away, until the course was strangely

empty except for Gaillard's Rally, which for some time refused to move.

Rose-Richards, driving Lord Howe's blue Alfa-Romeo, was first away, followed by Saunders-Davies in another Alfa, Raymond Sommer, the French favourite and winner of the previous year's race with Nuvolari, also with an Alfa, and then Veyron, with a big blue supercharged "four-nine" Bugatti. Brian Lewis, driving Arthur Fox's red Singer, was first of the English cars to round the bend after the start, in seventh place.

After the first lap Sommer screamed through already well in the lead, Rose-Richards second, and Etancelin, who was to play such a big part in the race, third, with Chinetti's Alfa-Romeo. First of the English challengers was now Ford's M.G. Magnette, travelling very fast in eighth place, and already in front of many larger cars.

"*Allô, Allô!*" The speakers gave out that Bertelli had spun round near Arnage, driving one of the Aston Martin "Rudge Cup" cars, with the result, as they said, that the clutch had become "deteriorated." Meanwhile, Sommer increased

his lead, and in ninth place, behind Ford, came Morris-Goodall's Aston Martin. But Thomas Fothringham made a hurried call at his pit with the other "Cup" Aston Martin to slack off his brakes, which had been rubbing. Soon Sommer had a lead of 27 sec. over Rose-Richards, which means quite a lot in distance when one considers that he was lapping at about 87 m.p.h., and the second car at 84 m.p.h.

At 4.30 a cheer went up, for Bertelli had got going again. It was now learnt that the gear box had been giving trouble, and "Bert" had had the top off and inspected the selectors. At five o'clock Ford was lapping at over 76 m.p.h. with the Magnette, and had moved up to seventh place. Brunet's beautifully built 3.3-litre Bugatti was holding sixth place behind Veyron's bigger "four-nine," both cars travelling finely, but the Dixon-Paul 1½-litre Riley had ousted Morris-Goodall from eighth place.

Shortly before 5.30, however, came a sensation, for it was given out that Sommer's car was on fire at the back of the course! Actually he had stopped

The animated scene at the pits, showing the cars lined up just before the start of the race.

near Arnage in a cloud of steam and smoke, while the disappointed spectators cried "*Fini! Fini!*" Later he was towed round to the pits by an official and retired. This let Rose-Richards into the lead with Lord Howe's Alfa-Romeo, Etancelin becoming second with Chinetti's car, only a few seconds behind, and Saunders-Davies third.

Brian Lewis' red painted Singer was in at the pits at this period, and leisurely adjustments were made; he got away after a stop of nearly three-quarters of an hour, two of the valve springs having been changed. About the same time Fourny's Bugatti ran out of petrol, and although he reached the pits, he was not allowed by the rules to replenish, so he retired.

When Rose-Richards came in after his allotted twenty-four laps to refuel, Lord Howe taking over, the stop let the other blue Alfa take the lead, Chinetti now driving. It was not long before the other cars began to come in one by one, and the huge crowd lining the railings, six or seven deep, below the grandstand, were quick to appreciate skilful pitwork, the Aston Martin team in particular working methodically to a set schedule.

The crowds were tremendous on this Saturday afternoon, and it was perhaps fortunate alongside the new road that all did not desire to watch the race at the same time. Taking refuge from the sweltering heat, many were picnicking in the woods. Others were dancing in the booths to typical French accordion music, the whole scene, amazing to English eyes, of a character indeed only seen in England on the downs at Epsom on Derby Day.

Yet the keenest interest was taken in the progress of the race, and many apparently of peasant class had their stop-watches clicking, so that if ever a driver had been absent at his pit for some time he frequently received applause all round the circuit on his rejoining the fray.

On the new road loud-speakers were arranged at intervals of about 100 yards, so that the French crowd, at all events, was supplied with a constant stream of information. Many were watching the interesting corner off the new road on to the old straight which leads to Mulsanne, and here a few notes might be made on cornering styles. Lord Howe was very polished and extremely fast, while his road manners were perfect, needless to say. On one occasion he politely gave precedence to Hendy's Singer where many drivers of fast cars would have snatched at the chance of getting by before the corner. Yet, regrettably, many drivers of the small, slower cars were not equally polite, especially on the long straight, and those travelling at speed were frequently baulked. Still more regrettably, on the authority of several noted drivers, the offenders were all too often on English cars.

Mahé's long-tailed 3-litre Bugatti was going round in a steady sweep, while Sebilleau leant out in more dashing fashion with his Riley. Still more dash-ing was Appleton, second driver in Fothringham's Aston Martin, but Donald Barnes toured round steadily with Wisdom's Singer. Trevoux' Riley was extremely neat, but Villeneuve's Derby less steady, while the seven-years-old Lorraine, one of the famous team of past Le Mans races, was good enough in its own ponderous fashion. Mme. Itier, with her M.G., was a little slow, but her cornering was neat, and the heroic Bedoignet, with what one would like to call a "G.P." Bugatti, was coming round skilfully, with perfect gear changes. Yet his car was already developing the misfiring which was to beset him throughout his run.

Penn-Hughes was making up for lost time with Bertelli's Aston Martin, and was one of the fastest, not only on this corner, but all round the course. He was lapping at round about the 80 m.p.h. mark. Appleton was chasing Roy Eccles, driving Martin's Magnette, and soon passed him. Mrs. Petre was lapping, to order of the *équipe*, at just over 63 m.p.h. very consistently with Miss Champney's Riley Imp, and, while her braking for the corner was a little unsteady at first, she soon settled down.

At Arnage wet tar on "Les Esses" bend was causing some trouble, but, on the right-angle following, some fine cornering was seen, especially by the Alfa-Romeos and Aston Martins, which were being driven round the sharp turn at about 40 m.p.h. quite steadily. The crowd had dubbed Lewis, clad in a red singlet with his blood-red Singer, "Le Diable Rouge," and he, too, cornered finely.

Chinetti in the lead was lapping at 85 m.p.h., and Lord Howe was fighting a ding-dong battle to catch him. First he was 16 sec. behind, then 11 sec., then 8 sec., then 4 sec. Great excitement was created, since "the Lord-Earl" is popular wherever he goes. rising to fever-pitch when at 8.15 p.m. he

A view of the start, with the grandstand in the background, taken from "The Autocar" pit.

The Alfa-Romeo which Etancelin and Chinetti drove to victory flashes past the stands.

broke the lap record at approximately 90 m.p.h., and on his forty-second lap passed his rival. Trouble had beset Saunders-Davies' Alfa-Romeo, and he suddenly dropped from third place to seventeenth, till on his fortieth lap he retired with a broken valve.

Thus there were only two of the proud Alfa-Romeos still running, but as "*le ciel de feu,*" as the French papers aptly put it, changed slowly from glaring blue to softer hues, and the sun began to sink behind the pine trees, Lord Howe drove smoothly on. Twilight grew apace, and the scene which has so often and so fitly been called "magic" developed. The lights in the pits twinkled out, and over towards Arnage and White House Corner the beams of hurrying head lights swung through the trees. Over behind the stands a long procession of twin shining eyes showed where spectators who had gone home for dinner were returning in their cars for that thrilling

Night falls over the scene, and the road in front of the pits is illuminated by floodlights.

spectacle, the night run at Le Mans!

But at half-past ten sensationally it was given out that *la voiture numero six*—Lord Howe's car—had stopped on the long straight. His lights had failed! And simultaneously it was announced that *numero neuf*—Chinetti's Alfa—had a leaking petrol tank, though he did not abate his speed. The two Alfas had such a lead over the rest, even over Veyron's Bugatti, which was lying third,

Etancelin with the Alfa-Romeo swoops past Mme. Itier driving her M.G. Midget.

and going well, that not for some time did Lord Howe lose first the premier position and then second place. An emissary was sent out from the pit to render verbal assistance, while Lord Howe himself frantically overhauled the electrical system.

Then, over an hour later, amid a burst of applause, the blue Alfa screamed through the pits again, the lights blazing, and the driver straining every nerve to catch up his lost ground. At midnight Fate struck again. It was a baleful hour for Veyron. His race was run, and so was a big-end. Hard luck indeed! He had been cornering splendidly with his big Bugatti, and with the Alfas in trouble had been looked upon as a likely winner.

At quarter-time the position of the Rudge Cup contest was Von der Becke and Peacock leading with their Riley, Ford and Baumer second with the Magnette, and Fothringham and Appleton third with the Aston Martin.

With Lord Howe now in eleventh place, though going up strongly, second position in the Grand Prix d'Endurance actually went to the 1,100 c.c. M.G. Magnette of Ford and Baumer, which was still travelling at an astonishing pace, while third came Appleton. Bertelli's Aston Martin had retired with gear box trouble, so the "A.M." hopes for the Rudge Cup were pinned on their second car.

Then came sensation after sensation. The Aston Martin *équipe,* pleased with

Morris-Goodall's Aston Martin cornering at the S-bend on the new road.

their success, for their third car, Morris-Goodall's, was lying fourth in the Grand Prix, though not qualified for the Cup, were suddenly startled by the non-appearance of Number Twenty-Two. Appleton was missing! He had taken the new corner on to the old straight at too great a pace, the car skidded right round on some loose sand, and up on to a bank he went. Breathless, he ran back to the pit for instructions, and then set out again. For two hours he laboured on his car, which at last was got away, so that the amazed Fothringham, who was having a quiet meal in *The Autocar* pit, despairing of his luck, suddenly saw his green car flash by the pits again, apparently undamaged and still in the race. Later, however, it transpired that outside assistance had been obtained, so that the car should have stopped there and then.

But, to return, a few laps later Ford, driving the Magnette, came upon Quinault's Tracta skidding just before White House corner. He had to brake heavily, and, turning round, collided with the tail of the French car. Blinded by the M.G.'s lights, momentarily facing in the reverse direction, Brunet too applied his brakes heavily, and his Bugatti spun into the ditch, side by side with the M.G. Both these cars were put out of the race, the M.G. with 83 and the Bugatti with 74 laps covered, and Mme. Itier also had a narrow escape from a bad collision in the *mêlée*, proceeding almost undamaged. The Tracta's tail was straightened out (more or less) and

(Left) Lord de Clifford's Lagonda Rapier, making its racing debut, enters the new road after the stands.

(Below left) The first corner on the new road after the start. The cars are Mahé's Bugatti and Alin's B.N.C.

ing easily for the Rudge Cup. Rileys, in addition, held fourth and fifth positions with Sebilleau's and Dixon's cars.

For a long time now the race pursued an even tenor, and dawn found the Alfa still increasing its lead in tireless manner. The Riley still led for the Rudge Cup, and Singers were second and third on formula, with Stanley Barnes and Brian Lewis. Hendy's Singer, however, retired with a puzzling trouble, later traced to a choked petrol supply.

Appleton was striving might and main to rejoin his colleague, Elwes, driving Morris-Goodall's car, at the top of the table, and just after five o'clock he came in, adjusted the brakes, refuelled, and handed over to Thomas Fothringham, the stop taking one second over three minutes, and at twenty to six Morris-Goodall came in, with a comfortable lead of two laps over the third man, and a broken steering column bracket was repaired, the stop taking 6¾ min., without appreciably altering the positions of the leading cars. Fothringham, whose cornering was amongst the best in the race, held

somehow the rear light was made to work, and he, too, continued. It was at White House, it will be remembered, where the famous Bentley crash took place in 1927, and where five cars crashed together in 1932—though this year's affair was not quite at the same place.

As though this were not enough, Lord Howe's lights failed again, but were put right, and at 1.0 a.m. the indomitable driver had got back to sixth place. Then clutch trouble developed, and this was serious. For a long time the crowd, still numerous, watched the mechanics work, then Lord Howe threw up his hands and the sleek blue car was sadly pushed away to the retired car park.

Only one Alfa left running! But that had a lead of over sixty miles, and pursued its way contemptuous of the small cars snarling at its heels. Yet there were still fifteen hours to go, and that leaking tank meant that anything might happen. There were still twenty-nine cars going strong. Morris-Goodall was now second, and Von der Becke third with the Riley, which was also still lead-

(Above right) At the top of the hill on the new road Von der Becke's Riley passes Bertelli's retired Aston Martin.

(Right) Martin's M.G. Magnette leads a bunch of small cars through the S-bend on the new road.

thirteenth place steadily, behind Brian Lewis' Singer, which was now going very well indeed. As his three-hour spell drew near its end he clapped on speed and, passing the Singer, came into his pit in twelfth place to hand over once more. The progress of these two is typical of the character of the race at this time. The Alfa was now over an hour ahead, and was obviously beyond catching, bar some serious trouble. Elwes remained second, Dixon had come up to third, and Sebilleau and Von der Becke maintained fourth and fifth places, Sebilleau having passed the Rudge Cup leader at about half-past five. Like Dixon, however, Sebilleau was not in the Rudge Cup contest, and the cars were merely running to instructions in order to qualify for next year's event, as also were the Singer Nines driven by Wisdom and Norman Black. Mahé's Bugatti actually held tenth place for 45 laps, or nearly six hours, at this period.

As the sun rose a cloudless sky gave promise of another scorching day, and *équipes* lay lazily on the pit counters

negligently holding out the "O.K." signal, nearly all cars holding their positions without incident. At half-past nine Elwes came in, refuelled the Aston Martin, and Morris-Goodall took over. The Aston management began to consider their chances for a place in the Rudge Cup contest with Appleton's car, which they thought was still in the race, when suddenly he came in. The oil pressure was ominously low, but he went on. Then just after ten o'clock the pit woke to life with a jerk. Appleton was overdue, and even as the worried chief pondered this development the cry went up that Morris-Goodall, too, was late, and then, by Heaven! "Vincent's" privately owned car of the same make, which had been running very steadily, was also missing! Such a calamity can never have befallen a team since the Bentley disaster in 1927—three cars in one lap! Then news filtered through that "Vincent" was coming round slowly with a flat tyre. He arrived with dire tales of his colleagues round the course, and went off at speed with a new wheel. Morris-Goodall's car had serious

Bertelli's Aston Martin makes a stop at the pits.

engine trouble, and Appleton's car had a broken oil pipe, but the driver was working on it. But both cars were out, Morris-Goodall's car having held, as an unblown "1,500," second place in the Grand Prix for 72 laps, or nearly eight hours. A remarkable performance!

The manner in which such cars as De Clifford's Special Lagonda Rapier and Norman Black's Singer Nine were running steadily to schedule, giving and receiving little challenge from other cars, may be noted from the fact that the Lagonda ran steadily in seventeenth place for forty-seven laps between four o'clock and eleven o'clock, while the Singer ran eighteenth for twenty laps, both cars moving up on their 133rd lap owing to the withdrawal of the Lorraine with piston trouble.

Then take the Tracta driven by Quinault and Danielault—one of the cars involved in the crash earlier on. From five o'clock until nearly noon the Tracta held nineteenth place, then moving up on its 133rd lap. For another ten laps Black's Singer was seventeenth and the Tracta twenty-first — then Appleton's withdrawal put them both up one place, and for another thirteen laps they were sixteenth and twentieth respectively. Then Morris-Goodall's lap total was passed, and they finished without further change in fifteenth and nineteenth places.

Another car which was running low in the list, but not quite so regularly, was de Gavardie's tank-like Amilcar, which travelled quite fast while on the road, but had many pit stops. The pits were on a slight slope, and this *équipe* had a neat little chock to place behind the wheels to avoid using the hand brake. Metchim's little Austin, too, was struggling against varied troubles.

The official Aston Martins' retirement *en masse* was indeed the last sensation of a race which had its thrills all crowded into three brief periods, and for the rest was singularly devoid of incident. Brian Lewis was making a bid for second place behind the Riley in the Rudge Cup with the gallant Singer, and was ahead of Barnes on formula at ten o'clock, maintaining this position at the finish. The Alfa went on like the clock, piling up its laps, the tank held out, and he was duly acknowledged as a worthy winner, at four o'clock on a day so hot that a sud-

den whirlwind at the grandstands to celebrate his victory tossed papers hundreds of feet into the air to meet the silvery shower of small leaflets spread like a vapour from a low-flying aeroplane.

It was all over. One by one the remaining twenty-two cars cruised in to receive the plaudits of the crowds—and everything else they may have won as a reward for their gruelling run of twenty-four hours. B. P. W. T.

Von der Becke's Riley, the Rudge Cup winner, is refuelled at the pit.

NOTES.

The Lagonda, basically, of course, one of the new Rapiers, was reduced within the 1,100 c.c. limit and modified in various permitted details, this being a model which is produced and catalogued as the De Clifford Special, Lord de Clifford being concerned with it in conjunction with Dobsons, of Staines, and with the co-operation of the works.

RESULTS.
GRAND PRIX D'ENDURANCE.

1. **Alfa-Romeo (Etancelin-Chinetti), 2,836.937 kms. (1,793.94 miles, 74.74 m.p.h.).**
2. Riley (Sebilleau-Delaroche), 2,706.730 kms. (1,681.96 miles, 70.07 m.p.h.).
3. Riley (F. W. Dixon-C. Paul), 2,688.156 kms. (1,670.41 miles, 69.60 m.p.h.).

4. M.G. Magnette (C. E. C. Martin-R. Eccles).
5. Riley (A Von der Becke-K. S. Peacock).
6. Riley (S. H. Newsome-E. McClure).
7. Singer (Hon. B. E. Lewis-J. Hindmarsh).
8. Singer (F. S. Barnes-A. Langley).
9. Bugatti (Mahé-Desvignes).
10. Aston Martin ("A. Vincent"-M. F. L. Falkner).
11. Aston Martin (J. C. Noel-Wheeler).
12. Riley (Trevoux-Carrière).
13. Riley (Miss D. Champney-Mrs. K. Petre).
14. Amilcar (J. De Gavardie-Duray).
15. Singer (Norman Black-J. R. H. Baker).
16. Lagonda Rapier (Lord de Clifford-C. Brackenbury).
17. M.G. Midget (Mme. Itier-Duruy).
18. Singer (T. H. Wisdom-J. D. Barnes).
19. Tracta (Quinault-Danielault).
20. Amilcar (Martin-Pousse).
21. B.N.C. (A. Alin-A. Alin).
22. Amilcar (Poiré-Robail).
23. Singer (R. P. Gardner-Belce).

1933-1934 RUDGE-WHITWORTH CUP FINAL.

1. **Riley (A. Von der Becke-K. S. Peacock), 1.3697.**
2. Singer (Hon. B. E. Lewis-J. Hindmarsh), 1.2549.
3. Singer (F. S. Barnes-A. Langley), 1.2389.
4. Amilcar (J. de Gavardie-Duray), 1.1767.
5. Alfa-Romeo (Etancelin-Chinetti), 1.1494.
6. Tracta (Quinault-Danielault), 1.1351.
7. B.N.C. (A. Alin-A. Alin), 1.0809.

Another view from the upper storey of the pits, showing Poiré's Amilcar.

CLASS WINNERS.

Over 3-Litres.—Alfa-Romeo (S.) (Etancelin-Chinetti).
3-Litres.—Bugatti (Mahé-Desvignes).
2-Litres.—M.G. (S.) (C. E. C. Martin-R. Eccles).
1,500 c.c.—Riley (Sebilleau-Delaroche).
1,100 c.c.—Riley (A. Von der Becke-K. S. Peacock).
S. denotes supercharged ; handicap, + 40% in c.c.

Victory at last after the long run ! The Alfa-Romeo comes home amid well-deserved cheers.

1935

The biggest number of cars so far came to the start this year: 58 cars were lined up on Saturday afternoon 15 June. British cars again dominated, with a total of 37 cars, most of them in the 1½ litre or smaller classes - Singer fielded the largest entry of nine cars, followed by Aston Martin and MG with seven cars each, six Rileys, four Austin Sevens (three works entries). Two Frazer-Nashes were the first representatives of this marque to race at Le Mans. But this year Britain also fielded a contestant in the big car class: two 4½ litre Lagonda Rapides, entered by Fox and Nichol. Among the drivers of the smaller British cars were Mr and Mrs Wisdom - Tommy and 'Bill' - but in separate cars, a Singer and a Riley respectively. Both retired without completing the race.

Among the French cars the La Lorraine made its final appearance - appropriately enough on the tenth anniversary of the win of this make. It was also the last year for entries from BNC and Derby. Bugatti was the only French make with more than a single entry; no less than seven cars of the Molsheim make took part, in assorted sizes from 1½ to five-litres. Talbot now under the control of Anthony Lago - made a welcome reappearance with a three-litre coupe; this operation was probably in the nature of testing the water, as was the first entry of a Delahaye. These two marques would be more prominent in the future. Undeterred by previous bad luck he was disqualified in 1933, and his engine seized in practice for the 1934 race - Prince Nicholas of Roumania once again brought his gigantic out-moded Duesenberg to the starting line. But popular imagination seized on the Alfa Romeos yet again; four of the 2.3 litre supercharged eight-cylinder cars which now had four wins to their credit, backed up by a 1,750 cc six-cylinder car. This year, however, there were two other Italian cars entered: a pair of Fiat Ballilla Sports with 995 cc engines, although their entry was due to Frenchman Amedee Gordini who had his first Le Mans drive in one of these cars.

As could be expected, the Alfa Romeos took the lead initially. Among their drivers this year were Sommer/de Sauge; but as the latter was taken ill, Sommer would have to drive solo. Lord Howe was partnered by Brian Lewis, Chinetti by Gastaud, and Stoffel by Pierre Louis-Dreyfus. Each of these cars took turns to lead the race, and were meanwhile challenged by the Lagondas of Hindmarsh/Fontes and Benjafield/Gunter, and also by the big Bugatti of Labric/Veyron. The Duesenberg retired before midnight; Sommer was in the lead at the time but a lengthy pit stop delayed him, and he ultimately abandoned the race before dawn on Sunday. He was followed by the Bugatti and the Alfa Romeo of Chinetti/Gastaud which twice had been in the ditch and the second time was too badly damaged to continue. Next to go was Lord Howe - his Alfa holed a piston so in almost a repeat of the sequence of events in 1934, there was now only one big Alfa left, the car of Stoffel and Louis-Dreyfus. The main challenger was now the Hindmarsh/Fontes Lagonda - the other Lagonda eventually dropped down the field with gearbox problems, although it did finish the race.

The Hindmarsh/Fontes car overtook the Alfa on Sunday morning; then in the final hours of the race its oil pressure failed and Dreyfus gained on the Lagonda as it made several pit stops with its speed dropping. When Dreyfus passed the British car, his pit manager was confused and signalled that he was now in the lead when in fact he still had one lap to make up; but when the mistake was realised it was too late. Hindmarsh and Fontes nursed their sickly Lagonda home to the first British victory since 1930, their distance was 1,868.33 miles and the average speed 77.847 mph they were just five miles ahead of the Alfa Romeo. But the 1933 record still stood.

In all 28 cars finished, third place went to Martin/Brackenbury in an Aston Martin and they also won the Index as well as the Biennial Cup. A Riley was fourth and the French newcomer, the Delahaye, placed fifth. Among the MGs, three PA-type Midgets driven by all female crews, managed by George Eyston, finished in twenty-fourth, twenty-fifth and twenty-sixth positions; they were followed home by two Austin Sevens. So ended a memorable race with a surprise finish - the Alfa Romeo robbed of its ultimate triumph by a British dark horse, and Britain confirming its supremacy in the smaller capacity classes.

A Record British Entry for Le Mans 24-hour Race

(Left) The special Austin Speedy Sevens which ran in the Land's End Trial at Easter.

(Right) The three P-type M.G. Midgets entered by George Eyston. They will all be driven by women. Eyston himself is standing by the leading car. (Below) A Riley taking the Arnage corner in last year's race.

AT four o'clock to-morrow afternoon 60 cars—37 of which are British—will burst into life opposite the elaborate permanent grandstands on the Sarthe Circuit at Le Mans and roar off towards the Pontlieue By-pass on the first lap of the 13th Grand Prix d'Endurance—the greatest sports car race in the world. Throughout the long summer evening they will run until, as darkness falls, the pits and grandstands will spring into floodlit life and the battle will continue by the beams of headlamps; dawn will see the cars still lapping the 8.34-mile road circuit and on throughout the heat of the following day the struggle will go on until, at 4 p.m. on Sunday, the cars —or what remains of the entry after 24 gruelling hours—will have lapped the circuit for the last time and the chequered flag will greet the victors.

The word "victors" is used advisedly, because the Le Mans 24-hour race is really three races in one. First, there is the Grand Prix d'Endurance, which is an annual affair and is won by the car which covers the greatest distance in the 24 hours; every car running takes part in it.

Next there comes the final of the Bi-ennial Rudge-Whitworth Cup, which is a handicap race open to those who qualified last year; actually, an Alfa-Romeo, four Aston-Martins, a Fiat, six Rileys and three Singers are competing in this final, which is the eleventh of the series. Finally, there is the eliminating race for the 1936 Biennial Cup, and in this all cars are competing.

All three events are open only to standard models, of which at least 30 must have been sold; certain modifications are, of course, allowed and non-standard bodies are permitted provided they comply with certain dimensions and are fitted with full touring equipment.

The entry of 60 this year is the largest ever received, and the British contingent of 37 is also a record. As a glance at the accompanying entry list will show, the majority are light cars.

In the smallest class—which has the unusual limit of 1 litre—all but two cars come from this side of the Channel. Austins have entered an official team of three and, except for modifications to make them suitable for racing, these cars will be the same as the new special Speedy Sevens which ran in the London-Land's End Trial at

Light Cars from This Country Outnumber Foreign Entries for World's Greatest Sports Car Race Starting To-morrow Afternoon.

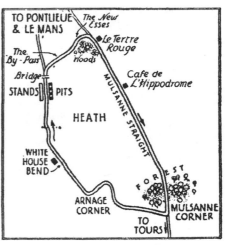

(Above) A map of the Sarthe circuit over which the race is run; it measures 8.34 miles round. (Left) One of the official Singer Nines; a very light body is fitted and weight reduction generally has been studied.

Easter. C. J. P. Dodson (of T.T. fame) and R. Richardson will drive one, L. P. (Record-breaker) Driscoll and D. Parish another, and C. Goodacre and R. F. Turner the third. An independent Austin entry comes from John Carr.

The backbone of the M.G. Midget contingent consists of six young ladies, who will be the first all-women team in a strenuous race. They are Miss Evans and Miss Skinner, Miss Allan and Mrs. Hugh Eaton, and Miss Joan Richmond and Mrs. Simpson. All are driving P-type Midgets. There is also a J4 Midget, to be driven by Bedille and Viale.

A works Singer team of "Nines" will have as its three pairs of drivers

F. S. Barnes and A. H. Langley, J. D. Barnes and T. H. Wisdom, and Norman Black and J. R. Baker.

Three independent entries—one from a Frenchman, Guy Lapchin—will complete the Singer contingent in this category. The only other 1-litre class entries are a Fiat and a B.N.C.

Of the 1½-litre class, Rileys with six entries, Aston-Martins with seven, M.G.s with four and Frazer-Nashes with two, account for all but three of the list. Amongst the Riley drivers will be the Freddie Dixon-C. Paul combination, whilst other cars will be driven by Newsome and McClure, Mrs. Wisdom and Mrs. Petre, and Von der Becke and C. Richardson.

Well-known Aston-Martin drivers in-

clude Brackenbury and Martin, Bertelli and Penn-Hughes and Faulkner and Clarke. "Tim Davies" and M. T. U. Collier account for the two Frazer-Nashes. George Eyston's M.G. Magnette entry has been scratched, but a K3 model has been entered by Maillard Brune, who won the recent Bol d'Or race, and another by E. Hertzberger.

Amongst the bigger stuff the most notable British car is the 4½-litre Lagonda to be driven by Hindmarsh and Fontes (of International Trophy fame). Rose-Richards is driving a 2.3-litre Alfa and another similar car will be manned by Lord Howe and the Hon. Brian Lewis. Also driving a 2.3-litre Alfa is Raymond Sommer, a famous Continental "independent" who has twice won at Le Mans in the past.

FOR SCOTS MOTORISTS.
The R.S.A.C. Year Book.

THE 1935-6 edition of the official Year Book of the Royal Scottish Automobile Club has now been issued to members of the Club. Its 300 pages contain much useful information, including a digest of the law as it relates to motor vehicles, and a guide to appointed hotels and repairers. Other useful features include outlines of suggested tours in Scotland and a series of maps of Great Britain to the scale of 16 miles to an inch.

ROAD CENSUS.
10,000 Officials to Count Traffic.

THE greatest traffic census ever taken in Great Britain will be carried out during the week commencing August 12, under the present arrangements of the Ministry of Transport. With the idea of obtaining

accurate data for highway authorities as to the amount and type of traffic in their districts, some 10,000 enumerators will be stationed at over 5,000 selected points.

Every type of road vehicle except steam rollers will be included in the census, and records will be kept daily of the average number and tonnage of vehicles passing each point. In addition, a count will be taken for the first time of pedestrians, with the object of finding out where footpaths are most urgently needed.

At certain of the points the census will be kept up for the whole of the 24 hours; elsewhere the count will begin at 6 a.m. and finish at 10 p.m. The census will not apply to the Metropolitan Boroughs, as separate records of the traffic are kept by the Commissioner of Police.

It is to be presumed that the week commencing August 12 has been chosen for the census because it is at the

height of the holiday season, and traffic will therefore be about at a maximum. The difficulty is, however, that a distorted view of traffic needs in certain districts will be obtained, owing to the general movement of holiday-makers towards the coast and other holiday resorts.

TYRE PRICES.
Slight Dunlop Increase

ALTERATIONS in the prices of their car and giant pneumatic tyres were announced last week by the Dunlop Rubber Co., Ltd. Dunlop Fort covers have been increased in price by 5 per cent., while standard covers and inner tubes are 10 per cent. up. This makes the price of a Dunlop standard 18 by 4.75 cover £2 9s. 6d. instead of £2 5s. as previously, while the same size Fort cover costs £3 3s. against the previous £3. New price lists will be available in the near future. Englebertts also announce increases as from June 3.

BRITISH CARS SWEEP THE BOARD AT LE MANS

Lagonda Wins at an Average Speed of 77.85 m.p.h.: British Cars First in Four Out of Six Classes, and Aston - Martin

Congratulations were showered on them—J. S. Hindmarsh and L. Fontes—winners with the 4½-litre Lagonda.

The great crowds rose to their feet as the cars swept away from the pits at the fall of the starter's flag. On the extreme right is Chinetti's 2.3-litre Alfa-Romeo with a new style radiator.

A MAGNIFICENT race, fraught with surprises, bitterly bad luck, plucky performances rewarded by victory and a sweeping demonstration of British sports car qualities. Driving Charles Fox's 4½-litre Lagonda, J. Hindmarsh and L. Fontes (International Trophy winner) won the 13th Grand Prix d'Endurance at Le Mans last week-end for this country, with an average speed of 125.283 k.p.h. (77.85 m.p.h.) for the 24 gruelling hours. Charles Martin and Charles Brackenbury won the Biennial Cup. F. S. Barnes and A. H. Langley, with one of the new model Singer Nines, were second, with A. Van der Becke and C. Richardson third with a Riley.

The weather was poor and unsettled throughout. The race opened after a heavy rainstorm, ran through many showers on the Saturday afternoon and early Sunday morning, but finished up under a fairly bright sky.

There was excitement from the word "Go!" Brian Lewis made a magnificent start in Lord Howe's 2.3-litre Alfa-Romeo and led on the first lap. He was passed by Sommer and then had pit stops. Sommer led until past 11 p.m., and then gave up. Hindmarsh and Fontes (4½-litre Lagonda) had driven steadily all the way through in second place, and took the lead before midnight.

Brian Lewis and Lord Howe worked the Alfa-Romeo forward, with Helde and Stoffel (2.3-litre Alfa-Romeo) always there, and at 2 o'clock on Sunday morning Lord Howe led the race. Pierre Veyron and Roger Labric (4.9 Bugatti) menaced his position for several hours and then blew up. Shortly before 6 a.m. on Sunday morning Lord Howe's car broke a piston. Helde led until 9 o'clock on Sunday morning, with Hindmarsh close on his tail.

Martin and Brackenbury's Aston-Martin, strongly opposed by Van der Becke's Riley, worked up into third position and stayed there to the end. Hindmarsh overtook Helde at 10 a.m., and from then led to the end, finishing with no oil pressure to speak of and with a pint of oil in the sump. There were the usual crop of incidents, and one accident, near White House, which might have proved serious. Fothringham (Aston-Martin) left the road, but escaped with cuts. Delaroche (Riley) turned upside-down near the same spot, without injury. Newsome's Riley ran off the road and there were several skids during the showers.

At 11 p.m. on Sunday the following telegram was received at Paris by Col. Lindsay Lloyd:—"This is really splendid. My congratulations to all concerned.— Hore-Belisha, Minister of Transport," to which the Colonel replied suitably.

IT seems impossible that a year has fled since we were here last. Nothing seems changed. The same excited crowds streaming to the course by car, on bicycles and on foot; the same crowded stands and busy restaurants; the line (surely a third of a mile long) of gaily decorated pits with their upper stories; and out there in front, drawn up in echelon facing down the course, very many of the same cars which ran last year.

There have been one or two changes. The pits were no longer equal to the record entry of 60 cars, and in several instances two pits' staffs were working from the same pit—but as this is Le Mans, the pits are even equal to that strain.

For once the weather seemed to have broken the tradition of sub-tropical heat

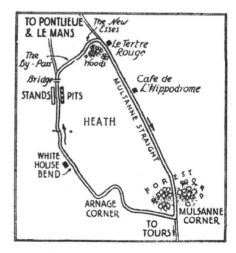

The 8.38-mile Le Mans circuit.

Takes the Rudge-Whitworth
Cup: 1,100 c.c. Supercharged
M.G. Wins 2-litre Class: Out
of 28 Finishers 22 were British

Winners of the Eleventh Biennial Rudge-Whitworth Cup—C. Brackenbury and C. E. C. Martin (Aston-Martin).

On his last lap; Luis Fontes, with the winning 4½-litre Lagonda passing the pits and the stands on his way to the new Esses bend

which has bathed the sweltering circuit for so many years past. Heavy showers of rain drifted over the course during the morning, and it rained heavily an hour before the start.

* * *

A shadow had been cast over the jollity which seems irradiated by the 24-Hours Race. On the last night of practice Vallence crashed his big 4.9 Bugatti on the fast bend just beyond the pits. The car hit the inside earth-bank and bounced back into the road. The front axle was torn clean off, Vallence himself was catapulted clear, but his mechanic was seriously injured.

Otherwise practising passed off without incident—if one does not count the people who found their cars far slower than they expected (which were balanced by those whose lap times were

higher than they had ever dared to hope). Lord Howe's Alfa seemed in perfect trim after the first night's practising, and the team intended to practise no more. Then a gasket went, and much work had to be done all over again.

* * *

With one or two exceptions, the British cars looked very much the smartest and best-turned-out of the whole entry. Each British marque seemed to have been on its mettle to produce glistening, clean cars, and it seemed a great pity that they had to stand there in the pouring rain for an hour on end.

The Aston-Martin works' team was finished in a magnificent red; the private entries were in British green. The two Lagonda Rapides were also in red, and very splendid they looked, reminding one by their air of perfect preparation of the old Bentley days. That driven by Dr. Benjafield and Sir Ronald Gunter had its steering wheel taped to provide grip in the wet.

* * *

As usual, there were many interesting features among the cars. Telecontrol shock absorbers were much in evidence, coloured rubber and cloth covers for the headlamps were as popular as ever, and the majority of cars had lights beneath the bonnet for night work.

The three P-type M.G.s were perfect standard models, but equipped with double S.U. fuel pumps. The new

ultra lightweight Singers had two pumps wired in unison, and, like the M.G.s, twin carburetters. The bodies were of the simplest and lightest design, with neat streamline tails.

* * *

Among the foreign cars, Lord Howe's beautiful blue 2.3 Alfa-Romeo was easily the best turned out. The most imposing was Prince Nicholas of Roumania's huge 5-litre Duesenberg, with its vast bonnet, high build, and outside exhaust pipes.

The 4.9 Bugattis looked low for their size. Rekip's had a torpedo-shaped wooden body built like a boat; De Souza Dantas's 3.3-litre model had the most gigantic exhaust pipe on the outside of any car on the course.

Mrs. Stewart's f.w.d. Derby, with canvas covers to the lamps, had an oil cooler carried further forward than any other similar device has ever projected before; it was protected by a small gauze screen. In somewhat similar fashion Duval's B.N.C. had a box out in front, but in this case it housed a pair of headlamps.

Vallee's Bugatti had the oddest body of all and carried a definite suggestion of home build. It was beetle-backed at the rear like those Bugattis of the old Grands Prix.

* * *

Much work has been done this year here and there on the circuit, but the stretch up from Mulsanne towards White House is still very steeply cambered and bumpy.

141

The New Esses

THE RACE COMMENTARY

AS the last hour ticked slowly away the rain poured steadily down. Drivers fidgeted, cleaned goggles and eye shields which had already been cleaned several times; some sat in the cars under tarpaulins and tonneau covers, others had umbrellas. With half an hour to go the rain slackened.

At a quarter to four (zero hour) the cars were parked in the due order of departure, the largest at the top of the line, and the air was filled with the "wump-wump" of engines as car after car was started up, to make sure of a thorough warming.

Ten Minutes to Go . . .

At ten minutes to the hour the rain positively stopped, and the hooded gendarmerie became even more energetic in casting those from the road who had no right there.

Five Minutes . . .

Five more minutes, and the drivers who were to take the first spell glanced ruefully at the lowering sky, and, buttoning up their collars, walked across the road to the far side of the course, ready for the sprint back to start the cars when the flag dropped. The minutes . . . the seconds ticked by, and the usual silence fell on the crowd. All eyes turned towards the top end of the line where the French tricolour went up.

They're Off!

A pause . . . down swept the flag, and with a quick scurry of feet in the silence, the men dashed across the road and vaulted into the driving seats, to start up and dash off on the long 24 hours of gruelling driving.

First in his seat and first to get his car moving was the Hon. Brian Lewis. A second before the flag fell he seemed the least interested person on the course. A second later it seemed he was in the seat, the Alfa-Romeo burst into life and was away.

As Lewis was several cars down the line, Hindmarsh's 4½-litre Lagonda actually took the road just ahead of the Alfa, but the car which led round the bend and off towards the Esses was Prince Nicholas of Roumania's 5-litre Duesenberg.

In a solid scrum the record field swept by the pits and streamed out for the first lap—all except Chaude's 2-litre Bugatti (destined to be in and out of the pits far too often) and Vallee's 2-litre Bugatti.

Squeezed out by those who had started higher up the line, Lewis hung back for a space, then he opened up, passed the Duesenberg and shot down to Mulsanne with Sommer (2.3-litre Alfa-Romeo) and Chinetti (last year's winner) with a beautifully turned out 2.3-litre Alfa.

Brian Lewis Leads

Back through the old Esses, round Arnage and through the twists and turns of the narrow road back to the start they streamed and as they crossed the line after the first lap, Brian Lewis (2.3 Alfa) was a few lengths ahead of Sommer (Alfa). Then came a 15-second gap before Chinetti shot by, followed in quick succession by Prince Nicholas's Duesenberg, Helde's Alfa, Veyron's 4.9 Bugatti, Hindmarsh, going great guns in the red

A dramatic moment at Mulsanne. Chinetti (Alfa), having skidded right round, has to drive against the competitors back to the corner in order to turn. He is waving his arm to direct Sommer (Alfa No. 15) and Lord Howe (Alfa No 10) as to his movements.

Lagonda Rapide, and Michel Paris in the Delahaye. Already these had set a big gap between themselves and the rest of the field, headed by the Viscomte Merlin's 2-litre Bugatti.

Order at 5 p.m. (after 1 hour)

1. Chinetti—Gastaud (2.3-Alfa-Romeo), 56 mins. 5.6 secs.—9 laps.
2. Sommer (2.3 Alfa), 56 mins. 10.4 secs.—9 laps.
3. —Helde—Stoffel (2.3 Alfa-Romeo), 56 mins. 22.7 secs.—9 laps.
4. Hindmarsh—Fontes (4½-litre Lagonda)—9 laps.
5. Veyron—Labric (4.9 Bugatti)—9 laps.
6. Prince Nicholas of Roumania (5-litre Duesenberg)—9 laps.
7. Merlin—d'Arnoux (2-litre Bugatti)—8 laps.
8. Penn-Hughes — Fothringham (1½-litre Aston-Martin)—8 laps.
9. Martin—Brackenbury (Aston-Martin)—8 laps.
10. Van der Becke—Richardson (1½-litre Riley)—8 laps.

Leading 1-litre Class
Baker-Black (Singer Nine)—7 laps.

On the second lap Sommer passed Lewis; then came Chinetti. Helde and Veyron both passed the Duesenberg and Hindmarsh clung tenaciously to his seventh place.

On the third lap Brian Lewis passed Sommer again, and the French driver came to his pit with shrieking tyres to adjust a plug lead and get going again "in a flash."

Then the threatening clouds rolled up and rain began again fitfully, so that the circuit shone wet, and the turns, particularly Arnage, became very tricky on so crowded a course. On the fifth lap Brian Lewis found his engine "woofling" on the pick-up and came in to his pit to investigate. While Chinetti flashed past in the lead they rapidly changed a distributor head on the Alfa, a matter which cost two laps.

Hindmarsh (Lagonda) Moves to Fourth Place

So Chinetti led, followed by Helde (Alfa) and Sommer (Alfa) going like smoke to win back his position—and going too fast to last, the experts said. Hindmarsh moved up to fourth place and Veyron and the Duesenberg thundered along just behind.

Chinetti was lapping in the region of 85 m.p.h., Sommer a little faster.

The Aston-Martins were tremendously fast, well in the picture in the general category, and fighting the good fight with the 1½-litre Rileys. Penn-Hughes (Aston-Martin) led the van, and the leading Riley was the Van der Becke—Richardson model. The Singers were travelling with a crisp exhaust note and surprisingly fast. The P-type M.G.s, driven to perfect team order by "George Eyston's young ladies," maintained a steady unhurried gait in numerical order, out to qualify at all costs; just behind came the three sports model Austins.

Order at 6 p.m.

1. Sommer (Alfa-Romeo), 1 hr. 55 mins. 16.8 secs.—19 laps.
2. Hindmarsh—Fontes (Lagonda), 1 hr. 58 mins. 22.1 secs.—19 laps.
3. Veyron—Labric (Bugatti), 1 hr. 58 mins. 54.3 secs.—19 laps.
4. Helde—Stoffel (Alfa-Romeo)—18 laps.
5. Prince Nicholas (Duesenberg)—18 laps.
6. Dr. Benjafield—Sir Ronald Gunter (Lagonda)—18 laps.
7. Merlin—d'Arnoux (Bugatti)—18 laps.
8. Martin—Brackenbury (Aston Martin)—18 laps.
9. Elwes—Morris Goodall (Aston-Martin)—18 laps.
10. Penn-Hughes — Fotheringham (Aston-Martin)—18 laps.
11. A. Van der Becke—Newsome (Riley)—18 laps.

Leading 1-litre Class
Gordini—Nazzaro (Fiat).

Just after 5 p.m. Sommer snatched the lead back from Chinetti and led by a few lengths, but gradually widening the gap between them, lap after lap. Two laps behind Brian Lewis was lapping at well over 80 m.p.h. and gaining ground every circuit.

Then came a heavy shower of rain, and more storm clouds were banking up behind. On the wet road the Elwes-Morris Goodall Aston-Martin got into a major slide on the bend just beyond the pits, ending up by clumping the bank and denting the tail to such effect

The Martin—Brackenbury Aston-Martin No. 29 (which finished third) tails Goodacre's Austin Seven through the new Esses, with Elwes (Aston-Martin) following.

Sweeping round Mulsanne Corner into a very fast straight: No. 24 (the Van der Becke—Richardson Riley, which finished fourth) hot on the heels of the Penn-Hughes—Fothringham Aston-Martin just before its crash.

that, at the subsequent pit stop, the shaped tail was thrown away and the car continued with the tank and spare wheel open to view.

On the 16th lap Helde stopped at the pit, and almost immediately Chinetti was signalled to come in for a tyre change. The work took the space of two laps, and was complicated by the leaking of oil from the back axle on to the brake shoes.

A few laps later Chinetti was in again with the same trouble (oil on the brake shoes), and Brian Lewis was steadily bringing the Alfa back well into the picture.

Petrol Refills After 24 Laps

At about half-past six the fastest cars concluded their regulation 24 laps and were able to come in to refill with petrol, oil and water. Veyron was first in, and got away again in 1 min. 22 secs.; Sommer came in next and took over two minutes, doing other things besides refuelling. Brian Lewis came in after, and, handing over to Lord Howe, had the car away again in 1 min. 29 secs.

Positions at 7 p.m.
1. Sommer (Alfa-Romeo), 2 hrs. 47 mins. 54.1 secs.—29 laps.
2. Hindmarsh—Fontes (Lagonda), 2 hrs. 53 mins. 7.1 secs.—28 laps.
3.—Veyron—Labric (Bugatti), 2 hrs. 56 mins. 24.7 secs.—28 laps.
4. Helde—Stoffel (Alfa-Romeo)—28 laps.
5. Dr. Benjafield—Sir R. Gunter (Lagonda)—27 laps.
6. Prince Nicholas (Duesenberg)—27 laps.

Leading 1½-litre Class
Martin—Brackenbury (Aston-Martin)—27 laps.

Leading 1,000 c.c. Class
Debille—Viale (M.G. Midget).

Just about 7 o'clock the big Duesenberg got out of hand at Mulsanne and went on up the escape road; Chinetti slid completely round at the same place, during which evolutions the Collier—Mitchell—Thompson Frazer-Nash had little room to go by.

Mulsanne provided one or two more excitements about this time. Rekip (Bugatti) charged the sandbank and then went on undismayed, and then Merlin (Bugatti) took the escape road, and, in returning to the course backwards, frightened Gaillard (Singer) into the hurdle-protected roadside. Next, a

Fothringham's Aston Martin skids and turns over at White House Corner. He was closely followed at the time by Gardner's Aston - Martin and Hindmarsh's Lagonda.

stone flew up from the Duesenberg and splintered Lord Howe's screen.

Shortly after 9 p.m., when the light was fading badly, but headlights were of little use—that perfectly beastly hour of the day when touring is trying and racing particularly wretched — Lord Howe came in for the second change of drivers, and Brian Lewis shot off with lamps aglow.

Just after Brian Lewis had sped off to commence the fast spell of night driving, Fothringham piled himself up on the bend just after White House. The Aston-Martin slewed round tail first and careered backwards off the road, where it turned over onto one side.

About the same time the Newsome—McClure Riley dived into the sand near Arnage, and was not only rather bent about, but was disqualified for being pushed out by over-enthusiastic spectators.

By 10 p.m. the rain stopped and a stormy moon rode above angry clouds. Here and there the circuit was very slippery, particularly on the accelera-

tion away from Mulsanne and Arnage, where several people slid about all over the place.

Singers Dominate Formula Race

About this time the Singers were dominating the Formula race, with first, second and fourth places (Coupe Biennial).

One of the features of the race up to now was the really few retirements. At 10 o'clock only six cars had given up out of the 58 starters. Mrs. Wisdom and Mrs. Petre (who deserve special mention for a fine show) had a big-end go in their Riley near Mulsanne. The Duesenberg ceased to come round any more and stood quietly near Mulsanne, Chaude's Bugatti after many weary pit stops finally gave in to obscure ignition bother, and the Singer Nine driven by Connell and Lloyd gave up at Arnage with mechanical trouble.

It was raining, and the road surface was extremely treacherous. Fothringham was thrown out and received bad cuts, but his injuries have proved to be not serious ones.

Shortly after 10.30 p.m., Sommer was firmly in the lead, the Hindmarsh—Fontes Lagonda running like a train, the Astons were coming higher up the general class with Van der Becke's Riley contesting every inch, the Singers still led the Coupe Biennial, the M.G. Midgets cruised round easily, Miss Skinner even tidying her hair as she took the slow section at Arnage; the Austins ran with similar regularity—and then came sensation. Sommer was overdue!

Frenzy! Sommer (Alfa) is Missing

Minutes ticked by, the Lagonda crept up and up, Sommer's pit became anxious, then agitated, then frenzied, and finally fell into despair. Still no Sommer.

Coming down to Mulsanne his engine had begun to splutter, and at the hairpin it dried right up. He restarted, went a few yards and stopped again. Leaping out he feverishly searched for the trouble. No fuel was coming through from the tank. Then began a nightmare journey back to the pit. Yard by yard he gradually jerked the car forward on the few drops which reached the carburetter.

The Lagonda Leads

A quarter of an hour slipped by, and Hindmarsh (Lagonda) roared into the lead. The clock crept on, Sommer, desperate, working the starter to death every few yards and watching his lights go dimmer and dimmer, painfully crawled back to his pit, arriving distraught and exhausted at 11.25 p.m. Frantically they worked to clear the blocked pipe, and amidst great clapping he restarted seven laps behind the Lagonda.

Order at Midnight (8th Hour)
1. Hindmarsh—Fontes (Lagonda). 7 hrs. 57 mins. 42 secs.—75 laps.
2. Helde—Stoffel (Alfa-Romeo)—74 laps.
3. Veyron—Labric (Bugatti)—74 laps.
4. Howe—Lewis (Alfa-Romeo)—74 laps.
5. Benjafield—Gunter (Lagonda)—72 laps.
6. Chinetti—Gastaud (Alfa-Romeo)—71 laps.
8. Van der Becke—Richardson (Riley)—71 laps.
Leading 1,500 c.c.

12. Hertzberger (M.G. Magnette)—70 laps.
27. Baker—Black (Singer)—62 laps. Leading 1,000 c.c.

Driving with that calm swing and ease which characterizes Brian Lewis at his best, he was bringing the Alfa rapidly forward. Fifth at 11 p.m., he gained another place before midnight, and in the succeeding hour brought the Alfa up to third, then second just over 3 mins. behind Hindmarsh.

Chinetti Back in the Picture

Veyron in third place stopped for a rapid refuel of the 4.9 Bugatti and dropped a place. At 1 a.m. Hindmarsh, Lewis, Helde and Veyron in that order were all on the same (84th) lap, and Chinetti, driving beautifully after his early troubles, was gradually creeping back and lay fifth again.

At 1.15 a.m. Sommer, 20 laps behind now, with the trouble only partially cured, came in to give up. He was driving single-handed, as his partner had gone sick on the eve of the race. He was tired out with battling the car along, and the case seemed hopeless. His pit, the crowd, everyone, exhorted him to keep going. With a gesture of despair he set off again, did two more laps and then threw his hand in.

Lewis Takes the Lead

Between 1 a.m. and 2 o'clock Lewis went up to first place and so regained the lead he had held on the first lap of all. A magnificent effort. Lord Howe took over at the refuel, and Veyron passed him to take the lead temporarily. A few laps later Lord Howe (Alfa) was back at the head of the procession, 1 min. 46 secs. ahead at 3 a.m., and in the next half-hour gained a lap.

Viscomte Merlin (Bugatti) retired owing to illness, leaving his car near Arnage, and Vallee's Bugatti retired about the same time.

On and on the cars roared through the night, the headlamps leaping and dancing among the pine woods, while all round the circuit thousands of spectators, despite the showery weather, stayed up all night. Camp fires burnt,

145

White House.

marquees did a roaring trade, and there was dancing in several big tents on very uneven board floors. The pits and stands were a blaze of light, dominated by the huge floodlit scoreboard, where men methodically changed the lap score hour after hour from billets passed up to them on the ends of long canes.

Over Two Minutes' Lead

At 4 a.m. Howe led by over 2 mins. from Veyron. Helde was a lap behind, and Hindmarsh lay a steady fourth.

The Singers were having trouble now. Wisdom's car went out with a starter which would do anything but start—and the Le Mans rules bar any other form of getting into motion. Chinetti lay fifth, Benjafield, in the

other Lagonda, sixth, and Martin and Brackenbury (Aston-Martin) came up to seventh place in the general classification, supplanting Van der Becke's Riley.

Order at 4 a.m.
1. Howe—Lewis (Alfa-Romeo), 11 hrs. 55 mins. 25 secs.—113 laps.
2. Veyron—Labric (Bugatti), 11 hrs. 57 mins. 43 secs.—113 laps.
3. Helde—Stoffel (Alfa-Romeo)—112 laps.
4. Hindmarsh—Fontes (Lagonda)—112 laps.
5. Chinetti—Gastaud (Alfa-Romeo)—108 laps.
6. Benjafield—Gunter (Lagonda)—106 laps.
7. Martin—Brackenbury (Aston-Martin)—105 laps. Leading 1,500 c.c. class.
8. Sebilleau—Delaroche (Riley)—105 laps.
20. Maillard Brune—Druck (M.G. Magnette)—97 laps.

2-litre Class
24. Baker—Black (Singer)—94 laps. Leading 1,000 c.c. class.

Retirements at 4 a.m.
Prince Nicholas (Duesenberg), Veyron—Labric (Bugatti), Porthault (Lorraine), Rekip (Bugatti), Chinetti (Alfa-Romeo), Sommer (Alfa-Romeo), Chaude (Bugatti), Mrs. Stewart (Derby), Mrs. Wisdom—Mrs. Petre (Riley), Penn-Hughes—Fothringham (Aston-Martin), McClure—Newsome (Riley), Ford—Baumer (M.G. Magnette), Hertzeberger (M.G. Magnette), Connell—Lloyd (Singer), Barnes—Wisdom (Singer).

The night's changes of fortune were not yet over. Veyron blew up just before 5 a.m. Chinetti retired at the same time, the Ford—Baumer Magnette broke a piston, and the Helde—Stoffel Alfa moved up to second place, a lap behind Lord Howe.

The Howe—Lewis Alfa Drops Out

Then, at about half-past five, disaster struck at the British entry, a piston broke, and the Howe—Lewis combination was out of the race after leading for over four hours. Wretched luck.

Helde led now by just over a minute from Hindmarsh, both having covered 131 laps at 6 a.m. Benjafield in the second Lagonda moved calmly up to third place, and Michel Paris (Delahaye), after a steady drive all night, came up to fourth, and the Martin—Brackenbury Aston-Martin took fifth position, just ahead of Sebilleau and Delaroche (Riley).

During the next hour Benjafield and Gunter (Lagonda) dropped back to fifth, the amazing Aston-Martin ran third, and the Delahaye was fourth.

Order at 8 a.m.
1. Helde—Stoffel (Alfa-Romeo), 15 hrs. 54 mins. 23.3 secs.—150 laps.
2. Hindmarsh—Fontes (Lagonda), 15 hrs. 56 mins. 13.6 secs.—150 laps.
3. Martin—Brackenbury (Aston-Martin)—142 laps. Leading 1,500 c.c.
4. Paris (Delahaye)—142 laps.
5. Benjafield—Gunter (Lagonda)—142 laps.
6. Sebilleau—Delaroche (Riley)—142 laps.
16. Maillard Brune (M.G. Magnette)—132 laps.

2-litre Class
20. Barnes—Langley (Singer)—121 laps. Leading 1,000 c.c.

British Cars Going Ahead

Hindmarsh and Fontes slowly but surely carved chunks off the Alfa's lead. At 8 a.m. they were 1 min. 50 secs. behind, at 9 a.m. just over a minute, and at 10 o'clock they passed and took the lead by nearly a minute and a half. The Aston-Martin steadily held third place, next came the Delahaye, and then Sebilleau skidded at Arnage after a shower of rain and shot off the road and out of the race. Desvigne (1,750 c.c. Alfa) moved into his position, sixth.

Failing to take the Mulsanne Corner at high speed, Prince Nicholas of Roumania (Duesenberg) just avoids disaster by dashing up the escape road.

Retirements at 7 a.m.

Connell—Lloyd (Singer), clutch; Chaude (Bugatti), ignition; McClure—Newsome (Riley), disqualified; Mrs. Wisdom—Mrs. Petre (Riley), engine.

Penn-Hughes—Fothringham (Aston-Martin), crashed at White House; Prince Nicholas of Roumania (Duesenberg), magneto; Barnes—Wisdom (Singer), starter; Porthault (Lorraine), fuel feed; Sommer (Alfa-Romeo), fuel feed.

Rekip (Bugatti), broken oil pipe; Hertzberger (M.G. Magnette), supercharger; Ford—Baumer (M.G. Magnette), piston; Mrs. Stewart (Derby), engine.

Veyron—Labric (Bugatti), broken spring shackle; Chinetti-Gastaud (Alfa-Romeo), broken spring shackle; Vallee (Bugatti), supercharger; Davis and Fane (Frazer-Nash), radiator.

Lord Howe—Brian Lewis (Alfa-Romeo), piston; Harvilleur (Amilcar), big-end; Debille—Viale (M.G. Midget), supercharger; Baker—Black (Singer), starter; De Souza Dantas (Bugatti), gearbox.

Shortly after 9 a.m. Delaroche, driving Sebilleau's Riley, skidded in a shower of rain on the Old Esses, leading into Arnage, and turned over. Fortunately the driver was not hurt, and at once set to work to dig his car clear of the sand where it was embedded. Two hours later he got it back on the road, unaided, of course, and was welcomed by great applause at the pits, where he retired.

Shortly after this accident a rocker in Freddie Dixon's Riley seized. He pulled into the pit to investigate, and the next moment there was a flash and the car was on fire. Thus Freddie made his exit from the race.

Order at 11 a.m. (after 19 hours)

1. Hindmarsh—Fontes (Lagonda)—178 laps. 1,492.3 miles in 18 hrs. 57 mins. 1.5 secs.
2. Helde—Stoffel (Alfa-Romeo)—176 laps. 1,475.5 miles in 18 hrs. 57 mins. 11.2 secs.
3. Paris (Delahaye)—169 laps.
4. Martin—Brackenbury (Aston-Martin)—169 laps.
5. Benjafield—Gunter (Lagonda)—169 laps.
6. Desvignes (Alfa-Romeo)—164 laps.

The Lagonda Rapide was lapping at about 131 k.p.h. (81 m.p.h.). Helde was doing 124 k.p.h. (77 m.p.h.), and then began to speed up until he also reached a lap speed of over 131 k.p.h., but he had now two laps to make up on the Lagonda.

Leaders for the R.-W. Cup

There was little alteration during the succeeding hours of the morning. Martin and Brackenbury were leading for the Rudge Cup, with Maillard Brune's blue and very noisy M.G. Magnette second, F. S. Barnes and Langley (Singer) third. At noon Dr. Benjafield lay third, and with Helde losing 7 mins. at the pits investigating plugs, looked like taking second place, when on the "by-pass" the gearbox cracked up, and Dr. Benjafield drove on top gear after that, to keep going to the end. The car had already covered enough distance to qualify for next year.

Coupe Biennial Positions at 12.30 p.m.

1. Martin—Brackenbury (Aston-Martin), 1,102 points.
2. Maillard Brune (M.G. Magnette), 1,089 points.
3. Barnes—Langley (Singer), 1,069 points.
4. Van der Becke (Riley), 1,060 points.
5. Falkner (Aston-Martin), 1,030 points.

At 1 o'clock, then, the Martin—Brackenbury Aston-Martin moved up into third place in the general category, besides leading the formula race. Paris (Delahaye) also moved up one, to fourth, and Van der Becke (Riley) came into fifth place.

Soon after 3 o'clock Nemesis fell

LE MANS RESULTS

Winners of the Grand Prix d'Endurance. — Hindmarsh and Fontes (4½-litre Lagonda). Distance 3,006.797 kiloms. Average speed, 125.283 k.p.h. (77.85 m.p.h.).

General Classification

1. J. S. Hindmarsh and L. Fontes (4½-litre Lagonda) (figures as above).
2. Helde and Stoffel (Alfa-Romeo), 2,998.308 kiloms. (77.37 m.p.h.).
3. C. E. C. Martin and C. Brackenbury (Aston-Martin), 2,905.576 kiloms.; 121.065 k.p.h. (75.22 m.p.h.).
4. Van der Becke and C. Richardson (Riley), 2,811.880 kiloms.; 117.45 k.p.h. (72.98 m.p.h.).

Over 4 Litres

1. Hindmarsh and Fontes (Lagonda, 4½-litre), 77.85 m.p.h.
2. Dr. Benjafield and Sir Ronald Gunter (Lagonda,. 4½-litre), 2,649.918 kiloms. (68.61 m.p.h.).

4-litre Class

1. Helde and Stoffel (Alfa-Romeo), 2,998.308 kiloms.
2. Paris and Mongin (3.3-litre Delahaye), 2,798.644 kiloms.

3-litre Class

1. Guy Don and Desvigne (Alfa-Romeo), 2,763.818 kiloms.
2. Villeneuve and Wagniez (Bugatti), 2,632.656 kiloms.

2-litre Class

1. Maillard Brune and Druck (M.G. Magnette), 2,734.332 kiloms; 113.930 k.p.h. (70.79 m.p.h.). (Running in this class because the car is supercharged.)

upon Fontes at the wheel for the last spell with the winning Lagonda. He came into his pit amidst universal consternation and reported lack of oil pressure. Three minutes later he went off gently, with one weary eye on the oil gauge and the other on Helde's Alfa-Romeo two laps behind. After one circuit he came in again more worried than before, but again they adjured him to go on, but very carefully. Hardly had Fontes restarted accelerating quite slowly from the pit when Stoffel brought in Helde's Alfa-Romeo and changed places with Helde so that the latter could have the satisfaction of bringing the car over the finishing line.

Unfortunate Wrong Time Announcement

Then occurred an extraordinary mistake. With 20 mins. to go the loud speakers announced that Helde was close on Fontes's tail. Off went the Alfa-Romeo, and, as they stood on the circuit, was 55 secs. behind the Lagonda. A lap later Helde overtook Fontes, who was little more than touring, and, according to the official loud speakers, led the race. A groan of sympathy went up for Fontes's bitter luck. With the Lagonda touring round, the Alfa-Romeo piled up the lead, and at once his pit slowed him down. With two minutes to go it was blandly announced that a mistake had been made and that Fontes was still ahead by a good three minutes.

1,500 c.c. Class

1. Martin and Brackenbury (Aston-Martin), 2,905.576 kiloms., 121.065 k.p.h. (75.22 m.p.h.).
2. Van der Becke and Richardson (Riley), 2,811.880 kiloms.
3. Trevoux and Carriere (Riley), 2,753.441 kiloms.
4. Falkner and Clarke (Aston-Martin).
5. Thomas and Kenyon (Aston-Martin).
6. Donkin and Lord Hamilton (Aston-Martin).
7. Elwes and Morris Goodall (Aston-Martin).
8. Gardner and Beloe (Aston-Martin).
9. Henon and Res (Singer)

1,000 c.c. Class

1. F. S. Barnes and A. H. Langley (Singer), 2,478.599 kiloms.; 103.274 k.p.h. (64.17 m.p.h.).
2. Mme. Itier and Jacob (Fiat Balilla), 2,327.169 kiloms.
3. Gordon Hendy and Boulton (Singer), 2,312.151 kiloms.
4. Marsh and Guest (Singer).
5. Duval and Treunet (B.N.C.).
6. Gaillard and Aime (Singer).
7. Savoye and Lapchin (Singer).
8. Miss Richmond and Mrs. Gordon Simpson (M.G.).
9. Miss Evans and Miss Skinner (M.G.).
10. Miss Allan and Mrs. Eaton (M.G.).
11. John Carr and Barbour (Austin).
12. C. Dodson and R. Richardson (Austin).

Eleventh Biennial Rudge-Whitworth Cup— 1934-1935

1. Martin and Brackenbury (Aston-Martin). Figure of merit, 1.31.
2. Barnes and Langley (Singer, 973 c.c.). Figure of merit. 1.28.
3. Van der Becke (1½-litre Riley). Figure of merit. 1.26.
4. Trevoux and Carriere (1½-litre Riley). Figure of merit, 1.25.
5. Tie between Elwes (Aston-Martin) and Mme. Itier (Fiat Balilla, 995 c.c.). Figure of merit, 1.19.
6. Tie between Hindmarsh (4½-litre Lagonda) and Gardner (1½-litre Aston-Martin). Figure of merit 1.16.

5 k.p.h. Faster than Last Year

When the true state of affairs was revealed poor Helde had lost all hope of victory for good, and the Lagonda led the procession over the finishing line, the first British win since the old Bentley days, and a glorious termination to a well-driven race, 5 k.p.h. faster than the winning Alfa-Romeo last year.

One by one the cars came in until the road in front of the stands was crowded with British cars. Out of 59 starters 28 had finished, and 22 of them were British. From first to last this country may be said to have dominated the race. The three P-type M.G. Midgets sailed gently home, followed by Charles Dodson on the remaining works Austin, and Carr with his privately owned model.

Dr. Benjafield (4½-litre Lagonda) finished to schedule after his plucky performance with the other Lagonda. Barnes's Singer came purring home second in the Biennial Cup, snatching that place from Van der Becke's Riley at the last moment. Maillard Brune (M.G. Magnette) sailed home as lustily as ever, winner of the two-litre class in the general category, in which he ran by virtue of his supercharger, and, of course, Brackenbury and Martin won the Biennial Cup besides being third with a 1,500 c.c. unsupercharged car in the general category of the Grand Prix proper.

A magnificent race in which British cars of all categories covered themselves with glory from first to last.

1936

A unique year in the history of the Le Mans 24-hour race - the year it was cancelled. If not quite on the brink of a civil war such as the one which broke out in Spain in June 1936, France was plagued by civil unrest, her industries paralysed by strikes not least of course the motor industry: this was the year when Ettore Bugatti was denied access to his factory at Molsheim; when 25,000 workers occupied the Renault factory at Billancourt for almost a month; when the strikes and occupations saved - for the time being . . .

But one casualty had been the Le Mans race which was cancelled only a week before it was scheduled to take place, at considerable cost to the A.C.O., not to mention the 60 entrants. There had been much increased support from the French manufacturers this year including works teams from Talbot, Delahaye and Delage (the two latter companies were now merged), and Amedee Gordini for Simca-Fiat. Aston Martin, Austin,

---

June 16, 1936. The **Motor**

Le Mans—Probably to be Held on August 1 and 2

French Motor Factory Employees Turn to Music During the Strike

From Our French Correspondent

THE Le Mans 24-hour race has now been fixed tentatively for August 1 and 2, having been postponed owing to the labour troubles in France. It cannot be confirmed, however, until all countries adhering to the International Association have given their approval in writing. The strike has caused petrol supply difficulties, while stoppages in the works put a finish to the preparation of the cars required for the race: had it been held it was as good as giving away the victory to a foreign competitor, which would probably have been a British driver.

The workpeople have been voluntary prisoners in the car manufacturers' factories now for over a week (at the time of writing). The patience and good humour shown everywhere by the men are astonishing, and they have won the sympathy of the public. Wages in French industry are low, and outside most factories the existing wage scale has been posted up alongside the scale asked for by the men.

So far there have been no disturbances of any kind, and no police have been sent anywhere near the factories. This certainly helps to keep things quiet, as nothing exasperates the independent Frenchman so much as the sight of massed police or municipal guards.

There are many picturesque aspects of the strike. At the Rosengart works, over which two huge red flags with the hammer and sickle are flying, the men have got up a band with home (or works) made instruments. This orchestra plays just inside the railings while men go out with collecting boxes for the strike fund. At Renaults (where there are 33,000 men on strike) they have an excellent negro choir, Senegalese and Soudanese. Everywhere there is music and dancing, wireless sets having been imported.

---

spread all over France until 5 million workers were involved. But with the Matignon agreements most of the demands of the workforce were met - a 40 hour week, paid holidays, and the recognition of collective agreements - and before the end of the year the socialist Leon Blum had formed his Popular Front government. The Third Republic was

Frazer-Nash and Riley continued to support the race, and there were numerous private entries from both France and Britain. Two Alfa Romeos were scheduled to defend the Italian colours, and an intriguing newcomer was the German Adler; after Mercedes-Benz, only the second German to enter Le Mans.

1937

The entry list for 1937 promised a more interesting race, particularly with the official return of a Bugatti works team - two of the stunning Type 57 G 'Tank' models with all-enveloping bodywork which had already proved their merit by winning the French Grand Prix at Montlhery in 1936 (run that year to a sports car formula when the French decided they could not compete with the new German Grand Prix cars). One car was entrusted to Le Mans veterans Veyron and Labric, the other to Benoist and Wimille - for the latter it was his first experience of the Sarthe circuit. Against the Bugattis were ranged no less than seven 3.6 litre Delahayes - part works, part private entries - a single Delage and two Talbots. There were also two privately entered Bugattis. Two other French makes made a return to Le Mans - Chenard et Walcker had two cars, appearing little different from their 1925 entries with the same streamlined bodywork; and Peugeot was seen at Le Mans for the second time, with a trio of the 402 based 'Darl' Mat' Specials.

Recalling past glories were single entries from Alfa Romeo - a 2.9 litre model driven by Sommer and Guidotti - and a Lagonda 4½ litre, but both these cars retired early on, leaving the big car class an all French preserve. Britain was well represented otherwise, by Aston Martin, Frazer-Nash - even if their entries were BMW's in all but name - Riley, Singer, MG and Austin Seven 'Grasshoppers' which this year were joined by a 1,500 cc HRG and a somewhat unlikely contender in the shape of a stripped-down Ford Ten, with the 1,172cc side valve engine. From Germany, the Adler entry promised for 1936 materialised - three outstanding cars, combining lowly-stressed 1.7 litre side valve engines with front wheel drive and stream-lined coupe bodywork in the manner of Jaray; on the track they looked like whales surrounded by sharks. Under the skin they were in fact remarkably standard Triumph models. They were joined by a single BMW 328. Finally, the main French entries in the smaller classes were three 1,100 cc Simca-Fiats and two Simca Cinqs - with the diminutive 569 cc Fiat 500 engine, much the smallest type of car ever to compete at Le Mans. Of the total field of 48 cars, 24 were French, 18 British, five German and one Italian.

As the race unfolded, the opening battle was between Sommer in the Alfa Romeo and Wimille in the Bugatti; but within the first hour of the race a multiple crash happened between the White House - scene of similar accidents in the past - and the pits. Six cars were involved; first Kippeurt rolled his Bugatti - he was thrown clear but had been killed instantly - then the single BMW ran into the wreckage, followed by Pat Farifield's Frazer-Nash-BMW and a Delahaye. Finally, one of the Talbots and a Riley added themselves to the pileup; only Forestier in the Riley was unharmed, and Pat Fairfield died from his injuries. The dual tragedy cast its shadow over Le Mans but the race continued. Kippeurt and Fairfield were the first two drivers to be killed while racing at Le Mans since 1925.

Soon after came Sommer's retirement, leaving the works Bugattis firmly in charge of the situation. Wimille and Benoist both set new lap records in turn; at midnight they had a three lap lead over the Delahaye which was running second, while the Veyron/Labric Bugatti was third. When this car retired on Sunday morning, another Delahaye automatically moved into third spot, and this was eventually the finishing order the Wimille/Benoist Bugatti, followed by two Delahayes and the Delage. The first non-French car was an Aston Martin in fifth place; two of the Adlers were placed sixth and ninth, and the Peugeots were seventh, eighth and tenth. Wimille's performance in his first Le Mans was outstanding; he was credited with a new lap record of 96.423 mph, and he and Benoist comfortably broke the 1933 records - their distance was 2,043.02 miles and the average speed 85.126 mph; furthermore they won the Index. The Biennial Cup went to the Aston Martin of Morris-Goodall and Hitchens. The Ford Ten actually finished, in fourteenth place.

France had her first Le Mans victory since 1926, and with French cars in the first four places, demonstrated her newly found supremacy in sports car racing in no uncertain way. For Bugatti, a most satisfactory outcome - their first Le Mans win at record speed helped to obliterate memories of the 1931 debacle; and for Wimille an outstanding personal triumph, winning at his first appearance at Le Mans, an achievement shared only by a few outstanding drivers, such as Barnato and Nuvolari.

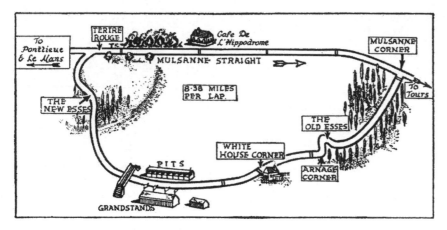

The Entries

GREAT BRITAIN.

Austin (4): C. J. P. Dodson and H. L. Hadley; C. L. Goodacre and C. D. Buckley; Mrs. K. Petre and G. Mangan, and two others.
Aston Martin (4): Debille and Hertzberger (2-litres); R. P. Hitchens and M. H. Morris Goodall; R. C. Murton Neale and J. M. Skeffington (1½-litres); M. Collier.
Bentley: Oliver Bertram and E. W. W. Pacey.
Ford (10 h.p.); Miss Joan Richmond and M. K. H. Bilney.
Frazer-Nash-B.M.W. (2): H. J. Aldington and A. F. P. Fane; D. H. Murray and P. G. Fairfield.
H.R.G.: A. C. Scott and E. A. Halford.
Lagonda: J. S. Hindmarsh and C. Brackenbury.
M.G. (PB Midget): Miss Dorothy Stanley-Turner and Miss Enid Riddell.
Riley: Jean Trevoux and Guy Lapchin.
Singer (4): Roy Eccles and Mrs. Eccles; J. D. Barnes and A. H. Langley; G. L. Boughton and F. H. Lye; P. Pichard and Jacques Savoye.

GERMANY.

Adler (4): Calaressano and Guilleaume; Von Hanstein and Lohr; Mme. Itier and Lesbros; Graf Orssich and Sauerwein.
B.M.W.: Henne and Roth.

ITALY.

Alfa-Romeo: Nuvolari and Chinetti; J. M. Dixon and another.

FRANCE.

Bugatti (5): Benoist and Leoz; Horvilleur and Kippeurt; Labric and Matra; Poulain and de Sauge; Veyron and Wimille.
Chenard Walcker (2): Cotet and Cabantous; Rigoulot and another.
Delage: Gerrard and de Valence.
Delahaye (7): Benazet and Carriere; Chabord and Dreyfus; Paul and Mme. Schell; Seylair and Tremouet; Villeneuve and Wagniez; and four drivers not nominated.
Peugeot (3): Contet and de Cortauze; Danniell and Pujol; Rigal and Serre.
Rallye: Audeux and Breillet.
Simca (Fiats): (7): Alin and Blot; Camerano and Ferrand; Gordini and Mme. Largeot; Maillard Brune and Molinari; Nazzaro and Robert; Vernet and Viale; Zanardi and one other.

TWICE ROUND the CLOCK

All Set for the World's Greatest Sports Car Race at Le Mans To-morrow

AT four o'clock to-morrow afternoon John Cobb, popular English driver and twice holder of the World's 24-hours record, will give the signal for close on 60 cars to burst into roaring life. Then will begin a battle that will go on ceaselessly into the night and on through the heat of the following morning and afternoon, until, when the hands of the clock once more point to the hour of four, the hopes of four nations will be settled and the 14th Grand Prix d'Endurance—the greatest sports car race in the world—will have come and gone.

The interval of two years that has passed since the previous Le Mans 24-hours Race—last year's event had to be cancelled owing to labour troubles in France—has made no difference to the popularity of this classic event, and the full total of 60 entries (the maximum) was received for to-morrow's race.

Of these, approximately half are French, and British cars are not far behind with an entry representing a third of the total, the remainder being made up of five German cars and two Italian. Thus the British entry, although not so large as in 1935, when 37 cars from this country took part, is a strong one, especially as it includes a representative of the marque which proved the winner two years ago—Lagonda.

The word "winner" is used rather loosely as there are in actual fact three winners each year, for three distinct races are contested simultaneously. First and foremost, there is the Grand Prix d'Endurance, which is an out-and-out scratch event in which every car running is taking part and the winner is the car which covers the greatest distance in the 24 hours.

Also including every car running, there is the first round of the Biennial Rudge-Whitworth Cup—a handicap event in which the winner is the car that exceeds its class handicap distance for the 24 hours by the greatest percentage. Although cars are "placed" in this event it is regarded mainly as an eliminating race for the final next year. Lastly, there is the final for the Rudge-Whitworth Cup, and, in this, only entries which qualified in the previous race are taking part.

The regulations on this point are rather confusing and not entirely logical. In the case of manufacturers' entries the cars running in the final must be of the same make as those which qualified in the previous race, although the drivers need not be the same; so far, so good; but when it comes to private entries not only may the drivers be changed, but so also may the make of car!

Pits Floodlit at Night.

The race is run on the famous Sarthe Circuit, with its huge permanent grand-stand and pits which are a blaze of light during the night. The circuit is quite close to the town of Le Mans and measures 8.38 miles to the lap.

As already indicated, the race is for sports cars, and they must be standard catalogued models. Coachwork, however, need not be standard provided that it conforms to the specified dimensions; certain mechanical modifications are also allowed, but only specified fuels may be used.

As for the race itself, all tools and spares must be carried on the car, with the exception of such items as spare wheels, jacks and tyre pumps or airbottles, whilst refuelling is allowed only at intervals of not less than 24 laps (about 200 miles), so that if a car runs out of petrol before this distance it is automatically out of the race.

Most prominent amongst the British entry this year are Aston Martin—winners of the 1934-5 Biennial Cup—Austin and Singer, each with four cars. Drivers for the Aston Martins (two drivers per car are allowed) include Debille and Hertzberger (2-litre), Hitchens, Morris Goodall, Murton-Neale and Skeffington.

For the Austin contingent—all "Sevens," of course—Dodson and Hadley, Goodacre and C. D. Buckley, Mrs. Petre and G. Mangan, and two others are the pilots.

The Singers (972 c.c. models) are in the hands of J. D. Barnes, M. Black, G. Boughton, Roy Eccles, Mrs. Roy Eccles, P. Pichard, F. H. Lye and Jacques Savoye.

Amongst the other British small cars are an H.R.G. with Halford and A. C. Scott up, an M.G. with an all-women combination in Miss Enid Riddell and Miss D. Turner, a Riley in the hands of two well-known French drivers, Guy Lapchin and Jean Trévoux, and a Ford Ten to be driven by M. K. H. Bilney and Miss Joan Richmond.

Two Frazer-Nash-B.M.W. models have a strong personnel in Aldington (H. J.) and Fane, and Fairfield and D. H. Murray, whilst amongst the big stuff Lycett's Bentley (Oliver Bertram and E. W. W. Pacey), and the Lagonda of Brackenbury and Hindmarsh, are two formidable entries.

They will, however, have to face very strong opposition—quite how strong can be seen at a glance when one examines the French, German and Italian entries in the list on this page.

Le Mans

Bugatti's Record Victory

FOR the first time since 1926 France has won the Le Mans 24-hour Race, the victors being Jean Pierre Wimille and Robert Benoist, with a 3.3-litre Bugatti. This pair beat all records for the race by covering 2,044.12 miles at an average speed of 85.13 m.p.h., or slightly over four miles an hour faster than in the 1933 event, when Tazio Nuvolari and Raymond Sommer averaged 81.6 m.p.h. with a supercharged Alfa-Romeo.

A British Victory

French cars also filled the next three places. J. Paul and Mongin (Delahaye) were second ; R. Dreyfus and H. Stoffel (Delahaye) were third, and de Valence and Gerard (Delage) were fourth. The Rudge-Whitworth Cup for the best performance on handicap· provided a British victory, the winners being M. H. Morris-Goodall and R. P. Hitchens (Aston Martin), while in second place were two newcomers to the race, the Misses Stanley-Turner and E. Riddell, with an M.G. Midget.

The race was marred with one of the worst smashes in motor-racing history, in which six cars were involved. Kippeurt, French amateur driver of a Bugatti, was killed outright, and Pat Fairfield, driving a Frazer-Nash-B.M.W., was so severely injured that he died a few hours later. Other drivers involved were Forestier (Riley), Raph (Talbot), Tremoulet (Delahaye), and Roth (B.M.W.). Of these, Forestier and Tremoulet escaped

The start of the race

unscathed. Raph broke a hip, and Roth sustained facial injuries.

Other cars following were only just stopped in time, and the race was

RESULT

1. **Wimille and Benoist** (Bugatti) 85.13 m.p.h. (2,044.12 miles).

2. **J. Paul and Mongin** (Delahaye).

3. **R. Dreyfus and H. Stoffel** (Delahaye).

4. De Valence and Gerard (Delage) ; 5, J. M. Skeffington and C. Murton-Neale (Aston-Martin) ; 6, Orssich and Sauerwein (Adler) ; 7, Pujol and Contet (Peugeot) ; 8, De Cortanze and Serre (Peugeot) ; 9, Lohr and Von Guilleaume (Adler) ; 10, Dannieli and Rigal (Peugeot) ; 11, Morris-Goodall and Hitchens (Aston Martin) ; 12, Vernet and Mlle. Largeot (Simca Fiat) ; 13, A. C. Scott and E. A. Halford (H.R.G.) ; 14, K. H. Bilney and Miss J. Richmond (Ford) ; 15, Calarasiano and Lesbros (Adler) ; 16, Miss D. Turner and Miss E. Riddell (M.G.) ; 17, Viale and Alin (Simca Fiat).

RUDGE-WHITWORTH CUP

1. Morris-Goodall and Hitchens (Aston Martin), 67.5 m.p.h. (1,618 miles).

2. Miss D. Turner and Miss E. Riddell (M.G.).

halted while the wreckage was dragged aside.

The race was started by John R. Cobb after the circuit had been formally closed by Mr. Alan P. Good at the wheel of a Lagonda. Of the 49 starters, Charles Brackenbury (Lagonda) was first away, with Raymond Sommer, with a supercharged Alfa-Romeo, in hot pursuit. Behind them, in a mass, were the Bugattis and the Delahayes.

J. P. Wimille at the wheel of the winning Bugatti during the race

Lap Record Shattered

After five laps it was Wimille who was the leader and from that period he and his co-driver, the veteran Robert Benoist, were never headed, as first one and then the other shattered the old lap record. By the end of an hour Sommer was virtually out of the race, and he eventually retired with valve trouble.

At quarter-distance no fewer than 15 were out of the race and the Wimille-Benoist Bugatti was four laps ahead of Schell and Carrière (Delahaye) and Veyron and Labric (Bugatti). At this stage most of the British cars were running well, with Hertzberger and Debille (Aston Martin) leading the 2,000 c.c. category ; Skeffington and Murton-Neale (Aston Martin) at the head of the 1,500 c.c. class, and Charlie Dodson and H. L. Hadley (Austin) first in the 750 c.c. class.

Drivers' Misfortunes

The Singers were also making a bold bid for the Rudge-Whitworth Cup, but when well in the lead they went out one after the other with ignition trouble. The Austin team was also well in the running, but misfortune overtook the drivers. Goodacre ran out of petrol three miles from the pits and the other two cars were withdrawn with engine trouble.

Meanwhile, the Rudge-Whitworth Cup had dwindled to two, with Morris-Goodall and Hitchens (Aston Martin), the leaders from the two women-drivers of an M.G. Midget, who put up a capital show.

Easy Winners

Wimille and Benoist continued to increase their lead, lap by lap, eventually to run out the easiest of winners from the two Delahayes and the lone Delage, which was fitted with a saloon body.

THE LE MANS

THE 1937 Le Mans Grand Prix d'Endurance was marred by a terrible multiple accident in the early stages of the race. Six cars piled into each other on a narrow section of road between Whitehouse and the Grand Stand. Rene Kippeurt (Bugatti) was killed instantly, Pat Fairfield (Frazer-Nash-B.M.W.), who hit the wreckage, was rushed to hospital with terrible internal injuries and was operated upon early in the morning. He lies at present in a critical condition, but the doctors now hold out hope of recovery

The four other drivers involved escaped with superficial injuries.

The opening stages of the race saw a great battle between Sommer (supercharged Alfa) and Wimille (streamlined unsupercharged Bugatti). The Alfa led for several laps, but was overtaken, and a little later blew up. Thereafter Wimille and Benoist, sharing the wheel, led the race until the finish at record speed. Time after time the lap record was broken at well over 90 m.p.h., and in 23 hours they broke the long-standing distance record set up in 24 hours in 1933.

The squadron of Delahayes dominated the rest of the field, although several fell out. Paul and Mongin, Dreyfus and Stoffel (Delahayes) chased the Bugatti right through the race and finished second and third. So many cars retired that comparatively slow and reliable cars came right into the picture during the last few hours.

A saloon Delage quietly worked up to fourth position, and Skeffington, private owner of a 1½-litre Aston Martin, just as quietly took fifth place. Very fine demonstrations were made by three Adlers and three Peugeots, which ran trouble-free.

The B.M.W.s had bad luck. Two cars were involved in the multiple collision, and Aldington and Fane on the third Frazer-Nash edition had to retire with complicated ignition trouble after lapping steadily at over 85 m.p.h. with plenty in hand.

The Austins and Singers were all eliminated. Hertzberger's 2-litre Aston Martin showed remarkable speed, but also retired, but Morris Goodall's similar car won the Biennial Cup on formula after a dramatic last-minute breakdown, after which it just crawled in to finish in time to win the cup. The only other car competing in the

FRENCH RECORD VICTORY AT 85.13 M.P.H.

24 HOURS RACE

Bugatti Record Win. Aston Martin Wins the Biennial Cup. Terrific Struggle Between the French and Italian Competitors: Lap Record Broken Many Times and Finally Left at over 96 m.p.h. by Benoist. Multiple Crash Results in One Death

Biennial Cup event was the M.G. Midget driven by Miss Dorothy Stanley Turner and Miss Joan Riddell, which had run steadily right through the race.

The 4½-litre Lagonda retired during the night. One of the most praiseworthy performances was that of a little 500 Fiat which finished the course. Miss Joan Richmond and M. K. H. Bilney (Ford Ten) qualified for next year, and after fighting trouble for some hours Scott and Halford just got their H.R.G. through in time to qualify also.

The getaway of the race was terriffic as the cars roared away in one grand massed start. The top picture shows the big cars, the first away amongst which was Hindmarsh's Lagonda—already well away and out of the picture—with the Dreyfus-Stoffel Delahaye, the Paul-Mongin Delahaye (No. 14) and a Bugatti (No. 18) following: the last two finished second and third.
The other picture shows the small cars with a strong contingent of Britishers, amongst them the Bilney-Miss Richmond Ford (No. 42), Goodacre-Seriwena Austin (No. 56), Dodson-Hadley Austin (No. 57), and Clifford-Mrs. Roy Eccles Singer (No. 50).

SWOOPING THROUGH THE ESSES. (Top) One of the Aston - Martins (J. Skeffington and Neale) which finished fifth, with Wimille (Bugatti) on his heels. The Goodall-Hitchens Aston Martin won the Biennial Cup.

(Centre) Congestion for Fane (white Frazer-Nash-B.M.W.), a Simca (No. 58), and the Seylair-Benazet Delahaye with the Black-Barnes Singer trailing them.

(Bottom) The saloon party—the streamlined enclosed Adlers and a Peugeot en masse through the bends.

By Air and Telephone from "Grande Vitesse."

Shortly before zero hour the cars were marshalled in echelon, tails to the long line of double-decker pits. Mr. Alan Good, head of Lagondas, with John Cobb as passenger, made a tour of the circuit (Lagondas won the race last time it was held). Then John Cobb took a tricolour flag and as twice holder of the World's 24-hour record and fastest man ever to lap Brooklands, was given the honour of starting the race as a gesture towards British motoring sport.

The loudspeakers ticked off the seconds, Cobb raised the flag, down it fell, and the drivers sprinted across the track, leapt to their seats and starting the engines tore off down the circuit.

First to move was Hindmarsh with the 4½-litre Lagonda, then in a compact mass when Raph (Talbot), Veyron (Bugatti), Wimille (Bugatti), Sommer (Alfa) and Dreyfus (Talbot).

At Tertre Rouge, where the new by-pass emerges on Mulsanne straight, Brunet's Delahaye led by a few lengths from Dreyfus (Talbot), Sommer (Alfa) and Kippeurt (old-type 3-litre Bugatti). As they tore down the straight past the famous Hippodrome Café, Raph (Talbot) passed the lot, with Sommer second. At 130 m.p.h. they streamed into Mulsanne hair-pin, braked with screeching tyres and slithering, turned into the narrow road leading to Arnage, and Sommer's acceleration took him into the lead, off-side wheels raising clouds of dust as he took the very verge of the road to get by. Brunet came second, then Veyron, then Raph.

Through the dangerous right-angle of Indianapolis Corner (the Old Esses) Sommer still led, and he came tearing down the slightly curving slope to the pits on the left-hand side of the road, leaving a trail of dust in his wake, leading Brunet by a good 5 secs., and having averaged over 87 m.p.h. for the standing lap.

On the first lap the order was Sommer, Brunet, Raph, Veyron, Dreyfus, Leoz (Bugatti), Paul (Delahaye), Tremoulet (Delahaye), Wimille (Bugatti) and Hindmarsh (Lagonda). Amazingly Aldington lay 15th in the 2-litre F.N.-B.M.W. travelling very fast and leading all the smaller cars and many of the bigger ones, Hertzberger's Aston close on his heels, then Roth (B.M.W.) and Trevoux (Riley Sprite). Gordini (Fiat) led the under 1,100 c.c. class, Boughton led the Singers, and Goodacre led the Austins.

For the next two laps Sommer led by five or six seconds from Brunet's Delahaye, averaging a shade over 90 m.p.h. and a fraction under Nuvolari's old lap record of 90.94 m.p.h. also with an Alfa. Sommer's double supercharger Alfa and Cabantous's Chenard with Cozette blower were the only forced-induction cars in the race.

On lap four Wimille opened up his unsupercharged Bugatti and went round at 92.58 m.p.h.—a new lap record—

DISASTER.—*Car after car crashing into one another near Whitehouse, depicted by Geo Ham, a well-known French artist. No. 12 is Tremoulet's spinning Delahaye; No. 30, Roth's B.M.W.; No. 20, ditched, is the unfortunate Kippeurt's Bugatti and in the foreground is Pat Fairfield (Frazer-Nash-B.M.W.).*

passed Brunet and took second place. Then began a great fight between Sommer and Wimille—Alfa v. Bugatti. A lap later Wimille passed him on the Mulsanne straight, and the rest of the field were 23 secs. behind these two flyers.

On the fifth lap Chiron came into his pit with engine trouble in the Talbot, and after a lengthy stop the car was withdrawn.

Thereafter Wimille began to leave Sommer and gained a half-minute lead after eight laps, lowering the lap record again, and Carriere (Delahaye) passed Brunet into third place.

The Tragic Crash

Then on the ninth lap came tragedy. A whole string of cars was streaking through the 100 m.p.h. curves just before the pits, headed by Kippeurt's old-type Bugatti. The car skidded, hit the bank, smashed down some fencing and rolled over and over down the road, throwing the driver face down into the fairway. Roth (B.M.W.) was on the wreckage like a flash, saw the inert form of the driver, and deliberately charged the hedge to avoid him. His car looped the loop into a field and Roth emerged with a cut face and holding a steering wheel in his hands. Meanwhile Fairfield bore down on the scene, braked hard, cannoned off the remains of the Bugatti, knocking its engine clean out of the frame, and the next instant he was charged from behind by Tremoulet's Delahaye and was catapulted end over end 100 yds. into a field. Raph (Talbot) banged head on into the Delahaye.

The road was completely blocked with the sliding cars, some upside down,

others on their side, and Forestier (Riley) crashed into two sliding cars. The air was full of flying metal. The Bugatti engine flew into the road, there was an incessant rending of metal, dust hung in the air, and agitated marshals dashed into the road with warning flags, while others ran to help the injured.

Kippeurt was past help and died almost at once. Fairfield was rushed to hospital with facial cuts and abdominal injuries. Raph was badly hurt. The rest escaped with bruises and concussion.

Sommer's Alfa Out!

One lap later Sommer's Alfa burst at Mulsanne, came slowly to the pit, and after a long pit stop retired—a bitter blow. Carriere thus ran second and Brunet third. Aldington continued to lead the small cars, with Hertzberger on his tail, and Wimille continued with increased speed.

The Lagonda was in trouble with a valve after 11 laps, but restarted; the H.R.G. was likewise in for maintenance, Trevoux cracked a cylinder in the Riley at Mulsanne, and that was roughly that. Wimille went round at

94.6 m.p.h. and a few laps later set a new record at 95.5 m.p.h. At half past six he had lapped every other car on the course and was going faster still.

At the same time Aldington came in, refuelled after his set minimum of 24 laps, handed over to Fane, and the car was away again in 1 min. 50 secs. Hertzberger passed in the meantime, but Fane soon began to gain on him again. Then Hertzberger stopped for his tanking, and the Frazer-Nash-B.M.W. went back into its place as leader of the small cars.

Benoist's Great Record

At half past seven Wimille stopped after his magnificent run, Benoist took over, tanks were filled, and on the next lap Benoist set a new record at 96.42 m.p.h.—an astonishing speed for an unblown car.

Huge dark clouds now rolled up, and at eight o'clock down came heavy rain and at the same time Fane disappeared.

The rain fell in torrents, so that young rivers flowed down the sides of the roads and the cars splashed through great pools. Flat out down the Mulsanne Straight at 140 m.p.h., the drivers sat blinded by the stinging rain, which tore their cheeks like whips. Braking became uncertain and the cars slid yards as they braked for the hairpin. Then, as suddenly as the downpour burst, it stopped. Lap speeds fell

PAT FAIRFIELD

AS we go to press, the regrettable news came through that Pat Fairfield died, as a result of his injuries, early Monday morning.

all round, but Benoist and the other leading drivers were still lapping at nearly 80 m.p.h.

Then the perturbed B.M.W. pit located Fane on the far end of the Mulsanne Straight trying to start a silent engine—bitter blow, for the car had been lying seventh in general classification and had been touring around with 1,000 r.p.m. in hand.

As the rain stopped the speeds began to go up again until the cars were again maintaining their original mad pace.

Half the Field out by Nightfall

With the coming of darkness the Permanent Circuit of the Sarthe underwent its customary but always mar-

(Right) THE WINNERS: Benoist and Wimille, at the finish, both looking surprisingly fresh, after having averaged over 85 m.p.h. for 24 hours.

(Below) NIGHT SCENE at the pits which are illuminated like a row of shops.

vellous transformation. The long line of double-decked pits sprang into life like a line of shops. The enormous scoreboard was floodlit, and with darkness came a perfect decimation of the large entry. Thirty-two cars were left at 8 p.m.

Fane at last got the remaining Frazer-Nash-B.M.W. to his pit, after having tried to retime the engine, and after a long time the car finally withdrew, having lost too much time to continue.

Throughout the night the order of the leaders remained unchanged. Always the Benoist-Wimille Bugatti sped along, lapping at around 90 m.p.h. as regular as a train, and three laps ahead of Schell and Carriere's Delahaye. Veyron and Paul were fighting a great battle between them and both were making a bold bid for second place.

The British Retirements

Car after car fell out. The Lagonda with its stretched valve, Fane's B.M.W. with timing trouble, then the Singers and the Austins, which had been running steadily well within their r.p.m. capacity, ran into annoying little troubles which put the cars one by one out of the race.

Thus at midnight Mrs. Roy Eccles

and Freddy Clifford (deputizing for Roy Eccles, who was sick just before the race) led the Biennial Cup handicap event from Morris Goodall's Aston Martin, with Savoye's Singer third, Villeneuve's Delahaye fourth, and Miss Stanley Turner and Miss Riddell (PB Midget) fifth.

At midnight in the 2-litre class the order was Hertzberger (Aston), Madame Itier (Adler) and Orssich (Adler), followed by the two Peugeots. Skeffington (Aston) led the H.R.G. in the 1,500 c.c. class, Gordini and Maillard Brune (Fiat) led two Singers in the 1,100 c.c. class, and two Austins led two 500 Fiats in the 750 c.c. class.

By 5 o'clock Dreyfus was third, and Valence's 2.9 saloon Delage, after a wonderfully steady run, was a firm sixth. Wimille was averaging 87 m.p.h. Then Veyron retired and Hertzberger (Aston) moved up to sixth place behind the Delage. A few hours later Savoye's Singer dropped out, and Boughton's with it.

At 8 o'clock Hertzberger's Aston cracked, and Villeneuve (Delahaye) moved up to sixth place behind the Delage, and Pujol, in one of the Peugeots which had run so reliably in line ahead, became seventh, and Orssich's Adler eighth.

The little M.G. ran into a spot of

bother also, with the clutch and one thing and another, and dropped into second place in the Biennial Cup. The next sensation was when the Schell-Carriere Delahaye, in second place in general category, arrived at its pit boiling like a kettle, and later retired. About the same time Villeneuve caught fire at his pit while filling up, and retired.

Wimille arrived at his pit with a damaged wing, evidently having touched something somewhere. But after a quick refill the car sped on again at a slightly abated pace, for it

A BRITISH SUCCESS—Morris Goodall (at the back) and R. P. Hichens who won the Biennial Cup with an Aston Martin: they covered 1,720.45 miles.

had a commanding lead. As the hours went on the Bugatti began repeated pit stops for a few seconds at a time.

By midday only 18 cars were left in the race, with Bugattis, Delahayes and the Delage dominating the scene. The H.R.G., after a gallant showing, ran into trouble about 10 o'clock with a broken internal oil pipe. In one hour and five minutes they dropped the sump without losing their oil or breaking the seals (clever that!) and were on their way again.

By 2 p.m., therefore, the additional retirements were Schell (Delahaye), 193 laps—no oil pressure, Gordini's

Fiat (139 laps), Cabantous (Chenard), 150 laps. Mrs. Eccles's Singer had gone out with ignition trouble when leading the Biennial Cup event.

Wimille's Commanding Lead

As the race neared its end the Wimille-Benoist Bugatti slowed right up, leading by many laps. It is noteworthy that this car, running on Dunlops, had worn its tyres only very slightly, and needed but three changes throughout the race, even at its record-breaking speeds. All but about half a dozen cars were running on Dunlops, incidentally.

The performance of Skeffington and Murton Neale on the 1½-litre Aston was outstanding, and on formula they were second to Wimille at 2.30 p.m. and fifth in the race. The H.R.G. was going rather slowly now, trying to qualify for next year, with eight laps to go and plenty of time to do it. The Ford Ten had at that time only one lap to go to qualify, the Midget had two laps to do, all with an hour and a quarter to do it in.

A few minutes after 3 p.m. Benoist, who was at the wheel of the winning

---

PERIODIC PLACINGS

After 1 Hour (5 p.m. Saturday)

1. Wimille (Bugatti), 10 laps in 55 mins. 35 secs.
2. Carriere (Delahaye), 10 laps in 56 mins. 54 secs.
3. Brunet (Delahaye), 10 laps in 56 mins. 55 secs.
4. Paul (Delahaye); 5, Veyron (Bugatti); 6, Dreyfus (Delahaye); 9, Hindmarsh (Lagonda); 11, Aldington (Frazer-Nash-B.M.W.); 13, Hertzberger (Aston Martin); 14, Trevoux (Riley); 33, Norman Black (972 Singer); 36, Dodson (Austin Seven), leading 750 c.c. class.

8 p.m.

1. Wimille-Benoist (Bugatti), 43 laps.
2. Schell-Carriere (Delahaye), 41 laps.
3. Veyron (Bugatti), 41 laps.
4. Paul (Delahaye), 41 laps; 5, Sauge (Bugatti), 40 laps; 6, Dreyfus (Delahaye), 39 laps; 9, Hertzberger (Aston), 37 laps; 10, Morris Goodall (Aston), 36 laps; 11, Fane and Aldington (Frazer-Nash-B.M.W.), 35 laps; 21, Gordini (Balilla Fiat), 32 laps; 23, Black (Singer Nine), 31 laps; 26, Hadley (Austin Seven), 30 laps.

11 p.m.

1, Wimille; 2, Schell; 3, Veyron; 4, Paul; 5, Sauge; 6, Dreyfus; 7, Hertzberger; 10, Lohr (Adler); 12, Cortauze (Peugeot).

2 a.m.

1, Wimille; 2, Schell; 3, Paul; 4, Dreyfus; 5, Veyron; 6, Sauge. Wimille averaging 87.97 m.p.h.

HALF-WAY. 4 a.m. 12 HOURS' RACING

1. Wimille-Benoist (3.3 Bugatti), 126 laps; 11:58:38 (87.144 m.p.h.).
2. Schell-Carriere (3.5 Delahaye), 120 laps.
3. Dreyfus (Delahaye), 119 laps.
4. Paul (Delahaye), 118 laps; 5, Veyron (3.3 Bugatti), 116 laps; 6, Valence (2.9 Delage), 106 laps; 8, Hertzberger (2-litre Aston Martin), 106 laps; 9, Orssich (2-litre Adler), 102 laps; 10, Pujol (2-litre Peugeot), 102 laps; 11, Morris Goodall (2-litre Aston Martin), 16, Gordini (990 Fiat), 95 laps; 17, F. E. Clifford and Mrs. Roy Eccles (Singer Nine), 92 laps.

BIENNIAL CUP AT 4 A.M.

1. Clifford and Mrs. Eccles (Singer Nine), 1.26 points.
2. Morris Goodall and Hichens (2-litre Aston Martin), 1.19.
3. Savoye (Singer Nine), 1.18.
4. Villeneuve (3.5 Delahaye), 1.13; 5, Miss Stanley Turner and Miss Riddell (M.G. P.B. Midget), 1.4.

7 a.m.

1, Wimille; 2, Schell; 3, Dreyfus; 4, Paul; 5, Valence; 6, Hertzberger. Wimille's speed: 87 m.p.h.

10 a.m.

1, Wimille; 2, Schell; 3, Paul; 4, Dreyfus; 5, Valence; 6, Pujol. Wimille's speed: 87.87 m.p.h.

FULL RESULTS

GENERAL CATEGORY

1. **Wimille and Benoist (3.3 Bugatti)**, 3,287.936 kiloms.; 2,043.11 miles (85.13 m.p.h.).
2. **Paul and Mongin (3.5 Delahaye)**, 3,193.43 kiloms. (1,993.38 miles).
3. **Dreyfus and Stoffel (Delahaye)**, 3,125.428 kiloms. (1,942.13 miles).
4. **Valence and Gerard (2.9 Delage)**, 2,907.59 kiloms. (1,806.77 miles).
*5. **J. M. Skeffington and R. C. Murton Neale (1½-litre Aston Martin)**, 2,768.68 kiloms. (1,720.45 miles).
6. **Count Orssich and Sauerwein (1,679 Adler)**, 2,766.89 kiloms. (1,718.79 miles).
7. Pujol and Contet (2-litre Peugeot).
8. Cortauze and Serre (2-litre Peugeot).
9. Lohr and Guilleaume (1,679 Adler).
10. Danniell and Rigal (2-litre Peugeot).
*11. M. H. Morris Goodall and R. P. Hichens (2-litre Aston Martin), 1,618 miles (67.5 m.p.h.).
12. Vernet and Mme. Largeot (996 Fiat).
*13. A. C. Scott and E. A. Halford (1,500 H.R.G.).
*14. M. K. H. Bilney and Miss Joan Richmond (1,099 Ford).
15. K. Calaraseano and Lesbros (1,679 Adler).
*16. Miss Dorothy Stanley Turner and Miss Joan Riddell (939 M.G. Midget).
17. Viale and Alin (568 Fiat).
  * Indicates British competitors.

BIENNIAL CUP
(On Formula Limited to Cars Qualified in 1935)

1. **Morris Goodall and R. P. Hichens (2-litre Aston Martin)**, 67.5 miles per hour.
2. **Miss Stanley Turner and Miss Joan Riddell (939 M.G. Midget)**.

CLASS RESULTS

750 c.c.

1. Viale and Alin (Simca Fiat).

1,100 c.c.

1. Vernet and Mme. Largeot (Simca Fiat).
2. Bilnet and Miss Richmond (Ford Ten).

1,500 c.c.

1. Skeffington and Murton Neale (Aston Martin).
2. Scott and Halford (H.R.G.).

Two-litres

1. Count Orssich and Sauerwein (Adler).
2. Pujol and Contet (Peugeot).
3. Cortauze and Serre (Peugeot).
4. Lohr and Guilleaume (Adler).

Three-litres

1. Valence and Gerard (Delage).

Five-litres

1. Wimille and Benoist (Bugatti).
2. Paul and Mongin (Delahaye).
3. Dreyfus and Stoffel (Delahaye).

Bugatti, came into his pit, having broken the distance record set up in 1933, with an hour in hand, having covered over 1,900 miles. He handed over to Wimille amidst applause, and the car was off again in 20 secs. At the same moment Morris Goodall retired with the second Aston. Sixteen cars remained out of nearly 50 starters!

Applause for the Aston Martin

Then a great shout went up. The Morris Goodall Aston, apparent winner of the Biennial Cup, had not retired but came limping into his pit where the mechanics flung themselves on the engine. Soon the car was moving slowly and painfully off again under its own power, and as the car was so far ahead of the only surviving competitor for the Biennial Cup, Miss Turner's M.G. Midget, there was a chance that the Aston could keep going until 4 o'clock and still win the Cup. With 10 minutes to go, the Aston's score on formula was 1.110 points to the M.G.'s 1.041, and the M.G. was lapping merrily while the Aston was creeping around.

Just before the end Paul (Delahaye) also beat the 1933 distance record of

---

Nuvolari. Wimille was simply touring round waiting for 4 o'clock.

Slowly the clock crept round and slowly the crippled Aston Martin crept round the Circuit. Scott in the lame H.R.G. had to do 164 laps to qualify for next year's Biennial Cup. He had done 163. On the 164th, with three minutes to go before the end of the race, the car stopped on the far side of the course. Then it slowly got going again, fluttered along, and, as the very last second of the 24 hours ran out, the H.R.G. cantered across the line amidst thunderous applause. Then all eyes searched the road for the Aston. If it stopped again the M.G. would win the Biennial Cup.

Wimille finished and the crowd thundered applause. Dreyfus finished. The little 500 Fiat finished. Each car was acclaimed with roars of applause and clapping from 50,000 people. Then a louder cheer. The little red Aston had come into sight. Slowly it crept down the road and finished, and Aston Martin was winner of the Biennial Cup yet again, even if by the skin of its paint. Then the Midget finished and received an ovation all to itself, Miss Turner at the wheel.

Thus ended the 1937 Endurance Race with just another Biennial Cup win for Great Britain, and the Grand Prix provided yet another win for Wimille and the marque Bugatti, with great glory to Delahaye and Delage, who were close behind. Only 17 cars finished out of nearly 50 starters.

THE FASTEST EVER ON I.o.M. MOTORCYCLE T.T. COURSE.

F. N. Frith, who won last Friday's motorcycle Senior Tourist Trophy Race in the I.o.M. at record speed. He was only the second string in the Norton team, but when the leader, James Guthrie, retired he received instructions to go all out and catch Stanley Woods (Velocette). After six laps (226½ miles) the two men were dead-heating at an average speed of 87.88 m.p.h., whereupon Frith made a further frantic effort and, by covering the final lap at the record speed of 90.27 m.p.h., won the race with 15 seconds to spare. A full report of the race will appear in to-morrow's "Motor Cycling."

1938

In view of their victory in 1937 the absence of Bugattis - either works entries or privately owned cars - from the 1938 line-up was remarkable. One supercharged 4.5 Litre Bugatti 'Tank', the Type 57 S 45, had taken part in the Le Mans practice run but was withdrawn, apparently because the factory did not consider that the car was ready to race. By contrast, Delahaye and Talbot were out in force; the former fielded two of their Type 145 4.5 litre V 12s - little more than camouflaged Grand Prix racing cars - in addition to five 3.6 litre sixes of the better known Type 135. There were six Talbots, one a 4½ litre, and the rest of four-litres; these were the favourite teams, together with two Alfa Romeos - one a supercharged 2.9 litre coupe driven by Sommer and Biondetti.

Other French entries were a single Delage, two women in an unusual 2.3 litre four-cylinder Amilcar based on the Pegase model but with an ohv engine - the last Le Mans entry for this make and the three Darl'Mat Peugeots. The one make fielding most entries was Simca, with eight 1,100 cc cars and two Simca Cinqs. There was a total of 28 French entries out of 42 cars altogether; other than the two Alfa Romeos and the two Adlers, there were ten British entries made up from two MGs, two Rileys (French owned), two Singers and single representatives of Aston Martin, HRG and two newcomers: Morgan and Atlanta. Morgan had an example of their first four-wheeler, the Coventry-Climax engined 4/4, and Atlanta a 1.5 litre engined car with fully independent suspension to smoothe out the bumps of the Sarthe circuit.

Raymond Sommer was the favourite, as so often before, and soon took the lead from the big Delahayes; he was briefly threatened by the 4½ litre Talbot driven by Etancelin and Chinetti, but all the three biggest French cars were soon out of the race with mechanical trouble, and Sommer/Biondetti could extend their lead over the following Talbots and Delahayes almost at their leisure. Among the smaller cars, Gordini and Scaron put up a magnificent drive in the 1,100 cc Simca-Fiat, and led not only their own class but all the 1½ litre cars as well. Two of the Peugeots had retired but the third was leading the two-litre class; the Adlers were circulating steadily and unobtrusively, like clockwork; and in a repeat of the 1935 race, a private husband and wife battle was being fought out between Tommy Wisdom in a Singer Nine, and Mrs Wisdom who this time shared a PB-Type MG - neither finished the race. Indeed, for most of the race the British cars were not doing very well.

But this was a Le Mans race with a sting in the tail, fully proving that to win, above all the car must stand the distance. While safely in the lead despite having burst a tyre - the Sommer/Biondetti Alfa Romeo broke a valve on Sunday afternoon. Suddenly, the Delahaye of Chaboud and Tremoulet, which ran for most of the race with only top gear, was promoted to race leader from having been 12 laps behind, and it was followed by another Delahaye in the hands of Serrauld and Giraud-Cabantous. There was little time left for any other competitor to come from behind and challenge the two leaders, and at 4 pm Sunday afternoon Delahaye could celebrate a 1-2 win, with the third surviving car of this make being placed fourth. A Talbot was third, and the Peugeot fifth - complete French dominance for the second year running, in marked contrast to previous years. But as the winner's distance was only 1,976.54 miles, at an average speed of 82.36 mph, no new records were set, nor was there a new lap record as Sommer's fastest lap was 96.177 mph, fractionally less than Wimille's 1937 record. Among the smaller cars, there had been another surprising change of fortune when Scaron crashed the leading Simca; this permitted the two Adlers to take sixth and seventh places, and Graf Orssich-Sauerwein in the leading Adler also won the Biennial Cup; but they were just beaten on Index by one of the tiny Simca Cinqs. Highest placed British car was a French-owned Singer Nine which finished eighth; altogether four Simcas finished, as did the HRG, a French-owned MG and the Morgan - there were no more than 15 finishers in 1938.

NEXT week-end we come to one of the biggest races of the year, and to the British industry, the most important of all Continental events— the 24-hour race at Le Mans, on the Sarthe Circuit, on Saturday and Sunday, June 18 and 19.

This is a race with a long history and a great tradition, bound up in British eyes with the triumphs of the Bentleys in the past, when they made a habit of winning this gruelling race year after year against the strongest Continental opposition and in spite of epic happenings like the multiple pile up at White House Bend in the dead of night.

The entry list comprises 56 cars, some of which are, as usual, still designated by the enigmatic letter

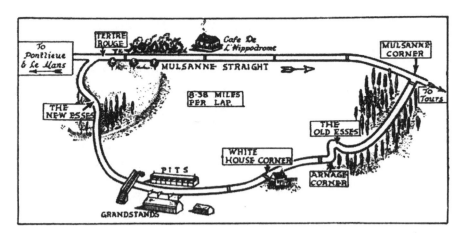

A sketch map of the Permanent Circuit of the Sarthe where the Le Mans 24-hours Race takes place. The course is 8.38 miles round and on the 3-mile Mulsanne Straight 130 m.p.h. is attained.

Le Mans

Next Week-end

Unusually Good Entry Should Provide an Exciting Race

" X." There are 30 French machines, 21 British, two German and four Italian, so the race is definitely International. Three Austins have been withdrawn.

This race is a little complicated, in that each year there are in fact three events being run concurrently. First of all there is the 15th Grand Prix d'Endurance, which is a scratch race for cars of any size, won by the machine which covers the greatest distance in the 24 hours. Secondly, there is the final round of the 13th Biennial Rudge-Whitworth Cup, which is an engine-size-handicap race for those cars which qualified last year, and thirdly there is the eliminating or qualifying round of the 14th Biennial Cup, the final round of which will be run next year, in which cars must cover set minimum distances according to engine size. In addition to all this there is a cup presented by the promoting club, the Automobile Club de l'Ouest, for the best performance of the day on handicap.

The handicapping is likewise a trifle complicated. It is worked out on an " index of performance " in which marks are given on a formula which takes into consideration the size of the engine, whether it is supercharged or not, and the mileage covered in excess of the set minimum for that engine size.

The race is for standard sports cars complete with lamps, wings and screens and proper touring bodies, including saloons. Several stream-lined saloons have done well in this race in the past few years.

Entrants of the cars which covered their minimum distance last year are entitled to enter one car for every car of theirs which qualified, and the car entered this year need not be the same one, nor even the same make or size. Manufacturers who qualified last year must, however, enter the same make of car this year.

In 1937 the qualified entrants

were:—F. S. Barnes, Ecurie Bleue (Laury Schell's group), George Eyston, Amedée Gordini, Roger Labric, H. Lesbros, Joseph Paul, A. C. Scott, J. M. Skeffington, Société R.V., R. P. Hichens and J. E. Vernet (with one car each) and the organization known as Darl'mat, who have three cars qualified. These entrants can dispose of their entries for this year to others, which explains why their names do not all appear in the programme.

Two drivers are obligatory for each

LE MANS ENTRIES
Great Britain
Aston Martin (2 litres): R. P. Hichens.
Atalanta (1½ litres): C. W. Morrison.
H.R.G. (1½ litres): A. C. Scott; Peter Clark.
M.G (939 c.c.): Miss Dorothy Stanley Turner; Bruxelles.
Morgan (1,100 c.c.): Miss P. M. Fawcett.
Riley (1½ litres): Pierre Ferry; Raoul Forestier.
Singer (1,100 c.c.): Jacques Savoye; F. S. Barnes.
Triumph (1½ litres): John Elliott.
Unspecified: Entries from Arthur Fox, T. H. Wisdom, St. John Horsfall.

France
Bugatti (3.3 litres): Roger Labric; T. A. S. O. Mathieson.
Delage (2.9 litres): One factory entry.
Delahaye (3½ litres): John Snow; Joseph Paul; two cars entered by Laury Schell to be driven by Dreyfus and Comotti; Chabaud and Tremoulet; Louis Villeneuve; Serraud.
Peugeot (2 litres): Three cars entered by Darl'mat.
Salmson (1,100 c.c.): Pierre Pichard.
Simca Fiat (571 c.c.): Amedée Gordini.
Simca Fiat (995 c.c.): J. E. Vernet.
Simca Fiat (1,100 c.c.): J. E. Vernet; Victor Camerano, and four cars entered by Amedée Gordini.
Darracq (3 litres): Norbert Mahé.
Darracq (4 litres): Jean Prenant; Jean Trevoux, and three cars entered by Luigi Chinetti.
Unspecified: Mme. Anne Itier.

Italy
Lancia (1,352 c.c.): T. E. Kenny.
Alfa-Romeo (3 litres): Hans Ruesch; Raymond Sommer; Marcel Horvilleur.

Germany
Adler (1½ litres): One factory entry.
Adler (1,679 c.c.): One factory entry.

car, since it must race all day and all night, from 4 p.m. on Saturday next until 4 p.m. on Sunday. The fuel to be used is what is known as " commercially obtainable " which prevents entrants using fantastic compression ratios. All spares and tools which are considered necessary must be carried actually on the cars right through the race and may not be kept in the pits until required, which sometimes leads to a good deal of heart-burning when a driver realizes he lacks something important.

Of recent years this country has not done too well in the scratch race, although the Lagonda broke a string of Alfa wins in 1935, but we have made a complete corner in the formula race. Last year Morris-Goodall and R. P. Hichens won this event with an Aston Martin at 67.5 m.p.h., with Miss Stanley Turner and Miss Riddell second with an M.G. PB Midget.

The Permanent Circuit of the Sarthe, where the race is run, is a D-shaped course a few miles out of Le Mans, in flat, sandy country and running through forests at one end. In all, the circuit measures 8.38 miles.

This year, with 3-litre Alfas, 3.3-litre Bugattis, 3-litre Darracqs and 3¼-litre Delahayes matched against each other, lap speeds of over 90 m.p.h. are expected, and the struggle between these teams should provide a memorable race. Not for a long time have there been so many very fast big cars in the race together.

The Motor, as usual, is making special arrangements to report the race in next Tuesday's issue, together with photographs and drawings made on the spot and sent over by special aeroplane.

IMPRESSIVE! The massed start as the cars begin their struggle against unrelenting time. (Below) The extraordinary appearance of the Orssich-Sauerwein Adler (not unlike a bomb-proof shelter) is clearly seen in this picture. It dropped a mild bombshell of its own by winning the Rudge-Whitworth Cup.

ON the face of it, the Le Mans 24-Hour race, run off over the famous Sarthe Circuit, was a disappointment from the British angle, since France, Germany, and Italy shared the major honours; but at least two British crews distinguished themselves and the marques they represented, namely, Miss Fawcett and G. Whitt (Morgan) and P. C. T. Clark and M. Chambers (H.R.G.). In addition, two French-entered British light cars finished, a Singer and an M.G. The former was eighth in the general classification and was the highest-placed British car. Here is the full story of the race—by "The Blower," who watched its progress throughout the 24 hours.

* * *

IN spite of a number of non-runners—including the works Bugatti, which could not be prepared in time and left the event, the first of the series for many years without a representative of the famous Molsheim factory—a field of 42 lined for the start of the classic Le Mans 24-Hour race last Saturday afternoon; and if the quantity was slightly reduced as compared with last year, the same certainly cannot be said for the quality. There was every indication of one of the greatest battles over the famous Sarthe Circuit for many years.

Ecurie Bleue were fielding their two 4½-litre 12-cylinder unblown cars as raced at Pau and Cork (where they carried off the first two events under the new International Formula) and had as their pilots Rene Dreyfus, partnered by Louis Chiron, and Comotti sharing the other car with Dreyfus.

Supporting these two formidable entries were five other Delahayes of the 3½-litre, six-cylinder type quite familiar to English crowds, and against them six very rapid French Talbots and a brace of Alfa-Romeos.

THE RESULTS

GENERAL CATEGORY—GRAND PRIX D'ENDURANCE

1. **Chaboud and Tremoulet** (3½-litre Delahaye), 3,180.9 kiloms. (1,976.628 miles), 82.36 m.p.h. **Also 5-litre class winner.**
2. **Serraud and Giraud-Cabantous** (3½-litre Delahaye), 3,153.8 kiloms. (1,959.59 miles).
3. **Prenant and Morel** (3.9-litre Darracq), 2,959.7 kiloms. (1,839 miles).
4. **Villeneuve and Biolay** (3½-litre Delahaye), 2,945.7 kiloms.
5. **de Cortanze and Contet** (2-litre Peugeot), 2,887.9 kiloms. **2-litre class winner** (at record speed).
6. **Orssich and Sauerwein** (1.6-litre Adler), 2,856.3 kiloms.
7. **Lohr and von Guilleaume** (1½-litre Adler), 2,765.0 kiloms. **1½-litre class winner.**
*8. **J. Savoye and P. Savoye** (974 c.c. Singer), 2,360.9 kiloms. (1,467.06 miles). **1,100 c.c. class winner.**
9. **Debille and Lapchin** (1,088 c.c. Simca Fiat), 2,329.5 kiloms.
*10. **Clark and Chambers** (1½-litre H.R.G.), 2,303.3 kiloms. (1,431.27 miles).
11. **Camerano and Robert** (1,088 c.c. Simca Fiat), 2,249.2 kiloms.
*12. **Bonneau and Mme. Itier** (954 c.c. M.G.), 2,227.5 kiloms. (1,384.16 miles).
*13. **Miss Fawcett and White** (1,098 c.c. Morgan), 2,209.4 kiloms (1,372.98 miles).
14. **Aime and Plantivaux** (568 c.c. Simca Fiat), 2,042.7 kiloms. **750 c.c. class winner** (at record speed of 52.7 m.p.h.).
15. **Leduc and Querzola** (568 c.c. Simca Fiat), 1,891.4 kiloms.
All the above qualified for the final of the Biennial Cup next year. There were no other finishers.
*British cars.

RUDGE WHITWORTH BIENNIAL CUP, 1937-1938
(For those who qualified in the 1937 Race)
1. **Orssich and Sauerwein** (1.6-litre Adler), 1,236 points, 73.7 m.p.h.
2. **Lohr and von Guilleaume** (1½-litre Adler), 1,230 points.
3. **de Cortanze and Contet** (2-litre Peugeot), 1,204 points.
No other runners finished in this class.

CLASSIFICATION ON FORMULA.
1, Aime and Plantivaux (Fiat); 2, Orssich and Sauerwein (Adler); 3, Lohr and von Guilleaume (Adler); 4, Chaboud and Trémoulet (Delahaye); 5, de Cortanze and Contet (Peugeot); 6, Serraud and Cabantous (Delahaye); 7, J. Savoye and P. Savoye (Singer); 8, Leduc and Querzola (Fiat); 9, Debille and Lapchin (Fiat); 10, Bonneau and Mme. Itier (M.G.), 11, Villeneuve and Biolay (Delahaye); 12, Prenant and Morel (Talbot); 13, Camerano and Robert (Fiat); 14, Miss Fawcett and White (Morgan); 15, Clark and Chambers (H.R.G.).

The Alfas were the only two blown cars in the race—one an old-type 2.3-litre Monza-type two-seater and the other a somewhat mysterious Alfa-Corse entry which turned out to be a recent 2.9-litre production model (Type C) based on the old eight-cylinder Monoposto racing car. Driving this machine, which was complete with a bright-red ultra-streamlined saloon body, were Raymond Sommer and Biondetti.

These cars alone would obviously provide a terrific scrap for honours in the general classification.

In the 3-litre class there were only Louis Gerard's Delage and a 2½-litre Amilcar, in the hands of two French women, Mmes. Roux and Rouault, whilst the 2-litre class comprised a trio of four-cylinder Peugeots, a saloon Adler and the Aston Martin with which R. P. Hichens and M. H. Morris-Goodall won the Biennial Cup last year. All the cars in this (the 2-litre) class, incidentally, were competing in the final for the 1937-8 Rudge Cup.

Barring the Aston Martin just mentioned, British entries and cars were entirely confined to the small-car classes. The 1½-litre class comprised two French-entered four-cylinder Rileys, a fairly standard H.R.G. privately entered by Peter Clark and Marcus Chambers, an Atalanta (C. H. W. Morrison and Neil Watson), and an Adler saloon.

In the 1,100 c.c. category, the five British cars were much outnumbered by no fewer than eight Simca-Fiats, one of which, in the hands of Gordini, won the Bol d'Or 24-hour race a week or two before.

GRUELLING LE MANS 24-HOUR RACE

Fastest Cars All Crack Up—French-entered Singer Wins 1,100 c.c. Class and Finishes Eighth—H.R.G., M.G. and Morgan also Complete the Course

precedes a great race came over all. Only the metallic voice over the loud-speakers ticked off the minutes.

Then, in a moment, a scurry of feet broke the silence, the whirr of starters coincided with an outburst of excited conversation in many tongues and the snarl of exhausts burst out, rose in a crescendo and they were off. First to break out of the line was Cabantous in one of the 3½-litre Delahayes, but Drey-fus, at the end of the line, was first round the right-hand corner under the Bridge and into the New Esses.

Round the right-angle corner at Terte Rouge he was still in front with Divo in the other 4¼-litre Delahaye hot on his heels, Carriere (Talbot) just behind and Mazaud (3½-litre Dela-haye) in fourth place. Out on to the undulating two-and-a-half-mile Mulsanne Straight Divo and Dreyfus still led, but Sommer in the Alfa screamed

SMILING happily are (above) Marcus Chambers and Peter Clarke in their H.R.G. and plucky Miss P. M. Fawcett and G. White (Morgan). (Left) The Annual Cup winners, Aime and Plantivaux (Simca-Fiat). (Below) Outright winners—Chaboud and Tremoulet (in No. 15). The other Delahaye was second.

The British cars were a pair of Singer Nines (one entered by F. S. Barnes and driven by his brother Donald and Tommy Wisdom, and the other a French entry, driven by Jacques and Pierre Savoye); two PB-type M.G. Midgets (one Miss Dorothy Stanley-Turner's very standard car which was taken over by Arthur Dobson and Mrs. Wisdom—and the other a special-bodied car in the hands of two French pilots, C. P. Bonneau and Mme. Itier); and the Morgan 4/4 which ran in the T.T. last year and was driven by Miss P. M. Fawcett and G. White.

The entry was completed by two Simca Cinq (Fiat " 500 ") models with extraordinary little streamlined bodies.

From early on Saturday morning there was a continuous exodus from the old city of Le Mans and long before zero hour (4 p.m.) every seat on the grandstand was occupied, all vantage points on the 8.38-mile course had been taken, flags fluttered, loud-speakers

blared, refreshment tents were doing a roaring trade . . . in fact, the unique Le Mans atmosphere had descended—and would remain until after the last exhaust note had died, over 24 hours later.

As starting time approached the drivers took up their stations in little circles on one side of the road opposite their cars, and that peculiar hush that

past the rest into third place. And so round Mulsanne Corner, down the twisty stretch through the Old Esses, round Arnage Corner leading back on to the " home " leg of the course and gently uphill past White House Corner of Bentley crash-fame and down to the Stands again.

When the field got away, two cars were left behind—Pierre Ferry's Riley and Clifford's Talbot. The former was off after a few seconds, but poor Freddie Clifford could not get his engine to fire until Dreyfus was flashing by on the end of his first lap.

Of the small cars, Viale's Simca Fiat was first away, followed by Gordini and Sarret in similar cars, Clarke's H.R.G., three more Fiats and then the two Singers.

At the end of the first lap Dreyfus and Divo in the two Delahayes flashed past with Sommer's Alfa and Carrière's Talbot only a few lengths behind, all putting up a terrific pace.

Leading the small cars, Gordini's Fiat was motoring extraordinarily rapidly for an 1,100 c.c. car. His speed for the standing lap was close on 70 m.p.h., and, together with Viale and another Fiat driver, was ahead of the leading 1½-litre car—Forestier's Riley.

At the back end of the field were the two M.G.s—obviously running with an eye to finishing—and, well behind, the two baby Fiats.

On the second lap, there was no doubt that the early part of the race, at any rate, was to see a terrific battle amongst the leaders.

On the Grass at 150 m.p.h.

At the end of the second lap, Dreyfus was still ahead, but Sommer's bright red saloon had passed Divo's Delahaye and was only a length behind the leader. On lap three Sommer took the lead at Arnage and there he stayed until the sixth lap when Dreyfus roared alongside approaching the Café de l'Hippodrome, found he hadn't room and so got past by using the grass and the open space in front of the café—all at something like 150 m.p.h.

A lap later Sommer was back in the lead again, Divo was at the pits with selector trouble in the gearbox, Etancelin in the 4½-litre Talbot had moved up into second place, Dreyfus was third and Carrière, in one of the other Talbots, fourth—a bare 5 secs. separating the four.

On the tenth lap, Etancelin took the lead. On the eleventh, Sommer put in

a turn at over 96 m.p.h., only .8 sec. outside the record for the course and got ahead again. Four laps later, Etancelin was once more in front and again Sommer won back his lead next time round.

Terrific!

But the pace was too hot for Dreyfus. On the fifteenth lap he came in for a rapid consultation, continued for a few more turns with nasty clanking noises going on and finally retired after 21 laps with no oil pressure.

Meantime, Gordini was setting a phenomenal pace for the small cars. On the second lap he passed the 2-litre Peugeots and was 16th in the general classification, lapping at 78 m.p.h. and taking the corners as fast as anybody on the course. A few laps later

(Above) The Simca-Fiats of (No. 41) Vernet and Mdme. Largeot and of Debille and Lapchin in the pits. (Below) The big cars getting away. Among them can be discerned (No. 2) the Comotti-Divo Delahaye and in the background the winning Delahaye.

he passed one of the 3½-litre Delahayes and by the tenth lap he was 14th in the race—in an 1,100 c.c. machine!

Forestier's Riley had been in to the pits twice and changed drivers twice—both looking worried—and the other Riley headed the 1½-litre cars; Peter Clark (H.R.G.) had also been in (to do things under the bonnet), and the Atalanta was out (after only three laps) with a broken rear hub.

Barnes's Singer was going round nicely, lapping at about 67 m.p.h., the other Singer came in with clutch slip but carried on, Mrs. Wisdom was lapping consistently at about 63 m.p.h., the Morgan at about 62 m.p.h. and the H.R.G. at over the "70" mark.

At the end of the first hour Sommer was still in front only a second ahead of Etancelin, with Carrière third; Ferry's bob-tailed Riley was at the head of the 1½-litre cars, but was several places behind Gordini's Fiat, which was still 14th in the general classification, and Plantivaux led the other Fiat 500.

By 7 p.m. these positions remained the same except that Gordini's Fiat had been passed by Viale's car.

About this time most drivers came in for their first refuel (which was not allowed under intervals of 24 laps) and changed drivers. The Alfa during this time temporarily lost the lead.

Two hours later the sun, which had blazed down on the scene since the start, went down behind the horizon, the light gradually faded and the flood lights on the pits came on, whilst behind the grandstand the scene was exactly like a fair, with refreshment tents, booths and even a marquee where a dance band competed with the hoarse loud-speakers outside whilst couples made the best they could of the result.

By 10 p.m. it was fully dark, most drivers had been in and removed the covers from their lamps and tore round with undiminished speed by the light of their head lamps.

At midnight the list of retirements had grown to a dozen. Ferry's Riley was out with gearbox trouble, Etancelin's Talbot damaged a valve, Mazaud's Delahaye had burst into flames and burnt itself out in the New Esses, and the British-entered M.G. had boiled all its water away as a result of a slipping clutch and limped round with constant stops to cool in the hope of completing its minimum refuelling distance and taking on water. Eventually the crew decided to give up.

Sommer and Biondetti were now a lap ahead of Carrière and Le Begue (Talbot), and Trévoux and Levegh, in another Talbot, with Trémoulet and Chaboud (Delahaye).

Leading the small cars, Gordini and Scaron in the Fiat were three laps ahead of the first 1½-litre car—now the Adler saloon driven by Otto Lohr and P von Guilleaume.

And so into the night the battle went on—and the list of retirements grew. Barnes's Singer, which had been running well but for slight plug trouble, broke an engine bearer, two more Fiats developed trouble, one of the Talbots and a Delahaye were out, and by 7 a.m. the field of 42 which had started had dwindled to 22.

In the general classification the Alfa had piled on a lead of six laps over Trévoux's Talbot and the Chaboud-Trémoulet Delahaye was third. Amongst the small cars the Adler had at last got ahead of Gordini's Fiat and was 10th in the general classification, with the Fiat 12th. The Riley, Singer and M.G. (all the French entries) were still running, and so were the H.R.G. and the Morgan, together with five other Fiats, including the babies.

On Formula, Gordini's Fiat led the whole race and the tiny Fiat of Aimé and Plantivaux was bracketed with the Alfa for second place Of those in the running for the final of the 1937-8

A little doodle-dicing by (top) the Villeneuve-Biolay Delahaye at Arnage, (centre) Sarret's Fiat at Mulsanne and (above) the Rosier-Huguet Talbot coupé which has spun round at Mulsanne and is being passed by the Amilcar.

Rudge Cup the Fiat was also in the lead, with the 1½-litre Adler next. Highest-placed British car in the running for the cup was Morris Goodall's Aston Martin, in fifth position.

Later in the morning the Aston came in with a burnt valve and the equipé promptly set about removing the head and changing it—a fine effort that unfortunately proved to be in vain.

Meanwhile, Mathieson's Talbot had burst into flames at White House when running second and was completely burnt out, and a little later Gordini's Fiat, Scaron driving, was rumoured to have crashed, but was later announced as retiring with a broken oil pipe.

By mid-day only 17 were left, the Alfa leading, 12 laps ahead of the Trémoulet-Chaboud Delahaye. The Adler still led the small cars and Savoye's Singer was best of the "eleven hundreds." On Formula. Aimé and Plantivaux had now come into the lead and the two Adlers were ahead in the Rudge Cup final.

It seemed that the result was a certainty with the Alfa running like clockwork and only a sixth of the race to go. Then, shortly before one o'clock, the Alfa came in with its off-side front tyre bereft of tread a bent wing and part of the panelling missing. The tread had come adrift when Sommer was travelling at 140 m.p.h. down Mulsanne Straight and for a few seconds the car dived wildly about with the thrashing tread tearing at the wings and coachwork.

Alfa Crippled

By a terrific effort Sommer kept control and toured round to the pits, where the wheel was changed and Biondetti took over. But that flying tread had damaged more than mere coachwork and the car came to rest with oiling trouble at Arnage.

There was only one hope—to push it into the pits and make some sort of temporary repair that would at least let the car tour round and, with its huge lead to help, finish well up—perhaps even win; but it was not to be. Pushing a ton of motorcar 2½ miles, part of it uphill, was an impossible task, and at about 3 p.m. Biondetti, exhausted, gave up.

After that, the race was a mere procession. The Tremoulet - Chaboud Delahaye had already exceeded the Alfa's distance and all the cars still running had covered their minimum distances with the sole exception of the H.R.G. which, limping round painfully with nasty clanking noises, had only a lap to go. When, soon after 3 p.m. it finished that lap, interest died—died, that is, until the very end, when, with true Continental enthusiasm the crowds flocked to the tribunes to honour the fifteen survivors.

The order they finished, the distances they covered and the honours they won are set out in the full results given at the beginning of this report.

(Left) Through the New Esses— the Forestier-Caron Riley followed by two of the Peugeots.

Le Mans!

Fight Between Alfa-Romeo (Sommer-Biondetti) and Twelve-cylinder Delahayes Sets a Cracking Pace : Race Eventually Won by 3½-litre Delahaye (Chaboud - Tremoulet) at 82.3 m.p.h. : 2-litre Adler Wins Rudge-Whitworth Cup

THE Le Mans 24-hour Race—*le Grand Prix d'Endurance*—this year provided a duel between France and Italy. And France won after one of the most gruelling races ever held. For 21 of the 24 hours an 8-cyl. 2.9-litre supercharged Alfa-Romeo —a streamlined coupé driven by Sommer and Biondetti—led the field at a terrific speed, only to retire, but not before the pace it set had served to crack up the really fast cars.

Two of the smaller Delahayes finished first and second. These were 3½-litre cars of more or less conventional type, the one driven by Chaboud and Tremoulet averaging 82.36 m.p.h. as compared with the 85.07 m.p.h. of the Bugatti driven by Benoist and Wimille last year.

For over 20 laps Sommer's Alfa covered the 8.38-mile circuit consistently in 5 min. 22 sec. (over 93 m.p.h.) which was only 7 sec. short of last year's record lap. The two 12-cylinder Delahayes were almost as fast, and during the initial stages there was a battle royal for the lead, which alternated between a Delahaye and the Alfa.

The two Delahayes meant to "break up" the Alfa or perish in the attempt. Then they could take things easier. But the Alfa, magnificently driven by Sommer at this stage, proved the victor. In six laps one of the Delahayes retired, and at 21 laps the other followed suit. This left the Talbots—the French

marque—and the smaller Delahayes to take up the challenge ; a large pack after a single fleeting red saloon. At the end of six hours the Alfa had a two-lap lead, followed by three Talbots, a Delahaye and another Talbot. In another six hours the Alfa's lead had increased to five laps, with three Talbots and two Delahayes battling for second place.

At eighteen hours the only change in the position was a thinning of the ranks of the pack, for Talbots had lost two out of four cars. The Alfa's lead was now as much as 11 laps.

(Top) The modernistic streamlined Alfa-Romeo which, driven by Sommer and Biondetti, dominated the race for twenty-one out of the twenty-four hours, passes the Lévy-Alin Simca-Fiat in front of the pits at speed.

(Left) An unusual aerial view as the field branches off on to the new road at the start.

With only three hours to go the red Italian machine paid the penalty of the killing pace and retired, leaving the Talbots and 3½-litre Delahayes to fight it out. It was no longer an international affair, and the average speed of the leaders fell considerably.

In the meantime one of the Simca-Fiats—an 1,100 c.c. model driven by Gordini—was astonishing the spectators by its speed. Never before had an 1,100 c.c. car held such an average. It, too, retired after a remarkable demonstration lasting over twelve hours,

The winning Delahaye pauses at Arnage for a minor adjustment as the H.R.G. of P. C. T. Clark and M. Chambers goes by.

and so gave some hope to the drivers of those cars which were competing for the Rudge-Whitworth Cup.

Eventually this biennial Trophy went to a German Adler streamlined saloon, after a run which was made impressive by its quietness, and the fact that with its sister car it gave no trouble whatsoever, the only cars in the race of which that could be said.

THE RACE DESCRIBED

IN all the world there is nothing quite like the 24-hour Race at Le Mans. It is the last event left to us which embodies the spirit of the old racing. The British entry excepted, the cars were as fine a group of racing sports cars as this race has ever produced.

In weather that was hot and oppressive to a point that augured an imminent thunderstorm, the machines came up to the start. Practice had proved that the opening battle would be between the Alfa-Romeo supercharged straight-eight, streamlined coupé and two twelve-cylinder V-engined Delahaye sports cars with the group of French Talbots, some of them saloons, as prospective rivals. As usual, an immense and deeply interested crowd watched every move as the cars assembled before the gaily flagged grandstand, and, being a French crowd, appreciated every move in the game.

In due order by fixed routine the machines were refilled, sealed, placed in position. That cheery streak of humour which is an attribute of Raymond Sommer led one of France's well-known

A mechanic takes a look at Sommer's Alfa-Romeo after a tyre tread had been flung, bursting the mudguard as shown.

drivers to appear in a most inappropriate straw hat, a thing appreciated to the full by the crowd.

And then, when the wait for the hour of 4 p.m. seemed eternal, the great Faroux dropped the flag, there was a hurried scampering of men, a whirring of starting motors, and the engines woke to life. And how great was the delight when Vial's tiny Simca-Fiat was away first of all, a hundredth of a second before the whole mass of brightly coloured cars roared away down the road, save for "Taso" Mathieson's Talbot!

Ensued that pause we all know so well. Then, in a minute or so, arose the shouts of the crowd who had seen, far down the road, the first approaching car. No. 1,

T. A. S. O. Mathieson had a narrow escape at White House when the Talbot he was driving caught fire. He jumped out just in time after pulling up on the grass.

twelve-cylinder Delahaye, Dreyfus at the wheel, flew by, leading with its sister car, Comotti's, second, and then the 2.9-litre Alfa coupé of Sommer's, which had gained some eleven places.

Next round, the red Alfa was second and Sommer was fanning himself with his hat, and on the next lap the red Italian car led. But it was to be no runaway victory. Howls of delight greeted the appearance of Dreyfus once more at the head of the line, only to be repassed by Sommer, and so the struggle went on.

But alas, Comotti's Delahaye came to its pit and instantly there was excitement, tragedy and comedy mixed. Comotti complained with much gesture that something was amiss with the gear box. The veteran Divo, now of important size, was promptly told to take the wheel. He did so, and on coming

in again delivered a curt, expressive diagnosis with a beautiful imitation of the noise caused by at least one tooth missing from a gear. The car had to retire.

That was the start of a series of disasters that filled the pits with cars in trouble and mechanics in distress. To cap it all Dreyfus' car fell right back, its driver signalling that the water was giving out. The louvres in the bonnet were opened to give air; everyone in the pit shouted at once. The car restarted, but slower and slower its lap time proved, while the meteoric Chiron at the pits encouraged it with hopeful signals, but that, too, failed, for the much-tried engine developed piston trouble and the second twelve-cylinder Delahaye was out.

A spectator in the pits was J. Paul, the French driver who was involved in the fatal accident at Brooklands recently, when his Delage caught fire and plunged into the spectators.

So the red Alfa coupé continued to lead, lapping at over 93 m.p.h.; the twelve-cylinder Delahaye challenge had failed! To show how the pace was telling, Vernet's Simca-Fiat was in trouble, Monneret's Delahaye had a fit of misfiring that a new coil and fuel pump failed to cure, Forestier's Riley was in the pits almost every five laps, Horvilleur's old type Alfa was hesitating, Mongin's Delahaye developed trouble, and the Atalanta most unfortunately sheared a pin in its axle driving shaft, all within two hours. Gerard's Delage and Debille's Simca-Fiat misfired violently, Savoye was in trouble with his Singer —no pleasant start for a 24-hour race.

The Lead Changes

Rain threatened, but did not develop. Mathieson, driving Mahe's Talbot, had got going well after being left on the line owing to a defect in the strangler gear. Meanwhile the other Talbots had tackled the Alfa and, gradually improving, Carriere's car temporarily captured the lead, followed by Etancelin's, when the Alfa fell to third place, due to a stop to refill.

The next spell saw Biondetti, in Sommer's place, once more regain the lead after a magnificent drive in which the red Alfa certainly demonstrated its speed. And there was still more trouble. The 936 c.c. M.G., driven by Mrs. Wisdom, once more developed alarming clutch slip, and a high temperature that threatened worse to come. Hichens' 2-litre Aston Martin, which had gone well, was badly delayed because a thoughtful plumber, repairing the pit fuel supply tank, saw fit to leave the main tap off, and the H.R.G. was delayed by a plug change.

But a car showing an amazing speed, being actually well up in the general classification, was Gordini's toad-like 1,100 c.c. Fiat. He was miles ahead for the Rudge Cup. The little Singer was going splendidly, and the Morgan quite steadily, according to plan. Not for a moment did the interest of the crowd relax. Various advertising stunts, such as feature at Le Mans, utterly failed to distract.

But the troubles continued. The Alfa sounded less happy now, and the Talbots pressed their rival hard. After six hours

Wheel to wheel race at Tertre Rouge. The Monza Alfa-Romeo of Horvilleur and Matra overtakes the Simca-Fiat of Lévy and Alin.

R. P. Hichens and Morris Goodall were involved in a pit stop of some two hours when their Aston Martin suffered valve trouble.

the order was: first, the Alfa, then close on its rear wheels Etancelin, Carriere and Trevoux on Talbots. Only thirty cars were still running. Some of those were not regularly in action, and Gerard's neat Delage went out with engine trouble. As dusk fell, Dobson, who had taken over from Mrs. Wisdom, made a great effort to keep the M.G. going when all the water had boiled away, but had to give up a hopeless contest.

Positions at 6 Hours (10 p.m.).
1. Sommer-Biondetti (Alfa-Romeo); 66 laps.
2. Etancelin-Chinetti (Talbot-Darracq); 64 laps.
3. Carriere-Le Begue (Talbot-Darracq); 64 laps.
4. Trevoux-Levegh (Talbot-Darracq); 62 laps.
5. Chaboud-Tremoulet (Delahaye); 61 laps.
6. Mathieson-Clifford (Talbot-Darracq); 60 laps.

The First Six Hours Kilometres Covered Compared with 1937.
Distance Covered by Leader.

	1937.		1938.
First hour	134.92	..	148.41
Second hour	283.33	..	296.82
Third hour	445.23	..	445.23
Fourth hour	580.15	..	593.64
Fifth hour	725.07	..	742.06
Sixth hour	863.48	..	890.47

Major repairs of a complicated and lengthy type were being executed on the suspension of Debille's Fiat, as the light of the grandstand created the true Le Mans atmosphere. News came through that Mongin's Delahaye had caught fire, and by the time eager helpers had finished throwing dirt into the engine to extinguish the flames the car was in no condition to continue, despite the Gallic argument that the driver had to face. The older Alfa developed a Vesuvius-like volcano of steam when refilling, which markedly made its driver peevish before he had to retire; in fact, the event was becoming a race of trouble.

Still the fleeting Alfa led, still the six-cylinder Talbots continued in a battle royal for leadership, and still Gordini's 1,100 c.c. Fiat maintained a speed that took the breath away. Ere midnight Etancelin's car fell out with engine trouble, but Carriere clung to second place, ably backed by Trevoux. British drivers and cars were still in the background.

The Aston and the Singer were running excellently, and but for the Fiat's amazing performance would have been right in the forefront for the Rudge Cup. The Morgan, now driven by Miss Fawcett, after White's spell, was steadily holding its qualifying speed, as ordered,

The three filler caps of the Villeneuve-Biolay Delahaye facilitated refuelling.

and the H.R.G., equally well controlled, was one lap ahead.

Time does not dull the beauty of the night scene at Le Mans, where an effect of indirect lighting makes grandstand and pits stand out sharply against the sky, while on the road in front, weirdly marked with circles and lines, car after car roars by with its head lamps ablaze, and still the crowd maintains its interest. True, here and there a worthy citizen calmly settles to well-earned repose, but in the main, with the music, the restaurants, and the excitement, most are very much awake.

By half-distance many things had happened. The Morgan's *commissaire*, pondering, no doubt, on that car's fair driver, fell through into the M.G. pit complete with a door, felling six bewildered people in the process. Only 23

cars were still running. A hard fate had smashed the little Singer's crankshaft just when Donald Barnes and Tommy Wisdom were bringing the car up apace.

Positions at 12 Hours (4 a.m.).
1. Sommer-Biondetti (Alfa-Romeo); 128 laps.
2. Trevoux-Levegh (Talbot-Darracq); 123 laps.
3. Mathieson-Clifford (Talbot-Darracq); 120 laps.
4. Chabaud-Tremoulet (Talbot-Darracq); 118 laps.
5. Serraud-Giraud Cabantous (Delahaye); 116 laps.
6. Villeneuve-Biolay (Delahaye); 114 laps.
7. Prenant-Morel (Talbot-Darracq); 109 laps.
8. de Cortanze-Contet (Peugeot); 108 laps.
9. Orssich-Sauerwein (Adler); 105 laps.
10. Otto Lohr-von Guilleaume (Adler); 102 laps.
11. Hichens-Goodall (Aston Martin); 101 laps.
12. Ferry-Noiraux (Riley); 100 laps.
13. Gordini-Scaron (Simca-Fiat); 98 laps.
14. Viale-Breillet (Simca-Fiat); 95 laps.
15. Clark-Chambers (H.R.G.); 86 laps.
16. Fawcett-White (Morgan); 85 laps.
17. Savoye-Savoye (Singer); 81 laps.
18. Debille-Lapchin (Simca-Fiat); 81 laps.
19. Bonneau-Itier (M.G.); 78 laps.
20. Camerano-Robert (Simca-Fiat); 76 laps.
21. Lévy-Alin (Simca-Fiat); 76 laps.
22. Aime-Plantivaux (500 Simca-Fiat); 74 laps.
23. Leduc-Querzola (500 Simca-Fiat); 68 laps.

The Aston lost all clearance for one exhaust rocker, considerable work by Hichens and the mechanic resulting in the car being able to continue with one weak cylinder. Gordini's fast Fiat was held up a good half-hour with front suspension trouble. Sommer, with Biondetti, had crept gradually ahead with the Alfa, for Carriere's Talbot had a stop, and Trevoux and Levegh with No. 7 Talbot annexed second place.

The "mice," otherwise the little 500 Simca-Fiats, continued to amble along

In contrast to the Delahaye, refuelling was a slow and messy job for the Prenant-Morel Talbot with a single narrow filler.

remarkably speedily for their size. Madame Itier drove Bonneau's M.G. with great verve, and the two streamlined saloon Adlers were impressively regular, one, handled by Lohr and Guilleaume, proudly bearing on its instrument board a miniature flower pot complete with exotic cactus. "Percy," the mascot turtle of the H.R.G. pit, thoughtfully sealed about the beak by a *plombeur*, seemed to look a little bored as the car continued with regularity without incident, and Mortimer Morris-Goodall grew a beard of porcupine consistency.

Of the 2-litre Peugeots, Cortanze's and Contet's was best and that without sign of stress, while Savoye's black Singer was now full of life, and Forestier's Riley was atoning for its past. That curious car, Camerano's Fiat, was now in the picture, outwardly the standard saloon of ordinary life save that the stridency of its engine's exhaust suggested that much had been done. T. A. S. O. Mathieson's and Clifford's Talbot had also settled down to hard work unstinted, with the facetious Mahe as chief adviser, at all times.

In the Sandbank

Dawn came very pleasantly, probably as a relief to the Alfa, which for some time had been carrying rather rakishly a single head lamp. *The Autocar* pit kitchen remained deep in the mysteries of eggs and bacon, without which no Englishman can drive with abandon.

Very unpleasant things happened to Viale's and Breillet's 1,100 c.c. Simca-Fiat which, like Gordini's, had been extremely fast. The Simcas certainly had patchy luck, for earlier on one car ran into Mulsanne sandbank, from which the driver eventually extracted it with hard work and a borrowed spade. The machine then left with one wing so hard on a tyre that the tread caught fire.

By 7.0 a.m. 22 cars were left, and Sommer and Biondetti, after rather convincing Franco-Italian messages from the pit, had definitely slowed, their pit work also being a little more leisurely, though neat and organised. Also the Chaboud-Tremoulet Delahaye had come up to third place by reason of a stop which delayed Mathieson and Clifford's Talbot, the second Talbot being also in trouble shortly afterwards and delayed long at the pit. That amazing vehicle, the Gordini-Scaron Simca-Fiat, had quite recovered from its indisposition, and urged on by the usual grand opera from the loud speakers was now going like a scared cat.

Then came a whole series of catastrophes. First the trouble in the Trevoux-Levegh Talbot proved irreparable, and the car that had held second place for so long retired. That put the

Panama hats for the Peugeot team : the 2-litre Peugeot driven by de Cortanze and Contet won the 2-litre class, was third in the Rudge Cup category, and fifth in the whole race.

Chaboud-Tremoulet Delahaye second, whereupon that car came in. Within a few seconds Mathieson would have been second, but time went on and he was overdue. Coming up from Arnage there was a pop, and Mathieson found the bonnet a mass of flames. He could not stop, he had to take White House, but

Raymond Sommer (right), that typical French personality, explains to Biondetti, his co-driver, just how he skidded. In his hand he brandishes a piece of tyre tread.

he shut off fuel, did his level best to stop a crash, succeeded, and actually got the car to the side of the road before it went up in flames. By a miracle Mathieson escaped injury. Meantime the Delahaye went on.

Then that wizard Simca-Fiat of Gordini's misfired badly, stopped, had all plugs changed, and the Aston, itself sounding unhealthy, gained two rounds. The Fiat got away seemingly right ; it was the Aston that came in next, and then the Fiat was overdue. Minutes later it was pushed to the pit.

Trouble for the Aston

The order now was Alfa, the Chaboud-Tremoulet Delahaye, then Serraud's and Giraud-Cabantous' Delahaye. Fate had indeed struck. The Aston's troublesome exhaust valve had finally decided to burn out, so when the car got going its exhaust note lacked all crack, which meant stop after stop, and finally led to Hichens and Morris-Goodall removing the cylinder head and fitting a new valve.

As though in sympathy with all this, the skies developed a gentle drizzle that lasted from 8.45 to nearly 10 o'clock, by which time only 18 cars were still in action. Of these, the two sweet-running Adlers continued impressively free from trouble ; the remaining Peugeot was still fast. But it was freely rumoured that the "mice," which continued as steadily as ever, would prove sole survivors, all the more because the Morgan had a bout of misfiring, and the note of Villeneuve's Delahaye was unpleasantly irregular. The scarcely recognisable M.G. of Bonneau and Madame Itier was now running extremely well, as was still the H.R.G.

Positions at 18 Hours (10 a.m.).
1. Sommer-Biondetti (Alfa-Romeo); 189 laps.
2. Chaboud-Tremoulet (Talbot-Darracq); 178 laps.
3. Serraud-Giraud Cabantous (Delahaye); 174 laps.
4. Prenant-Morel (Talbot-Darracq); 163 laps.
5. Villeneuve-Biolay (Delahaye); 163 laps.
6. de Cortanze-Contet (Peugeot); 162 laps.
7. Orssich-Sauerwein (Adler); 158 laps.
8. Lohr-von Guilleaume (Adler); 153 laps.
9. Hichens-Goodall (Aston Martin); 147 laps.
10. Clark-Chambers (H.R.G.); 132 laps.
11. Fawcett-White (Morgan); 129 laps.
12. Savoye-Savoye (Singer); 129 laps.
13. Debille-Lapchin (Simca-Fiat); 127 laps.
14. Bonneau-Itier (M.G.); 112 laps.
15. Camerano-Robert (Simca-Fiat); 112 laps.
16. Aime-Plantivaux (500 Simca-Fiat); 112 laps.
17. Lévy-Alin (Simca-Fiat); 109 laps.
18. Leduc-Querzola (500 Simca-Fiat); 105 laps.

Some humour enlivened the spectators when a chart-keeper suddenly made him-

Through " Les Esses " : Comotti with the twelve-cylinder Delahaye leads from Etancelin and Chinetti's Talbot. This was in the early stages before the twelve-cylinder Delahayes retired.

self a box seat outside on the pit counter, sat himself down in all solemnity, called on all persons to give him full view, then kept falling asleep, so that he never succeeded in recording the full number of cars running, and once lost his pencil, having forgotten its lodgment behind his ear.

From then on until 12 o'clock things went better with everyone, except that the changing of the Aston's head proved a longer job than expected, that Debille and Lapchin's Simca went out with rear axle defects, and that the Morgan's trouble persisted and appeared to be caused by a valve, the which caused Anthony much work. The Alfa toured comfortably round, and Sommer's rise in spirits displayed itself by the reappearance of the straw hat.

The End in Sight

After midday things were naturally much cheerier, for the end seemed suddenly closer, a thing devoutly wished by most, not least by Prenant and Morel, whose neat Talbot saloon exuded huge clouds of steam at a refill. At 12.20 p.m., amid enthusiastic applause, the Aston's engine was restarted, and a few minutes later it left, going much better. Things looked more promising from the British point of view, too, for the Aston, Morgan, H.R.G., M.G. and Savoye's Singer were all running.

But thrills still came. At 12.45 a tent in the spectators' enclosure caught fire, creating great excitement. Simultaneously the Alfa, which had led throughout, came limping in, making a horrible noise.

A front tread had torn off, smashing the mudguard. The car, according to Sommer's expressively gestured tale, had almost got out of control. After a change of wheels the car left slowly with Biondetti. But, alas, after two laps, it appeared no more. It had stopped near White House.

Thus ended what promised to be a new record for Le Mans. Throughout Sommer had held the attention of the crowds by the speed of his car and his own personality. Probably no driver was more popular, and, in spite of the fact that he was driving a foreign machine, the spectators seemed sorry for his defeat.

Almost simultaneously the Aston gave up, water having entered No. 1 cylinder, a tragic reward for much hard work and determination. Then the H.R.G. went fluffy, lost a cylinder, and thereafter was driven to finish at any cost.

Naturally, all this benefited Delahaye. Chaboud's and Tremoulet's now led, with Serraud's and Giraud-Cabantous' second, Prenant and Morel's Talbot third, a real feat of merit for all three, and the Adlers, which had given no trouble at all throughout the race, established themselves as first and second for the coveted Rudge cup.

For the last three hours the race was monotonous to watch; the spectators, a dense mass along the railings, watched the clock more than the cars now passing through at long intervals. The Delahayes were still travelling fast, and the two streamlined Adler saloons continued their demonstration of quiet running at high speed, but, barring accidents, the result was a foregone conclusion. The two Delahayes were fighting each other for first place, and there was a possibility that one or the other might crack up before the end, but as far as the crowds were concerned, it did not matter which car won. But they were enthusiastic enough when the winner crossed the line almost on the stroke of four. Had he been a moment or so earlier he would have had to complete another lap before receiving his flag.

Thus ended a great race and a gruelling one, remarkable for the number of retirements due to mechanical troubles. Out of 42 starters only 15 received the plaudits of the crowds at the finish, and of these four were British.

The drivers were glad enough to call it a day : twenty-four hours is enough for anyone.

RESULTS.
General Classification.

Pos.	Car.	Drivers.	Miles.	M.p.h.	Fig. of Merit.
1	Delahaye ...	Chaboud ; Tremoulet ...	1,976.40	82.35	1.209
2	Delahaye ...	Serraud ; Giraud-Cabantous	1,959.69	81.65	1.199
3	Talbot ...	Prenant ; Morel ...	1,839.07	76.62	1.110
4	Delahaye ...	Villeneuve ; Biolav	1,830.42	76.26	1.119
5	Peugeot ...	de Cortanze ; Contet	1,794.50	74.77	1.204
6	Adler ...	Orssich ; Sauerwein	1,774.85	73.95	1.236
7	Adler ...	Lohr ; von Guilleaume	1,718.16	71.59	1.230
8	Singer ...	J. Savoye ; P. Savoye	1,467.04	61.12	1.191
9	Simca-Fiat ...	Debille ; Lapchin ...	1,447.51	60.31	1.133
10	H.R.G. ...	Clark ; Chambers ...	1,431.19	59.63	1.024
11	Simca-Fiat ...	Camerano ; Robert	1,397.59	58.23	1.093
12	M.G. ...	Bonneau ; Mme. Itier	1,384.11	57.67	1.132
13	Morgan ...	Miss Fawcett ; White	1,372.84	57.20	1.072
14	Simca-Fiat ...	Aime ; Plantivaux	1,269.30	52.88	1.280
15	Simca-Fiat ...	Leduc ; Querzola ...	1,175.25	48.96	1.185

A.C. de l'O Cup.
Simca-Fiat (Aime, Plantivaux).

Class Winners.
5-litre.—Delahaye (Chaboud, Tremoulet).
2-litre.—Peugeot (de Cortanze, Contet).
1,500 c.c.—Adler (Lohr, von Guilleaume).
1,100 c.c.—Singer (J. Savoye, P. Savoye).
750 c.c.—Simca-Fiat (Aime, Plantivaux).

Rudge-Whitworth Cup.

	Fig. of merit.
1. Adler (Orssich, Sauerwein)	1.236
2. Adler (Lohr von Guilleaume)	1.230
3. Peugeot (de Cortanze, Contet)	1.204

WINNERS' EQUIPMENT.
The Delahayes, which finished first and second, used :
Dunlop tyres, Rudge-Whitworth wheels, Solex carburettor, Bosch sparking plugs, ignition, lighting, lamps and starter, Castrol oil, Shell petrol, Hartford shock absorbers and Jaeger instruments.
The Adler who won the Rudge-Whitworth cup used :
Englebert tyres, Bosch sparking plugs, lighting, lamps and starter.

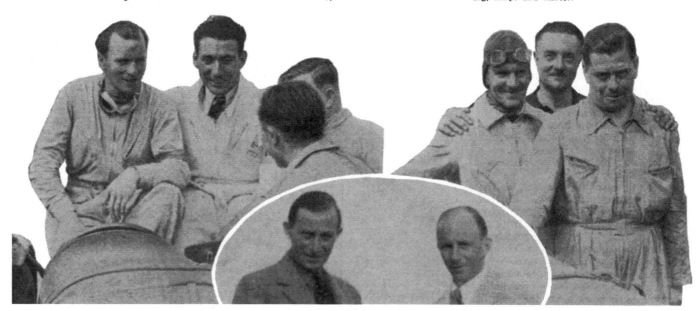

(Left, above) Drivers of the winning Delahaye, Chaboud and Tremoulet, who averaged 82.35 m.p.h. (Right, above) Serraud and Giraud-Cabantous who finished second, also with a Delahaye, at 81.65 m.p.h. (Inset) The German drivers Sauerwein and Orssich whose Adler won the Rudge-Whitworth cup for the handicap race at 73.95 m.p.h.

1939

Again there were only 42 cars in the race; the mixture was more or less as in the two previous years. Bugatti was back with a works entry, another Type 57 'Tank' with a supercharged 3.3 litre engine the sole example of this make, it was entrusted to the 1937 winning Wimille, partnered by Veyron who had driven in four previous races but never finished. By contrast, the French opposition was almost guilty of over-kill; the Delahaye-Delage combine had eight 3.6 litre cars of the former make and two three-litre Delages, and the Lagonda-Talbots were also present in force - six cars of which three were four-litre models, the other three 4½ litre cars with a close relationship with the company's Grand Prix racers. The home contingent was rounded off by eight Simcas taking the total number of French cars to 25.

Adler brought only one of their 'Rennlimousinen' to start this year; they had entertained hopes of repeating their success in a bigger class, and had brought an equally efficiently streamlined 2.5 litre six along, but this had to scratch after the engine blew up during practice. But German reinforcements came from BMW with three of the two-litre 328 models - one with coupe bodywork. Sommer brought a brand-new 2.6 litre Alfa Romeo coupe, forming an unusual Franco-Italian-Thai alliance as his co-driver was Prince Birabongse of Thailand, better known under his racing pseudonym of B. Bira.

The 12 British cars were mostly as before, small capacity models from Aston Martin, HRG, MG, Morgan, Riley and Singer, but with one very important addition two Lagondas, of the Bentley designed 4½ litre V12 model. One was driven by Lord Selsdon and Lord Waleran, the other by Charles Brackenbury and Arthur Dobson. W. O. Bentley had joined Lagonda some years after Rolls-Royce took over the original Bentley company, and while it must have given him some satisfaction to see one of his cars back at Le Mans, he was worried that the cars were not sufficiently prepared for the race - Lagonda chairman Alan Good had only allowed a few months in which to get the cars ready. In the circumstances, Bentley decided to run the cars at a set speed of 83 mph slightly faster than the 1938 winner and see what happened; this was intended mainly as a trial run for later Le Mans races.

Most of the initial excitement therefore centred round the dogfight of the big French cars- Chinetti's Talbot, Gerard's Delage, Mazoud's Delahaye and Wimille in the Bugatti. Sommer's performance must have disappointed his many supporters - the new Alfa misbehaved, and ultimately had to retire. Among the smaller cars, the Adler was an early retirement - a piston broke - while the BMW led the two-litre class, and Gordini and Scaron once again put up an excellent performance among the 1,100 cc cars.

The pace soon began to tell and several of the big cars retired; the Tremoulet/Forestier Delahaye spilled oil on the track, causing two accidents to other competitors, but fortunately without injury to the drivers. For most of the night the Delage of Gerard/Monneret was in the lead, gaining the lion's share of the newly instituted 1,000 franc bonus which the A.C.O. awarded to the leading car each hour. On Sunday morning they were still in the lead, followed by the Bugatti but the ranks of the French cars had thinned dramatically and the two Lagondas were third and fourth. Then the Delage ran into trouble; the engine ran rough, a plug change effected no improvement and the drivers suspected that a valve spring had broken - they carried no spare and were therefore unable to do anything about it. In the course of the Delage's pit stop, it was overtaken by the Bugatti which became the ultimate winner. The Delage still finished second, and the Lagondas - which appeared completely unperturbed by 24 hours of racing and had not needed even a tyre change - followed in third and fourth places. Wimille just beat his own 1937 records, with a distance of 2,084.54 miles at an average of 86.86 mph, while the honour of setting a new lap record fell to Mazoud in the Delahaye at 96.70 mph.

The three BMWs all finished in great style, in fifth, seventh and ninth places - the coupe was first home at a remarkable average speed of 82.55 mph. The surviving Delahayes were placed sixth, eighth and eleventh; and Gordini's Simca came home in tenth place, winning both the Index and the Biennial Cup at the same time, while none of the Talbots made it to the finish. The unanimous opinion was that for the 1940 race the Lagondas and the BMWs would have to be watched.

THE LAGONDA TEAM, after finishing third and fourth. Left to right are A. Dobson and C. Brackenbury (third); Lord Howe (R.A.C. observer); Lord Waleran and Lord Selsdon (fourth) neither of whom had seen their car until practice days, and Mr. A. P. Good, head of the Lagonda company.

RESULTS
(Provisional)

GRAND PRIX D'ENDURANCE, Wimille and Veyron (3.3-litre supercharged Bugatti), 2,083.3 miles, at 86.8 m.p.h. **New Record for the course.**
The old record for the full distance was held by Wimille and Benoist (3.3 Bugatti), in 1937, at 85.13 m.p.h.

RUDGE-WHITWORTH BIENNIAL CUP, on handicap.—Gordini and Scaron (1,100 Simca-Fiat), 1,789.7 miles, at 74.7 m.p.h.
New Lap Record.—R. Mazaud (3.5-litre Delahaye), 25th lap, 5 mins. 12.1 secs. (96.74 m.p.h.). **Old Record.**—Benoist (3.3 Bugatti, in 1937), 5 mins. 13 secs., 96.42 m.p.h.
Last year's winner, Chaboud and Tremoulet (3.5 Delahaye), 1,976.6 miles, at 82.3 m.p.h.

GENERAL CATEGORY

1, Wimille-Veyron (3.3 Bugatti S), 2,083.3 miles, 86.8 m.p.h.
2, Gerard-Monneret (3-litre Delage), 85.7 m.p.h. (26.4 miles behind the winner).
3, Arthur Dobson-Charles Brackenbury (4.5 Lagonda), 83.5 m.p.h. (77.7 miles behind the winner).
4, Lord Selsdon-Lord Waleran (4.5 Lagonda), 83.3 m.p.h. (83.9 miles behind the winner).
5, Prince Schaumburg Lippe-Wenscher (2-litre B.M.W. saloon), 82.5 m.p.h. (103.3 miles behind the winner).
6, Villeneuve-Biolay (3.5 Delahaye), covered 1,971.8 miles.
7, Roesse-Heinemann (2-litre B.M.W.), 1,926.3 miles.
8, B. Walker-G. Connell (3.5 Delahaye), 1,875.9 miles (78.1 m.p.h.).
9, Brien-Scholz (2-litre B.M.W.), 1,855.6 miles.
10, Gordini-Scaron (1,100 Simca-Fiat), 1,789.7 miles (74.7 m.p.h.).
11, Chotard-Feylair (3.5 Delahaye), 1,703.7 miles.
12, R. Hichens-Morris Goodall (2-litre Aston Martin), 1,654.1 miles.
13, Lapchin-Plaintivaux (1,100 Simca-Fiat), 1,638.2 miles.
14, P. Clark-M. Chambers (1,500 H.R.G.), 1,611.8 miles.
15 G. White-C. Anthony (1,104 Morgan), 1,545.8m iles.
16, Vernet-Bodard (1,500 Riley), 1,509.4 miles.
17, Camerano-Louveau (1,100 Simca-Fiat), 1,371.6 miles.
18, A. W. Jones-G. Wilkins (972 Singer), 1,296 miles.
19, Brothers Alin (570 Simca-Fiat), 1,239.7 miles.
20, Aimé-Leduc (570 Simca-Fiat), 1,232.1 miles.

CLASS WINNERS

Over 5 litres.—1, Wimille-Veyron (3.3 Bugatti), 2,083.3 miles. (This car is put into this class owing to its supercharger). **5 litres.**—1, Dobson-Brackenbury (Lagonda), 2,005.5 miles (83.5 m.p.h.); 2, Lord Selsdon-Lord Waleran (Lagonda); 3, Chotard-Feylair (Delahaye); 4, Walker-Connell (Delahaye). **3 litres.**—1,

---

Gerard (Delage), 2,056.9 miles (85.7 m.p.h.) **2 litres.**—Schaumburg-Lippe-Wenscher (B.M.W. saloon), 1,980 miles (82.5 m.p.h.); 2, Roesse-Heinemann (B.M.W.); 3, Brien (B.M.W.); 4, Hichens-Morris Goodall (Aston Martin). **1½ litres.**—1, Clark-Chambers (H.R.G.), 1,611.8 miles (67 m.p.h.); 2, White-Anthony (Morgan); 3, Vernet-Bodard (Riley). **1,100 c.c.**—Gordini-Scaron (Simca-Fiat), 1,789.7 miles (74.7 m.p.h.); 2, Lapchin-Plaintivaux (Simca-Fiat); 3, Camerano-Louveau (Simca-Fiat); 4, Jones-Wilkins (Singer). **750 c.c.**—1, Alin Brothers (Simca-Fiat), 1,239.7 miles (51.6 m.p.h.); 2 Aimé-Leduc (Simca-Fiat).

LE MANS

THE Le Mans 24-hour race run last Saturday and Sunday on the 8.4-mile Circuit of the Sarthe, for sports cars only, was won at record speed by Wimille and Veyron in a supercharged 3.3-litre Bugatti with two-seater super-streamlined body, after a magnificent race in which the car hung on the tail of the flyers and then moved into the lead.

For 20 hours the leader was Gerard's 3-litre unsupercharged Delage, which set up terrific speeds—a magnificent show—and ran into minor trouble two hours from the end, thereafter running second.

The two Lagondas, competing in their first and experimental race, also ran to time table and moved into third and fourth positions some hours before the end—a really fine performance.

The B.M.W. team (one a new streamlined car) ran like clockwork and immense speed, and finished as strongly as they began.

In the opening stages two Delahayes pursued the Delage, and one broke the lap record before they retired. Then a 4½-litre Darracq, driven by Chinetti and Mathieson, battled for the lead until a tyre burst and the car hit a sandbank. Hug, on a second Delage, was fourth, but collided with the Darracq and was forced out.

One Darracq spilt oil all over the circuit and caused skidding in all directions and two crashes, but fortunately none of the drivers was badly hurt.

Amedee Gordini's 1,100 c.c. Fiat easily won the handicap event. Sommer and Bira, on the new 2½-litre Alfa saloon, had to change a gasket, had brake trouble, and later retired.

All the British cars covered themselves with glory, and only four retired out of 12 starters, whereas 20 of the 42 starters failed to finish.

The Race by "Grande Vitesse"

LE MANS, *Saturday, Midnight.*
RACE day dawned somewhat doubtfully bright, and during the day heavy clouds banked up in a somewhat ominous manner. However, after the barometer had dropped for two days, it steadied and began to climb again. An enormous crowd streamed to the circuit by every means of conveyance known to man—even in aeroplanes—until half an hour before the start, at 4 p.m., the huge grandstand, the enclosures, and the fine, new ramp overlooking the pits, were crammed to capacity with a

GRAND PRIX—Wimille and Veyron (Bugatti) who also set up new course record.

typical French crowd in a typical state of French excitement.

The buffets did a roaring trade, so did the loudspeakers, and the big, permanent restaurant, with its white-coated waiters, just beside the circuit, was packed for hours. Flags flew, bunting danced in the breeze, and over all was that very Le Mans atmosphere of excitement and gaiety quite unknown anywhere else.

On the road in front of the pits was a bustle of activity. Mechanics put finishing touches to the long line of cars, drivers tried their driving seats for the thousandth time, or walked about, fiddling with goggles and gloves, officials darted about.

gendarmes swarmed everywhere, pushing people off the road who had no business there (only to have them return in larger numbers when they weren't looking), here and there an engine roared into life and died away again, and then the cars were pushed, with dead motors, into starting positions, tails to the pit counters, in echelon, facing down the circuit in a long, glistening line, while the drivers walked across to the far side of the road and stood somewhat sheepishly in the little numbered circles painted for them—except Sommer, who strolled across at the last moment.

Lagonda Away First

Half a minute to go . . . and a hush fell on the assembly. All eyes turned to the starter . . . down fell the flag . . . and there was the patter of flying feet as the drivers raced across the track. All down the line came the noise of banging doors, the grinding of

REGULARITY. The most regular team of all was the B.M.W. trio which won the 2-litre class. No. 26, Prince Schaumburg-Lippe and Wenscher in a saloon, finished fifth at 82.5 m.p.h.

won at record speed

starters, and in a few seconds the air was split by the roar of exhausts.

Sommer's Alfa, well down the line, was the first to move, but it was Arthur Dobson who shot out first from the top end and led the long string of cars howling down the circuit. For a few seconds the road was crammed with cars moving hub to hub, missing each other by inches, the drivers swerving in and out.

Bonneau's M.G. Midget was late away, too, but the rest were off like a flash.

On the first lap, Chinetti (4½-litre Darracq—the sports version of the

Battle was joined immediately. On the next lap the speed rose to 90 m.p.h. for the circuit, and Gerard shot past into second place, 4 secs. behind Chinetti, with the Bugatti third, and Dobson fell back to sixth place, Selsdon, in the other Lagonda, much further back—18th.

On the third lap Gerard took the lead at over 90 m.p.h., and put 7 secs.

Bugatti takes lead from Delage after 20 hours and wins by 26 miles at nearly 87 m.p.h. Magnificent performance by the two Lagondas finishing third and fourth at higher speeds than last year's winner. B.M.W. start and finish three cars high up

Grand Prix car) took the lead and went round at 88.7 m.p.h. from a standing start, leading by 7 secs. from a whole bunch, nose to tail, behind him —Dobson (Lagonda), Mazaud (3½-litre Delahaye), Wimille (3.3 blown Bugatti), Le Begue (Darracq 4-litre), and Louis Gerard (3-litre Delage).

BIENNIAL CUP WINNERS—Gordini and Scaron covered 1,789 miles in an 1,100 c.c. Simca-Fiat.

between himself and Chinetti. On the fourth lap Dobson fell back again, driving to schedule and refusing to be drawn into this dog fight so early in the race, and Gerard slammed round faster and faster, increasing his lead to nearly a minute. The Bugatti took second place after four laps, but dropped down again after another eight.

During these opening stages, with the leader lapping at nearly 95 m.p.h. and nearly a minute in the lead, those following were closely bunched, only a few seconds between them—Gerard, Mazaud and Paul (Delahayes) nose to tail, or abreast, at times, then the Bugatti, Chinetti, Helde (4½ Darracq), Le Begue (4.0 Darracq), Contet (Delahaye), and Hug (3.0 Delage). Dobson had fallen to 12th place. Selsdon stopped for a moment at his pit and went off again, running a lap behind, in 19th place, and after 18 laps (155 miles) Dobson lapped the other Lagonda.

Sommer's Usual Bad Luck

Sommer's usual Le Mans luck dogged him again. On the third lap, his Alfa stopped on the back of the course and lost a lap, and then, after 19 laps, he came to his pit spluttering, to find water in one cylinder. However, he blew the water out and went on, spluttering at first, but then the engine picked up again.

SECOND—the Delage drivers, Monneret and Gerard.

Sommer shot past, jammed between another car and the fence, and several drivers missed colliding more by luck than judgment. Belle-Croix's Delahaye was left at the pit with clutch slip, and he lost two laps fiddling about.

curves uphill round quite a sharp bend, several cars skated. Then Breillet (Simca Fiat) slid good and proper, spun round and round, hit the bank, was thrown out, and the car went sliding on.

Officials ran to flag down the other cars while the car was moved and the ambulance brought, and one car nearly collected the ambulance while it was turning on the track. Breillet was cut about the head.

At almost the same moment Mme. Itier (Simca-Fiat) crashed down at the Old Esses, before Arnage corner, and was thrown out but escaped with a shaking.

Oil on the Course

At once the officials tried to flag the oil-dropping Darracq, and flew a black flag at it. The driver took no notice.

24-HOUR SERVICE.—Bira (co-driver with Sommer of the streamlined Alfa-Romeo) came into the pits at about 10.30 p.m. with a rear brake binding. Sommer and a mechanic set to and put it right.

CLOSE FORMATION through the New Esses—No. 44 is the Scott-Wisdom Singer, No. 6, the Waleran-Selsdon Lagonda (which finished fourth) and No. 8 is the de Massa-Mahé Talbot.

Lap Record Goes, at 96.74 m.p.h.

However, on the next lap the engine passed out again and at the pit they set about lifting the cylinder head. They changed the gasket and rebuilt the engine in just about an hour, and once again Sommer set off. This time all was well, and he handed over to Bira just at dusk.

Meanwhile all sorts of things had been happening. Gerard was challenged

Race Progress

Order at 5 p.m.
1, Gerard (3.0 Delage), 10 laps in 54 mins 55.4 secs., leading by 43 secs.
2, Mazaud (3.5 Delahaye), 10 laps in 55:38.8.
3, Paul (3.5 Delahaye), 10 laps in 55:44.5.
4, Wimille (3.3 Bugatti S), 10 laps.
12, Dobson (4.5 Lagonda), 10 laps; 20, Lord Selsdon (4.5 Lagonda), 9 laps; 23, Hichens (Aston Martin); 26, Clark (H.R.G.); 27, Collier (M.G.); 28, Polledry (Aston Martin).

Order at 6 p.m.
1, Gerard-Monneret (Delage), 22 laps in 1:59:41.7
2, Mazaud-Mongin (Delahaye), 22 laps in 1:59:50.1.
3 Paul-Trevoux (3.5 Delahaye), 21 laps.
4, Wimille-Veyron (Bugatti).
11, Dobson-Brackenbury (Lagonda); 15, Selsdon-Waleran (Lagonda); 17, 18, 19, the B.M.W. team; 22, Hichens-Morris Goodall (Aston Martin).

Order at 7 p.m.
1, Gerard-Monneret (Delage), 32 laps in 2:55:52.8
2, Mazaud-Mongin (Delahaye), 32 laps in 2:56:2.
3, Chinetti-Mathieson (4.5 Darracq), 32 laps in 2:57:8.
4, Le Begue-Levegh (4.0 Darracq), 32 laps.

Order at 8 p.m.
1, Mazaud-Mongin (Delahaye), 43 laps in 3:56:59.8.
2, Gerard-Monneret (Delage), 43 laps in 3:57:0.8.
3, Chinetti-Mathieson (Darracq), 43 laps in 3:57:21.9
4, Wimille-Veyron (Bugatti), 42 laps.
11, Dobson-Brackenbury (Lagonda); 12, Selsdon-Waleran (Lagonda); 15, 16, 17, the B.M.W. team.

by Mazaud's Delahaye, and soon the two were in the throes of a dog fight, during which, on the 25th lap, Mazaud broke the long-standing lap record set up by Benoist's Bugatti (5 mins. 13 secs.—96.4 m.p.h.) with a lap in 5 mins. 12.1 secs.—96.74 m.p.h.

Thus at 6 p.m. Mazaud closed to within 8 secs. of Gerard's Delage, with Paul (Delahaye) third and the Bugatti always fourth.

Lagonda Lappery

At 6.25 Dobson brought in the Lagonda, refuelled and handed over to Charles Brackenbury, hatless as ever, who set off lapping at just under 89 m.p.h. Selsdon handed over the other Lagonda to Bill Waleran, who began lapping about 10 secs. a lap slower than Brackenbury.

All the faster cars had now covered their obligatory 24 laps (201 miles) before a refill is permitted, and during the pit stops the Paul-Contet Delahaye took the lead, only to lose it again.

At this juncture the Tremoulet-Forestier Darracq began dropping oil in quantity on the track, and just beyond the pits, where the road

Next lap the entire pit stood up and signalled him to stop, but again he took not the slightest. On the third lap they gave him the black flag again, plus a sign-board and dozens of officials leaping up and down, and this time he stopped, with the back of the car smothered in oil.

After a pit stop the trouble was rectified and he continued. As the officials had not shown his number with the flag apparently the driver couldn't make out what all the excitement was about!

At 7 p.m. the Gerard-Monneret Delage led by 9 secs., but during the next hour the Mazaud-Mongin Delahaye crept up and passed. Then the two cars passed and repassed, running a length or so apart, and at 8 p.m. it was the Delahaye which was in front —1 sec. in the lead.

There were in all four retirements out of the 40 starters by 9 p.m.—the 1½-litre Adler at five laps, Breillet (Simca) at 28 laps, Mme. Itier (Simca) at 25 laps and the Savoye Bros'. Singer Nine at three laps.

Night descended with Bira at the wheel of the Alfa, forbidden to exceed

CRASH—when car No. 40 (the Breillet - Debille Fiat) spun round, it hit the bank and ricochetted back into the fairway. The driver retrieved his seat cushion while helpers pushed the car away; then the ambulance arrived and swung out into the path of a 100 m.p.h. car (inset) whilst spectators gasped and waited for another crash . . . which happily did not come.

4,500 r.p.m. but still equalling Sommer's lap times, the Delage-Delahaye battle in full swing and the Bugatti hovering in fourth place a lap behind. The Lagondas were tooling round like trains, 11th and 12th, separated by three laps, and the team of three B.M.W.s ran in line ahead, one a lap ahead of the other two.

Slowly the light faded, and the pits and stands sprang into light, so that the track was floodlit and the pits took on their famous aspect of a street of shops. The car head lights came on, and the long beams could be seen dipping and waving over the tree tops in the distance.

A Battle Intense

LE MANS, *Sunday.*

DURING the long night—fortunately fine and star-lit—the battle began to develop. At 9 p.m. the Mazaud Delahaye was a second in the lead from Gerard's amazing Delage, with the 4½ Darracq of Chinetti and Mathieson on its tail, and the Bugatti, running 1,000 r.p.m. in hand, fourth, watching and waiting.

The Lagondas were going steadily, the drivers holding their horses and sparing their brakes for what might be needed later. They were running eighth and eleventh.

An hour later Chinetti took the lead by 21 secs. from Mazaud and the Delage was third after refuelling, but at 11 p.m. the Delage was back in the lead, a lap ahead of Chinetti, Mazaud and the Bugatti. At midnight the position was the same except that Mazaud was half a minute ahead of Chinetti.

Just over a minute separated first and second—Gerard and Chinetti—and in the next hour the flying Delage gained nearly four minutes on the Darracq, while the Lagondas came up to seventh and eighth, running two laps apart, Dobson ahead.

Shortly before 2 o'clock Mazaud caught fire and just got to his pit in time. The flames were put out, but too much damage was done, and after a gallant show, the Delahaye was out. This made the order Gerard, nearly a lap in the lead, Chinetti, the Bugatti, and fourth was Hug, on the second 3-litre Delage. This order remained for the next hour, but the Lagondas moved up again to sixth and seventh places, still two laps apart.

The whole point now was whether the Gerard Delage could keep going at this speed, and whether the Bugatti had enough reserve of speed to cope with the situation. At 5 a.m. it was only a lap behind and going well, but a little later it came to rest on the Mulsanne Straight while the driver did some tuning, and the car fell back to third place. The Lagondas were still sixth and seventh, and the three white B.M.W.s, which had gone with astonishing speed right through, were eighth, ninth and eleventh.

At 7 a.m. Gerard led by a lap still, but the Bugatti was second again, eight laps ahead of Mathieson, now at the wheel of Chinetti's Darracq, and lo, Dobson was fourth, Selsdon sixth, the B.M.W.s seventh, tenth and eleventh.

Shortly before 8 a.m. Mathieson threw a tread, and on a fast bend coming out on to the Mulsanne Straight, the tyre burst and the Darracq plunged sideways into the bank. Just behind was Hug in the second Delage, and as the Darracq went sideways, the Delage struck it and crashed. Neither of the drivers were really hurt, and Mathieson restarted—only to retire a couple of miles farther on.

This left Gerard three laps in the lead, the Bugatti second and—hurray—the Lagondas third and fourth. The B.M.W. team moved up to fifth, eighth and ninth.

Trouble Stalks

All during the night and the grim early hours of Sunday morning trouble stalked abroad among the cars, so that, by 9 a.m., 19 of 40 starters were out of the race. The Sommer-Bira Alfa, after the change of gasket, went off mightily well, and began to pick up, but then began brake troubles which put it right back. The Wisdom-Scott Singer retired with dirty fuel, water and rust and all sorts of things being therein, and the other Singer suffered the same bother.

Bonneau's M.G. broke its carburetter, the Hichens-Morris Goodall Aston Martin broke a valve spring, which let the valve down until it smacked the piston and bent up. The car carried on with three cylinders to finish its qualifying laps. Massa's Darracq had similar trouble.

Just after daybreak—and it was a lovely morning with bright sun and light clouds sailing on a gentle breeze—the handicap positions showed Gerard in the lead with an index of 1.33, Hug (Delage) and Gordini (1,100 Simca Fiat) equal second with 1.32, Chinetti and Prince Schaumburg-Lippe (B.M.W.) equal third with 1.27, and next up the Bugatti and the other two B.M.W.s, equal sixth with 1.25.

The race speed was still very high,

WINNER—Unusual angle on the imposing Bugatti—a streamlined 2-seater, with 3.3 litre supercharged engine.

well above the record speed of two years ago when the Bugatti averaged 85 m.p.h. Both the Lagondas were lapping at 87 m.p.h. or more, while the Bugatti was knocking out 92-94 m.p.h., speeding up now as the race position clarified. Gerard, in the Delage, was doing 5 mins. 28 secs. per lap, the Bugatti 5 mins. 21 secs., the Dobson-Brackenbury Lagonda 5:46.

Just after mid-day the Bugatti was a lap behind the Delage and all the time the B.M.W. team was going as strongly as when they started, with the saloon car in fifth place.

Then, after 20 hours' racing, what had long been expected happened: the Delage came into the pit with an enfeebled engine, and the Bugatti sailed past into the lead. The Delage restarted but stopped next lap, and the Bugatti rapidly piled up a lead of several laps and slowed down, still running with plenty in hand.

POSITIONS AT 1 P.M.
(After 21 Hours' Racing)

1, Wimille-Veyron (Bugatti), 219 laps.
2, Gerard-Monneret (Delage), 217 laps.
3, Dobson-Brackenbury (Lagonda), 208 laps.
4, Selsdon-Waleran (Lagonda), 208 laps.
5, Schaumburg - Lippe - Wenscher (B.M.W. saloon), 206 laps; 6, Villeneuve-Biolay (Delahaye), 204 laps; 7, Roese-Heinemann (B.M.W.), 201 laps; 8, Walker-Connell (Delahaye), 200 laps; 9, Briem-Sckolz (B.M.W.), 196 laps; 10, Gordini-Scaron (1,100 Simca Fiat), 187 laps; 11, Hichens-Goodall (Aston); 13, Clark-Chambers (H.R.G.); 15, White-Anthony (Morgan); 16, Vernet-Bodard (Riley); 18, Jones-Wilkins (Singer).
Only 20 left in race.

British Cars Doing Well

The British cars were doing extremely well, with very few retirements. The Morgan, H.R.G. and the French-entered Riley, the remaining Singer and, of course, the two Lagondas, were all going as hard as ever and were well up, and the three B.M.W.s were still amongst the fastest cars on the course, having hardly varied their pace since the start and lapping at about 86 m.p.h.

The Jones-Wilkins Singer ran into a spot of bother just after 2 p.m. and was at rest for some while, then restarted and tooled round and round at touring speed. The Delage stopped again to change drivers and soon went off, second now and sounding quite healthy, but three laps behind the Bugatti at 2 p.m. The Bugatti meanwhile had slowed right up and was rotating on the circuit at 85.5 m.p.h.—a reduction of 10 m.p.h. The H.R.G. lost a cylinder and went on to finish, having already done its minimum laps.

At 2 o'clock the Bugatti led by three laps, the Delage second, Dobson eight laps behind, Waleran fourth on the same lap, then the B.M.W. saloon two laps behind. The other two B.M.W.s were 7th and 9th, the Aston Martin 12th, H.R.G. 13th, Morgan 15th, Riley 16th and Singer 18th out of 20 runners.

Bugatti Set to Win

With two hours to go the Bugatti had the race in its pocket, the Lagondas were running to finish and the saloon B.M.W. was closing up on them.

At 3 p.m., after 23 hours motoring and with one hour to go, the Bugatti still led by three laps from the Delage, and was about to break the mileage record of the race (2,043 in 1937) set up by the 3.3 unblown Bugatti driven by Wimille and Benoist. Dobson was ten laps behind the leader, Selsdon a lap behind him, and the B.M.W. saloon two laps behind Selsdon.

The Bug. had slowed right up to 82 m.p.h., the Delage was doing 83.8 m.p.h., the saloon B.M.W. 86.9 m.p.h., and the Dobson-Brackenbury Lagonda 87.2 m.p.h. With 20 minutes to go the Singer had one lap to limp to qualify—and then a horde of officials strolled across the track and embarrassed the drivers flashing down past the pits, which occasioned howls of execration from the audience.

Lap by lap the remaining half-hour ticked away without any alteration in the order, and at 4 p.m. once again the marque Bugatti was the winner, and once again at record speed, then came the Delage after a wonderful performance, and then the two magnificent Lagondas, finishing their first race in as good order as when they started.

WRONG DIRECTION for the streamlined Talbot No. 8, which skidded right round, on an oil patch left by another car, in the face of a Simca Fiat.

Off to the States, as a Party

On Saturday last, 20 car loads of Junior Car Club members and passengers started on a rally to the United States and Canada. They sailed from Liverpool on the new S.S. Mauretania, which is making its maiden voyage. The cars include many famous British makes from Rolls-Royce downwards, and a very elaborate itinerary has been arranged for them. They are due to arrive at New York at the end of the week, their first call being the Waldorf Astoria Hotel, New York, at 8 a.m. on Saturday. Over the week-end they will visit the World's Fair and take part in an interesting programme arranged by the American Automobile Association.

The Veterans in Scotland

NEXT Saturday the R.S.A.C. will hold a veteran car run, starting from Glasgow at 11 a.m. and passing through Bishopbriggs, Kirkintilloch, Kilsyth, Falkirk and Linlithgow (about 50 miles). All cars competing will have been made before 1909.

Welsh Rally Entries Closing

THE final closing date for entries for the Welsh Rally (July 19-22) has been extended to June 26. Already over 100 have been received.

What Can You Do on a Gallon ?

THE well-known Vauxhall consumption tests whereby private motorists can drive a Vauxhall Ten over a selected route to see how far they can make it go on a measured quantity of petrol, without coasting, of course, is being held this month in the London area. Go to your local Vauxhall dealer and he will provide you with a Vauxhall Ten fitted with a special test tank on the dashboard so that the fuel remains visible until the last drop.

In the course of these tests in other parts of the country some extraordinarily good figures have been obtained—equal to 55 m.p.g. and over 60 m.p.g. by some competitors.

London is divided into different areas and the best from each will compete later in a final event, the winner of the all-London final being presented with a brand new Vauxhall Ten de luxe saloon, value £175. There will be numerous consolation prizes as well. It only costs 1s. to compete, the entrance fee being donated to the local hospitals.

This is a very amusing as well as instructional sort of competition, which is enjoying considerable popularity throughout the country.

Applications may now be made for the renewal of licences for next quarter.

LES 24 HEURES DU MANS

VICTORY FOR BUGATTI AT RECORD SPEED.   IMPRESSIVE DISPLAY BY NEW LAGONDAS.   H.R.G. WINS
1½-LITRE CLASS.   GORDINI'S WONDERFUL SIMCA-FIAT

ONE of the best races for years—was the general verdict of regular visitors to the Grand Prix d'Endurance which has been held here yesterday and to-day. It started with a magnificent duel between three or four cars which lasted for many hours; there were incidents and accidents full of drama in which nobody was badly hurt; big green British cars thundered round the course with the utmost regularity, as in days of old; the dashing driving of Louis Gerard was a tonic in itself; the race was run at record speed; a new lap record was set up; and the engine trouble of the Delage when it was leading by several laps after 20 of the 24 hours, thereby letting the Bugatti into the lead, could only be described as a *coup de theatre*.

The weighing and scrutineering of the cars took place in the Halle aux Toiles last Tuesday and Wednesday. There were few queries or delays. Earl Howe, acting as the R.A.C. representative on the A.I.A.C.R., spotted that the Adlers lacked the proper provision for sealing the petrol tank, and quite rightly insisted upon this being made. The interest on the second day centred on whether the Bugatti and Sommer's Alfa would get there in time. Sommer was reported to be having a terrible time getting through from Italy over the Mont Cenis Pass which was snow-covered. He himself turned up, looking quite fresh and fit, at about 2 o'clock, and at a quarter to four (1 o'clock was the deadline), his red Alfa saloon was pushed into the hall. Immediately after came the

course, it was a 2½-litre, fitted with a beautiful streamlined saloon body, painted bright red. Exactly the same type of body was used on Prince Schaumberg-Lippe's B.M.W. The Bugatti turned out to be a colossal affair, its streamlining being no doubt very efficient, but not too easy on the eyes. It was obviously very well prepared. An unusual feature

Five minutes before the start. The road is cleared of superfluous people and the drivers walk over to their allotted places.

The few days before the race passed pleasantly enough. All the hotels in Le Mans were full; the big shots staying at the Paris, the Lagondas being garaged in the yard of the Moderne as the Bentleys were ten years ago, the Adlers and the Jones-Wilkins Singer at the Central, the Barnes-Wisdom *equipe* at the Auberge, the Aston-Martin and Morgan crews at the Ifs. Practice was done every night between 1 a.m. and 6 a.m., and gossip about it was discussed at Gruber's and the Hippodrome. And what gossip! L'affaire Shrubsall kept everyone in suspense until Lord Howe returned from Paris to sit in conclave with the Commissaires Sportifs, who decided that it would be better if he did not start. This meant that a general switch round in the Darracq entries. Shrubsall's car was a dark red two-seater identical with the one shown at Earl's Court last October, and he was to have shared the driving of it with Antony Heal. Instead, this car was driven by Heldé and Schumann, and Bradley, the son of that famous journalist, W. F. Bradley, was called from Paris to share No. 7 Darracq with Morel. Meanwhile Lord Selsdon was dazzling everyone at Gruber's with his red cap, shirt of another shade of red, and tie of yet another—to say nothing of his bright blue trousers.

The weather was very pleasant as the time of the start drew near on Saturday afternoon, with high clouds motionless in a blue sky. Gradually the road was cleared of all unessential people, like the writer, the drivers stood in their little rings painted opposite their cars, and at last M. Charles Faroux raised and lowered the tricolour. There was a pattering of feet, a frantic getting into of cockpits and pressing of starter buttons, and almost immediately the first car was away. Very gratifying it was to see that it was Arthur Dobson on No. 5 Lagonda, and

The Lagonda driven by Lords Selsdon and Waleran receives a final rub-down before the start. It finished fourth after a fine, trouble-free run, covering 1999.4 miles and averaging 83.3 m.p.h.

huge, tank-like Bugatti, and so all was well. The engine size of the Alfa had not been declared, and there was some doubt as to whether it was the new twelve-cylinder 4½-litre, an eight-cylinder 3-litre, or a new 2½-litre "six." Actually, of

was a spotlight set into the side of the body on the right-hand side, pointing diagonally towards the kerb. The groove in which it was placed was covered with a talc window, so that it did not spoil the smooth contour of the body.

LES 24 HEURES DU MANS

he disappeared round the curve beyond the pits followed by Chinetti (Darracq) and the Bugatti, Wimille up. There were two unfortunates, Belle-Croix found that the gears of his Delahaye would not engage for some time, and Bonneau's M.G. took several minutes to get away.

All eyes were turned towards the end of the straight leading to the stands, while the announcer told us that Chinetti had passed Dobson at Mulsanne. Soon a speck appeared, grew rapidly nearer and Chinetti's blue Darracq swished by followed at a decent interval by Dobson, Mazaud (Delahaye), Wimille (Bugatti), Le Bégue (Darracq), and Gérard (Delage). Next time round Chinetti was still leading, but Gérard had moved up into second place and Dobson had dropped back to sixth. On the third lap Gérard took the lead, with Chinetti second, Wimille third, Mazaud fourth and Le Begue fifth.

Lapping at 93 m.p.h., Gérard went right ahead on the new Delage, driving superbly and cornering with all his well-known vigour. Wimille passed Chinetti for a few minutes, but before the first hour was out he had fallen back to fourth place behind Mazaud and Paul on their Delahayes, who were lying second and third respectively, while Chinetti was fifth, Heldé sixth and Le Bégue seventh.

Then Mazaud decided to set about Gérard. Lap by lap he gained on the blue Delage, and soon after six o'clock he caught up and passed it. In doing so he broke the previous lap record of 5 minutes 13 seconds, set up by Benoist on a 3.3-litre Bugatti in 1937, with a new time of 5 minutes 12.1 seconds (96 m.p.h.) which is pretty good going for an unblown 3½-litre car.

We will leave Mazaud and Gérard fighting it out for a moment, and see how the other people were getting on. The biggest surprise came when the single Adler (the second one had blown up in practice) came into the pits after 45 minutes and retired with an unspecified mechanical trouble. Selsdon made a quick stop at the pits for some sort of consultation, and Heldé was at the pits for some time while a broken push-rod was replaced. Dobson was going nicely, not hurrying, and was lapped by Gérard in 18 laps. Sommer came into the pits with the Alfa, which had been running extraordinarily quietly, at a lap speed of 88 m.p.h. to change some plugs, and at his refuelling stop after 24 laps the car was stationary for an hour while the gasket was changed. The necessary seat adjustments to allow for the difference in height of Sommer and "Bira" were made, and the Siamese took over. In practice he had suffered from car-sickness and an electric fan had been installed to assist ventilation.

At about this time Charles Faroux appeared with the black flag and waved it at Tremoulet's Darracq. But he neglected to hold up the car's number, and Tremoulet took no notice. Several times he came by while everyone in his pit, including the very charming Mme. Forestier, stood up and yelled at him. At last he came in, and then it was seen that his car was fairly dripping with oil, which had been making things very

difficult for other drivers all round the course. So difficult, indeed, that poor little Mme. Itier crashed quite badly at Arnage, turning her Simca-Fiat right over and giving herself painful bruises and no less painful shock. Another Simca-Fiat came to grief on the curve beyond the pits, the driver being Briellet, who won the 1,100 c.c. class in the T.T. at Donington last year. The car clipped the inside of the corner, swung round sideways, travelled like that for some distance (miraculously not turning over) fetched up against the outside fence with such a thud that Breillet was hurled out of the cockpit, and then bounced back into the fairway, which is fortunately very wide at this point.

This H.R.G., won the 1,500 c.c. class in the capable hands of P. C. T. Clark and Marcus Chambers, in spite of having its speed reduced by minor engine trouble, during the last two hours of the race.

Night fell with a tremendous scrap still going on between the Gérard-Monneret Delage, the Mazaud-Mongin Delahaye and the Chinetti-Mathieson Darracq, all of which led in turn as the refuelling stops altered the order. The lights in the pits were switched on, and electric torches flashed at drivers who failed to turn on their headlights at 9.30 At 10 o'clock, after a quarter of the race, the order was :

1. Chinetti-Mathieson (Darracq), 65 laps.
2. Mazaud-Mongin (Delahaye), 21s. behind.
3. Gerard-Monneret (Delage), 23.9s. behind.
4. Wimille-Veyron (Bugatti), 1 lap behind.
5. Loyer-Hug (Delage), 2 laps behind.
6. Contet-Brunet (Delahaye), 3 laps behind.
7. Chaboud-Giraud-Cabantous (Delahaye), 3 laps behind.
8. Dobson-Brackenbury (Lagonda), 4 laps behind.
9. Le Begue-Levegh (Darracq), 5 laps behind.
10. Villeneuve-Biolay (Delahaye), 6 laps behind.
11. Chotard-Seylair (Delahaye), 6 laps behind.
12. Selsdon-Waleran (Lagonda), 6 laps behind.

At about 11 o'clock we took a few lap times, with the following results : Wimille (Bugatti), 5.34 (90.362 m.p.h.) ; Gérard (Delage) 5.27 (92.296 m.p.h.) ; Dobson (Lagonda) 6.0 (83.836 m.p.h.) ; and Lord Waleran (Lagonda), 6.11 (81.35 m.p.h.).

When we left the stands last night Raymond Sommer was in at the pits again with the Alfa-Romeo, this time pouring buckets of water over its rear brakes, from which clouds of steam arose. Then we made our way to the car park and drove by devious ways to Arnage. Here there was a good crowd lining the fence beside the road, and the cars made a fine sight as they braked for the corner and swung into the straight back to White House and the pits. The Bugatti was

using its spotlight, and very effective it seemed in illuminating the inside of the right-hand swerve before the headlights had time to shine round the corner. We stumbled along in the pitch darkness to the preceding corner, called Indianopolis owing to its brick surface, and this was even better, for the cars approached it faster. Back at Arnage we had a final drink in a crowded tent lit by oil-lamps, and so back to bed at Le Mans.

We returned to the course next morning wondering what we should find. There was lots of news when we got there. Most important of all was the fact that the Delage was now leading by a street from the Bugatti, and was still going like a flash. But the two others of the four leading cars of the night before were both out of the race. At about 2 o'clock

LES 24 HEURES DU MANS

the Mazaud-Mongin Delahaye took fire while it was approaching the pits from the White House. The driver kept going, realising that his only hope lay in reaching fire-extinguishers. He pulled up in front of the Morgan pits, but it was too late. He himself was unhurt, but the fire had taken such a hold that it was all people could do to stop the petrol tank from blowing up, let alone save the car.

This retirement had altered the position of the leaders a bit, and at 4 a.m. twelve hours after the start and half-way through the race, the order had been.

1. Gerard-Monneret (Delage), 129 laps in 11h. 58m. 41.8s.
2. Mathieson-Chinetti (Darracq), 128 laps in 11h. 55m. 26s.
3. Wimille-Veyron (Bugatti), 128 laps in 11h. 56m. 13s.
4. Loyer-Hug (Delage), 2 laps behind.
5. Contet-Brunet (Delahaye), 7 laps behind.
6. Dobson-Brackenbury (Lagonda), 8 laps behind.
7. Selsdon-Waleran (Lagonda), 11 laps behind.
8. Prince Schaumberg Lippe-Wenscher (B.M.W.) 13 laps behind.
9. Villeneuve-Biolay (Delahaye), 14 laps behind.
10. Roese-Heinemann (B.M.W.), 15 laps behind.
11. Walker-Connell (Delahaye), 15 laps behind.
12. Briem-Scholz (B.M.W.), 15 laps behind.

There had been another accident in the night, and one which might have been very serious. Belle-Croix had for some unaccountable reason swerved while travelling fast along the tree-lined stretch of road at the beginning of the Mulsanne Straight. A hub-cap touched on the the trees, which are extremely thick and strong at this point, and the car spun round. Why it didn't hit another tree is a miracle. Instead, it plunged between two of them, careered along, turned over, and crashed through a garden up against the wall of a house. Belle-Croix was taken to hospital at Le Mans, and the worst was feared. However, it turned out that he was not badly hurt at all. Lucky man.

The next big change in the order was caused by Mathieson's retirement. One of his tyres lost a big chunk out of its tread, and at Terte Rouge, where the new road joins up with the main Tours road, the weakened tyre gave way under the strain. The Darracq skidded across the road smack into a sandbank. There was a report that the Loyer-Hug Delage was on the scene at the same time, but was struck by the Darracq, but Mathieson could not confirm this. He pluckily got out and began the terrible job of digging the car free of the sand. Eventually he succeeded, and then he changed

the wheel. At last he set off once more, but at the end of the Mulsanne Straight he came to rest with mechanical trouble—bad luck after so much work.

This left the Delage safely in the lead, a lead which was increased still more when the Bugatti stopped somewhere on the circuit with a broken wheel, limped back to its pits, and was there for ten minutes before restarting. Arthur Dobson also had quite a long pit stop in order to have his clutch adjustment attended to.

The Alfa-Romeo was still going, but at about 11 o'clock "Bira" came in and the car was finally abandoned. Tommy Wisdom and Scott had also withdrawn their Singer, for a most unfortunate reason. The pit fuel tank was full of rust and filth (as indeed were all of them, which was a bad thing) and a lot of it got into the Singer's fuel system. In cleaning this out they lost so much fuel that the car ran out of petrol after doing 23 of its specified 24 laps allowed between each refuel. The Aston-Martin went sick with valve trouble, and it was decided to keep going on three cylinders in the hope of qualifying. The Morgan and the H.R.G. were still going strong.

Twelve o'clock came, four hours to go, and with it a dramatic change in the outlook. At this time the race seemed a certainty for the Gérard-Monneret Delage, which was nearly two laps ahead of the Bugatti. True, Wimille had speeded up a bit, and was clipping off about 3 seconds a lap from the Delage's lead, but he could never hope to win at that rate. Then the Delage pulled into the pits. The bonnet was raised, plugs changed, and the car set off again—misfiring. Into the pits on the next lap, a consultation, and the seconds ticked by. The Bugatti had already gained one of its laps, and now it was due round again. The big blue car came into sight, swished up the straight and past the stationary Delage to take the lead. Gérard got going again, but still misfiring, and the most he could hope for now was second place.

There is little more to record. The H.R.G., after a splendid run, developed engine trouble a couple of hours from the end, but it kept going as the leader of the 1,500 c.c. class. The Morgan was quite monotonously consistent. And here it is time we said something about the Simca-Fiats of Gordini, one of which

he drove himself, which were doing simply amazing things, lapping at about 80 m.p.h. The B.M.W.s, too, were marvellous, the little streamlined saloon being the faster of the trio and frequently lapping at 87-88 m.p.h.

And so the end came, rather inconsequently, as is the way with Le Mans, without any chequered flag for the winner, but a quiet flagging in of each and every competitor as soon as the 24 hours was up. The French crowd were obviously delighted at the double French victory, as well as with Gordini's winning of the Rudge Cup, but they gave a rousing cheer to the Lagondas, the B.M.W.s, the Aston-Martin, the H.R.G. and its pipe-smoking driver, and the unobtrusive little Morgan.

RESULTS

Grand Prix D'Endurance : 1, Wimille-Veyron (Bugatti), 2,083 miles at 86.8 m.p.h. (New record. Previous best 85.13 m.p.h.): 2, Gerard-Monneret (Delage), 85.7 m.p.h.; 3, Dobson-Brackenbury (Lagonda), 83.5 m.p.h.; 4, Lord Selsdon-Lord Waleran (Lagonda), 83.3 m.p.h.; 5, Prince Schaumberg-Lippe-Wenscher (B.M.W.), 82.5 m.p.h.; 6, Villeneuve-Biolay (Delahaye); 7, Roese-Heinemann (B.M.W.); 8, Walker-Connell (Delahaye); 9, Breim-Scholz (B.M.W.); 10, Gordini-Scaron (Simca-Fiat); 11, Chotard-Seylair (Delahaye); 12, Morris-Goodall-Hitchens (Aston-Martin); 13, Lapchin-Plantivaux (Simca-Fiat); 14, Clarke-Chambers (H.R.G.); 15, White-Anthony (Morgan); 16, Vernet-Bodard (Riley); 17, Camerano-Loueau (Simca-Fiat); 18, Jones-Wilkins (Singer); 19 Alin-Alin (Simca-Fiat 500). 20, Aime-Leduc (Simca-Fiat 500).

Rudge-Whitworth Biennial Cup : Gordini-Scaron (Simca-Fiat).

Class Results

Over 5 litres : 1. Wimille-Veyron (3.3 supercharged Bugatti), 2,083.3 miles, (86.8 m.p.h.)

5-litres : 1, Dobson-Brackenbury (4,480 c.c. Lagonda), 2,000.5 miles, (83.5 m.p.h.); 2, Selsdon-Waleran (4,480 c.c. Lagonda), 1,999.4 miles, (83.3 m.p.h.); 3, Walker-Connell (3,575 c.c. Delahaye), 1,875.9 miles (78.1 m.p.h.); 4, Chotard-Seylair (Delahaye), 1703.3 miles (70.9 m.p.h.);

3-litres : 1, Gerard-Monneret (2981 c.c. Delage), 2,056.9 miles (85.7 m.p.h.).

2-litres : 1, Schaumberg-Lippe-Wenscher 1,976 c.c. B.M.W.), 1,980 miles (82.5 m.p.h.); 2, Roese-Heinemann (1,976 c.c. B.M.W.), 1,926.3 miles (80.2 m.p.h.); 3, Briem-Scholz (1,976 c.c. B.M.W.), 1,855.6 miles (77.3 m.p.h.); 4, Hitchens, Morris-Goodall (1,969 c.c. Aston-Martin), 1654.1 miles (68.9 m.p.h.)

1½-litres : 1, Clark-Chambers (1,496 c.c. H.R.G.), 1,611.8 miles (67 m.p.h.); 2, White-Anthony (1,104 c.c. Morgan), 1545.8 miles (64.4 m.p.h.); 3, Vernet-Bodard (1,496 c.c. Riley) 1,509.4 mils (62.8 m.p.h.)

1,100 c.c. 1, Gordini-Scaron (1,087 c.c. Simca-Fiat), 1,789.7 miles (74.7 m.p.h.); 2, Lapchin-Pnativaux (1,087 c.c. Simca-Fiat), 1,638.2 miles (68.2 m.p.h.); 3, Camerano-Louveau (1,087 c.c. Simca-Fiat) 1,371.6 miles (57.1 m.p.h.); 4, Wilkins-Jones (972 c.c. Singer), 1,296 miles (54 m.p.h.)

750 c.c. : 1, Alin-Alin (570 c.c. Simca-Fiat), 1,239.7 miles (51.6 m.p.h.); 2, Aime-Leduc (570 c.c. Simca-Fiat), 1,232.1 miles (51.3 m.p.h.)

Fastest Lap (record) : Mazaud (2,575 c.c. Delahaye), 5m. 12.1s., (96.74 m.p.h.)

RESULTS

The following tables are not a complete list of results but list the most important results of each race, as follows: first three cars finishing; all class and category wins; subsidiary awards, such as Biennial Cup and Index wins. The tables are in nine columns as follows:

Column 1: Overall placing.
Column 2: Make and nationality of car; nationalities: B Belgium, CS Czechoslovakia, D Germany, F France, GB Great Britain, I Italy, US U.S.A.
Column 3: Number of cylinders; where appropriate arrangement of engine if other than in-line as follows: F Flat (horizontally opposed), V V, t/s two-stroke.
Column 4: Capacity of engine in cc.
Column 5: Names of drivers; quotation marks indicate pseudonym.
Column 6: Distance covered, in miles.
Column 7: Average speed, in miles per hour.
Column 8: Class-winners only: indicates which capacity class won. Note changes in capacity class structure in 1960. NB: Not listed from 1975 onwards.

Column 9:
Category wins – particularly important from 1975 onwards – and subsidiary awards. Abbreviations used: Bi-cup, Biennial Cup; Tri-cup, Triennial Cup; Ind. Perf., Index of Performance; Index T.E., Index of Thermal Efficiency. Categories: 1959: Sport-prototype and Grand Tourisme; 1960–61: Sports Cars and Grand Tourisme; 1962: Experimental Cars and Grand Tourisme (with subsidiary category for under-2,000 cc GT); 1963–65: as 1962 but Prototypes replace Experimental Cars; 1966: as 1963–65 but with added Sports Car category; 1967: as 1966 but under-2,000 cc GT deleted, and under-1,300 cc Sports Car category added; 1968–71: Sports Car, Sports Prototype and Grand Tourisme – last category is called GT Special 1970–71; 1972–74: Group 5 sports cars, Group 4 GT special, Group 2 special touring; 1975: Group 6 sports-prototypes (with subsidiary two-litre class), and GTX – experimental GT cars – in addition to 1972–74 categories; 1976–81: Group 6, Group 5 and Group 4 as in 1975, GTX now unhomologated production GT cars, new class for GTP – Le Mans prototypes, and categories for I.M.S.A and N.A.S.C.A.R cars. Group 2 category deleted. N.A.S.C.A.R category only in 1976. 1981: Group C cars first admitted.
Note: There have not been entrants, or finishers, in all categories and classes every year.

All results listed in the Appendix have as far as possible been checked against official Automobile Club de l'Ouest figures and have been converted from kilometres to miles using 1.60935 kilometres equals 1 mile.

1	2	3	4	5	6	7	8	9

1st race—1923, 26–27 May. Circuit: 10.726 miles
33 cars starting, 30 cars finishing. Fastest lap: Clement (Bentley), 66.690 mph

1	2	3	4	5	6	7	8	9
1	Chenard et Walcker (F)	6 cyl	2,978 cc	A. Lagache/R. Leonard	1,372.937	57.206	3,000 cc	
2	Chenard et Walcker (F)	6 cyl	2,978 cc	R. Bachmann/C. Dauvergne	1,330.033	55.418		
3	Bignan (F)	4 cyl	1,979 cc	de Tornaco/P. Gros	1,287.130	53.629	2,000 cc	
6	Excelsior (B)	6 cyl	5,343 cc	A. Dills/N. Caerels	1,201.320	50.055	8,000 cc	
8	La Lorraine (F)	6 cyl	3,445 cc	G. de Courcelles/A. Rossignol	1,158.416	48.267	5,000 cc	
10	Bugatti (F)	4 cyl	1,495 cc	M. de Pourtales/S. de la Rochefoucauld	1,115.511	46.480	1,500 cc	
12	Salmson (F)	4 cyl	1,086 cc	L. Desvaux/G. Casse	1,051.155	43.798	1,100 cc	

2nd race—1924, 14–15 June. Circuit: 10.726 miles.
40 cars starting, 14 cars finishing. Fastest lap: Lagache (Chenard et Walcker), 69.076 mph

1	2	3	4	5	6	7	8	9
1	Bentley (GB)	4 cyl	2,995 cc	J. Duff/F. C. Clement	1,290.794	53.783	3,000 cc	
2	La Lorraine (F)	6 cyl	3,446 cc	H. Stoffel/E. Brisson	1,280.896	53.371	5,000 cc	
3	La Lorraine (F)	6 cyl	3,446 cc	G. de Courcelles/A. Rossignol	1,276.981	53.207		
4	Chenard et Walcker (F)	4 cyl	1,973 cc	Pisard/Chavée	1,191.829	49.659	2,000 cc	
11	Aries (F)	4 cyl	1,085 cc	F. Gabriel/H. Lapierre	979.706	40.821	1,100 cc	

3rd race—1925, 20–21 June. Circuit: 10.726 miles.
49 cars starting, 16 cars finishing. Fastest lap: Lagache (Chenard et Walcker), 70.206 mph

1	2	3	4	5	6	7	8	9
1	La Lorraine (F)	6 cyl	3,473 cc	G. de Courcelles/A. Rossignol	1,388.127	57.838	5,000 cc	
2	Sunbeam (GB)	6 cyl	2,942 cc	J. Chassagne/S. C. H. Davis	1,343.151	55.964	3,000 cc	
3	La Lorraine (F)	6 cyl	3,473 cc	Stalter/E. Brisson	1,335.621	55.650		
7	Rolland-Pilain (F)	4 cyl	1,997 cc	J. de Marguenat/L. Sire	1,255.360	52.306	2,000 cc	
8	Corre La Licorne (F)	4 cyl	1,493 cc	L. Balart/R. Doutrebente	1,185.680	49.403	1,500 cc	
10	Chenard et Walcker (F)	4 cyl	1,095 cc	R. Glaszmann/M. de Zuniga	1,169.572	48.723	1,100 cc	1st Bi-cup
13	Chenard et Walcker (F)	4 cyl	1,095 cc	R. Sénéchal/Loqueheux	1,126.691	46.945		Tri-cup

4th race—1926, 12–13 June. Circuit: 10.726 miles.
41 cars starting, 13 cars finishing. Fastest lap: de Courcelles (La Lorraine), 71.112 mph

1	2	3	4	5	6	7	8	9
1	La Lorraine (F)	6 cyl	3,446 cc	R. Bloch/A. Rossignol	1,585.991	66.083	5,000 cc	
2	La Lorraine (F)	6 cyl	3,446 cc	G. de Courcelles/M. Mongin	1,574.258	65.592		
3	La Lorraine (F)	6 cyl	3,446 cc	Stalter/E. Brisson	1,493.409	62.225		
4	O.M. (I)	6 cyl	1,990 cc	N. Minoia/G. Foresti	1,446.303	59.827	2,000 cc	2nd Bi-cup & Ind. Perf.
9	Salmson (F)	4 cyl	1,094 cc	G. Casse/A. Rousseau	1,189.810	49.575	1,100 cc	
10	Corre La Licorne (F)	4 cyl	1,425 cc	J. Errecalde/A. Galoisy	1,173.491	48.895	1,500 cc	

5th race—1927, 18–19 June. Circuit: 10.726 miles.
22 cars starting, 7 cars finishing. Fastest lap: Clement (Bentley), 73.409 mph

1	2	3	4	5	6	7	8	9
1	Bentley (GB)	4 cyl	2,989 cc	J. D. Benjafield/S. C. H. Davis	1,472.524	61.354	3,000 cc	
2	Salmson (F)	4 cyl	1,094 cc	A. de Victor/J. Hasley	1,255.165	52.280	1,100 cc	
3	Salmson (F)	4 cyl	1,094 cc	G. Casse/A. Rousseau	1,244.088	51.836		3rd Bi-cup & Ind. Perf.
4	S.C.A.P. (F)	4 cyl	1,493 cc	L. Desvaux/F. Vallon	1,190.053	49.585	1,500 cc	

1	2	3	4	5	6	7	8	9

6th race—1928, 16–17 June. Circuit: 10.726 miles.
33 cars starting, 17 cars finishing. Fastest lap: H. R. S. Birkin (Bentley), 79.289 mph

1	2	3	4	5	6	7	8	9
1	Bentley (GB)	4 cyl	4,392 cc	W. Barnato/B. Rubin	1,658.603	69.108	5,000 cc	
2	Stutz (US)	8 cyl	4,888 cc	E. Brisson/R. Bloch	1,650.725	68.780		
3	Chrysler (US)	6 cyl	4,076 cc	H. Stoffel/A. Rossignol	1,549.603	64.560		
6	Alvis (GB)	4 cyl	1,482 cc	C. M. Harvey/H. W. Purdy	1,420.687	59.195	1,500 cc	
7	B.N.C. (F)	4 cyl	1,099 cc	M. Doré/J. Truenet	1,410.548	58.773	1,100 cc	
8	Itala (I)	6 cyl	1,991 cc	R. Benoist/C. Dauvergne	1,403.157	58.465	2,000 cc	
10	Salmson (F)	4 cyl	1,095 cc	G. Casse/A. Rousseau	1,372.258	57.177		4th Bi-cup & Ind. Perf.

7th race—1929, 15–16 June. Circuit: 10.153 miles.
25 cars starting, 10 cars finishing. Fastest lap: H. R. S. Birkin (Bentley), 82.984 mph

1	2	3	4	5	6	7	8	9
1	Bentley (GB)	6 cyl	6,597 cc	W. Barnato/H. R. S. Birkin	1,767.067	73.627	8,000 cc	5th Bi-cup & Ind. Perf.
2	Bentley (GB)	4 cyl	4,398 cc	J. Dunfee/G. Kidston	1,695.951	70.665	5,000 cc	
3	Bentley (GB)	4 cyl	4,398 cc	J. D. Benjafield/A. d'Erlanger	1,614.544	67.273		
8	Lea-Francis (GB)	4 cyl	1,495 cc	K. S. Peacock/S. H. Newsome	1,380.644	57.526	1,500 cc	
9	Tracta (F)	4 cyl	985 cc	L. Balart/L. Debeugny	1,299.678	54.153	1,100 cc	

8th race—1930, 21–22 June. Circuit: 10.153 miles.
17 cars starting, 9 cars finishing. Fastest lap: H. R. S. Birkin (Bentley), 89.696 mph

1	2	3	4	5	6	7	8	9
1	Bentley (GB)	6 cyl	6,597 cc	W. Barnato/G. Kidston	1,821.023	75.876	8,000 cc	6th Bi-cup
2	Bentley (GB)	6 cyl	6,597 cc	F. C. Clement/R. Watney	1,760.017	73.727		
3	Talbot (GB)	6 cyl	2,276 cc	B. Lewis/H. S. Eaton	1,647.856	68.661	3,000 cc	Ind. Perf.
5	Alfa Romeo (I)	6 cyl	1,752 cc	Lord Howe/L. C. Callingham	1,620.319	67.513	2,000 cc	
6	Lea-Francis (GB)	4 cyl	1,496 cc	K. S. Peacock/S. H. Newsome	1,424.107	58.716	1,500 cc	
8	Tracta (F)	4 cyl	986 cc	J. A. Gregoire/F. Vallon	1,306.664	54.444	1,100 cc	

9th race—1931, 13–14 June. Circuit: 10.153 miles.
26 cars starting, 6 cars finishing. Fastest lap: B. Ivanowski (Mercedes-Benz), 86.515 mph

1	2	3	4	5	6	7	8	9
1	Alfa Romeo (I)	8 cyl	2,337 cc	Lord Howe/H. R. S. Birkin	1,875.076	78.128	3,000 cc	7th Bi-cup & Ind. Perf.
2	Mercedes Benz (D)	6 cyl	7,100 cc	B. Ivanowski/H. Stoffel	1,805.163	75.215	8,000 cc	
3	Talbot (GB)	6 cyl	2,970 cc	T. E. Rose-Richards/A. C. Saunders-Davies	1,763.071	73.461		
5	Aston Martin (GB)	4 cyl	1,496 cc	W. Cook/J. Bezzant	1,420.693	59.195	1,500 cc	
6	Caban (F)	4 cyl	1,100 cc	J. E. Vernet/F. Vallon	1,300.019	54.167	1,100 cc	

10th race—1932, 18–19 June. Circuit: 8.383 miles.
26 cars starting, 9 cars finishing. Fastest lap: N. Minoia (Alfa Romeo), 88.506 mph

1	2	3	4	5	6	7	8	9
1	Alfa Romeo (I)	8 cyl	2,337 cc	R. Sommer/L. Chinetti	1,835.547	76.481	3,000 cc	Ind. Perf.
2	Alfa Romeo (I)	8 cyl	2,337 cc	F. Cortese/G. B. Guidotti	1,818.919	75.788		
3	Talbot (GB)	6 cyl	2,970 cc	B. Lewis/T. E. Rose-Richards	1,517.138	63.214		
4	Alfa Romeo (I)	6 cyl	1,746 cc	Mme. Siko/J. Sabipa	1,502.218	62.592	2,000 cc	
5	Aston Martin (GB)	4 cyl	1,495 cc	S. H. Newsome/H. Widengren	1,459.497	60.812	1,500 cc	
7	Aston Martin (GB)	4 cyl	1,495 cc	A. C. Bertelli/L. P. Driscoll	1,409.319	58.094		8th Bi-cup
8	Amilcar (F)	4 cyl	1,089 cc	C. A. Martin/A. Bodoignet	1,269.504	52.896	1,100 cc	

11th race—1933, 17–18 June. Circuit: 8.383 miles.
29 cars starting, 13 cars finishing. Fastest lap: R. Sommer (Alfa Romeo), 90.959 mph

1	2	3	4	5	6	7	8	9
1	Alfa Romeo (I)	8 cyl	2,336 cc	R. Sommer/T. Nuvolari	1,953.607	81.400	3,000 cc	9th Bi-cup
2	Alfa Romeo (I)	8 cyl	2,336 cc	L. Chinetti/P. Varent	1,953.358	81.389		
3	Alfa Romeo (I)	8 cyl	2,336 cc	B. Lewis/T. E. Rose-Richards	1,891.059	78.809		
4	Riley (GB)	4 cyl	1,091 cc	A. W. K. van der Becke/K. S. Peacock	1,604.077	66.836	1,100 cc	Ind. Perf.
5	Aston Martin (GB)	4 cyl	1,495 cc	L. P. Driscoll/S. C. Penn-Hughes	1,583.677	65.986	1,500 cc	
6	MG (GB)	4 cyl	745 cc	J. L. Ford/M. H. Baumer	1,482.208	61.756	750 cc	
8	Alfa Romeo (I)	6 cyl	1,742 cc	A. Rousseau/F. Paco	1,404.726	58.271	2,000 cc	

12th race—1934, 16–17 June. Circuit: 8.383 miles.
44 cars starting, 23 cars finishing. Fastest lap: P. Etancelin (Alfa Romeo), 88.506 mph

1	2	3	4	5	6	7	8	9
1	Alfa Romeo (I)	8 cyl	2,336 cc	L. Chinetti/P. Etancelin	1,793.853	74.744	3,000 cc	
2	Riley (GB)	6 cyl	1,458 cc	J. Sebilleau/G. Delaroche	1,681.078	70.078	1,500 cc	
3	Riley (GB)	6 cyl	1,458 cc	F. W. Dixon/V. Paul	1,670.336	69,597		
4	MG (GB)	6 cyl	1,087 cc	C. E. C. Martin/R. Eccles	1,655.967	68.998	1,100 cc	
5	Riley (GB)	4 cyl	1,087 cc	A. W. K. van der Becke/K. S. Peacock	1,640.845	68.368		10th Bi-cup & Ind. Perf.

13th race—1937, 15–16 June. Circuit: 8.383 miles.
58 cars starting, 28 cars finishing. Fastest lap: Lord Howe (Alfa Romeo), 86.751 mph

1	2	3	4	5	6	7	8	9
1	Lagonda (GB)	6 cyl	4,451 cc	F. S. Hindmarsh/L. Fontès	1,868.330	77.847	5,000 cc	
2	Alfa Romeo (I)	8 cyl	2,331 cc	P. L. Dreyfus('Heldé')/H. Stoffel	1,863.055	77.627	3,000 cc	
3	Aston Martin (GB)	4 cyl	1,494 cc	C. E. C. Martin/C. Brackenbury	1,805.434	75.226	1,500 cc	11th Bi-cup & Ind. Perf.
6	Alfa Romeo (I)	6 cyl	1,774 cc	J. Desvignes/G. Don	1,717.350	71.553	2,000 cc	
9	MG (GB)	6 cyl	1,083 cc	C. Druck/P. Maillard-Brune	1,699.029	70.896	1,100 cc	
27	Austin (GB)	4 cyl	749 cc	J. Barbour/J. Carr	1,189.111	49.546	750 cc	

1936: Race cancelled

14th race—1937. 19–20 June. Circuit: 8.383 miles.
48 cars starting, 17 cars finishing. Fastest lap: J-P Wimille (Bugatti), 96.423 mph

1	2	3	4	5	6	7	8	9
1	Bugatti (F)	8 cyl	3,266 cc	J-P Wimille/R. Benoist	2,043.022	85.126	5,000 cc	Ind. Perf.
2	Delahaye (F)	6 cyl	3,580 cc	J. Paul/M. Mongin	1,979.335	82.472		
3	Delahaye (F)	6 cyl	3,580 cc	R. Dreyfus/H. Stoffel	1,942.044	80.918		
4	Delage (F)	6 cyl	2,984 cc	J. de Valence/L. Gerard	1,806.686	75.278	3,000 cc	
5	Aston Martin (GB)	4 cyl	1,493 cc	J. M. Skeffington/R. C. Murton-Neale	1,720.375	71.682	1,500 cc	
6	Adler (D)	4 cyl	1,679 cc	Graf Orssich/R. Sauerwein	1,719.262	71.636	2,000 cc	
11	Aston Martin (GB)	4 cyl	1,942 cc	M. H. Morris-Goodall/R. P. Hitchens	1,624.186	67.674		12th Bi-cup
12	Simca (F)	4 cyl	996 cc	J. E. Vernet/Mme. Largeot	1,434.682	59.778	1,100 cc	
17	Simca (F)	4 cyl	569 cc	J. Viale/A. Alin	1,222.878	50.953	750 cc	

15th race—1938. 18–19 June. Circuit: 8.383 miles.
42 cars starting, 15 cars finishing. Fastest lap: R. Sommer (Alfa Romeo), 96.177 mph

1	2	3	4	5	6	7	8	9
1	Delahaye (F)	6 cyl	3,558 cc	E. Chaboud/J. Trémoulet	1,976.537	82.356	5,000 cc	
2	Delahaye (F)	6 cyl	3,558 cc	G. Serraud/Y. Giraud-Cabantous	1,959.719	81.655		
3	Talbot-Lago (F)	6 cyl	3,985 cc	J. Prenant/A. Morel	1,839.064	76.627		
5	Peugeot-Darl'mat (F)	4 cyl	1,998 cc	C. de Cortanze/M. Contet	1,800.094	75.004	2,000 cc	
6	Adler (D)	4 cyl	1,679 cc	Graf Orssich/R. Sauerwein	1,774.867	73.952		13th Bi-cup
7	Adler (D)	4 cyl	1,485 cc	O. Löhr/P. von Guilleaume	1,718.108	71.587	1,500 cc	
9	Simca (F)	4 cyl	1,090 cc	A. Debille/P. Lapchin	1,447.514	60.313	1,100 cc	
14	Simca (F)	4 cyl	568 cc	M. Aimé/C. Plantivaux	1,269.307	52.887	750 cc	Ind. Perf.

16th race—1939. 17–18 June. Circuit: 8.383 miles.
42 cars starting, 20 cars finishing. Fastest lap: R. Mazaud (Delahaye), 96.701 mph

1	2	3	4	5	6	7	8	9
1	Butatti (F)	8 cyl	3,251 cc	J-P. Wimille/P. Veyron	2,084.543	86.856	5,000 cc	
2	Delage (F)	6 cyl	2,991 cc	L. Gerard/G. Monneret	2,058.112	85.754	3,000 cc	
3	Lagonda (GB)	V-12	4,479 cc	A. Dobson/C. Brackenbury	2,006.680	83.611		
5	BMW (D)	6 cyl	1,976 cc	von Schaumburg-Lippe/F. Wenscher	1,981.204	82.550	2,000 cc	
10	Simca (F)	4 cyl	1,087 cc	A. Gordini/J. Scaron	1,793.212	74.717	1,100 cc	14th Bi-cup & Ind. Perf.
14	HRG (GB)	4 cyl	1,496 cc	P. C. T. Clark/M. Chambers	1,615.378	67.307	1,500 cc	
19	Simca (F)	4 cyl	566 cc	A. Alin/A. Alin	1,242.410	51.705	750 cc	

Made in the USA
Middletown, DE
27 August 2020